The Power of the In-Between

Intermediality as a Tool for Aesthetic Analysis and Critical Reflection

Edited by Sonya Petersson, Christer Johansson, Magdalena Holdar, and Sara Callahan

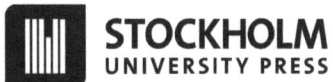

Published by
Stockholm University Press
Stockholm University
SE-106 91 Stockholm, Sweden
www.stockholmuniversitypress.se

Text © The Author(s) 2018
License CC-BY

Supporting Agency (funding): The publication of this book has been made possible by generous grants from Magnus Bergvalls stiftelse, Stiftelsen Konung Gustaf VI Adolfs fond för svensk kultur, Stiftelsen Lars Hiertas minne, Sven och Dagmar Saléns stiftelse, and Åke Wibergs stiftelse.

First published 2018
Cover Illustration: Dick Higgins, Intermedia chart, 1995. From Dick Higgins, "Intermedia," *Leonardo* 34, no.1 (2001): 50, 49–54. Photo: Charles Deering, McCormick Library of Special Collections, Northwestern University Libraries.
Cover License: Copyright. Courtesy of the Estate of Dick Higgins. License: CC-BY-NC-ND.
Cover Design: Karl Edqvist, SUP

Stockholm Studies in Culture and Aesthetics ISSN: 2002-3227

ISBN (Paperback): 978-91-7635-067-6
ISBN (PDF): 978-91-7635-064-5
ISBN (EPUB): 978-91-7635-065-2
ISBN (Mobi): 978-91-7635-066-9

DOI: https://doi.org/10.16993/baq

This work is licensed under the Creative Commons Attribution 4.0 Unported License. To view a copy of this license, visit creativecommons.org/licenses/by/4.0/ or send a letter to Creative Commons, 444 Castro Street, Suite 900, Mountain View, California, 94041, USA. This license allows for copying any part of the work for personal and commercial use, providing author attribution is clearly stated.

Suggested citation:
Petersson, Sonya, Christer Johansson, Magdalena Holdar, and Sara Callahan, eds. *The Power of the In-Between: Intermediality as a Tool for Aesthetic Analysis and Critical Reflection*. Stockholm: Stockholm University Press, 2018. DOI: https://doi.org/10.16993/baq. License: CC-BY.

To read the free, open access version of this book online, visit https://doi.org/10.16993/baq or scan this QR code with your mobile device.

Stockholm Studies in Culture and Aesthetics

Stockholm Studies in Culture and Aesthetics (SiCA) (ISSN 2002-3227) is a peer-reviewed series of monographs and edited volumes published by Stockholm University Press. SiCA strives to provide a broad forum for research on culture and aesthetics, including the disciplines of Art History, Heritage Studies, Curating Art, History of Ideas, Literary Studies, Musicology, and Performance and Dance Studies.

In terms of subjects and methods, the orientation is wide: critical theory, cultural studies and historiography, modernism and modernity, materiality and mediality, performativity and visual culture, children's literature and children's theatre, queer and gender studies.

It is the ambition of SiCA to place equally high demands on the academic quality of the manuscripts it accepts as those applied by refereed international journals and academic publishers of a similar orientation. SiCA accepts manuscripts in English, Swedish, Danish, and Norwegian.

Editorial Board

Jørgen Bruhn, Professor of Comparative Literature at the Centre for Intermedial and Multimodal Studies at Linnaeus University in Växjö

Karin Dirke, Senior Lecturer in History of Ideas at the Department of Cultur and Aesthetics at Stockholm University

Elina Druker, Associate Professor of Literature at the Department of Culture and Aesthetics at Stockholm University

Johanna Ethnersson Pontara, Associate Professor of Musicology at the Department of Culture and Aesthetics at Stockholm University

Kristina Fjelkestam, Professor of Gender Studies at the Department of Ethnology, History of Religions and Gender Studies at Stockholm University

Malin Hedlin Hayden, Professor of Art History at the Department of Culture and Aesthetics at Stockholm University

Christer Johansson (coordination and communication), PhD Literature, Research Officer at the Department of Culture and Aesthetics at Stockholm University

Jacob Lund, Associate Professor of Aesthetics and Culture at the School of Communication and Culture - Aesthetics and Culture, Aarhus University

Catharina Nolin, Associate Professor of Art History at the Department of Culture and Aesthetics at Stockholm University

Ulf Olsson (chairperson), Professor of Literature at the Department of Culture and Aesthetics at Stockholm University

Meike Wagner, Professor of Theatre Studies at the Department of Culture and Aesthetics at Stockholm University

Titles in the series

1. Rosenberg, T. 2016. *Don't Be Quiet, Start a Riot! Essays on Feminism and Performance*. Stockholm: Stockholm University Press. DOI: https://doi.org/10.16993/baf. License: CC-BY 4.0
2. Lennon, J. & Nilsson, M. (eds.) 2017. *Working-Class Literature(s): Historical and International Perspectives*. Stockholm: Stockholm University Press. DOI: https://doi.org/10.16993/bam. License: CC-BY 4.0
3. Tessing Schneider, M. & Tatlow, R. (eds.) 2018. *Mozart's* La clemenza di Tito: *A Reappraisal*. Stockholm: Stockholm University Press. DOI: https://doi.org/10.16993/ban. License: CC-BY 4.0
4. Petersson, S., Johansson, C., Holdar, M. & Callahan, S. (eds.) 2018. *The Power of the In-Between: Intermediality as a Tool for Aesthetic Analysis and Critical Reflection*. Stockholm: Stockholm University Press. DOI: https://doi.org/10.16993/baq. License: CC-BY 4.0

Peer Review Policies

Stockholm University Press ensures that all book publications are peer-reviewed in two stages. Each book proposal submitted to the Press will be sent to a dedicated Editorial Board of experts in the subject area as well as two independent experts. The full manuscript will be peer reviewed by chapter or as a whole by two independent experts.

A full description of Stockholm University Press' peer-review policies can be found on the website: http://www.stockholmuniversitypress.se/site/peer-review-policies/

Recognition for reviewers

The Editorial Board of Stockholm Studies in Culture and Aesthetics applies single-blind review during proposal and manuscript assessment. We would like to thank all reviewers involved in this process.

Special thanks to the reviewers who have been doing the peer review of the manuscript of this book.

Contents

List of Illustrations   ix

Introduction   1
Christer Johansson and Sonya Petersson

PART ONE: ARTEFACTS

In between Life and Death: Sophie Calle's *Rachel, Monique* (2014)   25
Jørgen Bruhn and Henriette Thune

The Intersection between Film and Opera in the 1960s: Ingmar Bergman's *Hour of the Wolf* as an Example of Formal Imitation   49
Johanna Ethnersson Pontara

Figures of Migration: Intertextuality in Michelangelo's *Night*   75
Peter Gillgren

The Unlimited Performativity of Instruction Art: *Space Transformer* by Yoko Ono   99
Magdalena Holdar

From Folk Tale to Photomontage: A Transformation through a Stage Performance   129
Rikard Hoogland

Today's Cake is a Log: Remediating the Intermediality of Hotel Pro Forma's Works in an Exhibition   149
Daria Skjoldager-Nielsen and Kim Skjoldager-Nielsen

PART TWO: NETWORKS

Panoramic Visions: Sven Hedin in "Transhimalaya" 1906–1909   185
Staffan Bergwik

The Lithographic Album 1873: Reproductive Media and Visual Art in the Age of Lithographic Reproduction   213
Anna Dahlgren

Stages of Consumerism: Mass Advertising and Children's Literature in Early Twentieth-Century Sweden   239
Elina Druker

Mediating Public Cultural Policy: Buildings, Bills, and Films as Governmentality   261
Fredrik Krohn Andersson

PART THREE: CONCEPTS

"The Analogue": Conceptual Connotations of a Historical Medium   287
Sara Callahan

Unfixing the Concept of Illustration: Its Historiographical Ambivalence and Analytical Potential   321
Sonya Petersson

Song as Event: On Intermediality and the Auditory   349
Erik Wallrup

Old and New Media: On the Construction of Media History   375
Christer Johansson

About the Authors   407

Index   411

List of Illustrations

Photograph of the film projection of Sophie Calle's dying mother on the wall in the chapel. Sophie Calle, 2014. Photo: Henriette Thune, University of Stavanger. License: CC-BY-NC-ND. Rights holder has not responded after repeated requests about copyright claims. Copyright claims are welcomed. 26

Overview of the exhibition from the entrance at the Western wall. Sophie Calle, 2014. Photo: Henriette Thune, University of Stavanger. License: CC-BY-NC-ND. Rights holder has not responded after repeated requests about copyright claims. Copyright claims are welcomed. 34

Photograph of the open coffin of Monique Sindler. Sophie Calle, 2014. Photo: Henriette Thune, University of Stavanger. License: CC-BY-NC-ND. Rights holder has not responded after repeated requests about copyright claims. Copyright claims are welcomed. 35

Night. Michelangelo, c. 1530. Marble. The Medici chapel, San Lorenzo, Florence. Reproduction and permission: Bildarchiv Foto Marburg. License: CC-BY-NC-ND. 79

Belvedere Cleopatra. Unknown artist, 2nd century BC. Marble. Vatican Museums, Rome. Reproduction and permission: Bildarchiv Foto Marburg. License: CC-BY-NC-ND. 82

Sculptures for Lorenzo de' Medici's tomb. Michelangelo, c. 1530. Marble. The Medici chapel, San Lorenzo, Florence. Reproduction and permission: Bildarchiv Foto Marburg. License: CC-BY-NC-ND. 86

Sculptures for Giuliano de' Medici's tomb. Michelangelo, c. 1530. Marble. The Medici chapel, San Lorenzo, Florence. Reproduction and permission: Bildarchiv Foto Marburg. License: CC-BY-NC-ND. 86

Madonna with Saint Cosmas and Saint Damian. Michelangelo, c. 1530. Marble. The Medici chapel, San Lorenzo, Florence. Photo: Private, Wikimedia Commons. License: CC-BY-SA-3.0. Available at Wikimedia Commons: https://commons.wikimedia.org/wiki/File:Madonna_mit_Kind_von_Michelangelo_Cappelle_Medicee_Florenz-1.jpg. 89

Reconstruction of the Medici chapel during mass. Petter Lönegård, 2017. Photo and copyright: Petter Lönegård and Peter Gillgren. License: CC-BY-NC-ND. 90

Migrant Sleeping in the Streets of London. Hannah McKay, 2014. Photo and copyright: National Picture/Hanna McKay. License: CC-BY-NC-ND. 92

Space Transformer. Yoko Ono, c. 2010. Multiple, print on paper, 9 × 5 cm. Photo: Magdalena Holdar. License: CC-BY-NC-ND. 100

Intermedia chart. Dick Higgins, 1995. Photo: Charles Deering, McCormick Library of Special Collections, Northwestern University Libraries. Copyright: Courtesy of the Estate of Dick Higgins. License: CC-BY-NC-ND. 104

Ljungby horn tournée, 1894–95. Reproduction: National Library of Sweden/Kungliga biblioteket, Stockholm. License: CC-BY-NC-ND. 130

Justus Hagman in *Ljungby horn*, Stora Teatern in Gothenburg 1893, photographed by Alfred Peterson. Permission: Swedish Performing Arts Agency/Statens musikverk, Stockholm. License: CC-PD. Available at Wikimedia Commons: https://commons.wikimedia.org/wiki/File:Justus_Hagman,_rollportr%C3%A4tt_-_SMV_-_H9_188.tif. 133

Montage of stage images from *Why Does Night Come, Mother*. Hotel Pro Forma, 1989. Photo: Roberto Fortuna. Copyright: Hotel Pro Forma. License: CC-BY-NC-ND. 162

War Sum Up. Hotel Pro Forma, 2011. Photo: Roberto Fortuna. Copyright: Hotel Pro Forma. License: CC-BY-NC-ND. 165

Clothes rag, *Today's Cake is a Log*. Hotel Pro Forma, 2015. Photo: Daria Skjoldager-Nielsen. Copyright: Hotel Pro Forma. License: CC-BY-NC-ND. 170

Mirror room, *Today's Cake is a Log*. Hotel Pro Forma, 2015. Photo: Torben Eskerud. Copyright: Hotel Pro Forma. License: CC-BY-NC-ND. 170

Text collages, *Today's Cake is a Log*. Hotel Pro Forma, 2015. Photo: Kim Skjoldager-Nielsen. Copyright: Hotel Pro Forma. License: CC-BY-NC-ND. 172

Photo/video montage, *Today's Cake is a Log*. Hotel Pro Forma, 2015. Photo: Torben Eskerud. Copyright: Hotel Pro Forma. License: CC-BY-NC-ND. 173

The ghost, *Today's Cake is a Log*. Hotel Pro Forma, 2015. Photo: Daria Skjoldager-Nielsen. Copyright: Hotel Pro Forma. License: CC-BY-NC-ND. 174

Readhead reader, *Today's Cake is a Log*. Hotel Pro Forma, 2015. Photo: Daria Skjoldager-Nielsen. Copyright: Hotel Pro Forma. License: CC-BY-NC-ND. 175

UV room, *Today's Cake is a Log*. Hotel Pro Forma, 2015. Photo: Torben Eskerud. Copyright: Hotel Pro Forma. License: CC-BY-NC-ND. 176

A photographic panorama consisting of interlaced images by Sven Hedin. From *Sven Hedins Kartsamling* (vol. G1 0917-958, no. 720811: 954). Copyright: The Sven Hedin Foundation and National Archive of Sweden/Sven Hedins stiftelse and Riksarkivet, Stockholm. License: CC-BY-NC-ND. 196

Photograph from Transhimalaya by Sven Hedin. From *Sven Hedins Kartsamling* (vol. G1 0917-958, no. 720811: 945). Copyright: The Sven Hedin Foundation and National Archive of Sweden/ Sven Hedins stiftelse and Riksarkivet, Stockholm. License: CC-BY-NC-ND. 196

Hand-drawn panorama by Sven Hedin. From *Southern Tibet: Atlas of Tibetan Panoramas* (illustrations 494–497). Reproduction: National Library of Sweden/Kungliga biblioteket, Stockholm. License: CC-BY-NC-ND. 199

Panoramic photograph by Sven Hedin. From *Sven Hedins Kartsamling* (vol. G1 0917-958, no. 720811: 931). Copyright: The Sven Hedin Foundation and National Archive of Sweden/Sven Hedins stiftelse and Riksarkivet, Stockholm. License: CC-BY-NC-ND. 199

Watercolour sketch by Sven Hedin. Copyright: The Sven Hedin Foundation and National Archive of Sweden/Sven Hedins stiftelse and Riksarkivet, Stockholm. License: CC-BY-NC-ND. 202

Unfolded panoramic image where the lower section is a continuation of the upper, together forming a 360° panorama, by Sven Hedin. From *Southern Tibet: Discoveries in Former Times Compared with My Own*

xii List of Illustrations

Researches in 1906–1908, vol. 2. Reproduction: National Library of Sweden/Kungliga biblioteket, Stockholm. License: CC-BY-NC-ND. 206

The cover of *Lithographic Album*, 1873. Reproduction: National Library of Sweden/Kungliga biblioteket, Stockholm. License: CC-BY-NC-ND. 215

Cabinet portrait of Prince August by Gösta Florman. Photo: Lisa Raihle Rehbäck. Copyright: Swedish Royal Court/Kungl. Hovstaterna, Stockholm. License: CC-BY-NC-ND. 221

Lithographic reproduction of Florman's photograph of Prince August. *Lithographic Album*, 1873. Reproduction: National Library of Sweden/Kungliga biblioteket, Stockholm. License: CC-BY-NC-ND. 221

Hjalmar's Farewell. Mårten Eskil Winge, 1866. Oil on canvas. Reproduction and permission: Nationalmuseum/Nationalmuseum, Stockholm. License: CC-PD. Available at Wikimedia Commons: https://commons.wikimedia.org/wiki/File:Hjalmars_avsked_av_Orvar_Odd_efter_striden_på_Samsö.jpg. 223

Hjalmar the Brave. Lithographic reproduction of Mårten Eskil Winge's oil painting. *Lithographic Album*, 1873. Reproduction: National Library of Sweden/Kungliga biblioteket, Stockholm. License: CC-BY-NC-ND. 223

A Wounded Danish Soldier. Maria Elisabeth Lisinska Jerichau-Baumann, 1865. Oil on canvas. Photo and copyright: National Gallery of Denmark/Statens Museum for Kunst, Copenhagen. License: CC-BY-NC-ND. 225

A Wounded Danish Soldier. Lithographic reproduction of Anna Maria Elisabeth Lisinska Jerichau-Baumann's oil painting. *Lithographic Album*, 1873. Reproduction: National Library of Sweden/Kungliga biblioteket, Stockholm. License: CC-BY-NC-ND. 225

Lithographic depiction of Bellman statue by G. Alfred Nyström, erected in Stockholm 1872. *Lithographic Album*, 1873. Reproduction: National Library of Sweden/Kungliga biblioteket, Stockholm. License: CC-BY-NC-ND. 229

Lithographic depiction of Molin's fountain, erected in Stockholm 1873. In *Lithographic Album*, 1873. Reproduction: National

Library of Sweden/Kungliga biblioteket, Stockholm. License: CC-BY-NC-ND. 230

Advertising short film *The Pastille Dance*. Produced by Marabou, 1938. Permission: Swedish Film Institute/Svenska Filminstitutet, Stockholm. License: CC-PD. Available at http://www.filmarkivet.se/movies/marabou-pastilldansen/. 240

Anthropomorphized consumer articles in the children's picture book *Per och Lisas julkök*. Unknown illustrator, most likely Marie Walle. Produced by Atelier E.O., Kooperativa förbundet, 1935. Reproduction: Swedish Children's Literature Institute/Svenska Barnboksinstitutet, Stockholm. License: CC-BY-NC-ND. Location of rights holder for this work has been unsuccessful after a diligent search. Copyright claims to this work are welcomed. 243

Advertising short film *Crisp Bread Parade*. Produced by Öhmans Spisbrödfabrik, 1933. Permission: Swedish Film Institute/Svenska Filminstitutet, Stockholm. License: CC-PD. Available at http://www.filmarkivet.se/movies/ohmans-spisbrodsfabrik-knackebrodsparaden/. 244

Advertising short film *The Ideal Baking Powder*. Produced by Marabou, 1945. Permission: Swedish Film Institute/Svenska Filminstitutet, Stockholm. License: CC-PD. Available at http://www.filmarkivet.se/movies/marabou-bakpulver-den-idealiska-burken/. 247

View of Sergel square, Stockholm, with the northern façade of the Culture house to the left. Sune Sundahl, 1985. Permission: Swedish National Centre for Architecture and Design/Statens centrum för arkitektur och design, Stockholm (ARKM 1988-111-SX2423-4). License: CC-BY. Available at DigitaltMuseum: https://digitaltmuseum.org/011015021173/kulturhuset-och-sergelstorg-stockholm-vinterbild-exterior. 274

Damaged Negatives: Scratched Portrait of Mrs. Baqari. Akram Zaatari, 2012. Inkjet print, framed. Made from 35 mm scratched negative from the Hashem el Madani archive. Copyright: Akram Zaatari. Courtesy of Thomas Dane Gallery, London. License: CC-BY-NC-ND. 289

Message from Andrée. Joachim Koester, 2005. 16 mm film animation. Copyright: Jocahim Koester. Courtesy of Jan Mot, Brussels and Gallery Nicolai Wallner, Copenhagen. License: CC-BY-NC-ND. 302

Zeppelin, Friedrichshafen, I: August 10–13, 1999. Vera Lutter, 1999. Unique, silver gelatin print. Copyright: Vera Lutter/Bildupphovsrätt 2018. License: CC-BY-NC-ND.   308

Sans Titre (hommage á B. Lategan). Lotta Antonsson, 2008. Silvergelatin photography, collage. Copyright: Lotta Antonsson. License: CC-BY-NC-ND.   311

Selection from the Analogue Portfolio. Zoe Leonard, 1998/2009. Dye transfer prints, 20 × 16 inches each/50.8 × 40.64 cm each. Copyright: Zoe Leonard. Courtesy of the artist, Hauser & Wirth, New York and Galerie Gisela Capitain, Cologne. License: CC-BY-NC-ND.   312

Front page of *Ny Illustrerad Tidning*, 1884. Reproduction: National Library of Sweden/Kungliga biblioteket, Stockholm. License: CC-BY-NC-ND.   336

"Sprich nicht immer … ." Arnold Schoenberg, 1908–09. From Schoenberg's *15 Gedichte aus Das Buch der hängenden Gärten von Stefan George für Stimme und Klavier* op. 15. Copyright: Copyright 1914, 1941 by Universal Edition A.G. Vienna UE5338. License: CC-BY-NC-ND.   360

Introduction
Christer Johansson and Sonya Petersson

In the present volume, intermediality is inclusively defined as *relations between media conventionally perceived as different*. It covers themes such as relations between old and new media, intermedial concepts such as remediation and illustration, and explorations of mixed-media objects as well as of objects in intermedial networks.[1] These and other intermedial issues are elaborated in this volume's fourteen individual chapters that bring together a number of highly diverse cases, ranging from present-day installation art, to twentieth-century geography books, to renaissance sculpture, and to public architecture of the 1970s.[2] This inclusive understanding of intermediality makes it possible for each individual study to narrow it down and specify it according to particular demands, methods, and research questions. Instead of stipulating a fixed definition, our shared concern is precisely to

---

[1] Cf. Irina O. Rajewsky's characterization of intermediality in the broad sense as "a generic term for all those phenomena that (as indicated by the prefix *inter*) in some way take place *between* media." Irina O. Rajewsky, "Intermediality, Intertextuality, and Remediation," *Intermediality: History and Theory of the Arts, Literature and Technologies*, no. 6 (2005): 46, 43–64. Italics in the original. See also note 37 below for a reference to Rajewsky's discussion about the assumption of conventional media differences included in the concept of intermediality.

[2] The authors are with few exceptions affiliated with the cross-disciplinary Department of Culture and Aesthetics at Stockholm University, where "Mediality" is established as a profiled research area.

How to cite this book chapter:
Johansson, Christer, and Sonya Petersson. "Introduction." In *The Power of the In-Between: Intermediality as a Tool for Aesthetic Analysis and Critical Reflection*, edited by Sonya Petersson, Christer Johansson, Magdalena Holdar, and Sara Callahan, 1–21. Stockholm: Stockholm University Press, 2018. DOI: https://doi.org/10.16993/baq.a. License: CC-BY.

explore the concept of intermediality. The key is to combine it with other perspectives, to provide it with particular methods and materials, and to make it the object of both aesthetic and media-historical approaches. While we take "aesthetic" to include issues of formal analysis, the arts, and experience, "media-historical" designates the specificity of media practice in time, space, and particular environments. Our aim to integrate these two lines of inquiry is intended to overcome what we understand as an unhappy divide between, on the one hand, the intermedial subfields of semiotically and formalistically oriented studies and, on the other, media-historical ones.[3] Consequently, "intermediality" in this volume is not only a concept employed to cover an inclusive range of cultural objects, cultural contexts, and methodological approaches, but is also modelled out by the particular cases it is brought to bear on.

The following introduction has a three-part structure. First, in the most general section, we discuss intermediality as a field of research in a broad and cross-disciplinary sense. Then, in the second section, the perspective is centered upon the present volume and its overarching objectives. The third and last section is the most specific and introduces the volume's outline and individual chapters.

---

[3] In this ambition, we complement a range of available edited volumes on intermediality, as, e.g.: *Changing Borders: Contemporary Positions in Intermediality*, eds. Jens Arvidson, Mikael Askander, Jørgen Bruhn, and Heidrun Führer (Lund: Intermedia Studies Press, 2007); *Framing Borders in Literature and Other Media*, eds. Werner Wolf and Walter Bernhart (Amsterdam: Rodopi, 2006); *Intermedial Arts: Disrupting, Remembering and Transforming Media*, eds. Leena Eilittä, Liliane Louvel, and Sabine Kim (Newcastle upon Tyne: Cambridge Scholars Publishing, 2012); *Intermedialitet: Ord, bild och ton i samspel*, ed. Hans Lund (Lund: Studentlitteratur, 2002); *Media Borders, Multimodality and Intermediality*, ed. Lars Elleström (Basingstoke: Palgrave Macmillan, 2010); *Intermedialities: Philosophy, Arts, Politics*, eds. Henk Oosterling and Ewa Plonowska Ziarek (Lanham: Lexington Books, 2011); *Media Inter Media: Essays in Honor of Claus Clüver*, eds. Claus Clüver and Stephanie A. Glaser (Amsterdam: Rodopi, 2009).

Intermediality as a Field of Research: Traditions, Rationales, and Subdivisions

The term "intermediality" may variously designate 1) certain cultural phenomena involving the interrelations between two or more media; 2) a cross-disciplinary subfield usually termed intermediality studies, starting to evolve during the 1990s; and 3) a larger field of research, including not only subfields like intermediality studies, but also allied fields like media theory and media history. Our presentation of the field of intermediality is informed by the third, inclusive, sense of the term.

Starting with intermediality studies in the narrower sense, as we know it today, it is often demonstrating its dependence on three interrelated research traditions: intertextuality, semiotics, and interart studies.[4] Its reliance on the first two, intertextuality and semiotics, is, for instance, clearly manifested in Werner Wolf's well-known model of intermedial relations, where intertextuality and intermediality are conceived of as two analogous phenomena of semiotic referentiality, or "intersemiotic relations."[5] For Wolf, intertextuality is the "mono-medial" variant of these

---

[4] This account of traditions is fairly presentist. Of course, it could be added that discussions on and investigations of media and relations between media are as old as Western thought. The examples that immediately come to mind are Horace's for centuries rehearsed phrase from *Ars Poetica*, "ut pictura poesis" ("as is painting so is poetry") and Lessing's *Laocoön*, still often acknowledged as an important instance of media studies *avant la lettre*. Both texts are available in early translations: Quintus Horatius Flaccus, *Q. Horatius Flaccus: His Art of Poetry*, trans. Ben Jonson (London: 1640 [c. 19 BC]); Gotthold Ephraim Lessing, *Laokoön: An Essay upon the Limits of Painting and Poetry*, trans. Ellen Frothingham (Boston: 1887 [1766]). For a discussion on the concept of medium in early modern and modern philosophy, see John Guillory, "Genesis of the Media Concept," *Critical Inquiry* 36, no. 2 (Winter 2010): 321–362.

[5] Werner Wolf, *The Musicalization of Fiction: A Study in the Theory and History of Intermediality* (Amsterdam: Rodopi, 1999), 46, 35–50. For a historiographic overview and a critical discussion of the concept of intertextuality, see Mary Orr, *Intertextuality: Debates and Contexts* (Cambridge: Polity, 2003). For an introduction to semiotics, see Daniel Chandler, *Semiotics: The Basics* (London: Routledge, 2002).

co-working and meaning-producing relations, while intermediality is the "cross-medial" one.⁶ The third tradition, interart studies, has been especially significant in the disciplines of comparative literature and art history, and may broadly be characterized by its comparative approach—not to media—but to the arts. The comparative approach proceeds from investigating how separate art forms differ from or resemble each other,⁷ often under the guidance of concepts such as ekphrasis ("the verbal representation of visual representation," e.g., poems about paintings), so-called artistic *Doppelbegabungen* (artists expressing themselves in more than one art form), or adaptation (a transfer of qualities from novel to film, from music to poetry, etc.).⁸ A typical product of the interart tradition is the edited volume *Interart Poetics: Essays on the Interrelations of the Arts and Media* (1997).⁹ Besides its typicality, the book should also be noted as an example of the differences between interart and intermediality studies and the emergence of the latter. The chapter written by Jürgen E. Müller, "Intermediality: A Plea and Some Theses for a New Approach in Media Studies," already in its title launches intermediality as a "new approach" and further describes it as a challenge to "specialized disciplines for different arts/media."¹⁰ Intermediality is

---

⁶ Wolf, *Musicalization of Fiction*, 46.
⁷ For a critical evaluation of the comparative tradition, see W. J. T. Mitchell's chapter "Beyond Comparison: Picture, Text, and Method," in *Picture Theory: Essays on Verbal and Visual Representation* (Chicago: University of Chicago Press, 1994), 83–107.
⁸ The definition of *ekphrasis* is taken from Mitchell, *Picture Theory*, 152. For studies on ekphrasis and adaptation, both in line with the interart tradition and deviating from it, see *Pictures into Words: Theoretical and Descriptive Approaches to Ekphrasis*, eds. Valerie Robillard and Els Jongeneel (Amsterdam: VU University Press, 1998); Stephen Cheeke, *Writing for Art: The Aesthetics of Ekphrasis* (Manchester: Manchester University Press, 2008); *Adaptation Studies: New Challenges, New Directions*, eds. Jørgen Bruhn, Anne Gjelsvik, and Eirik Frisvold Hanssen (London: Bloomsbury Academy, 2013).
⁹ *Interart Poetics: Essays on the Interrelations of the Arts and Media*, eds. Ulla-Britta Lagerroth, Hans Lund, and Erik Hedling (Amsterdam: Rodopi, 1997).
¹⁰ Jürgen E. Müller, "Intermediality: A Plea and Some Theses for a New Approach in Media Studies," in *Interart Poetics: Essays on the Interrelations of the Arts and Media*, eds. Ulla-Britta Lagerroth, Hans

thus presented as the successor of interart studies, which replaces the comparative tradition with a more wide-ranging crossing of borders between media and disciplines. Instead of making the canonized art forms the center of attention, the rationale for intermediality studies is to foreground the more inclusive concept of medium, embracing not only the arts but also medial multimodality, different forms of popular culture, and new digital media.

The traditions of intertextuality, semiotics, and interart studies are especially interwoven in the intermedial subfield oriented toward formal analysis mentioned above.[11] Again, Wolf's model of intermediality is one of the prime examples, since it is concerned with schematizing media interrelations in typologies based on formal qualities, such as "intracompositional" as opposed to "extracompositional," "overt/direct" as opposed to "covert/indirect," and in modes of "showing" as opposed to "telling."[12] Similarly, Irina O. Rajewsky's distinctions between "medial transpositions" ("transformation" in Wolf's terminology, or the production of one media object out of qualities of another, "first," medium), "medial combinations" (two distinct media present in one object in their own materiality), and "intermedial references" (references to an absent medium by way of the first medium's own media specific means), are structured by formal qualities of absent or present media objects.[13]

A rationale for studying intermedial relations that is not so much based on formal typologies but more pointing to the role and function of sensory, perceptual, and interpretative interaction

---

Lund, and Erik Hedling (Amsterdam: Rodopi, 1997), 295 (quote), 295–304.

[11] Cf. Jørgen Bruhn's discussion of the "'formalistic' line of intermediality studies." Jørgen Bruhn, "Heteromediality," in *Media Borders, Multimodality and Intermediality*, ed. Lars Elleström (Basingstoke: Palgrave Macmillan, 2010), 231, 225–236.

[12] Wolf, *Musicalization of Fiction*, 37–46; for "intracompositional" and "extracompositional" cf. Werner Wolf, ed., "Metareference across Media: The Concept, its Transmedial Potentials and Problems, Main Forms and Functions," in *Metareference across Media: Theory and Case Studies* (Amsterdam: Rodopi, 2009), 19–20, 1–85.

[13] Rajewsky, "Intermediality, Intertextuality, and Remediation," 51–53. See also Irina O. Rajewsky, *Intermedialität* (Tübingen: Francke, 2002). Cf. Wolf, *Musicalization of Fiction*, 42.

with media is developed by W. J. T. Mitchell and Lars Ellestrōm and may be called the multimodal conception of mediality. This concept recognizes media as operative by what Mitchell calls "sensory, perceptual and semiotic elements" and what Ellestrōm terms "modalities." Mitchell's argument, in the article "There Are No Visual Media" (first published in 2005), is basically that a medium and its mediation always entail some mixture of the sensory, perceptual, and semiotic elements.[14] All media are necessarily approached by the senses (sight, hearing, touch, etc.) and prompted by "semiotic operators," such as the Peircean triad of iconic, indexical, and symbolic signs.[15] Mitchell's point is therefore that all media are "mixed media," but all media are emphatically not "mixed in the same way."[16] The latter, and sometimes forgotten, part of Mitchell's famous phrasing is perhaps the most important, since it entails a more qualified concept of medium specificity than is warranted by the traditional mono-modal perspective. For Mitchell, the acknowledgement of the mixedness of all media makes it urgent to describe and analyze individual objects by their various specific media elements or making a "more precise differentiation of mixtures."[17] Ellestrōm's multimodal concept follows the logic of Mitchell's: four "modalities" are understood as present in all media, but in different ways, to different degrees, and in different combinations. Ellestrōm distinguishes between "the material modality," "the sensorial modality," "the spatiotemporal modality," and the "semiotic modality."[18] The

---

[14] Mitchell's article "There Are No Visual Media," *Journal of Visual Culture* 4 (2005): 257–266, has later been reprinted with minor amendments in W. J. T. Mitchell, "There Are No Visual Media," in *MediaArtHistories*, ed. Oliver Grau (Cambridge: MIT Press, 2007), 395–406 and in W. J. T. Mitchell, *Image Science: Iconology, Visual Culture, and Media Aesthetics* (Chicago: University of Chicago Press, 2015), 129 (quote), 125–135.

[15] Mitchell, *Image Science*, 130. In Peirce's semiotics, symbolic signs work by convention, iconic by resemblance, and indexical by cause and effect or existential relations. Cf. Charles S. Peirce, "Logics as Semiotic: The Theory of Signs," in *Semiotics: An Introductory Anthology*, ed. Robert E. Innis (Bloomington: Indiana University Press, 1985), 1–23.

[16] Mitchell, *Image Science*, 129.

[17] Mitchell, *Image Science*, 129.

[18] Lars Ellestrōm, ed., "The Modalities of Media: A Model for Understanding Intermedial Relations," in *Media Borders, Multimodality*

latter coincides with Mitchell's semiotic element in its reliance on Peirce's sign functions. The sensorial modality regards the physical and mental acts of perceiving the medial interface, the material modality includes the "latent corporeality of the medium," whereas the spatiotemporal modality covers "the structuring of the sensorial perception of sense-data of the material interface into experiences and conceptions of space and time."[19] In other words, Elleström's modalities, just like Mitchell's elements, enable media to function as media; that is, to mediate and signify. The material interfaces condition sensory inputs, which give rise to perceptions that are structured in space and time and understood as signifying.[20] It should also be stressed that the multimodal concept of medium designates intermedial relations as present from the start: media objects, from television shows to epic poems, are media specific only by virtue of their perceived mixtures.

The field of intermediality thus offers a range of terms and approaches designed to describe and analyze media and media interrelations. Nevertheless, there is one fundamental question that needs to be answered by anyone taking an interest in using the tools on offer: Why should they be used in the first place? Are formal, synchronic investigations of medial modes and intermedial relations in artworks and other kinds of artefacts motivation enough, or are the intermedial categories and concepts just tools to be used in studies with additional and greater ambitions? No doubt the formalistic answer to these questions will differ from an answer with media-historical, diachronic, points of departure—a subdivision of the intermedial field that will be more directly addressed in the next section. Here, it should only be noted, firstly, that media history and what is commonly called media theory rarely approach relations between media as ends in themselves, but rather as means to explore larger questions of, for instance, media's role in maintaining or subverting social and cultural power, performing cultural agency, or taking part in the formation of epistemological ruptures and traditions.

---

and *Intermediality* (Basingstoke: Palgrave Macmillian, 2010), 17–24, 11–48.
[19] Elleström, "Modalities of Media," 17 (first quote), 18 (second quote).
[20] Elleström, "Modalities of Media," 17–24.

Secondly, we insist on including media history and theory in intermediality as an area of research, since these fields' exploration of media history cannot but take relations between media into consideration.[21] Such relations are, for example, those between oral and written media on the one hand, and between old and new media on the other. The relationship between oral and written media have been frequently discussed in the context of diachronic relations, media revolutions, and historical junctures and networks by the pioneering media theorists Eric A. Havelock, Walter Ong, and Marshall McLuhan (as well as by later exponents of the field, such as Friedrich Kittler and Jan Assmann).[22] The relationship between old and new media have both been understood as a question of what Lisa Gitelman calls media-historical specificity (see more in the next section),[23] and closely associated with Jay

---

[21] This is also the case with the field of media archaeology (not to be confused with media history in the sense of, e.g., Lisa Gitelman). In his account of the rationales and interests of the media-archaeological project, Jussi Parikka singles out "intermediality" as one of its issues. Jussi Parikka, *What is Media Archaeology?* (Cambridge: Polity, 2012), 10, 19, 25–27, 34, 37, 38, 154.

[22] Eric Alfred Havelock, *The Muse Learns to Write: Reflections on Orality and Literacy from Antiquity to the Present* (New Haven: Yale University Press, 1986); Walter J. Ong, *Orality and Literacy: The Technologizing of the Word* (London: Methuen, 1982); Marshall McLuhan, *The Gutenberg Galaxy: The Making of Typographic Man* (London: Routledge and K. Paul, 1962); Friedrich A. Kittler, *Gramophone, Film, Typewriter* (Stanford: Stanford University Press, 1999); Jan Assmann, *Cultural Memory and Early Civilization: Writing, Remembrance, and Political Imagination*, 1st English ed. (Cambridge: Cambridge University Press, 2011).

[23] Lisa Gitelman, *Always Already New: Media, History, and the Data of Culture* (Cambridge: MIT Press, 2006), 1–22. For further discussions of media-historical approaches to old and new media see Lisa Gitelman and Geoffrey B. Pingree, eds., "Introduction: What's New About New Media?," in *New Media, 1740–1915* (Cambridge: MIT Press, 2003), xi–xxii; David Thornburn and Henry Jenkins, eds., "Introduction: Toward an Aesthetics of Transition," in *Rethinking Media Change: The Aesthetics of Transition* (Cambridge: MIT Press, 2003), 1–16. The historical perspective on new media in these volumes is opposed to the view that new media are confined to present digital media and that its distinguishing factor is its unprecedented possibilities of embodiment, as in Mark B. N. Hansen, *New Philosophy for New Media* (Cambridge: MIT Press, 2004), 21–46.

David Bolter and Richard Grusin's concept of "remediation."[24] The latter designates a kind of intermedial relationship in which both old and new media, by way of processes of medial refashioning, are involved in "competition or rivalry," and struggling for cultural status, either through "immediacy" (concealing media) or through "hypermediacy" (foregrounding media).[25] Investigating digital media, Bolter and Grusin argue that "all current media function as remediators," and thus pay homage to as well as rival earlier media through the particular ways in which they refashion them.[26] The same is however true of old media: "remediation operates in both directions: users of older media such as film and television can seek to appropriate and refashion digital graphics, just as digital graphics artists can refashion film and television."[27] Bolter and Grusin maintain remediation to be a "defining characteristic" of the new digital media and, at the same time, a fundamental characteristic of all medial practices.[28]

The previous attention to relations between doublets such as orality and literacy, and old and new media, motivates the method of triangulation introduced by Mitchell and Mark B. N. Hansen in a recent textbook in media studies.[29] At its most general level, the method is designed to sidestep the binarism exposed above and, more particularly, explore the way media do more than just passively participate in culture—that is, have actual agency in interconnecting the specific cultural and historical domains of aesthetics, society, and technology. The question "[h]ow are media distributed across the nexus of technology, aesthetics, and society, and can they serve as points of convergence that facilitate communication among these domains?" deliberately seeks to bridge

---

[24] Jay David Bolter and Richard Grusin, *Remediation: Understanding New Media* (Cambridge: MIT Press, 1999). The concept is defined on p. 45.
[25] Bolter and Grusin, *Remediation*, 45, cf. 5. "Immediacy" and "hypermediacy" are explained on pp. 11–12, 21–44, 54–55, 70–71.
[26] Bolter and Grusin, *Remediation*, 55, cf. 14–15.
[27] Bolter and Grusin, *Remediation*, 48.
[28] Bolter and Grusin, *Remediation*, 45, 65.
[29] W. J. T. Mitchell and Mark B. N. Hansen, eds., "Introduction," in *Critical Terms for Media Studies* (Chicago: University of Chicago Press, 2010), vi–xxii.

conventionally un-bridged areas.³⁰ Mitchell and Hansen make the concept of media their rationale for bridging and interconnecting, by recognizing it as that which "mediates" between binaries and also, relying on McLuhan, as that which impacts experience through its content as well as through its formal and technological qualities. Ultimately, media are envisioned as opening "onto the notion of a form of life, of a general environment for living—for thinking, perceiving, sensing, feeling."³¹ Mitchell and Hansen's reconceptualization of media as an environment for living is not only based on the obvious fact that media are "everywhere," from human bodies to newspapers, but also on the way it both conditions and makes experiencing and understanding possible.³²

So far, we have presented intermediality as a much wider field than intermediality studies in the narrower sense. The gained insight, which informs our objectives below, is the benefit of moving between subfields rather than fixing our position in one of them.

Exploring Intermediality as a Tool for Aesthetic Analysis and Critical Reflection

The function of intermediality in this volume can be described as a "travelling concept."³³ First, it travels between different disciplines. It is employed in studies emanating from art history, comparative literature, theatre studies, musicology, and history of ideas. But more to the point of our aim to explore it and fuse it with other perspectives, the concept of intermediality travels from

---

[30] Mitchell and Hansen, "Introduction," viii.
[31] Mitchell and Hansen, "Introduction," xii.
[32] Mitchell and Hansen, "Introduction," x–xiv. Closely connected to Mitchell and Hansen's widened concept of medium is John Durham Peter's conceptualization of media as environments or ecosystems: "Once communication is understood not only as sending messages—certainly an essential function—but also as providing conditions for existence, media cease to be only studios and stations, messages and channels, and become infrastructures and forms of life." John Durham Peters, *The Marvelous Clouds: Toward a Philosophy of Elemental Media* (Chicago: University of Chicago Press, 2015), 14.
[33] "Travelling concept" as defined in Mieke Bal, *Travelling Concepts in the Humanities: A Rough Guide* (Toronto: University of Toronto Press, 2002), 22–55.

Jørgen Bruhn and Henriette Thune's combination of it with the Bakthinian aesthetic object, to Peter Gillgren's connection of it to Kristeva's intertextuality, and to Elina Druker's insertion of it in a Baudrillarian socio-ideological economy of signs. Throughout the volume, intermediality is both the concept that informs the studies and a concept modelled out in encounters with their particular materials, methods, and research questions.

However inclusive, in all cases intermediality concerns something that takes place *in between* media.[34] One first sense of the in-between is that it is *productive*. For instance, in Bruhn and Thune's study of Sophie Calle's exhibition *Rachel, Monique*, the authors demonstrate how the space in between the media objects juxtaposed in the exhibition gives rise to "formal content," or themes that not only correspond to more explicit themes in the exhibition, but also add values like multiplicity and irony to the latter.

Anything that is in-between is also about the *crossing of borders*. As noted above, intermediality has, from its launch in the 1990s, been promoted as a field of research that transgresses borders between disciplines as well as between the specific media conventionally studied within them.[35] If keeping with the conventional view that disciplines are fairly separated and that their objects are fairly media specific, one could say that this volume testifies to the often-recognized promise of exchange over disciplinary borders. It includes, for example, literary scholars working with an art exhibition, art historians working with text and film, a musicologist studying film, and a historian of ideas studying images. But one could also leave the conventional view and, to paraphrase Mitchell, say that the disciplines are just like media in being mixed from the outset. Take art history and one of its traditional objects, painting, as an example: Has not painting

---

[34] Cf. the discussion of "in-between" in relation to the etymology and historiography of the term in Stephanie A. Glaser, "Dynamics of Intermedial Inquiry," in *Media Inter Media: Essays in Honor of Claus Clüver*, eds. Claus Clüver and Stephanie A. Glaser (Amsterdam: Rodopi, 2009), 12–15.

[35] The latter is a pattern of association that permeates Werner Wolf's discussion about "metareferentiality" as a transdisciplinary and transmedial category in Wolf, "Metareference across Media," 1–85.

"always" been the object of art historical/academic interpretation in words, disseminated in the medium of writing and in the package of books? Has not painting, by the practices in and of art history, been reproduced in slides and photographs, not to mention by digital interface?[36] This is not an argument that in any way denies the infrastructural compartmentalization of the academy, but points to the already mixed character of *both* the disciplines *and* their assumed media objects. The very difference between the traditional, comparative approach to intermedial phenomena and the mixed-media approach is that the latter conceives of the object—a sculpture or a painting just as well as a comic strip or a film—as always a product of more than one medium. Accordingly, that which takes place in between media may also take place *within* one object, as distinct from between two separate objects, taken to represent specific media. But importantly, in each case there must still be, as Irina O. Rajewsky writes, an "assumption of tangible borders between individual media, of media specificities and differences."[37] In short, the concept of intermediality—relations between media conventionally perceived as different—demands that media borders and differences are presupposed from the start. Otherwise there would be no borders to transgress, destabilize, and challenge.

The idea of the in-between as a transgression of borders is not restricted to the borders between disciplines or between media. As will be demonstrated in detail in the chapters that follow, it may, by analogy, be transferred to various other conventionally separated categories. For instance, Anna Dahlgren takes Walter Benjamin's classic argument further and highlights the transgression between the original work of art and its reproduction,[38] Peter

---

[36] For disciplinary/institutional practices, "protocols," structuring media use, cf. Lisa Gitelman, *Always Already New*, 7–8.

[37] Irina O. Rajewsky, "Border Talks: The Problematic Status of Media Borders in the Current Debate about Intermediality," in *Media Borders, Multimodality and Intermediality*, ed. Lars Elleström (Basingstoke: Palgrave Macmillan, 2010), 52 (quote), 61, 63, 51–68.

[38] The new translation of Benjamin's essay "The Work of Art in the Age of Its Technological Reproducibility: Second Version" is available in *The Work of Art in the Age of Its Technological Reproducibility and Other Writings on Media*, eds. Michael W. Jennings, Brigid Doherty, and

Gillgren makes a point of transgressing the border between past and present by analyzing the themes of night and sleep as "migrating" between renaissance sculpture and present-day photography, while Daria and Kim Skjoldager-Nielsen's argument about media embodiment transgresses the border between object and subject. These are indeed examples of the power of the in-between.

Our attempt to integrate aesthetic and media-historical approaches to intermediality is, as noted, an attempt to integrate formal and historical lines of analysis. Needless to say, the benefit of Wolf's and Rajewsky's typologies of intermediality is a fine-tuned terminology that specifies the complexities of formal relations. Nonetheless, it should be stressed that neither Wolf's nor Rajewsky's elaboration of distinctions need to be media-historically framed or demonstrated as culturally, socially, politically, epistemologically, or institutionally embedded in the particularity of time and space. The latter approach is precisely what Lisa Gitelman argues for when she succinctly writes that "specificity is key."[39] Rather than essentializing media as, well, "media," Gitelman calls for the specificity of media in history. To take another example from the present volume, this corresponds to the difference between what would, in Sara Callahan's study, be digital photography in general as opposed to the specificity of the present-day artistic genre of digital photography, discursively established as a new medium against the preceding medium of analogue photography. Our conviction is that the call for historical specificity does not rule out, but may very-well include attention to formal qualities. Likewise, formal considerations of media interrelations may very-well be simultaneously treated as issues of social, cultural, and political use and abuse in particular media environments. Throughout this book, our integrative perspective also takes different forms. One example is Johanna Ethnersson Pontara's close analysis of the "formal imitation" of opera in Ingmar Bergman's film *The Hour of the Wolf*. The author pays considerable attention to how media combination and intermedial references interact with the modalities of sound, image,

---

Thomas Y. Levin, trans. Edmund Jephcott, Rodney Livingstone, Howard Eiland, and Others (Cambridge: Harvard University Press, 2008), 19–55.
[39] Lisa Gitelman, *Always Already New*, 7.

and speech. The formal analysis is, however, intersected by considerations of the film's narrative (which is another perspective combined with intermediality) and its early reception (which is a historical issue). Another example is Magdalena Holdar's study, in which the argument is built around the performative character of Yoko Ono's work *Space Transformer*. In Holdar's case, intermediality takes on exactly the historical role Lisa Gitelman and Geoffrey B. Pingree has described as an "agent […] of cultural definition and cultural change."[40] For Holdar, the historical articulation of a theory of intermediality (by Dick Higgins) and the artistic and political intermedial practices of the Fluxus movement are cultural-historical factors that contributed to make the radical agenda of Ono's work possible.

The last aspect to highlight here is the critical potential of media history, a recurring theme in Mitchell's writings. In discussing text and image relations in film, Mitchell presents them as "a site of conflict, a nexus where political, institutional, and social antagonisms play themselves out in the materiality of representation."[41] Put differently, any mix of media and modalities matter, as vehicles for, or signs of, corresponding social, ideological and discursive borders, convergences, and power relations.[42] These are critical considerations of media and of qualities in media that are historical through and through: As when, for example, Elina Druker examines how a network of references between the inter-war era's avant-garde film, music, window display, artistic styles, and branded advertising furthered a market-driven media aesthetics in the service of the ideology of the "welfare state."

Artefacts, Networks, and Concepts

The present volume is divided into three parts, under the headings "Artefacts," "Networks," and "Concepts." These headings are intended to describe how intermedial considerations enter and are

---

[40] Gitelman and Pingree, "Introduction: What's New About New Media?," xvi.
[41] Mitchell, *Picture Theory*, 91.
[42] Cf. Mitchell, *Image Science*, 167–179.

put to work in the different contributions. In characterizing the authors' use of intermediality, they both target the objects studied and the way the objects are approached. It goes almost without saying that all studies include medial artefacts, concepts, and networks, even if not to the same extent. Nonetheless, the criterion for inclusion is in all cases qualitative. The studies are included under the heading that best corresponds to their approach and line of argument, rather than to any quantitative amount of artefacts, networks, and concepts.

The first part, "Artefacts," includes six studies that all focus on a particular object or exhibition. This is the case in Johanna Ethersson Pontara's analysis of Bergman's film *The Hour of the Wolf*, Peter Gillgren's analysis of Michelangelo's sculpture *Night*, Magdalena Holdar's analysis of Yoko Ono's instruction artwork *Space Transformer*, and Rikard Hoogland's analysis of a photomontage of a Swedish late nineteenth-century theatre performance. In these studies, the intermediality of one particular object is targeted and determines other considerations. In Bruhn and Thune's and Daria and Kim Skjoldager-Nielsen's contributions, dealing with Sophie Calle's exhibition *Rachel, Monique* and the theatre group Hotel Pro Forma's exhibition *Today's Cake is a Log*, relations between media are studied within the totality of the exhibitions.

All studies further demonstrate different approaches to intermediality. While Ethnersson Pontara is making a careful formal analysis of operatic qualities in the film, Gillgren's focus is on the themes of night and sleep. Spurred by Kristeva's concept of intertextuality, these themes are examined as realized in the sculpture's sixteenth-century multimodal environment and "migrating" across then contemporary poetry and philosophy as well as into present-day culture. Holdar's case, which centers on the performative transgression of human and non-human agency, makes the argument that part of the performative force of Ono's work stemmed from the intermedial theory and practice in the artistic milieu of the Fluxus movement. Daria and Kim Skjoldager-Nielsen share Holdar's interest in performativity, but combine it with attention to remediation as an aesthetic strategy in the Hotel Pro Forma exhibition. Hoogland makes a theatre historical case of the complex "layers" of the photomontage, layers that are traced to the media practices of illustrative drawings, light, play script, and theatre photography. Bruhn and Thune share the interest in intersubjectivity with Gillgren, but derive it from Mikhail Bakhtin (rather than Kristeva). Besides making an analysis of Calle's exhibition as a Bakhtinian aesthetic and notably intersubjective object, the authors also use the study to develop a method of analysis where the introductory step is to make an inventory of "medialities" as a framework for analyzing meaning production.

The four studies in part two, "Networks," more symmetrically deal with, on the one hand, networks of different media, and, on the other, networks of media in networks of societal distribution and ideological, political, and scientific discourses.[43] Both aspects of networks are present in all four studies, albeit not equally stressed. Anna Dahlgren and Staffan Bergwik emphasize networks of media. In Dahlgren's case, the central issue is the reproduction of art. One of the important points demonstrated by Dahlgren challenges any notion of a direct relationship between art and reproductive media. The late nineteenth-century lithographic album, around which she builds her media network, is a reproduction. It is, however, shown to remediate not only the original works of art, but also photography as yet another medium of reproduction. In Bergwik's case, the widely distributed geography books by the Swedish explorer Sven Hedin are analyzed as media technological nexuses of "descriptive layering." Bergwik investigates how the book's interlayered photographs, drawings, and texts are both transgressive of any particular media technology and merging with the idea of a "panoramic vision" in early twentieth-century geographical discourse. Elina Druker and Fredrik Krohn Andersson, respectively, lay stress on networks of media as vehicles for ideology and politics: the consumer society of the inter-war era and the Swedish cultural policy of the 1970s. Druker shows how the mass advertising of branded picture books and short films echoes avant-garde and entertainment media genres and thus not only interconnects media but also traditionally

---

[43] Cf. the double sense of "networks of remediation" in Bolter and Grusin, *Remediation*, 65–84.

separated categories like art and advertising. Krohn Andersson traces the mediations of "the new cultural policy" in governmental bills, the architectonic space of the newly built cultural center in Stockholm, and an information film as media channels for the infected political issue of culture's inherent openness. However, it is Krohn Andersson's contention that these mediations do more than just realize the "new cultural policy"; in less controllable ways, they introduce an element of uncertainty to it.

Part three, "Concepts," also consists of four studies, that all have a concept (or concepts) as object of study, although it is derived from and elaborated against various materials. In this last section, the reader will get acquainted with, in Sarah Callahan's case, the contemporary art genre of digital photography and criticism of analogue photography; in Sonya Petersson's study, historiographic texts on the genre of illustration and the late nineteenth-century illustrated press; in Erik Wallrup's text, intermedial theory and a song by Arnold Schoenberg; and in Christer Johansson's case, media theory or, more specifically, the conceptualizations of the relations between old and new media in the well-known books of Bolter and Grusin and Lev Manovich. Callahan's name for the conceptual category she both tentatively starts out from and offers as outcome is "the analogue." It refers both to a corpus of texts revealing a cluster of associations around analogue photography and to an analytical strategy. From the point of view of relations between old and new media, Callahan importantly points out that "the analogue" is made visible by being folded against digital photography, which also means that the later medium has, *a posteriori*, created that which preceded it. The remaining three studies are all in different ways engaged in critical readings. Petersson deconstructs the concept of illustration by attending to the inherent ambiguity of the "conventional concept" and offers a demonstration of a tentatively defined alternative concept. Wallrup's concern is with the "song as event" or an argument elaborated in reconsideration of what the author argues to be "a semiotic overstatement" in intermedial theory, where meaning in music is reduced to a sign. Lastly, Johansson undertakes a "metatheoretical" re-reading of the works by Bolter and Grusin and Manovich that discloses the internal architecture of the texts: their conceptual transfers, use of metaphors, and patterns of inference. The analysis shows how Bolter and Grusin's and Manovich's concepts are a mix of traditional theorizing and postmodern strategies, underpinning the author's concluding suggestion of new directions for future explorations of the relations between old and new media.

References

Adaptation Studies: New Challenges, New Directions, edited by Jørgen Bruhn, Anne Gjelsvik, and Eirik Frisvold Hanssen. London: Bloomsbury Academy, 2013.

Assmann, Jan. *Cultural Memory and Early Civilization: Writing, Remembrance, and Political Imagination.* 1st English ed. Cambridge: Cambridge University Press, 2011.

Bal, Mieke. *Travelling Concepts in the Humanities: A Rough Guide.* Toronto: University of Toronto Press, 2002.

Benjamin, Walter. "The Work of Art in the Age of Its Technological Reproducibility: Second Version." In *The Work of Art in the Age of Its Technological Reproducibility and Other Writings on Media*, edited by Michael W. Jennings, Brigid Doherty, and Thomas Y. Levin, translated by Edmund Jephcott, Rodney Livingstone, Howard Eiland, and Others, 19–55. Cambridge: Harvard University Press, 2008.

Bolter, Jay David, and Richard Grusin. *Remediation: Understanding New Media.* Cambridge: MIT Press, 1999.

Bruhn, Jørgen. "Heteromediality." In *Media Borders, Multimodality and Intermediality*, edited by Lars Elleström, 225–236. Basingstoke: Palgrave Macmillan, 2010.

Chandler, Daniel. *Semiotics: The Basics.* London: Routledge, 2002.

Changing Borders: Contemporary Positions in Intermediality, edited by Jens Arvidson, Mikael Askander, Jørgen Bruhn, and Heidrun Führer. Lund: Intermedia Studies Press, 2007.

Cheeke, Stephen. *Writing for Art: The Aesthetics of Ekphrasis.* Manchester: Manchester University Press, 2008.

Durham Peters, John. *The Marvelous Clouds: Toward a Philosophy of Elemental Media*. Chicago: University of Chicago Press, 2015.

Elleström, Lars, ed. "The Modalities of Media: A Model for Understanding Intermedial Relations." In *Media Borders, Multimodality and Intermediality*, 11–48. Basingstoke: Palgrave Macmillan, 2010.

Flaccus, Quintus Horatius. *Q. Horatius Flaccus: His Art of Poetry*. Translated by Ben Jonson. London: 1640 [c. 19 BC].

Framing Borders in Literature and Other Media, edited by Werner Wolf and Walter Bernhart. Amsterdam: Rodopi, 2006.

Gitelman, Lisa. *Always Already New: Media, History, and the Data of Culture*. Cambridge: MIT Press, 2006.

Gitelman, Lisa, and Geoffrey B. Pingree, eds. "Introduction: What's New About New Media?" In *New Media, 1740–1915*, xi–xxii. Cambridge: MIT Press, 2003.

Glaser, Stephanie A. "Dynamics of Intermedial Inquiry." In *Media Inter Media: Essays in Honor of Claus Clüver*, edited by Claus Clüver and Stephanie A. Glaser, 11–31. Amsterdam: Rodopi, 2009.

Guillory, John. "Genesis of the Media Concept." *Critical Inquiry* 36, no. 2 (Winter 2010): 321–362.

Hansen, Mark B. N. *New Philosophy for New Media*. Cambridge: MIT Press, 2004.

Havelock, Eric Alfred. *The Muse Learns to Write: Reflections on Orality and Literacy from Antiquity to the Present*. New Haven: Yale University Press, 1986.

Interart Poetics: Essays on the Interrelations of the Arts and Media, edited by Ulla-Britta Lagerroth, Hans Lund, and Erik Hedling. Amsterdam: Rodopi, 1997.

Intermedial Arts: Disrupting, Remembering and Transforming Media, edited by Leena Eilittä, Liliane Louvel, and Sabine Kim. Newcastle upon Tyne: Cambridge Scholars Publishing, 2012.

Intermedialitet: Ord, bild och ton i samspel, edited by Hans Lund. Lund: Studentlitteratur, 2002.

Intermedialities: Philosophy, Arts, Politics, edited by Henk Oosterling and Ewa Plonowska Ziarek. Lanham: Lexington Books, 2011.

Kittler, Friedrich A. *Gramophone, Film, Typewriter*. Stanford: Stanford University Press, 1999.

Lessing, Gotthold Ephraim. *Laokoön: An Essay upon the Limits of Painting and Poetry*. Translated by Ellen Frothingham. Boston: 1887 [1766].

McLuhan, Marshall. *The Gutenberg Galaxy: The Making of Typographic Man*. London: Routledge and K. Paul, 1962.

Media Borders, Multimodality and Intermediality, edited by Lars Elleström. Basingstoke: Palgrave Macmillan, 2010.

Media Inter Media: Essays in Honor of Claus Clüver, edited by Claus Clüver and Stephanie A. Glaser. Amsterdam: Rodopi, 2009.

Mitchell, W. J. T., and Mark B. N. Hansen, eds. "Introduction." In *Critical Terms for Media Studies*, vi–xxii. Chicago: University of Chicago Press, 2010.

Mitchell, W. J. T. *Image Science: Iconology, Visual Culture, and Media Aesthetics*. Chicago: University of Chicago Press, 2015.

Mitchell, W. J. T. *Picture Theory: Essays on Verbal and Visual Representation*. Chicago: University of Chicago Press, 1994.

Mitchell, W. J. T. "There Are No Visual Media." *Journal of Visual Culture* 4 (2005): 257–266.

Mitchell, W .J. T. "There Are No Visual Media." In *MediaArtHistories*, edited by Oliver Grau, 395–406. Cambridge: MIT Press, 2007.

Müller, Jürgen E. "Intermediality: A Plea and Some Theses for a New Approach in Media Studies." In *Interart Poetics: Essays on the Interrelations of the Arts and Media*, edited by Ulla-Britta Lagerroth, Hans Lund, and Erik Hedling, 295–304. Amsterdam: Rodopi, 1997.

Ong, Walter J. *Orality and Literacy: The Technologizing of the Word*. London: Methuen, 1982.

Orr, Mary. *Intertextuality: Debates and Contexts*. Cambridge: Polity, 2003.

Parikka, Jussi. *What is Media Archaeology?* Cambridge: Polity, 2012.

Peirce, Charles S. "Logics as Semiotic: The Theory of Signs." In *Semiotics: An Introductory Anthology*, edited by Robert E. Innis, 1–23. Bloomington: Indiana University Press, 1985.

Pictures into Words: Theoretical and Descriptive Approaches to Ekphrasis, edited by Valerie Robillard and Els Jongeneel. Amsterdam: VU University Press, 1998.

Rajewsky, Irina O. "Border Talks: The Problematic Status of Media Borders in the Current Debate about Intermediality." In *Media Borders, Multimodality and Intermediality*, edited by Lars Elleström, 51–68. Basingstoke: Palgrave Macmillan, 2010.

Rajewsky, Irina O. "Intermediality, Intertextuality, and Remediation." *Intermediality: History and Theory of the Arts, Literature and Technologies*, no. 6 (2005): 43–64.

Rajewsky, Irina O. *Intermedialität*. Tübingen: Francke, 2002.

Thornburn, David, and Henry Jenkins, eds. "Introduction: Toward an Aesthetics of Transition." In *Rethinking Media Change: The Aesthetics of Transition*, 1–16. Cambridge: MIT Press, 2003.

Wolf, Werner, ed. "Metareference across Media: The Concept, its Transmedial Potentials and Problems, Main Forms and Functions." In *Metareference across Media: Theory and Case Studies*, 1–85. Amsterdam: Rodopi, 2009.

Wolf, Werner. *The Musicalization of Fiction: A Study in the Theory and History of Intermediality*. Amsterdam: Rodopi, 1999.

PART ONE: ARTEFACTS

In between Life and Death: Sophie Calle's *Rachel, Monique* (2014)
Jørgen Bruhn and Henriette Thune

Abstract

This chapter is dedicated to Sophie Calle's aesthetically rich and existentially moving art exhibition *Rachel, Monique* (2014), representing her mother's death in 2006. Calle's well-known dichotomies between private and public, random acts and aesthetic form are repeated in a new dichotomy between life and death, and the nuances in between these. The authors suggest a combination of some of the fundamental notions of intermedial studies combined with the aesthetic theory of Mikhail Bakhtin in order to grasp the exhibition and the experience of it.

Introduction

The art exhibition *Rachel, Monique* is Sophie Calle's artistic representation of her mother's death. It is shown in a side chapel of The Episcopal Church of the Heavenly Rest on the Upper East Side, New York City. At the back of the room, which is the sanctuary and thus the front of the chapel, there is a reading going on, emerging through loudspeakers. There are butterflies meticulously pinned on the right-hand wall, forming the word "souci"—French for "worry" or "care"—close to a large photograph of an open coffin in full size, horizontally placed on the left-hand side floor. Numerous photographs and texts are displayed on walls and floors. It is difficult not to be drawn towards a large projection on

---

How to cite this book chapter:
Bruhn, Jørgen, and Henriette Thune. "In between Life and Death: Sophie Calle's *Rachel, Monique* (2014)." In *The Power of the In-Between: Intermediality as a Tool for Aesthetic Analysis and Critical Reflection*, edited by Sonya Petersson, Christer Johansson, Magdalena Holdar, and Sara Callahan, 25–48. Stockholm: Stockholm University Press, 2018. DOI: https://doi.org/10.16993/baq.b. License: CC-BY.

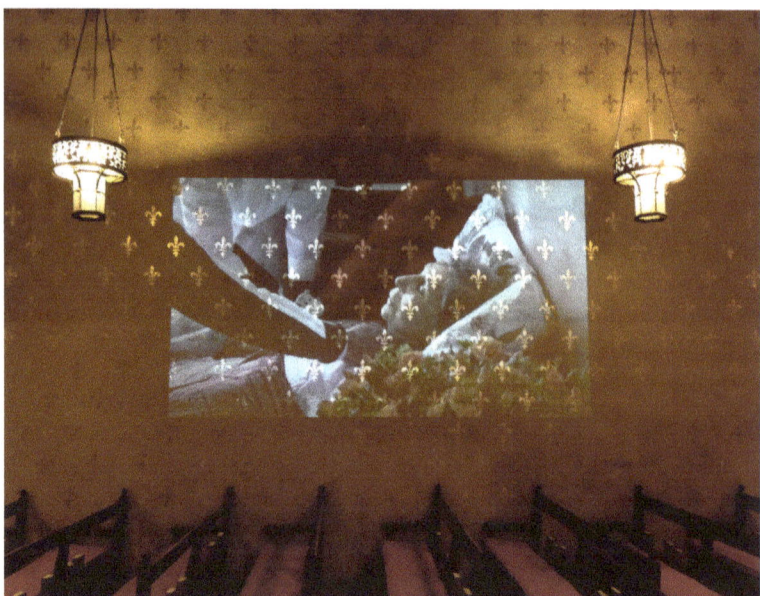

Figure 1. Photograph of the film projection of Sophie Calle's dying mother on the wall in the chapel. Sophie Calle, 2014. Photo: Henriette Thune, University of Stavanger. License: CC-BY-NC-ND. Rights holder has not responded after repeated requests about copyright claims. Copyright claims are welcomed.

the right-hand wall closer to the altar: at first it appears to be a photograph, but at a second glance it turns out to be moving images, with a dead or dying woman in a semi close-up (Figure 1).

As visitors to the exhibition we intuitively and with pleasure follow our natural curiosity. Moving around the exhibition—which was open to visitors from May 9 to June 25, 2014—this curiosity sometimes turns into a less comfortable sensation of nosey prying. This latter sensation, however, is over and over again pushed back by the feeling that the exhibition is a crafted, formed, work of art.

Rachel, Monique is a complex composition of a wide range of media and art forms (which we will call "medialities" in the following).[1] *Rachel, Monique* analyses as well as problematizes thresholds

---

[1] In the following we employ the terms "mediality" and "medialities" (instead of "media" or "art forms"). Mediality refers to a constellation

between life and death, relations between mother and daughter, closeness and distance, and investigates the ethical implications of the distinctions between real life and aesthetic representation. *Rachel, Monique* materialises the spectrum and borders between life and death of Monique Sindler; she is dying, remembering, being remembered and even, in one of the works, she is depicted as when she was living. Our text will work through Calle's exhibition suggesting an interpretation of *Rachel, Monique*, and an important distinction will be existential or psychological content on the one hand versus what we shall call a "formal content" on the other hand. Furthermore, a second, important aim of this chapter is to demonstrate how combining an intermedial approach with the Russian theorist Mikhail Bakhtin's concept of "the aesthetic object," makes for a fruitful method for analysing and interpreting works of art.[2] We will only briefly refer to the entire oeuvre of Calle, and we do not go into the extensive Sophie Calle reception.

---

of communicative, aesthetic and material dimensions of communicative acts that blend a limited number of medial or modal aspects. Our understanding is inspired by Rajewsky's discussion of the nature of media borders and Ellström's discussion of media and modalities. See also Bruhn's general reflections concerning intermediality and textual analysis. Irina O. Rajewsky, *Intermedialität* (Tübingen: Francke, 2002); Lars Ellström, ed., *Media Borders, Multimodality and Intermediality* (Basingstoke: Palgrave Macmillan, 2010); Jørgen Bruhn, *The Intermediality of Narrative Literature: Medialities Matter* (London: Palgrave Macmillan, 2016).

[2] Mikhail Bakhtin's concept of the aesthetic object was first introduced in "The Problem of Content, Material and Form in Verbal Art" in *Art and Answerability: Early Philosophical Essays*, eds. Michael Holquist and Vadim Liapunov (Austin: University of Texas Press, 1990). Here Bakhtin introduces the concept of the aesthetic object as an interwovenness of the ethical, the epistemological and the aesthetic. The aesthetic object comes into being as the meaning produced between an author/artist and a reader/spectator in their contemplation of an external work. For a full application of Bakhtin's concept of the aesthetic object as method for aesthetic analysis—including a critical discussion of how to incorporate the unavoidably subjective experience of a work of art as an a priori prejudice to any analytical approach—see Henriette Thune's dissertation discussing this question: Henriette Thune, *Mikhail Bakhtin's Aesthetic Object: Adaptation Analysis of Sara Stridsberg's Novel The Dream Faculty and Its Theatre Adaptation Valerie Solanas Will Be President of America* (PhD diss., University of Stavanger: Faculty of Arts and Education, 2012).

Entering the chapel is a serene experience, but inside the conventionally peaceful and solemn frame, contradiction reigns. The feeling of simultaneously being attracted *and* shoved away, pulled in *and* pushed off, is particularly poignant around the beautiful but also disturbing film of the dying Monique Sindler. The film goes on and on in 11 minutes' looped circuits, leaving only three to four seconds after the image and music have faded away before it starts over again. During the first six to seven minutes, the dying woman is all we see. The only motion to be detected, if any, is a very marginal movement of the woman's chest, granted she breathes. During the last four minutes of the film, we hear whispering from behind the camera and three different persons come over to the bed, one after the other, trying to detect pulse, heartbeats or breathing. Being invited in as observers to this deeply private moment, next to a bed where she is lying to die, and at the same time being in a public exhibition in a church chapel, activates deviating sensations. These sensations are, for instance, related to the private, the sacred, the emotionally moving, the elevated, the down-to-earth, the intimate, the real-life as opposed to the aesthetic, the genuine, and the composed. The visitors are witnessing acts of personal and professional care-taking and love. At the same time, the visitors are confronted with Sophie Calle's bluntness (or exhibitionism) when she displays in an artwork the private and, particularly in modern and contemporary Western culture, extremely privatized moment of her mother dying. *Rachel, Monique* exhibits a number of contradictions that seem apt for being included in even more abstract dichotomies, but also internally contrasting and inconsistent oppositions, such as life in relation to art and private in relation to public. The exhibition's processing and negotiation of conventional oppositions such as distance and intimacy, pathos and humour, formal sophistication and banal simplicity will interest us particularly. In the following, we will attempt to stay with the contrasting sensations and impressions of both the movie and the exhibition as a whole, instead of trying to explain and thereby overcome or exceed this tension, and we wish to balance the thematic "content" with the formal aspects of the exhibition.

It is in order to better understand and describe Calle's apparently exorbitant display of the uttermost, private experience—that at the same time, metonymically, represents each and every human being's unavoidable death—that we suggest the application of a combination of intermediality and media theory with the concept of Bakhtin's aesthetic object.

Bakhtin introduced his concept of the aesthetic object as an attempt to understand the basic form of being of a work of art. Bakhtin uses the term "the external work" for the concrete compositional forms that may be described and agreed upon by multiple perceivers. The aesthetic object, according to Bakhtin, is the dynamically produced meaning of artists or perceivers related to such an external work when they try to make sense of it. It is this aesthetic object—a dynamic meaning production going on in contemplation of an external work—we will refer to when we in the following speak of the "content" or the "meaning" of a work of art.

With the 1924 introduction of Bakhtin's concept of the aesthetic object follows his suggested guidelines for analysis. Henriette Thune has developed and operationalized these guidelines into a framework of analysis in her PhD thesis on Bakhtin's aesthetic object in 2012, emphasizing the necessity of the initial, subjective experience of a work of art for the choice of analytical strands to pursue.[3] Following the inner logic of the concept of Bakhtin's aesthetic object, it is thus completely on purpose when we begin this article by letting the reader follow some of our experiences of *Rachel, Monique*—even though it is not our aim here to see through an analysis conforming strictly with details of the framework operationalized by Thune.

Investigating the forms of the external work, we will nonetheless pursue what we experience as the capital meaning-producing elements of *Rachel, Monique*, attempting to describe and understand the heterogeneous, but nevertheless systematically ordered, range of different medialities that together comprise this complex art exhibition. We shall distinguish between the exhibition as the overall main work in this analysis and the respective single works that together form *Rachel, Monique* as individual constituents of the main work. Three of these stand out as particularly central.

---

[3] Thune, *Mikhail Bakhtin's Aesthetic Object*, 320.

Having already introduced our experience of *Rachel, Monique* as a frame of reference, the first step of our analysis involves a description and inventory of the material of the exhibition, the surroundings and the respective works of which the exhibition consists. The second step, building upon the first, establishes some of the thematic and more abstract structures shortly mentioned above. The third step brings our findings in the mediality analysis into a discussion of *Rachel, Monique* as a Bakhtinian aesthetic object.

We are fully aware that it is impossible to draw clear and undisputed lines between experience, description of experience, description of material (inventory), and interpretation of a work of art, as if a work of art and the experience of it were things that could be efficiently dissected:

> The aesthetic object is also the threshold where the author/artist as the origin of the external work and the reader/spectator as a co-creative contemplator meet. In this sense the aesthetic object is the threshold of an existential meeting between two subjects. This is why, as Bakhtin says in "Toward a Methodology for the Human Sciences," the activity of the researcher in human sciences needs to be "the activity of one who acknowledges another subject, that is, the *dialogic* activity of the acknowledger."[4]

Bakhtin, with his idea of the aesthetic object and indications for a methodology for analyzing it, thus forefronts the necessity to strive for grasping the event-like aesthetic object as a whole, even if he well understands the utopian character of "succeeding" in such a quest.[5] And we do, of course, assume the hermeneutical

---

[4] Thune, *Mikhail Bakhtin's Aesthetic Object*, 327 quoting Bakhtin in *Toward a Philosophy of the Act*, eds. Michael Holquist and Vadim Liapunov (Austin: University of Texas Press, 1993), 161. In one of his very last texts, "Toward a Methodology of the Human Sciences," Bakhtin argues that the objects of the so-called exact sciences are things and may be treated like things, while the human sciences' objects represent subjects, therefore cognition of the objects of human sciences must always be dialogic. See Mikhail Bakhtin, Vern W. McGee, Michael Holquist, and Caryl Emerson, *Speech Genres and Other Late Essays* (Austin: University of Texas Press, 1986). See also Thune, *Mikhail Bakhtin's Aesthetic Object*, 68.

[5] That is, if "succeeding" means attaining one "true" answer or conclusion.

circle and both individual and more general a priori prejudices in the form of situated positions as fundamental for understanding any approach to art analysis.[6]

Rachel, Monique as Part of Sophie Calle's Oeuvre

Sophie Calle is a French writer, photographer, installation artist, and conceptual artist. She started working as an artist in the late 1970s, and her early photographs were of tombstones, marked simply—and in this context interestingly—"mother" or "father." One of the photographs of the exhibition *Rachel, Monique* is a black-and-white photograph of a tombstone with "Mother" engraved (1990), another black and white photo is of a white cross in a cemetery and says "Maman" (2013). The exhibition also includes a black-and-white digital print showing Monique Sindler's tombstone, with a picture of herself making a face and the inscription and title "I'm getting bored already!" (2010).[7]

Generally, Calle's work orchestrates numerous aesthetic processes into myriad, rhizomatic exhibitions, where a network of medialities challenge any assumption of the existence of pure art forms or media. All through her artistic career, Sophie Calle mixes medialities, real life, fiction, public, and private in a narrating way that provokes engagement, affect, and emotion in the public, and she explicitly uses her own and other peoples' personal lives in her praxis. As also in *Rachel, Monique*, she often delves into questions and problematizations of identity, intimacy, and vulnerability.

Calle was chosen as the official representative of France at the 2007 Venice Biennale where her main presentation was the monumental exhibition *Prenez soin de vous* (*Take care* [of yourself]),

---

[6] See Thune, *Mikhail Bakhtin's Aesthetic Object*, 51–54 on the development of a reception aesthetical frame for the aesthetic object.

[7] The inscription is in French: "Je m'ennuie déjà!" This was part of Monique Sindler's own preparation for her funeral, as explains this quotation from what we shall refer to as the Pulpit Text—the text displayed at the pulpit upon entering the chapel: "She organized the funeral ceremony: her last party. Final preparations: she chose her funeral dress—navy blue with a white pattern—; a photograph showing her making a face for the tombstone, and her epitaph: I'm getting bored already!"

which deserves a brief presentation here. It has strong affinities with *Rachel, Monique* because of its equally systematic, mixed mediality representation of a personal experience that blends humor and pathos. *Prenez soin de vous* is named after the last words of a break-up e-mail Calle received from a lover at some point in the early 2000s. Devastated and incapable of making sense of the e-mail and the accompanying sensation of shock and loss, she decided to ask 107 women, all outstanding in their respective, very different, professional occupations, skills and experience, to read, analyze, and interpret the letter for her as a way to do what her ex-lover had encouraged her to do—*take care of herself*. The result was gathered and documented in what has become a central feminist artwork, which after the Venice Biennale has been shown in amongst other England, Denmark, USA, Finland, Norway, and Mexico. *Prenez soin de vous* is at the same time a massive and refined demonstration of Calle's experimentation with how different medialities affect meaning production. The analyses, interpretations and representations of Sophie Calle's break-up letter may be seen as a variety of "adaptations" (in the broad sense of the term[8]) of the e-mail, along with certain responses. The adapted medialities including various musical genres, loud readings, short stories, advertisements, dances, theatrical performances, and so on—a lot of them produced as short films, also available on DVD in the artist's book *Take Care of Yourself* (2007).[9]

Experiencing *Rachel, Monique*

As mentioned above, *Rachel, Monique* offers a rich and complex network of interrelated individual works. As a first step toward an interpretation and understanding of the exhibition, we propose a relatively systematic description of what meets the visitor, or

---

[8] On this understanding of adaptation, see Linda Hutcheon with Siobhan O'Flynn, *A Theory of Adaptation* (London: Routledge, 2013); for a short overview of the field of adaptation studies, see Jørgen Bruhn, Anne Gjelsvik, and Eirik Frisvold Hanssen, eds., *Adaptation Studies: New Challenges, New Directions* (London: Bloomsbury Academic, 2013).
[9] Sophie Calle, *Take Care of Yourself*, trans. Charles Penwarden (LeMéjan: Actes Sud, 2007).

rather the participant of the exhibition, when entering the space. This will enable us to afterwards establish an initial register of the represented medialities. We have chosen to describe the experience of walking through *Rachel, Monique* in present tense in order to furnish an idea of the exhibition as a living perceptual experience. Whether described in past or present tense, it is impossible either way for the reader to go back and visit the exhibition that ended June 25, 2014.[10]

In order to enter the exhibition, the visitor is led through the main entrance of the Episcopal Church of the Heavenly Rest on Fifth Avenue facing the east side of Central Park on Manhattan. Once inside the church, one turns right before making a left into one of the rather large side chapels which lie parallel to the main church nave. Entering the large rectangular space of about 8 meters' breadth and 20 meters' length, one can take in a view of the entire chapel and (almost) the entire exhibition.

The light in the exhibition is turned somewhat down without being dark, and instead of the murmur of other churchgoers in a conventional religious space, the visitors of the exhibition can hear the sound of a female voice reading aloud from the far end of the room. The exhibition consists of 14 named and numbered individual works of different sizes, textures, and medialities (listed in a printed folder). The works all weigh differently in the medial economy of the exhibition.

Entering from the west end of the chapel (Figure 2), one immediately sees a pulpit with what we shall refer to as the Pulpit Text, describing all Monique Sindler's "lasts" taking place between January 31 and March 15, 2006, when she died (text on paper, not listed in the folder). One's attention is attracted to what we consider the three major works of the exhibition. The first of these is the audio recording of Kim Cattrall reading Sophie Calle's selections of Monique Sindler's diaries out loud to the right of the altar close to the south-eastern corner of the chapel. Letting

---

[10] For an artist's book/exhibition catalogue, where several of the objects are reproduced, see Sophie Calle and Xavier Barral, *Elle s'est appelée successivement Rachel, Monique, Szyndler, Calle, Pagliero, GonThier, Sindler: Ma mère aimait qu'on parle d'elle* (Paris: Xavier Barral, 2012).

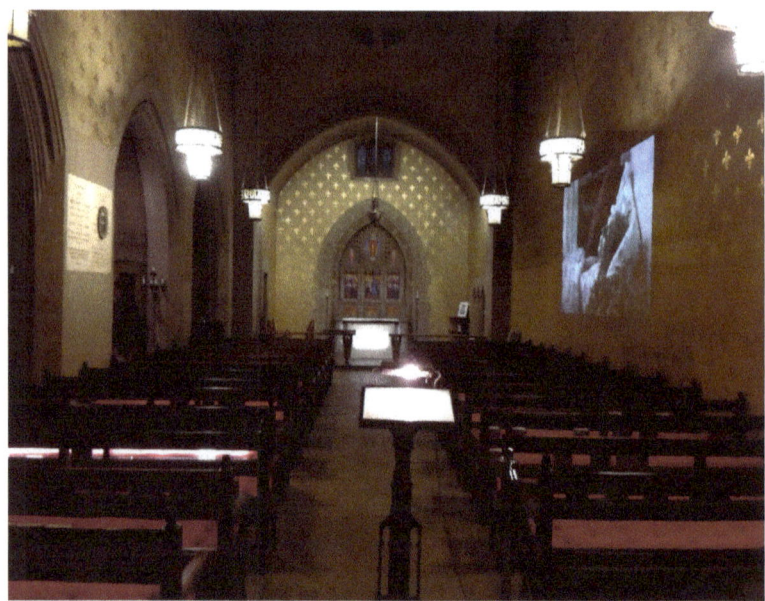

Figure 2. Overview of the exhibition from the entrance at the Western wall. Sophie Calle, 2014. Photo: Henriette Thune, University of Stavanger. License: CC-BY-NC-ND. Rights holder has not responded after repeated requests about copyright claims. Copyright claims are welcomed.

one's eyes be swept towards the altar and the sounds, make them pass by the video installation, an 11-minute loop, projected on the south wall—"Couldn't capture death." The installation represents Monique Sindler's last minutes alive. Being drawn towards the front of the chapel, one discovers a life-size photograph of Monique Sindler's open coffin on the left of the nave (Figure 3). The rather sinister but also peaceful aspect of the deceased woman is softened by the numerous objects included with her in the coffin—and by the fact that all these objects are also listed and framed on the wall over the coffin. Monique Sindler's open coffin is what we consider to be the last of the three major works of the exhibition as the overall main work.

Around the three capital works are situated the less-dominant works. On the eastern wall, occupying a central place, immediately visible when entering the chapel, is the altar table with the "Souci" centerpiece in front (sandblasted paper). The visitor

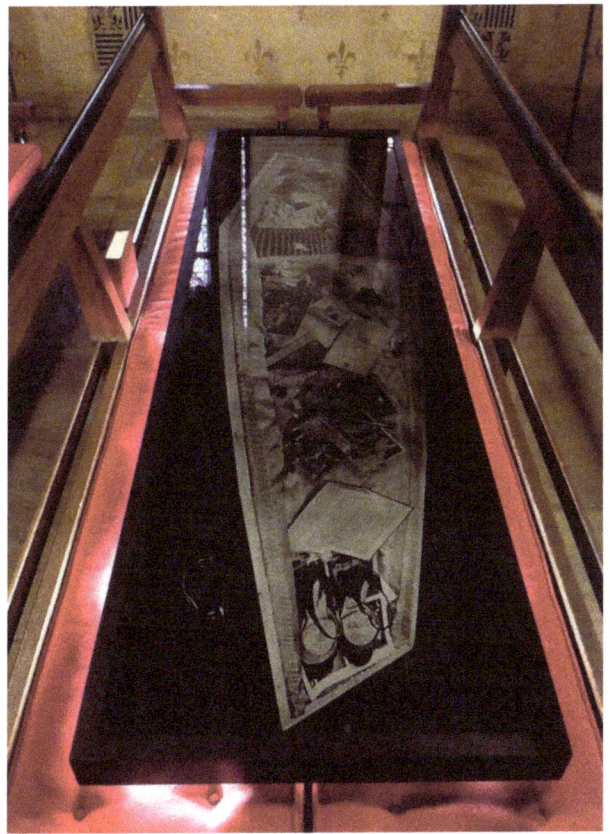

Figure 3. Photograph of the open coffin of Monique Sindler. Sophie Calle, 2014. Photo: Henriette Thune, University of Stavanger. License: CC-BY-NC-ND. Rights holder has not responded after repeated requests about copyright claims. Copyright claims are welcomed.

can see photos and digital prints of numerous tombstones, particularly along the southern wall, including a photo of Monique Sindler's tombstone (sculpturesque with text "Je m'ennuis déjà!" ["I'm bored already"] and a photo of a smiling Monique), as well as a number of individual photos and digital prints symbolically relating to aspects of motherhood, either in writing or sculpture.[11]

---

[11] "Les Mains" (photo), "Maman" (photo on marble epitaph), "Mother" (black and white photo), "Daddy Mother" (digital print), "Mama" (digital print), "Maman" (digital print), and "Souci"—stitched butterfly poem.

The word "souci" appears on the same wall, close to the entrance, and only up close it becomes clear that the word is put together of dried, pinned butterflies forming the five letters.

Near the altar on the northern wall, the work "Gênes," three kneelers, are situated, facing three different enlargements of the same photo of a girl lifting a cover to peek in under it, seemingly at the head end of a bed or table where a body lies.

Finally, turning around and looking towards the western wall of the entrance appear lace curtains hung above the entrance door. The curtains are visible only from well inside the room as one turns around and looks back, and embroidered in the lace we once again see the word "souci."

Even a quick trajectory through the exhibition reveals a thematic core message, which is what we will refer to as the content of the work concerning a number of related existential or affective notions such as grief, loss, death, subordinated under the broader idea of *souci* (worries, sorrow, and care).

Inventory of Medialities

Before we go closer into such a thematic investigation, however, we shall go through the exhibition in line with our proposed method in this article by way of listing an inventory of the different medialities at play. This is because it seems obvious to us that Sophie Calle has chosen to convey a relatively clear-cut thematic message in an unusually differentiated medial constellation.

We begin with the 18-minute audio recording of selections of Monique Sindler's diaries, which is—medially speaking—complex. Initially, Calle has selected parts of her mother's diaries. The diaries, conventionally being a semi-literary and private genre, have been read aloud and recorded, not by Calle or her mother, but by actress Kim Cattrall. The private diaries are not only made public as such—they are also "contaminated" with the exhibition participants' knowledge of *Sex and the City*-celebrity Cattrall's character in the NYC-based TVshow for which she is known.

"Couldn't capture death,"[12] the 11-minute video installation projected on the south wall representing Monique Sindler's last minutes in life, is also a complex mediality product. Calle placed a camera beside Monique Sindler's deathbed in order to record the first extremely weak and later absent movements of her dying mother. Sophie Calle said about this project and her mother:

> My mother liked to be the object of discussion. Her life did not appear in my work, and that annoyed her. When I set up my camera at the foot of the bed in which she lay dying—I wanted to be present to hear her last words, and was afraid that she would pass away in my absence—she exclaimed: "Finally!"[13]

The sound is diegetic; what we hear is whispering and a few everyday noises. Extradiegetic sound is added only in the last minute or two when Monique Sindler is dead, and the music is a Mozart sonata, that she had demanded be played upon her death.[14]

Beside the life-size photography of Monique Sindler's open coffin a written list is hung on the wall just above it, specifying the many objects put in the coffin along with the body. We here quote the entire list:

> Before the lid of her coffin was closed, the following objects were laid on her body:
> Her white polka-dot dress and her red and black shoes, because that is what she chose to wear for her death.
> Handfuls of sour candies, because she gorged on them.
> Stuffed cows and rubber cows, because she collected cows.
> Volume I of *À la recherche du temps perdu* by Marcel Proust, in the Pléiade edition, because she knew the first page by heart and recited it whenever she got the chance.
> A postcard of Marilyn Monroe with Humphrey Bogart and Lauren Bacall, because Marilyn was her idol.

---

[12] The video installation was screened for the first time at the French pavillion of the 2007 Venice Biennale, one year after Monique Sindler's death in 2006.
[13] Quoted from the gallery's web material, now deleted.
[14] See Sadie Stein, "Worry," accessed January 16, 2016, https://www.theparisreview.org/blog/2014/05/14/worry/.

A postcard of Ava Gardner, because when people met her for the first time, that is who she claimed to be.

A Christian Lacroix silk scarf, because she was a coquette.

A book from the "Que sais-je?" collection on Spinoza and Spinozism, because she began studying the subject a month before she died.

Mozart's sonatas for violin and piano K. 376, K. 377, K. 357 and K. 360, because at the end, Mozart was all she listened to.

A photograph of a sailboat on the Atlantic, because she loved the ocean.

Marlboro cigarettes and matches, because she smoked a lot.

Vodka, rum and whisky, because she loved to drink.

Paper, a pencil, and an eraser, because she dreamed of writing.

A MoMA membership card, because of New York.

Photographs of the love of her life, her friends, her children, her brother, and a few lovers, because she loved them.

Photographs in which she felt she looked young and beautiful.

A photograph of a parasol pine, because it was planted at Courtonne-le-Deux-Églises the day after her death, and it bears her name.

A few flowers—*souci* (marigolds), because *souci* (worry) was her last word.

This list—enumerating what can also be seen on the photograph—is on the one hand an emotional tribute to the mother, but on the other hand also an almost systematic list of different medialities related to different sense perceptions, different aesthetic conventions, and different technical media being present in the coffin. We have objects relating to fashion, to literature, to music, to philosophy, to the technical ability of writing, to museum activities, and more.

The remaining photos and digital prints represent either words or tombstones: the "Gênes" refer to the religious design and architectural space of churches with three kneelers, an appropriation of the architectural trend continued in the implementation of the word "souci" on the centrally placed altar table. The word "souci" made from dried butterflies on the southern wall, close to the entrance, is mixing the iconic images (or shapes) of the butterflies with the symbolic signs of the five letters.

Making a rather coarse but perhaps necessary distinction between qualified artistic medialities in themselves as opposed to remediated forms enables us to produce two lists.[15] On the one hand *Rachel, Monique* consists of the qualified artistic medialities of photography, digital prints, stitched butterflies, a video recording, an audio recording, texts, and a lace embroidery. On the other hand, these medialities mediate and represent a range of other medialities: several tombstones (sculpture), a diary (in Cattrall's reading), the photograph of the contents of the coffin (specified also in a verbal list exhibited on the wall resembling an epitaph) is representing by way of synecdoche *literature* (the Proust volume), *music* (the Mozart CD in the coffin), *philosophy* (the Leibniz volume in the coffin), and *fashion* (the scarf and the dress and shoes).

The medialities could also be further ordered into groups according to different criteria and following different theoretical interests and positions, for instance by means of a relatively simple and conventional division into predominantly visual media or audio-visual media or media focused on verbal text. This, however, is not necessary for our argument, since the purpose of naming and listing all the medialities of the exhibition is of course not to produce the list in itself, but to acknowledge and truly perceive the widespread presence of medialities in the show. The many medialities of the exhibition demonstrate, consciously or unconsciously, that Calle's thematic requires the widest possible array of medialities.

In other words: what interests us is neither the list in itself nor the multiple presence of medialities. It is, instead, the *function* as well as the artistic and existential *meaning* produced by this conspicuous presence of different medialities. As mentioned from the outset: the core of the exhibition establishes a dichotomy between two strongly related but nevertheless distinctly different systems related to two thematic dimensions. We have the conventional

---

[15] "Qualified media" in Lars Elleström's terminology roughly equates conventional art forms. See Elleström, ed., *Media Borders*. "Remediation" is here simply referring to medialities being mediated once again; thus the term does not refer to Bolter and Grusin's influential concept of remediation in Jay David Bolter and Richard Grusin, *Remediation: Understanding New Media* (Cambridge: MIT Press, 1999).

thematic, or content, established early on as the question of souci (loss, sorrow, absence—death), but we also find that there is a "formal" thematic in the exhibition, that seems to consist of multiplicity, perspectivism, irony, and heterogeneous medialities. We will argue that *Rachel, Monique* exhibits a systematic "testing" and opposing and questioning of how the different medialities opposed to each other create a "formal content" of its own. The goal of the following discussion will consequently be to establish the relations between the explicit conventional content and the implicit "formal" content.

Formal Content in *Rachel, Monique*

The internally conflictual presence of medialities in *Rachel, Monique* produces two closely related impressions, we believe. The mere presence tends, on the one hand, to dominate the message of the exhibition—and on the other hand the medialities seem to exhibit a certain kind of systematization. In other words, the medialities dominate the visitors' experience of the show, but they dominate in an almost systematic, structured way.

Conventionally, the meaning and the function of such medial plurality is located in one of three different positions: either it is located in the position of the exhibition or it is seen from the viewpoint of the visitor or that of Sophie Calle. That is, from the receiver or sender or the work in the basic communicative model, so to speak. We want to avoid this pragmatic but also limiting and rather destructive division of the meaning production taking place through the artwork to either *sender* or *work* or *receiver* by employing the aesthetic model sketched by the early Bakhtin, namely, what we have already introduced as the aesthetic object.

Thune develops this model in her thesis about Bakhtin's aesthetic object, where she defines both:

> contemplating subjects [as being] engaged from their respective ethical-epistemological situated positions. From these situated positions the artist and the contemplator co-produce meaning related to contemplation of the external work, that is, they co-produce the

content of the aesthetic object. [...] the artist creates a form-bound, external work where meaning and ideas are represented almost statically through compositional forms. The meaning and ideas represented develop through the co-creation of architectonic forms.[16]

While conventional communication models tend to focus on analyzing *either* semiotic content *or* formed material *from* sender *to* receiver—and often with the idea of communication as a finalizable process where a more or less static content is communicated—the model sketched by Bakhtin[17] enables us to systematically approach the elements of form and content and complex ethical-epistemological situated positions of the sender, the receiver, and the work of art, and simultaneously look upon these as a complex constellation where meaning is dynamically and dialogically produced.

Following this model we interpret the myriad presence of media in *Rachel, Monique* not as a pêle-mêle of diverse medialities for the sake of difference and plurality itself, but rather as a necessary strategy following from the fact that the work aims to represent something that is in essence more or less unrepresentable. What may look like an uncommitted artistic experimentation with forms and medialities, should in our opinion be interpreted as a necessarily non-consummated attempt to track the incomprehensible, the absent presence, the fact of death and the resulting feelings of absence, loss, and grief.

These remarks are necessarily very general, almost abstract, but by way of Bakhtin's idea of the aesthetic object it becomes possible to narrow down slightly the thematics of the work.

Rachel, Monique as a Bakhtinian Aesthetic Object

In Thune's model of Bakhtin's aesthetic object, the concept of situated positions is central and we need this terminology in order to be able to approach the question of the meaning of the exhibition. This necessitates a few terminological clarifications. The artist creator, following this model, occupies a given situated position at the moment of creation of the external work. The

---

[16] Thune, *Mikhail Bakhtin's Aesthetic Object*, 41.
[17] Thune, *Mikhail Bakhtin's Aesthetic Object*, 27–68.

visitor, on the other side, occupies another situated position at the moment s/he relates to the external work and makes sense of it. Finally, the external work (which in this case amounts to all the works adding up to the exhibition) occupies a third given complex situated position when the artist and the visitor create and relate to it.

Within the external work—in our case the exhibition—the different works of art represent different situated positions that internally stand in dynamic relations to one another. For our purposes here, the interesting situated positions of *Rachel, Monique* are the different medialities and how they are situated in relation to one another within each and every work, and within the exhibition as a whole. Meaning production in the aesthetic object takes place as the visitor, from her/his situated position, relates to and intellectually and bodily-emotionally interprets the situated positions of the external work—in our case *Rachel, Monique* or any of the works constituting it. The dynamic meaning production taking place between the artist creator and the visitor in contemplation of any of these external works *is* the aesthetic object. One may thus approach Sophie Calle's exhibition *Rachel, Monique* and the three major and the other less dominant works of which it is constituted, as aesthetic objects on a number of levels.

Corresponding to the main external work, the main aesthetic object is *Rachel, Monique*, the exhibition, as a whole. In this case the artist creator is of course Sophie Calle but also the visitors experience the exhibition from their respective situated positions. The external work *Rachel, Monique* may be described as an attempt to capture Monique Sindler's life and death in a greater perspective of living and dying, and the aesthetic object—that is; the meaning we produce in contemplating this external object—may be summarized as *Monique Sindler remembered*.

When it comes to the movie, "Couldn't capture death," one of the three major works of the exhibition, the artist creator is still Sophie Calle and the visitor whoever sees this death bed film, making sense of it from their situated positions at any given time. The external work is an attempt to capture Monique Sindler's death in the moment it occurs, and its aesthetic object may thus be summarized as *Monique Sindler dying*.

In case of the audio of Monique Sindler's diaries read out loud by Kim Cattrall, the artist creator may still be seen as Sophie Calle, but also as Kim Cattrall (producing the reading from Monique Sindler's diaries) or even as Monique Sindler herself having produced the read text. One therefore questions the situated position(s) of the artist creator, as it involves boundaries between several situated positions at different times; Kim Cattrall and Sophie Calle's roles here are as mediating instances to purvey Monique Sindler's written utterances. Sophie Calle offers her dead mother, Monique Sindler, the position of a living situated position and an active utterer, so that the external work is an attempt to re-present Monique Sindler's life and living after her death. The visitor is whoever listens to the audio recordings from their, at any given time, situated positions. In this context, the aesthetic object of the reading aloud of the diaries may be summarized as *Monique Sindler living*.

Regarding the photo of Monique Sindler's coffin, the artist creator is Sophie Calle and the perceiver (in this specific analysis we call this the visitor) is whoever contemplates the coffin text and/or the photograph of the coffin from their, at any given time, situated positions. The external work "the coffin," is an attempt of through a pile of qualified medialities capturing Monique Sindler's life, or—alternatively—Sophie Calle's story of Monique Sindler's life, after her death, and its aesthetic object may in the following be summarized as *Monique Sindler's life*.

In the remaining works of the exhibition, the artist creator remains Sophie Calle and the visitor, whoever contemplates any single of these subworks from their, at any given time, situated positions. The external subworks themselves represent several independent medially situated positions that in different constellations represent other more complex medially situated positions. It is our opinion that the composition and mixture of these medialities and the boundaries between them are fundamental to what we see as Sophie Calle's attempt to capture the process of dying as the ungraspable but nevertheless indisputable boundary between life and death. The aesthetic object of these less dominant external works may be summarized as exactly different variations of *the process of dying marking ungraspable boundaries between life and death*.

Conclusion

The immediate impetus for writing this text was our slightly confusing experience of Sophie Calle's *Rachel, Monique*: the feeling of calm solemnity of the church space that was met with the complex medial mixture of the show. Another, slightly confusing—not to say disturbing—feeling was created in the exhibitions' confrontation of deeply private material that was represented. We decided to approach the exhibition by way of two theoretical frameworks: the aesthetic philosophy of Bakhtin combined with a more general media theoretical approach, and it is this combination that we wish to lift forth as a fruitful means of sharpening the tools that intermediality can provide for researchers in meetings with aesthetic objects. Bakhtin's theory helped us establish a fundamental understanding of the basic nature of the objects of the art exhibition, while the mediality approach gave us the analytical tools to describe and distinguish between the different aspects of the rich exhibition.

Beginning with the role of the artist in this composite work, our description and analysis shows that through *Rachel, Monique*—as was also the case with *Prenez soin de vous*—Sophie Calle aesthetically processes and thus transforms highly personal and private material, giving it general relevance by turning it into art. Sophie Calle starts off by setting up severe dichotomies, for instance between the private and the public, then only to permit the excessively public experience of this exhibition to become inherently private.

Characteristic in this exhibition, and this is typical for Calle's entire work (and of course of much of what is going on in contemporary art), is that it does away with the conventional, often romantic, idea of the artist as an autonomous creative instance behind the work of art. The exhibited works here are rather "found" or recorded, and often consists of conventionally non-aesthetic objects, most of which in another setting would primarily have pragmatic or to some extent symbolic functions: The coffin's list (or *Wunderkammer*-like form), the stable camera (ref. Warhol's experiment with putting a camera in front of the Empire State building), not to forget the reading of Monique Sindler's diaries, that in their written form were not created by Sophie Calle, but simply found, selected, and adapted. Calle's creative input is to gather and put on display rather than creating *ex nihilo*, and she hides herself behind her findings while at the same time relating every single detail to a specific, personally related life situation. As mentioned already, Monique Sindler was upset that her daughter didn't let her be part of any of her earlier artworks. "Finally"—as it turns out—when Sophie's mother is on her deathbed, Sophie Calle starts a long process where the mother becomes the center of several projects through many years.

Why did this happen just then? Why didn't Sophie try to grasp the relation to her mother while she was alive? Were they too close—or too distant, too different—or too much alike? These psychological questions are of course out of reach of our analysis, but it seems to be the case that only when her mother is vanishing, can Sophie get close to her. Only at the threshold between life and death are the borders between mother and daughter, a parental intimacy and distance, being explicitly worked into Calle's personal artistic production. Only in her death, as an object, can Sophie's mother become a subject for Sophie's art.

Unsurprisingly, we found that the content thematized in *Rachel, Monique* is grief and loss and the absent presence of death. Without ever stating directly that Sophie Calle is in grief or that she misses her mother, the meticulousness and detailed care, her *souci*, by which the exhibition gives us an impression of her mother, nevertheless demonstrates the magnitude of the loss. We have suggested that this overarching theme of grief and loss branch into differentiated emotional subthemes: On the level of the exhibition, the emotional content is Monique Sindler *remembered*; the main theme of the death-bed movie is Monique Sindler dying, whereas the reading aloud of her diaries deals with Monique Sindler *living*, which is also the case of all the "gifts" Sophie Calle's gives to her mother's coffin. Several of the other works rather take positions in life or in death, and negotiates the borders between them by representing death, dead people, or symbols of love and resurrection (the butterflies forming the word "souci"), *life*.

One could have expected an exhibition about life and death and a dying mother to be terrifying or uncomfortable. Depending upon the visitor's experienced life and situated position, it would not be surprising if some visitors experienced such feelings or were quite simply reminded about their anxieties related to their own deaths. For the two authors of this article, from our situated positions, the dominating sensations became more about humbleness for being invited to witness a very private, caring, loving event, motivated by a wish on behalf of Sophie Calle to share, to keep alive, and to understand. We ask ourselves whether *sharing* and *reworking* existentially devastating experiences such as a parent's or another close person's death makes it possible to grasp a little more of what is ungraspable in our living, ongoing lives, always on the threshold of the unknown.

The formal setting is at least as engaging and demanding as the thematics, and by employing a relatively broad concept of mediality we have endeavored to describe a formal system underlying the exhibition. From a formal point of view, our initial observation was the quite overwhelming presence of different medialities of the show. However, our main argument concerning this medial multiplicity has been centered around our conviction that the variety of different medialities is not a mere coincidence, nor should it be understood as a superficial multiplicity of forms. Instead, it is our belief that the abundance of medialities mimics the thematic content of the exhibition.

The ungraspable nature of death, or to be more precise: the indefinability of the threshold dividing life from death (and despite the fact that at least the outer borders of this very moment is "caught" on film), seems to have forced Sophie Calle to orchestrate a number of found or recorded materials in several different medialities. The number of medialities reflects the impossibility of representing death, or perhaps the exact moment of death (if such a moment exists), and thus the thematic content of the exhibition is beautifully, and necessarily, represented by way of the formal complexity of the show.

Sophie Calle, in a manner typical for most of her work, builds dichotomies, only to make them collapse, and consequently the meaning inherent in *Rachel, Monique* as polyphonic, ungraspable, and dynamic. In a way, this relation between structure and collapse of structure corresponds to a tension in our own methodology in this investigation: from a rather narrow point of departure, with an indeed very structural approach to trying to grasp a meeting with a work of art as a living aesthetic experience. As we were well aware of before we began thinking about this work, the aesthetic object exceeds the limits inherent in any structured analytical framework. But nevertheless we find this Bakhtinian intermedial framework apt to include the subjective experience of art as the core of aesthetic meaning production, as well as permitting us to understand some of the formal intermedial aspects at play in the work.

References

Bakhtin, Mikhail. *Art and Answerability: Early Philosophical Essays*, edited by Michael Holquist and Vadim Liapunov. Austin: University of Texas Press, 1990.

Bakhtin, Mikhail. *Speech Genres and Other Late Essays*, edited by Vern W. McGee, Michael Holquist, and Caryl Emerson, Austin: University of Texas Press, 1986.

Bakhtin, Mikhail. "Supplement: The Problem of Content, Material and Form in Verbal Art." In *Art and Answerability: Early Philosophical Essays*, edited by Michael Holquist and Vadim Liapunov, 257–325. Austin: University of Texas Press, 1990.

Bakhtin, Mikhail. "Toward a Methodology of the Human Sciences." In *Speech Genres and Other Late Essays*, edited by Vern W. McGee, Michael Holquist, and Caryl Emerson, 159–172. Austin: University of Texas Press, 1986.

Bakhtin, Mikhail. *Toward a Philosophy of the Act*, edited by Michael Holquist and Vadim Liapunov. Austin: University of Texas Press, 1993.

Bolter, Jay David, and Richard Grusin. *Remediation: Understanding New Media*. Cambridge: MIT Press, 1999.

Bruhn, Jørgen. *The Intermediality of Narrative Literature: Medialities Matter*. London: Palgrave Macmillan, 2016.

Bruhn, Jørgen, Anne Gjelsvik, and Eirik Frisvold Hanssen, eds. *Adaptation Studies: New Challenges, New Directions*. London: Bloomsbury Academic, 2013.

Calle, Sophie, and Xavier Barral. *Elle s'est appelée successivement Rachel, Monique, Szyndler, Calle, Pagliero, GonThier, Sindler: Ma mère aimait qu'on parle d'elle*. Paris: Xavier Barral, 2012.

Calle, Sophie. *Take Care of Yourself*. Translated by Charles Penwarden. LeMéjan: Actes Sud, 2007.

Elleström, Lars, ed. *Media Borders, Multimodality and Intermediality*. Basingstoke: Palgrave Macmillan, 2010.

Hirschkop, Ken, and David Shepherd, eds. *Bakhtin and Cultural Theory*. Manchester: Manchester University Press, 2002 [1989].

Holquist, Michael. "Introduction: The Architectonics of Answerability." In *Art and Answerability: Early Philosophical Essays*, edited by Michael Holquist and Vadim Liapunov, ix–xlix. Austin: University of Texas Press, 1990.

Hutcheon, Linda, with Siobhan O'Flynn. *A Theory of Adaptation*. London: Routledge, 2013.

Rajewsky, Irina O. *Intermedialität*. Tübingen: Francke, 2002.

Shepherd, David. "Bakhtin and the Reader." In *Bakhtin and Cultural Theory*, edited by Ken Hirschkop and David Shepherd, 91–108. Manchester: Manchester University Press, 2002 [1989].

Stein, Saide. "Worry." Accessed January 16, 2016. https://www.theparisreview.org/blog/2014/05/14/worry/.

Thune, Henriette. *Mikhail Bakhtin's Aesthetic Object: Adaptation Analysis of Sara Stridsberg's Novel The Dream Faculty and Its Theatre Adaptation Valerie Solanas Will Be President of America*. PhD diss., University of Stavanger: Faculty of Arts and Education, 2012.

The Intersection between Film and Opera in the 1960s: Ingmar Bergman's *Hour of the Wolf* as an Example of Formal Imitation

Johanna Ethnersson Pontara

Abstract

The topic of this article is the intersection between media genres in 1960s Sweden. In a case study of Ingmar Bergman's *Hour of the Wolf* (1968) it is shown how the music contributes to intermedial qualities through the film's connection with opera. It is argued that the film, by how the music is related to sound effects and images, can be seen as an example of formal imitation. The imitation of opera is created through technical media of film, such as foregrounding of media in the audio-visual space, and manipulations of sounds, music, and images. Of special interest is how, by alternating between synchronicity and counterpoint between images, sound effects, and music, Bergman attracts attention to the media as visual and sonic experiences and creates formal structures that deviate from the overall character of the film. The intermedial dimension of the film revealed by the analysis is contextualized in relation to the historical discussion of mixed versus pure medialities. The film is seen in the light of an interest in media genre mixedness versus media genre specificity in 1960s Sweden.

Introduction

In a review of Ingmar Bergman's *Hour of the Wolf* (*Vargtimmen*, 1968) published in the American film journal *Film Quarterly*

How to cite this book chapter:
Ethnersson Pontara, Johanna. "The Intersection between Film and Opera in the 1960s: Ingmar Bergman's *Hour of the Wolf* as an Example of Formal Imitation." In *The Power of the In-Between: Intermediality as a Tool for Aesthetic Analysis and Critical Reflection*, edited by Sonya Petersson, Christer Johansson, Magdalena Holdar, and Sara Callahan, 49–74. Stockholm: Stockholm University Press, 2018. DOI: https://doi.org/10.16993/baq.c. License: CC-BY.

in the summer 1968, film critics Richard Corliss and Jonathan Hoops posited that the film drew upon an operatic mode. The critics took into consideration how the film alluded to W. A. Mozart's *The Magic Flute* (*Die Zauberflöte*, 1791); however, they also characterized the film as "frankly operatic," and described how it pointed to opera through structural devices:

> In *Hour of the Wolf*, the model is Mozart's *The Magic Flute* and, though a specific reference to it during the party seems at first superfluous, we later realize that it is doubly relevant: because the film is a retelling of the *Magic Flute* story, and because, whereas the dramas from *Through a Glass Darkly* to *Persona* were "chamber" films (described by Jörn Donner as covering "short spans of time with few actors" and possessing "something of the character of intimate music"), *Hour of the Wolf* is frankly operatic. The settings are expansive rather than constrictive; there are many characters, and each is given a verbal aria; the treatment, like most libretti, is melodramatic in the extreme. The film draws its inspiration from *The Magic Flute's* artful conglomeration of magic, music, farce, and fragmentary statements of high-sounding philosophy.[1]

Corliss and Hoops' description of the film focused on visual and verbal media: the configuration of the settings, the number of characters, and how the characters appeared verbally. Then, which intermedial qualities can be revealed through the film's connection with opera? Moreover, how does the music, a central medium of the film as well as of opera as a media genre, contribute to such qualities?

The film genre's relationship with opera, one of its precursors, is an issue that has attracted attention among scholars during the last decades.[2] The interest in combining traits from the two media genres in innovative productions was strong in the 1920s and 1930s (examples of this are Alban Berg's *Lulu* and the screen

---

[1] Richard Corliss and Jonathan Hoops, "Hour of the Wolf," review of *Hour of the Wolf*, by Ingmar Bergman, *Film Quaterly* 21:4 (1968): 38, accessed October 29, 2015, http://www.jstor.org/stable/1210600?seq=1#page_scan_tab_contents.

[2] Cf. Joe Jeongwon and Rose Theresa, eds., *Between Opera and Cinema* (New York: Routledge, 2002); Marcia Citron, *When Opera Meets Film* (Cambridge: Cambridge University Press, 2010).

version of Richard Strauss' *The Cavalier of the Rose*). Recently, however, scholars have also paid attention to how film and opera intersect in multimedia products from the 1960s, a period of time when genre-specific traits were called into question. It has been shown how composers and directors drew on experiences with cinema and television in attempts to reinvigorate the opera genre,[3] and how European art film directors created spectacular and distancing effects by drawing on aesthetics of opera.[4]

The film production of Bergman from the 1960s provides interesting objects of investigation in this context. Just like contemporary art film directors such as Andrei Tarkovsky (1932–86) and Jean-Luc Godard (born 1930), Bergman often challenges a traditional narrative cinematic discourse, and an important means by which this is achieved is the music.[5] Per F. Broman has shown how an important characteristic of Bergman's use of music is to let it dominate the narrative to the extent that the domains of diegetic and extra diegetic is blurred.[6] Furthermore, it has been shown how Bergman reveals an awareness of the film viewer through the way in which he combines images and sounds. Alexis

---

[3] Cf. Harriet Boyd, "Remaking Reality: Echoes, Noise and Modernist Realism in Luigi Nono's *Intolleranza 1960*," *Cambridge Opera Journal* 24:2 (2012): 177–200; Andrea Santini, "Multiplicity – Fragmentation – Simultaneity: Sound-Space as a Conveyor of Meaning, and Theatrical Roots in Luigi Nono's Early Spatial Practice," *Journal of the Royal Musical Association* 137:1 (2013): 71–106; Johanna Ethnersson Pontara, "Music as Excess: *Die Reise* and Neo-Baroque Aesthetics in Opera from the 1960s," *STM-Online* 16 (2013), accessed December 30, 2013, http://musikforskning.se/stmonline/vol_16/ethnersson/index.php?menu=3; Johanna Ethnersson Pontara, "Narrative and Performative Modalities in the Swedish Opera-in-the-round *Dreaming about Thérèse*," *STM-SJM* 96:2 (2014), accessed December 12, 2014, http://musikforskning.se/stm-sjm/node/19.

[4] Cf. Claudia Gorbman, "Auteur Music," in *Beyond the Soundtrack: Representing Music in Cinema*, ed. Daniel Goldmark et al. (Berkeley and Los Angeles: University of California Press, 2007), 154–158.

[5] On Tarkovsky, see Tobias Pontara, "Bach at the Space Station: Hermeneutic Pliability and Multiplying Gaps in Andrei Tarkovsky's *Solaris*," *Music, Sound, and the Moving Image*, 8:1 (2014): 1–23.

[6] Per F. Broman, "Music, Sound, and Silence in the Films of Ingmar Bergman," in *Music, Sound and Filmmakers: Sonic Style in Cinema*, ed. James Wierzbicki (New York: Routledge, 2012), 16, 19.

Luko has observed how he, through the collage-like structure of autobiographical images and film-clips in the opening scene of *Persona* (1966), "bypasses all pretense of diegesis and communicates directly with the spectator."[7]

In the present article concepts and approaches recently developed in the field of intermediality are drawn upon in order to reveal the intermedial qualities of Bergman's *Hour of the Wolf* (Stockholm 1964–68), as an artefact situated in a specific historical context.[8] Besides with historical issues, the intermedial analysis intersects with considerations of the film's narrative. *Hour of the Wolf* is, just like *Persona*, set to music by art-music composer Lars Johan Werle (1926–2001). The film includes modernist music by Werle and Western art music references.[9] I will argue that *Hour of the Wolf* can be seen as an example of what Werner Wolf denominates "formal imitation," implying that the media product is shaped "in such a manner that it acquires a formal resemblance to typical features or structures of another medium or heteromedial work."[10] Lars Elleström's distinction between three dimensions of a media product: the basic, the qualified ("the art form," formed by basic media under certain conditions), and the technical (the material-technological display of basic or qualified media) is adapted. I attempt to show how opera (a qualified medium/art form) is suggested in the underlying structure of the film (a qualified medium/art form) through the way in which the included

---

[7] Alexis Luko, *Sonatas, Screams, and Silence: Music and Sound in the Films of Ingmar Bergman* (New York: Routledge, 2015), 144.
[8] The film had its original release in 1967 and was re-released in 1968. For more on this see Luko, *Sonatas, Screams, and Silence*, 130.
[9] The study is based on the second version of the film from 1968, and on Werle's score of *Hour of the Wolf*. On the extensive deviances between Bergman's soundtrack and Werle's score, see Broman, "Music, Sound, and Silence," 25–26.
[10] Werner Wolf, "(Inter)mediality and the Study of Literature," *Comparative Literature and Culture* 13:3 (2011): 6, accessed January 8, 2018, http://docs.lib.purdue.edu/cgi/viewcontent.cgi?article=1789&context=clcweb. Cf. how Jørgen Bruhn makes use of this concept in *The Intermediality of Narrative Literature: Medialities Matter* (London: Palgrave Macmillan, 2016), 27.

basic media music, sound effect, image, and speech are combined and displayed through technical media of film.[11]

The analysis of the film is also informed by Irina O. Rajewsky's division into two sub-categories of intermediality: "media combination" and "intermedial reference." The category of media combination entails that "two medial forms of articulation" are "present in their own materiality and contribute to the constitution and signification of the entire product in their own specific way."[12] The category of intermedial reference overlaps with Wolf's concept formal imitation, entailing that a media-product "thematizes, evokes, or imitates elements or structures of another, conventionally distinct medium through the use of its own media-specific means."[13] Framed by the historical context (the early reception and debated ideas) the intermedial analysis will show how the two media genres film and opera both contribute to the constitution of the film by being "present in their own materiality" (that is through media-specific means), and how specific means of the media genre film are used in ways that "evoke an illusion of" operatic qualities.[14]

I will pay attention to two formal attributes by which the film imitates opera: a division into set numbers or tableaux,[15] and an emphasis of a double role of the music: as a means by which to construct the diegesis (the illusion of a fictive world), on the one hand, and as a sound object attracting attention to itself, on the other. I draw on recent discourses in opera studies where the genre

---

[11] Lars Elleström, "The Modalities of Media: A Model for Understanding Intermedial Relations," in *Media Borders, Multimodality and Intermediality*, ed. Lars Elleström (Basingstoke: Palgrave Macmillan, 2010), 26. See also Bruhn, *Intermediality of Narrative Literature*, 19–20.
[12] Irina O. Rajewsky, "Intermediality, Intertextuality, and Remediation: A Literary Perspective on Intermediality," *Intermédialités* 6 (2005): 52.
[13] Rajewsky, "Intermediality, Intertextuality, and Remediation," 53.
[14] Rajewsky, "Intermediality, Intertextuality, and Remediation," 57. On the importance of framing intermedial analysis by the historical context, see Rajewsky, "Intermediality, Intertextuality, and Remediation," 50.
[15] For how film may refer to opera in this way, see Marcia Citron, *When Opera Meets Film*, 20.

as a whole has been seen as characterized by this double role of the music both ideologically and structurally.[16]

Coming to the creation of illusion versus distance through the interaction between visual, verbal, and aural media recent research on the theatrical modes of film and opera is taken into consideration. Broadly speaking, it is a distinction between two ways of creating an audio-visual space: the theatrical (entertaining, spectacular, and rhetorical), implying that the labour behind the way in which the basic media is combined is exposed for the audience, and the cinematic (narrative and affective), implying that the combination of basic media by technical media has the effect of creating illusion and may contribute to absorption.[17] In her investigation of the dialectical relationship between film and theatre in Bergman's production, Maaret Koskinen has shown how Bergman makes use of the image in a way that enhances oscillation between a cinematic mode of creating affect in the frame of the narrative and a theatrical mode of creating spectacular entertainment, in accordance with film theorist Tom Gunning's concept of "cinema of attractions."[18] Gunning's concept attracts attention to how media can enhance the film viewer's awareness and arouse curiosity.[19] According to Koskinen, through the close-ups of faces in *Persona*, for example, diegetic absorption (through transparent narration) is challenged by exhibitionistic confrontation (an

---

[16] Cf. Christopher Morris, "'Too much Music': The Media of Opera," in *The Cambridge Companion to Opera Studies*, ed. Nicholas Till (Cambridge: Cambridge University Press, 2012), 95–116.

[17] Cf. Maaret Koskinen, *Ingmar Bergman: "Allting föreställer, ingenting är": Filmen och teatern – en tvärestetisk studie* (Nora: Nya Doxa, 2001), 114–115; Nicholas Ridout, "Opera and the Technologies of Theatrical Production," *The Cambridge Companion to Opera Studies*, ed. Nicholas Till (Cambridge: Cambridge University Press, 2012), 167; Robynn Stilwell, "Audio-visual Space in an Era of Technological Convergence," *The Oxford Handbook of New Audiovisual Aesthetics*, ed. John Richardson et al. (New York: Oxford University Press, 2013), 8.

[18] Koskinen, *Ingmar Bergman*, 115–117.

[19] Tom Gunning, "The Cinema of Attractions: Early Film, its Spectator and the Avant-Garde," *Wide Angle* 8:3/4 (1986): 63–70.

exposition of performance) in a way that reveals an awareness of the film viewer.[20]

Koskinen argues that this dialectics between cinematic and theatrical modes is important also in Bergman's production of the 1960s, consisting of films (for example *Persona* and *Hour of the Wolf*) previously being seen as permeated by a cinematic mode.[21] As to aural media she pays attention to Bergman's use of extended concrete sounds as a means by which to "arouse" the spectator's curiosity.[22] Gunning's concept, however, is highly useful also for analyzing the roles played by music in relation to sound effects and images.[23] Moreover, Bergman's experience as opera director and his interest in this media genre are factors that make it interesting to take the audio-visual space as a whole into consideration when analyzing the film.

In his autobiographical book *Images* (*Bilder*, 1990) Bergman described how he had been fascinated with opera, and more specifically with Mozart's *The Magic Flute* since childhood. At twelve years old, he attended a performance of this opera at the Royal Opera in Stockholm, and thereafter he wanted to set it at his puppet theatre; however, he did not have the right equipment for the project.[24] Although interested in staging *The Magic Flute* as employed at Malmö City Theatre, he got the opportunity first in 1974 with a TV production celebrating the fiftieth anniversary of Swedish National Radio and Television.[25] Already in 1961, however, Bergman had a successful opera production with Igor Stravinsky's *The Rake's Progress* at the Royal Opera in Stockholm.[26] The production was revived at the Montreal's

---

[20] Koskinen, *Ingmar Bergman*, 114–115.
[21] Koskinen, *Ingmar Bergman*, 49–50.
[22] Cf. Koskinen, *Ingmar Bergman*, 150.
[23] Cf. Martha Feldman, *Opera and Sovereignty: Transforming Myths in Eighteenth-Century Italy* (Chicago: University of Chicago Press, 2007), 95.
[24] Ingmar Bergman, *Bilder* (Stockholm: Norstedt, 1990), 307.
[25] Luko, *Sonatas, Screams, and Silence*, 14.
[26] Luko lists the operettas and operas that Bergman directed over his lifetime: Bertolt Brecht and Kurt Weill's *The Threepenny Opera* (1950), Franz Lehár's *The Merry Widow* (1954), Andreas Randel's *The Inhabitants of Värmland* (1958), Igor Stravinsky's *The Rake's Progress* (1961, 1967), Mozart's *The Magic Flute* (1974), and Daniel Börtz's *The Bacchantes*

World's Fair in 1967, and Bergman had plans on directing the same opera at the Hamburg Opera.[27] Bergman was also as film director influenced by opera and music; at various occasions he compared the film medium to the medium of music, and he described some of his films in relation to operas.[28] Recently, it has been conveyed how this influence was manifested both structurally and aesthetically in his production.[29]

Hour of the Wolf: Synopsis and Key Scenes

Hour of the Wolf has attracted attention among scholars for its mixture of realities and ambiguity of point of view, an ambiguity created by alternations between various narrative levels (for example the film producer Bergman, Alma, and Johan).[30] It has been shown how the music also contributes to this ambiguity.[31] With the re-release of the film in 1968, the film was interpreted as a horror movie by critics in Swedish daily journals, and the film was praised for its visual and sonic qualities, above all.[32]

(1991) in *Sonatas, Screams, and Silence*, 9. See also Broman, "Music, Sounds, and Silence," 18–19; Luko, *Sonatas, Screams, and Silence*, 8–19.

[27] These plans were cancelled when Bergman became ill in the spring of 1965. Cf. Luko, *Sonatas, Screams, and Silence*, 12–15.

[28] Cf. Michael Bird, "Music as Spiritual Metaphor in the Cinema of Ingmar Bergman," *Kinema: A Journal for Film and Audiovisual Media* (Spring 1996), accessed January 4, 2017, http://www.kinema.uwaterloo.ca/article.php?id=315&feature.

[29] Cf. Luko, *Sonatas, Screams, and Silence*, xxiii, 45–70.

[30] Cf. Luko, *Sonatas, Screams, and Silence*, 151; Mark B. Sandberg, "Rewriting God's Plot: Ingmar Bergman and Feminine Narrative," *Scandinavian Studies* 63:1 (1991): 1–29.

[31] Luko has shown how in *Hour of the Wolf*, just like in *Persona*, Werle's music is used where "fantasy blends with reality," in *Sonatas, Screams, and Silence*, 134.

[32] Jurgen Schildt, "Demoner i konstnärshuset," review of *Hour of the Wolf*, by Ingmar Bergman, *Aftonbladet*, February 20, 1968; Lasse Bergström, "'Vargtimmen' Skön och rik," review of *Hour of the Wolf*, by Ingmar Bergman, *Expressen*, February 20, 1968; Mauritz Edström, "'Vargtimmen' Mörkerrädsla för livet," review of *Hour of the Wolf*, by Ingmar Bergman, *Dagens Nyheter*, February 20, 1968; Carl Henrik Svenstedt, "Kontaktsvårigheter," review of *Hour of the Wolf*, by Ingmar Bergman, *Svenska Dagbladet*, February 20, 1968; "För och emot

Critic Karl Henrik Svenstedt described in *Svenska Dagbladet* on February 20, 1968, how the dimension of the images and the (sound) effects were "ear splitting." The film narrates the story of the painter Johan Borg and his wife, Alma, during a period of time when they are settled on a desolate island. Alma initially narrates about the disappearance of Johan and of her reading of his diary. She recalls what happened after their arrival to the island, and these events are visualized for the film viewer. The couple discover that the desolated island is inhabited and the inhabitants get in touch with Alma, first directly (an old lady), then indirectly through Johan's diary, which she reads (Veronica Vogler and Therapist Heerbrand). One of the inhabitants is Johan's former lover Veronica Vogler, who Alma encounters indirectly by way of reading about a love meeting between her and Johan in the diary (visualized in the film). A key scene of the first part of the film is the performance of a puppet show during a dinner party in the castle of baron von Merken, where Johan and Alma are guests, together with the inhabitants of the island. During the party, the atmosphere increasingly becomes oppressive with a culmination at the puppet show, where Johan appears to be the target of the performance.

In the second part of the film, the inhabitants' influence on the lives of Johan and Alma intensifies. A key scene is a flashback of Johan, which has a dreamlike character and narrates how he, while fishing on the rocks, encounters a young boy and finally kills him. An important sequence is also when Johan, having fired a pistol shot on Alma, returns to the castle in search for Veronica Vogler and becomes the laughing-stock of the inhabitants. The film ends as it begins, with Alma as narrator of Johan's destiny. Her final glimpse of Johan is shown in a flashback, which, just like the earlier scene of Johan and the boy on the rocks, has a dreamlike character. Eventually it is suggested that the inhabitants are demons of Johan's disturbed interior, which also Alma has begun to see.[33]

'Vargtimmen,'" *Svenska Dagbladet*, February 21, 1968; "Vargtimmen," *Expressen*, March 15, 1968.

[33] Cf. Luko, *Sonatas, Screams and Silence*, 151.

Formal Imitation of Opera through the Combination of Speech and Sound Effects

Considering the storyline and the characterization of certain characters *Hour of the Wolf* alludes to *The Magic Flute*. Johan's search for Veronica Vogler is a parallel to Tamino's search for Pamina,[34] and the character Archivist Lindhorst, in the film named "the bird man," is based on the character Papageno.[35] The title of the film is repeated in the middle of the film, the words in white against a dark backdrop, a device that, just like the drop curtain of a theatre (and opera) performance, emphasizes a division into two parts and has a distancing effect.[36] Each part of the film is verbally configured as an alternation between monologues, dialogues, and ensembles, in a set numberlike structure. Rather than interacting verbally with each other, the characters (above all the inhabitants) formulate themselves in long one-way monologues resembling verbal arias.

In the first part of the film inhabitants of the island are introduced in the narrative presenting themselves in one verbal monologue each. The part culminates at the dinner party in baron von Merken's castle, where Alma and Johan are dinner guests. The scene is introduced as a chaotic sonic space of various speeches of foregrounded voices. Gradually, however, individual speeches come to the fore, whereas the web of voices forms a sonic background. The intertwined speeches come to function as an accompaniment to individual monologues. This texture is occasionally broken by outbursts of unison laughter. By filmic technical media (such as sonic extension, foregrounding, and backgrounding) the voices are related to each other in textures evoking the illusion of an ensemble number in the qualified medium opera. It is an interchange between monologues with accompaniment, counterpoint,

---

[34] Cf. Broman, "Music, Sound, and Silence," 24.
[35] Cf. Martin Nedbal, "Live Marionettes and Divas on the Strings: Die Zauberflöte's Interactions with Puppet Theatre," *The Opera Quarterly* 28:1–2 (2012): 29; Luko, *Sonatas, Screams and Silence*, 133.
[36] On the "Brechtian alienation effect" of this device see Luko, *Sonatas, Screams, and Silence*, 145.

and unison texture.³⁷ This aural and verbal construction make the scene appear as a separate number.

The tableau-like structure of the film is also created through a combination of speech with sound effects that are manipulated by cinematic technical media. The vocal monologues of the inhabitants in the first part of the film are accompanied by extended natural sounds. Each monologue is surrounded by a certain soundscape, and these environmental sounds may occasionally dominate the sonic space whereas the voices are muted. The monologue of Veronica Vogler is surrounded by the sound of waves, whereas the monologue of Therapist Heerbrand is surrounded by the sound of a strong wind. The combination of sonic and vocal performance is especially remarkable in the monologue of the old lady, the first inhabitant introduced in the film, who appears before Alma directly. Her appearance is preceded by an extension of the environmental sounds, a strong wind, bird calls, and waves, and when she is discovered by Alma, the woman performs a one-way monologue against this soundscape. There is an interchange between vocal and sonic phrases, and at the second part of the monologue, the natural sounds occasionally substitute for the voice and dominate the sonic space entirely.³⁸ The soundscape continues after the end of the monologue, and ties the event together as a sonic unit. However, as Alma enters the house it is abruptly broken.

Framing the monologue by foregrounded sound effects, and alternating between speech and sound effects in the audio-visual space, Bergman uses technical media of film in a way that structures the monologue as a set piece. Just like in an opera aria individual media (the speech and the sound effects) occasionally attract the attention of the film spectator, appearing as qualified media (individual aesthetic entities) rather than basic media (the entities of

---

[37] Luko characterizes the conversation as "a cacophony resulting from a confluence of one-way monologues," and the "beakdown of verbal conversation," in *Sonatas, Screams, and Silence*, 133.

[38] Cf. Luko, who interprets this moment as an "aural out-of-focus moment," in *Sonatas, Screams, and Silence*, 132.

qualified media). This is achieved through the use of technical media of film, such as manipulations of tape of sound effects and tape of speech.

Formal Imitation of Opera through the Use of Opera

Although music is used sparingly in the film, it is an important structural device in the scenes where it occurs. Of certain importance is the introduction of an actual opera number towards the end of the first part of the film: Tamino's "O ewige Nacht" from *The Magic Flute*. This was one of the moments mentioned by Corliss and Hoops in their review of the film, and it motivated their characterization "frankly operatic."[39] The scene also attracted attention among the critics in Swedish daily papers.[40] In *The Magic Flute* this aria-like number is a vocal gesture of resignation performed by Tamino in his search for Pamina, and a choir of priests responds to his expression.[41] In his autobiographical book *Laterna Magica* (1987), Bergman stated that this was the scene affecting him most in the opera.[42] *The Magic Flute* number is featured during the puppet show performed in the scene following the dinner conversations, mentioned earlier, at the dinner party in the castle.

The dinner guests are gathered in front of a puppet stage and Archivist Lindhorst acts as puppeteer, standing behind the stage. On his command the instrumental prelude of Tamino's "O ewige Nacht" starts. The descending musical movement is synchronized with a descending movement of the camera, followed by an ascending movement as the curtain of the theatre raises. As the vocal part begins, a puppet appears on stage; however, it is a puppet

---

[39] Corliss and Hoops, "Hour of the Wolf," 38.
[40] Schildt, "Demoner i konstnärshuset"; Bergström, "'Vargtimmen' Skön och rik"; Edström, "'Vargtimmen' Mörkerrädsla för livet."
[41] Broman draws an existential parallel between Tamino's words and Bergman's intentions in "Music, Sound, and Silence," 25. Nedbal, in turn, argues that Bergman makes use of puppets in order to distance the film's audience from the opera's conventional meaning in "Live Marionettes and Divas on the Strings," 27.
[42] Ingmar Bergman, *Laterna Magica* (Stockholm: Norstedt, 1987), 251.

of flesh and blood, a miniaturized human puppet in a twisted pose with raised hands.[43] The moment is built up of a mixture of pre-recorded performance (the technical media of film is taken into consideration), a representation of a fictive reality (a part of the qualified medium film), and a representation of a dreamlike twist of this reality through the image of the performer (a manipulation through technical media). The use of an actual human being on stage suggests the performative mode of the qualified media opera and theatre. The illusion of an opera performance is also created through the use of technical media of film; when the music starts, the action "freezes" as Bergman lets the camera move around the audience with close-ups of experiencing faces.[44] At the same time, the live puppet representation in small proportion is a clearly filmic device.

The scene reveals how certain intermedial qualities are at play coming to how modes of the qualified media film and opera are combined. In accordance with the intermedial quality Rajewsky has labelled "media combination" it appears at first glance as two medial forms of articulation are "present in their own materiality and contribute to the constitution and signification of the entire product in their own specific way."[45] Opera is present musically and verbally through a specific number played in its entirety. Borrowing the words of Marcia Citron, the medium "is present in an obvious way that makes it recognizable."[46] Bergman, however, also calls attention to the musical number as sound object through the camera work (freezing the action through close-ups of faces of attentive spectators/listeners).[47] A closer analysis of the film shows

---

[43] Cf. Broman, "Music, Sound, and Silence," 24.
[44] On how the music may freeze the narrative, see Nicholas Cook, *Analysing Musical Multimedia* (Oxford and New York: Oxford University Press, 1998), 227.
[45] Rajewsky, "Intermediality, Intertextuality, and Remediation," 52.
[46] Citron, *When Opera Meets Film*, 246.
[47] Broman has paid attention to how the section emphasises music's ability to immerse its audience, humans as well as demons in "Music, Sound, and Silence," 25. See also Luko's consideration of Bergman's way of "watching the listener," in *Sonatas, Screams, and Silence*, 31–33.

that various modes are emphasized in the scene through a process of change in the configuration of the audio-visual space.

As to the configuration of the audio-visual space in film, film music scholar Robynn Stilwell has distinguished between a theatrical and a filmic mode. Each mode is based on audio-visual conventions, including for example the placement of music, "the way sound/speech are represented through sound design, camera, editing, lighting, performance, style."[48] She shows how the music-image relationship can differ coming to shape and texture and thereby may create theatrical versus cinematic experiences.[49]

The way in which the music is used initially in the scene conveys a theatrical mode. As the *Magic Flute* excerpt is introduced, the music is diegetic through its connection to the puppet show; it is experienced as music by the fictive characters. Also the sound quality (created by technical media) contributes to this position as the music is muted, which indicates that it emanates from a recording. It is a re-mediation of opera that takes the technological consequences of the production and distribution of the music into consideration in the representation, which means that a theatrical mode is at play. The technological implications of the mediation are revealed for the film viewer.[50]

However, successively the mode of using the basic media becomes cinematic, as the music comes to be subordinated to the narrative role of creating illusion. The camera moves around the audience with close-ups of faces of listening persons at the same time as the sound quality changes. The sound becomes clearer and the volume is elevated. The status of the music appears to transform from diegetic to non-diegetic. The production of music is in a cinematic mode subordinated to the narrative and integrated in the cinematic apparatus of production. As the camera moves around the spectators/listeners with close-ups of faces the music gets a foreground position with a build-up at Tamino's culminating outbreak of despair.

---

[48] Stilwell, "Audio-visual Space in an Era of Technological Convergence," 2.
[49] Stilwell, "Audio-visual Space in an Era of Technological Convergence," 1.
[50] Cf. Stilwell, "Audio-visual Space in an Era of Technological Convergence," 1–2; Ridout, "Opera and the Technologies of Theatrical Production," 167.

With this vocal climax, the mode becomes operatic, as the music attracts attention to itself as a sound object. The music is foregrounded in the audio-visual space to such an extent that it attracts the attention also of the real audience (the film viewer), and it is its status as qualified medium (a work of art) that is emphasized as much as its status as a means of creating a fictive world (how it works as a basic medium). The way in which Bergman lets the footage follow the musical development with hesitating movements that reinforce the vocal climax and the following decrescendo contributes to this impression. He lets the music guide the filmic apparatus of the production. In this way a technical medium of opera, the vocal climax, is reinforced. This is an example of what Citron labels "operaticness," implying that opera is "celebrated" through a specific trait.[51] Accordingly, the technical media of film are used in a way that reinforces a characteristic trait of opera as a media genre.[52]

Formal Imitation of Opera through the Combination of Music, Sound Effects, and Images

In the second part of the film, the music plays an important structural role in combination with sound effects and images. The music having this role is the modernist music by Werle. This part of the film includes two mute flashbacks, transcending from a dialogue, and a monologue respectively, each connected to the characters Johan and Alma. The dialogue and monologue are set in a theatrical mode visually, verbally, and sonically. The way in which the characters appear in front of the camera, and express themselves surrounded by environmental sounds is realistic and the means of production is revealed to the film viewer.[53] The two flashbacks, on the contrary, have an abstract and dreamlike character. Together with the Mozart excerpt, these two scenes set to

---

[51] Citron, *When Opera Meets Film*, 246.
[52] Cf. Rajewsky, "Intermediality, Intertextuality, and Remediation," 57.
[53] Cf. Koskinen, *Ingmar Bergman*, 114–117; Ridout, "Opera and the Technologies of Theatrical Production," 167; Stilwell, "Audio-visual Space in an Era of Technological Convergence," 8.

music by Werle, were the moments above all attracting attention among the Swedish critics of the film.[54]

The two scenes open up new audio-visual modes that differ from the theatrical mode of the framing monologue and dialogue, respectively, and gives them the character of what Stilwell terms "cinematic bubbles."[55] However, the effect of them is spectacular rather than affective cinematic through Werle's obtrusive modernistic score upon which Bergman superimposes sound effects and through oscillations between gestural synchronicity and counterpoint.

The flashback of Johan is mute and shows Johan encountering a boy on the rocks above the sea. The audio-visual configuration of the scene makes it deviate from the film at large. The footage is overexposed, and the sonic world is made up of modernistic sound constellations and of silence. Also the structure of the scene as a whole contributes to the creation of a self-sufficient entity with an exposition, a build-up to a climax, and a recapitulation. Initially, Johan and the boy are seen from a distance; Johan is fishing and the boy observes him. Eventually, the boy runs to look at Johan's things, which are put on the ground nearby. The music has a sighing character with sounds that are cut in separately and are suspended. As Johan and the boy suddenly make eye contact, a dissonant chord in low register creates a tense character. At this moment there is a build-up of sonic intensification, which culminates in a chaotic sonic world as the boy is shown in close-up from behind standing right behind Johan. A moment of relaxation is followed by the return of the initial sonic "sighing" character as Johan and the boy leaves their positions on the rocks. Thereafter a second section of intensification leads to a climax where Johan confronts the boy. The climax consists of a combination of drastic images and sounds oscillating between reinforcing and contradicting each other coming to movement and content.

---

[54] Cf. Svenstedt, "Kontaktsvårigheter"; Edström, "'Vargtimmen' Mörkerrädsla för livet."

[55] Stilwell, "Audio-visual Space in the Era of Technological Convergence," 6, 8.

Broman has paid attention to how expectations are contradicted through this combination of music and synthetic sounds with the forceful images:

> Musically the scene is remarkable, with a combination of conventional Hollywood suspense clichés, mickey-mousing, and stingers. The insertion of the boy's screams, in a scene devoid of natural sounds, is very effective and adds a layer of almost comic absurdity. Importantly, the music challenges the images by renouncing and contradicting them.[56]

The images show actions appearing to demand realistic sounds: the conniption of Johan shouting furiously at the boy, the boy screaming and biting Johan, Johan furiously hitting the boy and throwing him into the water. However, the scene is mute, and synthetic sound effects substitute for the natural sounds. Through synthetic sound effects and abrupt silence the actions are contradicted and exaggerated. At some moments the use of rhythmic and dissonant intensification and of silence is foregrounded to the extent of intruding upon the film viewer. In these moments the footage appears to be "enveloped by" the sonic and the mute world, respectively.[57] As Johan has thrown the body of the boy into the water the musical character initiating the scene returns, the musical gestures following the movements of the image; the body of the boy rising to the surface of the water.

The scene can be seen as a realization of Rajewsky's intermedial quality "intermedial reference," as the means of film (its technical media) is used in a way that create an audio-visual structure that evokes an effect of the qualified medium opera.[58] The scene is audio-visually configured as a self-contained number that deviates from the audio-visual space of the film at large. Moreover, individual media are foregrounded as visual and sonic objects (that is as qualified media rather than as basic media) through the synthetic quality and through unexpectedness of the action-sound combination with oscillations between gestural synchronicity and

---
[56] Broman, "Music, Sound, and Silence," 26.
[57] Cf. Stilwell, "Audio-visual Space in the Era of Technological Convergence," 23.
[58] Rajewsky, "Intermediality, Intertextuality, and Remediation," 57.

counterpoint at the climax. It is a modernist audio-visual space where the media attract attention to themselves as visual and sonic objects. In this way they also evoke an illusion of the double role of media in an opera aria. As to the music its role as sonic attraction (that is as qualified medium) is emphasized at the expense of its role as diegetic construction (that is as a basic medium of the qualified media of opera or film) through the way in which it is combined with sound effects.

Bergman also lets Werle's modernistic music substitute for vocal expression at the climax of the second part of the film where Johan becomes the laughing-stock of the inhabitants. Johan's monologue is suddenly muted and substituted by a sound that successively expands at the same time as the camera zooms in on Johan's face to the extent of blurriness. The image dissolves into the image of the boy's body floating in the water from the scene of Johan and the boy on the rocks. Just like in this other scene, the music and the images are reinforced as visual and sonic objects (making them appear as qualified media as much as of basic media) through the substitution of the vocal expression for the extended dissonant sound constellations in combination with the camera work.

The film ends as it starts, with a monologue of Alma; looking into the camera, she gives details about Johan's disappearance and of his diary. Eventually, her narration turns into a flashback (a visualization of the narrated events) breaking with the realistic mode of the scene through an overexposed footage in combination with extended natural sounds. It is shown how Alma searches for Johan in the forest, finds him, and they embrace with eyes closed. The camera zooms in on Alma's face and there is a cut with a doubling of the image. Alma appears to wake up, Johan has disappeared and instead she is confronted with one of the inhabitants, baron von Merken. As she discovers Johan the sequence dissolves into a montage of close-ups of Johan being beaten and injured and of Alma screaming. The images are combined with constellations of synthetic sounds in an audio-visual montage that oscillates between synchronization and counterpoint regarding the audio-visual movements.

In *Analysing Musical Multimedia* Nicholas Cook has shown how the music can be foregrounded in a narrative through structural devices, such as the da capo form of an aria, and in this way contribute to an experience of "formal intrusion."[59] At the end of Alma's flashback in *Hour of the Wolf*, the combination of montage technique, technologically manipulated images and sounds, and alternation between gestural synchronization and counterpoint (that is, through technical media) contribute to such formal quality.[60] The excessive sonic world of the scene of Johan and the boy on the rocks is re-established (this sonic world also recurs in the scene where Johan fires a pistol-shot on Alma)[61] and is foregrounded in relation to the images. A steady editing of close-ups is combined with manipulated, tape-recorded sound constellations. An initial stinger consisting of a foregrounded stylized sound effect is synchronized with the cut to a close-up of the mute scream of Alma. A forward-driving, metallic sound effect, overlaps the cut to an image where Johan is beaten and falls, mickey mousing his gesture. Thereafter sounds are cut in separately and are suspended (it is a re-establishment of the dissonant sonic world that initiates and appears at the end of the scene with Johan and the boy on the rocks) over cuts between close-ups.

The oscillation between synchronicity and counterpoint coming to visual and sonic movements creates the impression of two abstract montages being at play at the same time, a visual and a sonic. Together with the cutting rhythm and gestural movements the synthetic sonic and visual quality highlights the opacity of visual and sonic media and contributes to the stylized effect. The cinematic visual working through close-ups in steady editing is foregrounded and juxtaposed with foregrounded sound constellations in a way that makes the scene appear as a spectacular tableau.[62] Just like at the climax of the scene of Johan and the boy on the rocks the narrative is subordinated to the abstract beauty of the audio-visual space in a way that creates an illusion of an aria in the qualified medium opera.[63]

---

[59] Cook, *Analysing Musical Multimedia*, 220.
[60] Cook, *Analysing Musical Multimedia*, 226.
[61] Cf. Luko, *Sonatas, Screams, and Silence*, 157–161; Broman, "Music, Sound, and Silence," 26.
[62] Cf. Citron, *When Opera Meets Film*, 26.
[63] Cf. Rajewsky, "Intermediality, Intertextuality, and Remediation," 54–55.

Historical Contextualization: Medial Mixedness versus Medial Purity

The intermedial dimension of formal imitation being highlighted in *Hour of the Wolf,* with emphasis of the role played by the music, can be framed by the historical discussion of mixed versus pure medialities.[64] The film should be seen in the light of the debates around the relationship between music and other media and between various media genres among the Swedish avant-garde during the period 1940–50, discussing in what sense the arts could be seen as separated by distinctive properties or exchangeable coming to expressive means and aesthetic conventions.[65] A key figure in these debates was art-music composer Karl-Birger Blomdahl, who proclaimed that music should participate in film and other media genres in a manner appropriate to the medium and not be subordinated to visual and verbal media.[66] He meant that the aesthetic value of film, just like of opera and ballet, was enhanced if the arts included were joined on equal conditions, without any art dominating another.[67] Moreover, he posited that the film music composer should be free to avail himself of any sound and also of silence.[68]

It has been shown how Blomdahl's ideas about how music should be related to sound and image in film coincided with similar ideas of Bergman, who in turn was influenced by the aural language of the plays by August Strindberg.[69] An important issue of Blomdahl's and Bergman's ideas was the relationship between music and sound effect. Luko has pointed to how the distinction between music and sound effect is blurred in Bergman's film *Sawdust and Tinsel* (1953), in the scene where the clown Frost

---

[64] Cf. Bruhn, *Intermediality of Narrative Literature,* 12. See also Morris, "'Too much Music,'" 95–97.
[65] Cf. Christina Tobeck, *Karl-Birger Blomdahl: En Musikbiografi med inriktning på förhållandet mellan ord och ton i hans tidiga produktion,* vol. I–II, (PhD diss., University of Gothenburg, 2002), 355, 359–360, 385–386.
[66] Cf. Tobeck, *Karl-Birger Blomdahl,* I: 409, II: 75–76.
[67] Tobeck, *Karl-Birger Blomdahl,* II: 75–76.
[68] Luko, *Sonatas, Screams, and Silence,* 50.
[69] Luko, *Sonatas, Screams, and Silence,* 50, 181–195.

finds his wife, Alma, as she is bathing naked with soldiers. Here, Blomdahl's soundtrack not only has the character of sound effect through dissonant and rhythmic irregular ostinatos where individual pitches are emphasized and through a setting dominated by wind instruments and percussions, but Bergman also superimposes sounds of cannon firing on this music. Moreover, the aural media music, sound effect, and later in the sequence silence, are foregrounded in the audio-visual space and contribute, together with an over-exposed footage, to an abstract character that makes the scene unique in the film.[70]

The two scenes in *Hour of the Wolf*, scored by Werle, have affinity audio-visually with this scene in *Sawdust and Tinsel*.[71] The view of music's position in relation to other media, presented by Blomdahl, appears to have been of importance also for Werle during this period of time. In an interview published in a Swedish daily journal in the late 1960s Werle posited that his ambition was to create contradiction between music and other media rather than interaction.[72] Bergman's *Persona* (1966) and the ballet *Zodiak* (1966) are mentioned as examples of how counterpoint is created between Werle's music and images and bodily movements respectively.[73]

Besides in media mixedness versus media specificity, the media production of the Swedish 1960s, conveys an interest in media genre mixedness versus media genre specificity. In, for example, the music theatrical productions of Werle and director and librettist Lars Runsten: *Dreaming about Thérèse* and *The Journey*, the media genres opera, TV, and film intersect.[74] The media genres are

---

[70] Luko, *Sonatas, Screams, and Silence*, 51–59, 67–68; cf. Broman, "Music, Sound, and Silence," 26; Koskinen, *Ingmar Bergman*, 149.
[71] Cf. Broman, "Music, Sound, and Silence," 26.
[72] "En socialt anpassad rebell i folkhemmets lugna trygghet," *Svenska Dagbladet*, February 12, 1967.
[73] "En socialt anpassad rebell." The image-music-sound relationship is also interesting in the scenes having music by Werle in Alf Sjöberg's film *The Island* (1966). Here, forceful images are combined with a chaotic sonic world of free jazz where the distinction between music and sound effect is dissolved.
[74] Cf. Ethnersson Pontara, "Music as Excess," and "Narrative and Performative Modalities."

mixed, however, in ways enhancing their specific traits. Bergman's film production of the 1960s can be seen as belonging to this category of productions too, not only visually, but also through the way in which music is used in relation to sound effects and images.[75] Accordingly, the structural imitation of another media genre in *Hour of the Wolf* conveys a modernist approach where individual media are distinguished in the moment of combination, an approach that also was used on the level of media genre, where media genres were distinguished within one and the same media product.

Final Reflections

With point of departure in a specific historical context this article has highlighted how certain intermedial qualities can be revealed by the film *Hour of the Wolf*'s connection to opera.[76] It has been shown how the film imitates opera through a division into set numbers and through the double role of music as subordinated to a narrative in order to create illusion (that is, as a basic medium), on the one hand, and as attracting attention to itself as a sound object and arousing the film viewer's curiosity, on the other (that is, as a qualified medium). The disclosure of the intermedial quality of formal imitation highlights how the film was integrated in discourses on the relationship between media in the 1960s, not only coming to visual and verbal media, but also regarding the music. In this modernistic context, media objects were not only characterized by media specificity as to individual media, but also coming to how they structurally were indebted to other media genres.

The way in which Bergman foregrounds music as a sound object in the film *Hour of the Wolf* can be compared to the way in which he foregrounds the spectacular effect of images in the film, which has been shown by Koskinen. The investigation of the scenes in *Hour of the Wolf* suggests that sound and music are as

---

[75] Cf. Koskinen, who, however, posits that the modes of theatre and film are fused, in *Ingmar Bergman*, 16.
[76] Cf. Bruhn, *Intermediality of Narrative Literature*, 24.

important as the image for a challenge of "diegetic absorption" through "exhibitionistic confrontation."[77] To this challenge contributes not only the use of an actual opera number in the film, but also the way in which Werles music is combined with sound effects and images. The two scenes of Johan's and Alma's flashbacks in the second part of the film appear as autonomous montages freezing the narrative, as images, sounds, and music have the effect of opacity instead of transparency. Musical opacity is displayed through sound constellations generated by new technology and through oscillations between synchronicity and counterpoint coming to the relationship between musical and visual movements and expressions. Through these devices, these media appear as aesthetic entities (rather than basic media subordinated to the narrative). The music thereby contributes to the dialectical relationship between diegetic absorption and attracting entertainment that is an important experience of much art film,[78] which points to opera. The way in which sounds, music, and images are foregrounded makes the effect of spectacular excess enhanced at the expense of the affective absorbing. Borrowing the word of Koskinen, the scenes are experienced as audio-visual shocks.[79]

References

Books and Articles

Bird, Michael. "Music as Spiritual Metaphor in the Cinema of Ingmar Bergman." *Kinema: A Journal for Film and Audiovisual Media* (Spring 1996). Accessed January 4, 2017. http://www.kinema.uwaterloo.ca/article.php?id=315&feature

Bergman, Ingmar. *Bilder*. Stockholm: Norstedt, 1990.

Bergman, Ingmar. *Laterna Magica*. Stockholm: Norstedt, 1987.

---

[77] Koskinen, *Ingmar Bergman*, 114–115.
[78] Cf. Koskinen, *Ingmar Bergman*, 117; Gunning, "The Cinema of Attractions," 63–70.
[79] Koskinen, *Ingmar Bergman*, 115–117.

Boyd, Harriet. "Remaking Reality: Echoes, Noise and Modernist Realism in Luigi Nono's *Intolleranza 1960*." *Cambridge Opera Journal* 24:2 (2012): 177–200.

Broman, Per F. "Music, Sound, and Silence in the Films of Ingmar Bergman." In *Music, Sound and Filmmakers: Sonic Style in Cinema*, edited by James Wierzbicki, 16–31. New York: Routledge, 2012.

Bruhn, Jørgen. *The Intermediality of Narrative Literature: Medialities Matter*. London: Palgrave Macmillan, 2016.

Citron, Marcia. *When Opera Meets Film*. Cambridge: Cambridge University Press, 2010.

Cook, Nicholas. *Analysing Musical Multimedia*. Oxford and New York: Oxford University Press, 1998.

Corliss, Richard, and Jonathan Hoops. "Hour of the Wolf," review of *Hour of The Wolf*, by Ingmar Bergman. *Film Quarterly* 21:4 (1968): 33–40. Accessed October 29, 2015. http://www.jstor.org/stable/1210600?seq=1#page_scan_tab_contents.

Elleström, Lars. "The Modalities of Media: A Model for Understanding Intermedial Relations." In *Media Borders, Multimodality and Intermediality*, edited by Lars Elleström, 11–48. Basingstoke: Palgrave Macmillan, 2010.

Ethnersson Pontara, Johanna. "Music as Excess: *Die Reise* and Neo-Baroque Aesthetics in Opera from the 1960s." *STM-Online* 16 (2013): 1–32. Accessed December 30, 2013. http://musikforskning.se/stmonline/vol_16/ethnersson/index.php?menu=3.

Ethnersson Pontara, Johanna. "Narrative and Performative Modalities in the Swedish Opera-in-the-round *Dreaming about Thérèse*." *STM-SJM* 96:2 (2014). Accessed December 12, 2014. http://www.musikforskning.se/stm-sjm/node/19.

Feldman, Martha. *Opera and Sovereignty: Transforming Myths in Eighteenth-Century Italy*. Chicago: University of Chicago Press, 2007.

Gorbman, Claudia. "Auteur Music." In *Beyond the Soundtrack: Representing Music in Cinema*, edited by Daniel Goldmark, Lawrence Kramer, and Richard Leppert, 149–162. Berkeley and Los Angeles: University of California Press, 2007.

Gorbman, Claudia. "Ears Wide Open: Kubrick's Music." In *Changing Tunes: The Use of Pre-existing Music in Film*, edited by Phil Powrie and Robynn Stilwell, 3–18. Aldershot: Ashgate, 2006.

Gunning, Tom. "The Cinema of Attractions: Early Film, its Spectator and the Avant-Garde." *Wide Angle* 8:3/4 (1986): 63–70.

Jeongwon, Joe, and Rose Theresa, eds. *Between Opera and Cinema*. New York: Routledge, 2002.

Koskinen, Maaret. *Ingmar Bergman: "Allting föreställer, ingenting är": Filmen och teatern – en tvärestetisk studie*. Nora: Nya Doxa, 2001.

Luko, Alexis. *Sonatas, Screams, and Silence: Music and Sound in the Films of Ingmar Bergman*. New York: Routledge, 2015.

Morris, Christopher. "'Too much Music': The Media of Opera." In *The Cambridge Companion to Opera Studies*, edited by Nicholas Till, 95–116. Cambridge: Cambridge University Press, 2012.

Nedbal, Martin. "Live Marionettes and Divas on the Strings: Die Zauberflöte's Interactions with Puppet Theatre." *The Opera Quarterly* 28:1–2 (2012): 20–36.

Pontara, Tobias. "Bach at the Space Station: Hermeneutic Pliability and Multiplying Gaps in Andrei Tarkovsky's Solaris." *Music, Sound, and the Moving Image* 8:1 (2014): 1–23.

Rajewsky, Irina O. "Intermediality, Intertextuality, and Remediation: A Literary Perspective on Intermediality." *Intermédialités* 6 (2005): 43–64.

Ridout, Nicholas. "Opera and the Technologies of Theatrical Production." In *The Cambridge Companion to Opera Studies*, edited by Nicholas Till, 159–176. Cambridge: Cambridge University Press, 2012.

Sandberg, Mark B. "Rewriting God's Plot: Ingmar Bergman and Feminine Narrative." *Scandinavian Studies* 63:1 (1991): 1–29.

Santini, Andrea. "Multiplicity – Fragmentation – Simultaneity: Sound-Space as a Conveyor of Meaning, and Theatrical Roots in Luigi Nono's Early Spatial Practice." *Journal of the Royal Musical Association* 137:1 (2012): 71–106.

Stilwell, Robynn. "Audio-visual Space in an Era of Technological Convergence." In *The Oxford Handbook of New Audiovisual Aesthetics*, edited by John Richardson, Claudia Gorbman, and Carol Vernallis, 125–145. New York: Oxford University Press, 2013.

Tobeck, Christina. *Karl-Birger Blomdahl: En Musikbiografi med inriktning på förhållandet mellan ord och ton i hans tidiga Produktion*, vol. I–II. PhD diss. University of Gothenburg, 2002.

Wolf, Werner. "(Inter)mediality and the Study of Literature," *Comparative Literature and Culture* 13:3 (2011): 1–9. Accessed January 8, 2018. http://docs.lib.purdue.edu/cgi/viewcontent.cgi?article=1789&context=clcweb.

Reports and Reviews from Daily Papers

Anonymous ("Ulrika"). "En socialt anpassad rebell i folkhemmets lugna trygghet." *Svenska Dagbladet*, February 12, 1967.

Anonymous. "För och emot 'Vargtimmen.'" *Svenska Dagbladet*, February 21, 1968.

Anonymous. "Vargtimmen." *Expressen*, March 15, 1968.

Bergström, Lasse. "'Vargtimmen' Skön och rik." *Expressen*, February 20, 1968.

Edström, Mauritz. "'Vargtimmen' Mörkrädslan för livet." *Dagens Nyheter*, February 20, 1968.

Schildt, Jurgen. "Demoner i Konstnärshuset." *Aftonbladet*, February 20, 1968.

Svenstedt, Carl Henrik. "Kontaktsvårigheter." *Svenska Dagbladet* February 20, 1968.

Film and Score

Bergman, Ingmar. *Vargtimmen (Hour of the Wolf)*, 1968.

Werle, Lars Johan. Score for *Vargtimmen (Hour of the Wolf)*, 1968.

Figures of Migration: Intertextuality in Michelangelo's *Night*

Peter Gillgren

Abstract

Migration is a central feature of contemporary culture, bringing to our attention—among other things—certain problematic aspects of the concept intermediality. It may be asked if the concept is at all relevant in relation to such cultural phenomena. Below, it is argued that a return to Julia Kristeva's original concept of intertextuality could be the way forward. Discussing the example of Michelangelo's sculpture *Night*, it is argued that the specific work must be interrelated not only to the multimedia context of the Medici chapel but also to political and personal experiences of migration in the artist's own time and cultural sphere. Such perspectives, however, demand the consideration of psychological and political contexts that are commonly absent in intermedia studies. The Kristevian concept of intertextuality, on the other hand, allows for intermedia phenomena to take place in relation to the full complexities of art, life, and culture.

Cultures of Migration

"If we think of culture today," says Mieke Bal, "it is impossible not to think of migration." There is an analogy to be made here, she continues, "between the movement of people and the movement of images, a double movement through spacetime,

---

How to cite this book chapter:
Gillgren, Peter. "Figures of Migration: Intertextuality in Michelangelo's *Night*." In *The Power of the In-Between: Intermediality as a Tool for Aesthetic Analysis and Critical Reflection*, edited by Sonya Petersson, Christer Johansson, Magdalena Holdar, and Sara Callahan, 75–97. Stockholm: Stockholm University Press, 2018. DOI: https://doi.org/10.16993/baq.d. License: CC-BY.

where time is short and space is large."[1] It should be added that migration is a central feature not only of culture today but in a much longer European perspective. Looking back over the epochs, migration appears as a continuous phenomenon no less in pre-history, Antiquity, or the Renaissance than today. It is unsurprising, therefore, that migration is a reoccurring theme in the visual arts as well. One of the most well-known themes is the flight of Aeneas, narrating how the hero, his family, and their followers flee from Troy over the Mediterranean Sea, about their settlement in Italy, and ultimately the establishment of the Roman Empire. The story is told, over and over again, in hymns and opera, poetry and literature, as well as sculpture and painting all through the centuries. For a true and thorough understanding, an analysis that goes beyond what is purely media specific seems essential. It should encompass the multimodal reality of historical circumstances and the multimedia assemblages of artistic practice as well as a discussion of the relationship between such aspects and the specific work of art.

The figure of migration is truly a figure of in-betweenness, being on the move from one place to the other and, as a consequence, from one mode of existence to another. Often the image or metaphor of sleep has been used to represent this state of being, in philosophy and poetry as well as in the visual arts. Theories of intermediality may help to clarify these relationships, but in most cases they will fall short of including intersubjective features or cultural contexts in the analysis. The in-betweenness considered in formalist intermedia studies is focused on what is taking place between different media forms. The relationship to social and cultural practices or what is going on between the artist and the public becomes secondary. One way around this restriction is—perhaps paradoxically—a return to Kristeva's original concept of intertextuality.[2]

---

[1] Mieke Bal, "Intercultural Story-Telling," in *Kultur – Wissen – Narration: Perspektiven transdisciplinärer Erzählforschung für die Kulturwissenschaften*, ed. Alexandra Strohmaier (Bielefeld: Transcript Verlag, 2013), 289–306.
[2] Julia Kristeva, "Le mot, le dialogue et le roman," in *Sēmeiōtikē: Recherches pour une sémanalyse* (Paris: Seuil, 1969), 143–173; translated in *Desire in Language: A Semiotic Approach to Literature and Art*, ed.

Kristeva's Intertextuality

Following other important semioticians such as Jan Mukařovský and Roland Barthes, Kristeva considered everything a text; not only the visual arts and music but also everyday life and private imagination.[3] They all belong to the intertextual network of the artistic enterprise that makes art readable. One of her primary examples is the multimodal event of a carnival: Through an intertextual process it may take the artistic form of for example a poem, a painting, or a song. Even more important, though, was Kristeva's opposition to the formalistic schools of semiotics. Using Bakhtin's concept of dialogism as well as Freud, she opposed the analysis of isolated cultural artefacts and insisted on regarding them as parts of a lived experience—on behalf of both artists and public. Associated with this original concept of intertextuality is therefore also the intersubjective or psychological dimension of artistic practices. The *thetic* drive, the struggle to break loose from patriarchal traditions, is one of the main forces behind every urge to signify, she insisted. On the one hand, all texts are grounded in the *chora*—the unspoken conditions behind any articulation. On the other hand, a work of art is a struggle with the symbolic Father and with authority. Artistic creations can therefore be understood as efforts to undo and overwrite the predecessors. Paradoxically, the poetic work is an effort to start anew and to get rid of all authoritative interferences, just as much as it is an embracing of those very confining and intertextualizing premises.

It is telling that Kristeva herself gave up the concept of intertextuality only a few years after coining it, finding it watered-out and unproductive when it was used simply as an equivalent to literary influence.[4] The more precise meaning of the concept has

---

Leon S. Roudiez, trans. Thomas Gora, Alice Jardine, and Leon S. Roudiez (New York: Columbia University Press, 1980). Also published as "Word, Dialogue and Novel," in *The Kristeva Reader*, ed. Toril Moi (New York: Columbia University Press, 1986), 34–61.

[3] Roland Barthes, "De l'oeuvre au texte," *Revue d'esthétique* 3 (1971): 225–232; translated as "From Work to Text," in *Image–Music–Text*, trans. Stephen Heath (London: Fontana, 1977), 155–164.

[4] Julia Kristeva, *La révolution de langage poétique* (Paris: Seuil, 1974), 57–61; translated as *Revolution in Poetic Language*, trans. Margaret Waller (New York: Columbia University Press, 1984), 57–61.

been debated ever since Kristeva, and in relation to the concept of intermediality it has been understood both as subordinate and as the more profound.[5] In the former case, intertextuality is usually defined as concerned only with the relationship between verbal utterances. This is limiting enough, of course. Even more important is that all further cultural contexts and active subjects are excluded from such systems. Aspects of creativity or reception are missing, and the focus is very much on the formal analysis of fixed artefacts. Below, however, the idea of intertextuality is applied in its original Kristevian meaning, in order to present a close-up reading of Michelangelo's *Night* in the Medici chapel as a figure of migration. Analysis encompasses intermedia aspects of the work, but the ultimate focus is on the process of semiosis itself.[6]

Michelangelo's *Night*

The statue *Night* was produced under the most difficult of circumstances (Figure 1). After completing the Sistine ceiling in triumph in 1512 followed some years of unfulfilled promises for the artist as he was thrown between the efforts of completing the monument for Julius II's tomb in Rome on behalf of the Della Rovere family and doing works at San Lorenzo in Florence for the Medici. In connection with the Sack of Rome in 1527, he had chosen to return once again from Rome to his native Florence, only to be ensnared by the political and military conflicts of the Italian Wars and the struggles for power within the city walls.

---

[5] The relationship is thoughtfully problematized in Valerie Robillard, "Beyond Definition: A Pragmatic Approach to Intermediality," in *Media Borders, Multimodality and Intermediality*, ed. Lars Elleström (Basingstoke: Palgrave Macmillan, 2010), 150–162. It is also well presented in Werner Wolf, *The Musicalization of Fiction: A Study in the Theory and History of Intermediality* (Amsterdam: Rodopi, 1999), 35–50. Wolf is on the formalist side of the debate but gives further references also to opponents.

[6] This aspect was followed up also in Julia Kristeva, "Le sujet en procès," in *Polylogue* (Paris: Seuil, 1977); translated as "The Subject in Process," in *The Tel Quel Reader*, eds. Patrick Ffrench and Roland-François Lack (London: Routledge, 1998), 133–178.

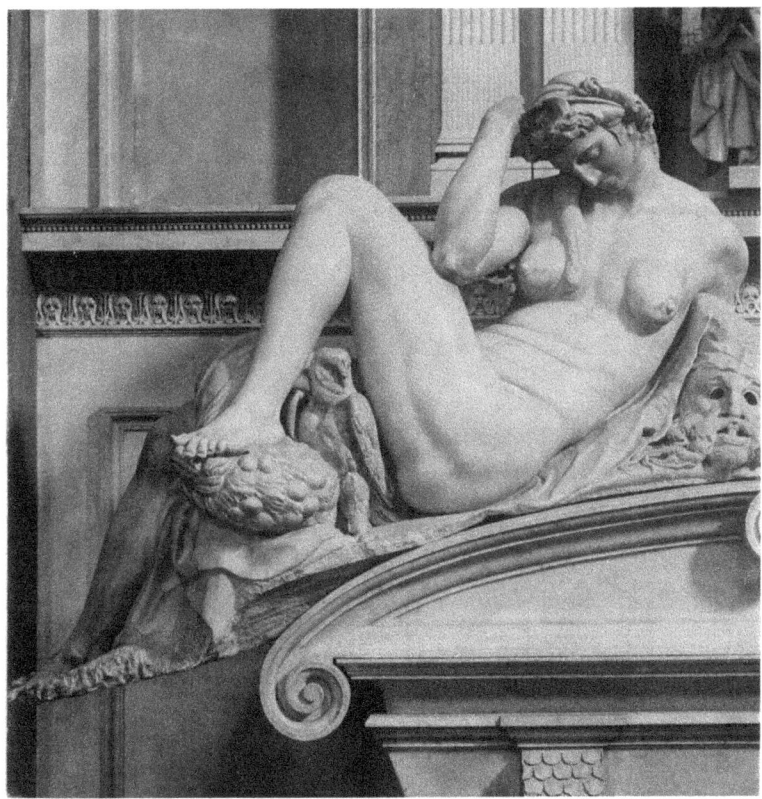

Figure 1. *Night.* Michelangelo, c. 1530. Marble. The Medici chapel, San Lorenzo, Florence. Reproduction and permission: Bildarchiv Foto Marburg. License: CC-BY-NC-ND.

In the same year, the Medici family was—once again—expelled from Florence, and Michelangelo interrupted his work at San Lorenzo to join the Republican government. His main responsibility was the fortifications of the city, their maintenance, strengthening, and extension. In September 1529, however, the political intrigues become too difficult for him and he decided to flee the city together with two of his friends, Antonio Mini (b. 1506) and the goldsmith Piloto (Giovanni di Baldassarre, c. 1460–1536). Michelangelo's plan was to go Venice and then, most likely, to France. The three companions were not the only ones at flight during these difficult times, though, and Giorgio Vasari (1511–1564) writes:

> It happened that because of the tumult caused by the wars, and the alliance between the emperor and the Pope, who were besieging Ferrara, wanting to know from those who gave lodgings to travellers the names of all arrivals from day to day; and every day he had brought to him a description of all foreign visitors and where they came from. So when Michelangelo dismounted with his companions, intending to stay in Ferrara without making himself known, his arrival was notified to the Duke [...].[7]

The companions were prevented to leave Ferrara until Michelangelo promised the Duke a painting of his own hand. A painting representing Leda and the Swan was indeed begun by the artist, but it was never delivered. Instead, Michelangelo gave it to his traveling companion Antonio Mini, perhaps as a memorial of their flight. The main figure is close to the figure of *Night* in the Medici chapel and, unusually, the motif includes the offspring of the seduction, the twins Castor and Pollux. In the Renaissance (as well as later) they were commonly interpreted as representations of Republicanism. The three companions avoid staying at the Duke's castle, insisting on returning to the hostel and to stay with the other travelers and refugees. From Ferrara they went to Venice, but after being "much sought after by various people" and being "strongly urged to return home" Michelangelo did so in December 1529. According to both Vasari and Ascanio Condivi (1525–1574), he feared for his life already at this point, but even more so when, in 1530, the Florentine Republic fell and the Medici family returned to power. He went underground, but was found by the Medici and, ultimately, pardoned under the explicit

---

[7] Giorgio Vasari, *Lives of the Painters, Sculptors and Architects* II, trans. Gaston du C. de Vere (New York: Everymans Library, 1996 [1568]), 370. "Et a Ferrara condotti, riposandosi, avvenne che per gli sospetti della guerra e per la lega dello imperatore e del papa, ch'erano intorno a Fiorenza, il Duca Alfonso da Este teneva ordini in Ferrara e voleva sapere secretamente da gli osti che alloggiavano, i nomi di tutti coloro che ogni dí alloggiavano, e la lista de' forestieri, di che nazione si fossero, ogni dí si faceva portare. Avvenne dunque che, essendo Michele Agnolo quivi con li suoi scavalcato, fu ciò per questa via noto al duca [...]."

demand that he would now obediently and without further delay continue work on the tomb sculptures for the Medici chapel. According to Condivi, he set out at once with the work and even though it was now 15 years since he had handled the tools of a sculptor, he produced all the statues to be seen in the New Sacristy of San Lorenzo in just a few months, including *Night*, "driven more by fear than by love."[8]

Night and the *Belvedere Cleopatra*

As for the character of Michelangelo's figure, Vasari's description is both convincing and questionable:

> And what can I say of the Night, a statue not only rare but unique? Who has ever seen a work of sculpture of any period, ancient or modern, to compare with this? For in her may be seen not only stillness of one who is sleeping but also the grief and melancholy of one who has lost something great and noble.[9]

Despite Vasari's words, and while it must be admitted that the sculpture is unique, the figure of *Night* does have some forerunners. The closest one is probably the so-called *Cleopatra* at the Belvedere court in Rome (Figure 2). She too is a reclining female in an uncomfortable sleep, twisting her torso and folding one arm over the head—as if to suggest difficult dreams and an undefinable anguish. This Antique statue was acquired by Julius II in 1512 and installed as a fountain in the same year at the Vatican (the very same year that Michelangelo completed the Sistine chapel ceiling).[10] Today the statue is believed to represent Ariadne but during the Renaissance the snake armlet of the left arm made

---

[8] Ascanio Condivi, *Vita di Michelangelo Buonarroti* (Pisa, 1823 [1553]), 49; translated as "Life of Michelangelo Buonarroti," in *Michelangelo: Life, Letters and Poetry*, trans. George Bull (Oxford: Oxford University Press, 1987), 45: "più della paura, che dall'amore."

[9] Vasari, *Lives* II, 369. "E che potrò io dire della Notte, statua unica o rara? Chi è quello che abbia per alcun secolo in tale arte veduto mai statue antiche o moderne cosí fatte? Conoscendosi non solo la quiete di chi dorme, ma il dolore e la maninconia di chi perde cosa onorata e grande."

[10] Brian Curran, *The Egyptian Renaissance: The Afterlife of Ancient Egypt in Early Modern Italy* (Chicago: University of Chicago Press, 2007), 167–177.

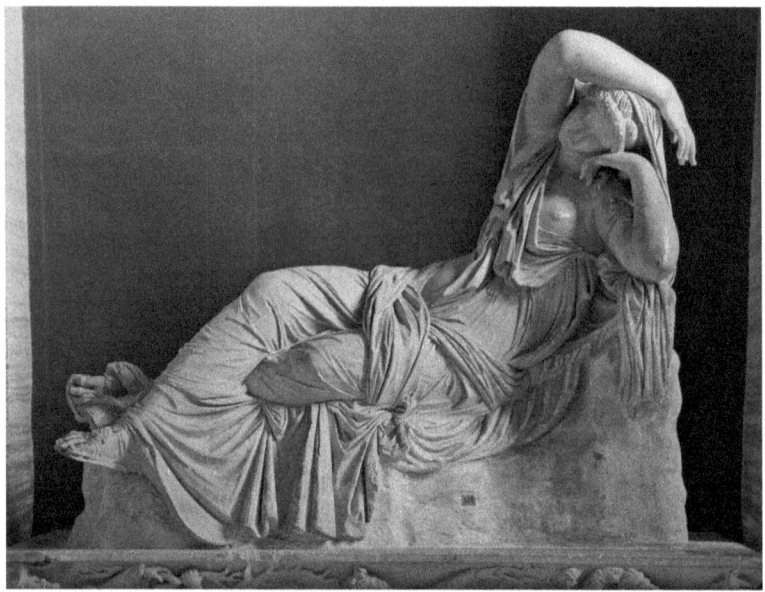

Figure 2. *Belvedere Cleopatra*. Unknown artist, 2nd century BC. Marble. Vatican Museums, Rome. Reproduction and permission: Bildarchiv Foto Marburg. License: CC-BY-NC-ND.

scholars associate her with the dying Cleopatra. According to Vasari this was one of the classical works—together with the Apollo, the Laocoon, the torso etc. at the Belvedere court—that inspired the *bella maniera*, the style of the High Renaissance acquired by Leonardo da Vinci, Raphael, and Michelangelo.[11] Like *Night*, *Cleopatra* belonged to an assembly of sculptures that attracted great attention among artists and poets of the time; they were both parts of courtly and multimodal arenas, where poems were written and exclaimed, music was performed, and artists gathered to exercise the art of drawing.[12]

---

[11] Vasari, *Lives* I, 618.
[12] Sylvie Deswarte-Rosa, "Francisco de Holanda el le *Cortile di Belvedere*," in *Il cortile delle statue: Der Statuenhof del Belvedere im Vatikan* (Mainz: von Zabern, 1998), 394–395, describes mostly the literary scene and understands the sculpture court as a site for *orti letterati*.

Sculpture and Poetry

For both of these sculptures a number of poems were written. We know more about the ones for *Cleopatra*. Best known is the poem by Baldassare Castiglione, composed during the pontificate of Leo X (1513–1521). Castiglione describes how the Egyptian Queen is taken prisoner by the Romans and their plans to bring her to Rome in a triumphal procession. Instead, she manages to kill herself with snake poison and escape such a destiny. Among "blazoned inscriptions and enslaved peoples, [is] led through the Capital [instead] the luckless image of a dead woman."[13] Julius II then placed her "among the figures of ancient heroes, and set the stone beneath eternal tears"—referring to her function as a fountain. Tears, Cleopatra insures us, is her only comfort now: "Restore, I beg, that weeping, a weeping which is almost a gift for me, since now heartless fortune has left me nothing else […]." Other epigrams speak of the figure as sleeping, or rather about the uncertainty as to whether she is dead or still alive. They all seem to go back to an epigram for a sleeping nymph by a well, claimed during the Renaissance to be of Antique origin but today usually attributed to the Roman humanist Gianantonio Campano and dated to around 1470:

> Here I, the Nymph of this place, guardian of the sacred fountain
> Slumber, while the murmur of gentle water is what I hear.
> Whoever touches this hollow marble, take care not to wake me;
> Whether you have in mind drinking or bathing, do not speak.[14]

This poetic fascination with sleep goes back at least to Heraclitus' writings, as transmitted to us in fragments by for example St Clement of Alexandria and Plutarch. One of the most well-known fragments notes that "the waking have one world in common, but the sleeping turn aside each into a world of their own."[15] Other fragments are even more intriguing and hard to interpret. Somehow, though, they all come down to the fact that we

---

[13] Curran, *Egyptian*, 173.
[14] Curran, *Egyptian*, 175.
[15] Heraclitus, "Fragments," in *Early Greek Philosophy*, trans. John Burnet (London: Black, 1912), fragment 89; Plutarch, "On Superstition," in

do not know the dreams and thoughts of the sleeping. We cannot grasp their mode of experience, because dreaming and sleeping is so fundamentally different from knowing the world as when awake. Finally, we do not know, either, if they are dead or alive. And so we ask ourselves: Should we make the effort to awaken them, try make them part of our world again, or are they better off on their own?

The reception and use of the Medici chapel was in many respects similar to the Belvedere complex and Vasari notes that many poems were written for *Night* as well.[16] In a few poems that were probably penned down before the sculpture was produced the artist himself celebrates night as a *dolce tempo*—a pleasant time (Sonnets 102, 103, and 104).[17] It is a time praised by all with good judgment, he says, for it breaks tiresome thoughts and sweeps them into dark shadows.[18] The topology of Night is an enclosed and narrow little place—every closed room, every covered site, everything that is circumscribed by *materia*, is protected by Night. Man is procreated in the night and it is therefore more holy than the day. Continuing on the same theme Michelangelo observes that God created both the sun and the moon and that the latter is closer to man; man is a sublunary being.

Night is also a central deity of Orphic Theogony.[19] In an alternative version of Biblical cosmology, the Orphists claimed that Chaos gave birth first to Nyx (Night) and then to her brother Erebos. Night then gave birth to Aither and Hemera, also a brother

---

    Moralia II, trans. F. C. Babbitt (Harvard: Loeb Classical Library, 1928), 3, 166 C.

[16] Vasari, *Lives* II, 682–683. These epigrams also relate to a wider tradition from the late fifteenth century of poems dedicated to "sleeping nymphs," often poets connected with humanistic societies gathering in gardens ornamented with fragments of classical sculpture. See Leonard Barkan, "The Beholder's Tale: Ancient Sculpture, Renaissance Narratives," *Representations* 44 (1993): 133–166 (with further references).

[17] Michelangelo, *The Poetry of Michelangelo*, trans. James M. Saslow (New Haven: Yale University Press, 1991).

[18] "tu mozzi e tronchi ogni stancho pensiero, che l'umid' ombra e ogni quiet' appalta."

[19] Edgar Wind, *Pagan Mysteries in the Renaissance* (New York: Norton & Co., 1968 [1958]), 165 ff.

and a sister.[20] The same genealogy is given already by Boccaccio in the fourteenth century, but then without the positive connotations that we find for example in Michelangelo.[21] Traditionally the allegorical figures of the Medici chapel have been identified as the Night with the Day beside her and the Morning together with the Evening on the other sarcophagus. Such an iconography is strangely dull, though, given the otherwise high aspirations of the Medici chapel project. An Orphic and cosmological approach seems more in line with its original overall pretensions. The identity of the allegorical figures is also better in line with the gender of the figures—a brother and a sister on each tomb—as well as with their formal rendering. *Night* and *Darkness* are ungraspable and diffuse, while *Day* and *Light*, on the other side of the chapel, are more sharply defined (Figures 3 and 4).[22] Such an identification of the figures suggests that the New Sacristy was conceived as an Orphic site, perhaps a select place for chanting and hymns. At one point a relief of Orpheus himself, singing and playing for the animals, was included in the chapel decoration.[23] It only came to sketches and all such direct Orphic motifs were finally aborted, but the idea of the chapel as a place for praying

---

[20] William Keith Chambers Guthrie, *Orpheus and Greek Religion* (Princeton: Princeton University Press, 1993 [1952]), 84.

[21] Giovanni Boccaccio, *Genealogy of the Pagan Gods* I, trans. Jon Solomon (Cambridge: Harvard University Press, 2011 [1370s]), 88–95.

[22] It may well be asked why Vasari (in case the above interpretation is correct) gave us the wrong identity of the figures. He could of course be uninformed, but it is also likely that he wanted to conceal the true identity of the figures and an iconology rivalling Christian cosmology. Writing during the early Counter Reformation, he had every reason to evade cultural ideas that were so much more problematic around 1560 than 1520.

[23] The motif of Orpheus and the animals occurs in funerary monuments already in Antique and Early Christian art. It is disputed if this is meant as a figuration of Christ or an image of how hymns, singing, and prayers comforts the deceased and their relatives; Laurence Vieillefon, *La figure d'Orphée dans l'Antiquité tardive: Les mutations d'un mythe: Du héros païen au chantre chrétien* (Paris: Editions De Boccard, 2003), 95–103; Marek Titien Olszewski, "The Orpheus Funerary Mosaic from Jerusalem in the Archeological Museum at Istanbul," in *11th International Colloquium on Ancient Mosaics 2009*, ed. Mustafa Sahin (Istanbul: Zero Books, 2011), 659.

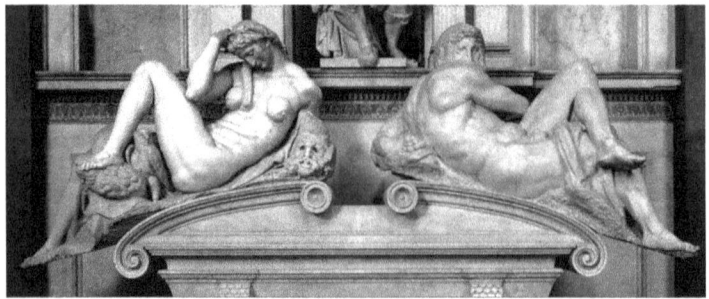

Figure 3. Sculptures for Lorenzo de' Medici's tomb. Michelangelo, c. 1530. Marble. The Medici chapel, San Lorenzo, Florence. Reproduction and permission: Bildarchiv Foto Marburg. License: CC-BY-NC-ND.

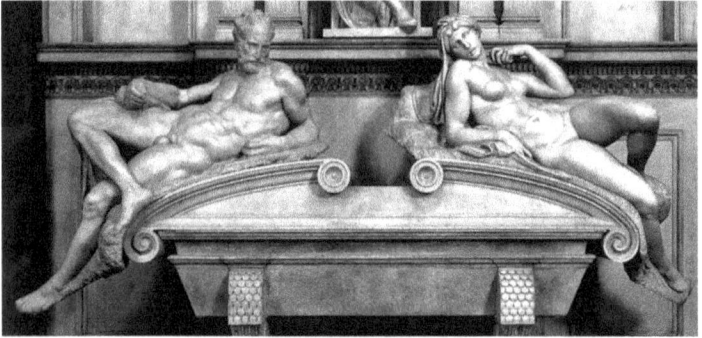

Figure 4. Sculptures for Giuliano de' Medici's tomb. Michelangelo, c. 1530. Marble. The Medici chapel, San Lorenzo, Florence. Reproduction and permission: Bildarchiv Foto Marburg. License: CC-BY-NC-ND.

and singing remained.[24] The Medici chapel received a soundscape of its own, a sonic environment, that included soft whispers just as well as music.

Soundscapes

In a dialogue published by Donato Giannotti an epigram by Giovanni Strozzi is discussed, where it is said that Michelangelo's *Night*, seen sleeping, must have been sculptured by an angel—a

---

[24] Paul Joannides, "A Newly Unveiled Drawing by Michelangelo and the Early Iconography of the Magnifici Tomb," *Master Drawings* 29:3 (1991): 255–262.

play with the artist's name, of course. Since the Nymph is sleeping she must also be alive, and the spectator is asked to awaken her if he does not believe it, in which case she will certainly wake up and speak to him. In response Michelangelo is supposed to have written a short epigram (Poem 247), where *Night* answers that sleep is dear to her and so is being made out of stone: Not to see and hear during these difficult times is a blessing, so do not wake me up but speak softly.[25] If these and similar poems were read out loud before *Night* we do not know, but it is not impossible. The literal content certainly implies so, insisting on the presence of the sculptured figure.

Even though a quiet place, the Medici chapel was never meant to be altogether silent. It was not mute; it had a voice of its own.[26] With its foundation followed a bull issued in 1532 by pope Clement VII, giving instructions for the eternal prayers that were to be read in the chapel.[27] The ceremonies probably did not begin until in 1561, though, since work was still being done in the chapel during the 1550s.[28] The bull allowed for four chaplains to be employed. Two priests were to pray together in the chapel, day and night, *a voce inelligibile*—with intelligible voices. The couple was to be replaced every two hours. Praying together two and two is an unusual arrangement and it was probably meant to strengthen the powerfulness of the invocation. Another consequence was that the two priests could control each other, making sure that

---

[25] "non mi destar, deh, parla basso."
[26] Regarding the differentiation between being silent and mute, see Salomé Voegelin, *Listening to Noise and Silence: Towards a Philosophy of Sound Art* (New York: Continuum, 2010).
[27] The documents were published already in the early nineteenth century but have received little attention among art historians. Domenico Moreni, *Delle tre sontuose cappelle Medicee sitate nell'imp. basilica di S. Lorenzo* (Florence, 1813), 152–156. An attempt at an iconographical interpretation on its basis is done by L. D. Ettlinger, "The Litugical Function of Michelangelo's Medici Chapel," *Mitteilungen des Kunsthistorischen Institutes in Florenz* 22 (1978): 287–304.
[28] Raphael Rosenberg, *Beschreibungen und Nachzeichnungen der Skulpturen Michelangelos: Eine Geschichte der Kunstbetrachtung* (Munich: Deutscher Kunstverlag, 2000), 135. The conclusion is drawn by Rosenberg from letters written by Giorgio Vasari during this period.

none of them escaped their duties. It also meant that the priests were made to pray out loud, so that they could be in synch or relay, giving the ambience a definite and continuous soundscape, not unlike the present one with the soft murmuring of art-loving visitors. The recitations were only interrupted for Mass and the singing of psalms three or four times a day. Some of the psalms may have been especially composed for the site by one of the many composers attached to the Medici court. The two priests would be the third couple of the chapel, so to speak, together with *Night* and *Darkness* as well as *Day* and *Light*. Like the sculptured figures they represented the continuous coming and going of time, the quiet shifting of positions and the long, long wait for the final coming of Christ. The bull of Clement VII was softened somewhat by Urban VIII in the early seventeenth century but did not lose its impact altogether until the nineteenth century.[29]

The French visitor Nicolas Audebert made a note in his diary of 1576 on the soundscape of the chapel. "It should be mentioned that in the chapel there are always and at all times, by day as well as by night, two priests kneeling in prayer to God for the dead resting in their sepulchers. They are changed every two hours, without any interruption except to sing the high mass or vespers, when all pray together."[30] Though taking note of the praying, Audebert did not refrain from also taking extensive notes on the sculptures, which obviously interested him more. He also took time to produce a small drawing after the most impressive of the statues, the *Night*.[31]

The two priests were positioned behind the altar of the Medici chapel, both during prayer and mass, as indicated by another sixteenth-century visitor, Francesco Bocchi:

---

[29] Moreni, *Cappelle*, 154–156.
[30] Published by Rosenberg, *Beschreibungen*, 149. The full manuscript is in the British Library, Department of Manuscripts. Signature: Landsdowne 720. "Fault remerquer que en ceste chapelle y à tousjours & et en tout temps soit de jour ou de nuit, deux prestres a genoux à prier Dieu pour les deffuncts qui ont la leur sepulchres eslevez, ce qui se change de deux en deux heures, sans aucune intermission sinon quand lon chante la grande messe ou vespres lors que tous prient ensamble."
[31] The drawing is reproduced by Rosenberg, *Beschreibungen*, 137.

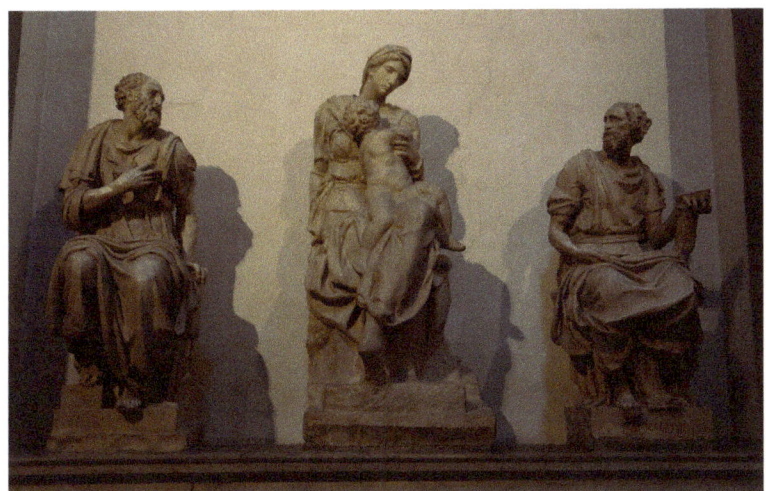

Figure 5. Madonna with Saint Cosmas and Saint Damian. Michelangelo, c. 1530. Marble. The Medici chapel, San Lorenzo, Florence. Photo: Private, Wikimedia Commons. License: CC-BY-SA-3.0. Available at Wikimedia Commons: https://commons.wikimedia.org/wiki/File:Madonna_mit_Kind_von_Michelangelo_Cappelle_Medicee_Florenz-1.jpg.

For on the altar of this Sacristy, dedicated to the Resurrection, he [Clement VII] wanted—and it is indeed inviolably observed by two priests at every hour and in all seasons—prayers to be said for those souls of the living and the dead of the Medici Family, and for those who are united to them by blood [...] and at least four masses to be said every morning for two hours.[32]

The small exedra joined to the otherwise square chapel plan gives room not only for the two priests but for assistants and a small choir as well (Figure 5). An oddity about the altar is its orientation towards the center of the chapel, rather than towards the wall.

---

[32] "Per che all Altare di questa sagrestia, che ha il titolo della Resurrezione, egli volle, come si offerna innuiolabilmente due sacerdoti ad ogni ora, in ogni tempo facessero orazione per quelle Anima de'vivi, e de morti, che sono della Casa de Medici [...] e che la mattina poscia per due hore si dicessero messe, almeno quattro." Francesco Bocchi, *Le belezze della città di Fiorenza* (Florence, 1677 [1591]), 539–540. English translation from *The Beauties of the City of Florence: A Guidebook of 1591*, trans. Thomas Frangenberg and Robert Williams (London: Harvey Miller, 2006), 254.

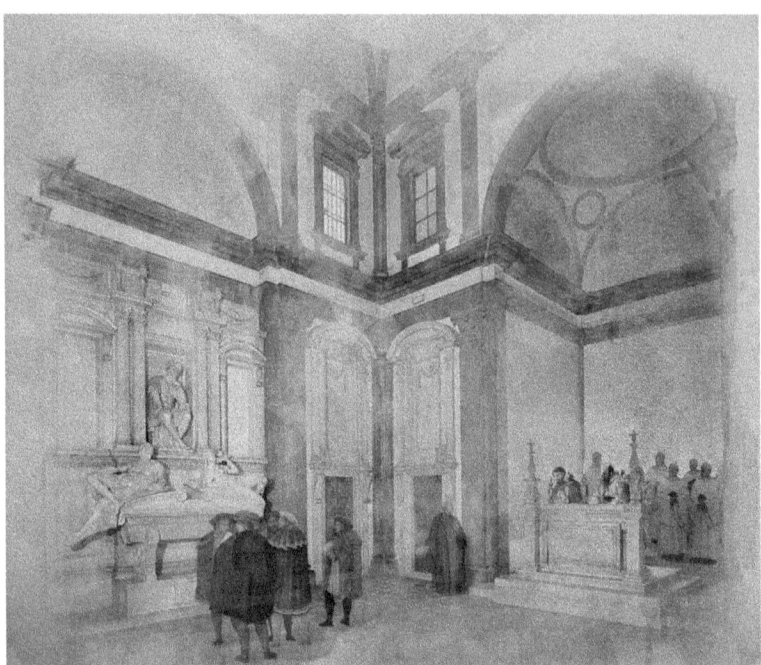

Figure 6. Reconstruction of the Medici chapel during mass. Petter Lönegård, 2017. Photo and copyright: Petter Lönegård and Peter Gillgren. License: CC-BY-NC-ND.

The general rule was otherwise that the priest should stand by the altar with the congregation behind him.[33] In the Medici chapel, however, the clergy would be confronting, watching, and directing their attention towards the sculptured tombs and the visitors of the chapel. Likewise, the slowly twisting and turning bodies of the allegorical figures and the captains would be in direct relation to the priests in the choir. It has recently been pointed at the unusualness of this arrangement, suggesting that instead of the placement of a panel above the altar the chapel itself appears as a pictorial installation.[34]

In the chapel we have also, of course, important Christian representations (Figure 6). They differ from the Orphic deities in

---

[33] Joseph Braun, *Der Christliche Altar in seiner geschichtlicher Entwicklung* (Munich: Alte Meister Guenther Koch, 1924), 407.
[34] Alexander Nagel, *Medieval Modern: Art Out of Time* (London: Thames and Hudson, 2012), 84–90.

their uprightness and active gesturing. Especially the *Madonna* is praised by Vasari for its beauty and perfection. Both *Saint Cosmas* and *Saint Damian* are probably executed by assistants, but nevertheless they were clearly meant to be more extravert and dynamic than the semi-anonymous and passive pagan gods or allegories. It may well be that in 1521, when the chapel was first conceived, creating a syncretic ambience of pagan and Christian gods seemed like an excitingly good idea. The Medici fascination for and interest in the Orphic tradition is well-known and documented, not least through the visual arts.[35] Less than ten years later, when Michelangelo was forced into carving the sculptures, the idea must already have seemed less appealing. When Vasari, finally, wrote about and ultimately completed the installation in the 1550s, even less so. The Christian theme became the dominant one and the presence of the pagan gods is carefully disguised and suppressed. Their identity is uncertain and probably it is meant to be. Instead of an Orphic goddess the figure of *Night* appears as an anonymous guardian of obscure symbolism with the owl, the mask, and the little clutch of poppies beside her. The transformation gives credence to the old claim that there is an essential affinity between the struggle against the pagan gods and the triumph of allegory.[36]

Pathos Formula

Loss of home and of identity is the unavoidable fate of both the allegorical figure and the refugee migrant, it seems (Figure 7). There is no more fundamental representation of this than the figure of sleep, functioning as its most efficient pathos formula throughout the ages.[37] Watching contemporary photographs of slumbering,

---

[35] At the same time as the Medici chapel was begun the statue of Orpheus for the Medici Palace in Florence was commissioned from Baccio Bandinelli; J. Rogers Mariotti, "Selections from a ledger of Cardinal Giovanni de' Medici, 1512–1513," *Nuovi Studi: Rivista di Arte Antica e Moderna* VI–VII, 2001–2002 (2003): 103–146.

[36] Walter Benjamin, *The Origin of German Tragic Drama*, trans. John Osborne (London: Verso, 1992 [1928]), 220.

[37] The concept of pathos formula originates with Any Warburg and is typically defined as "an emotionally charged visual trope"; Colleen

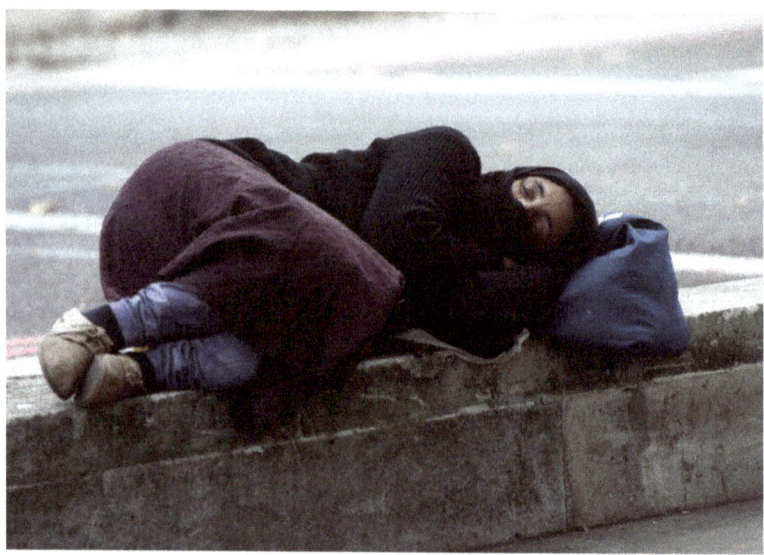

Figure 7. Migrant Sleeping in the Streets of London. Hannah McKay, 2014. Photo and copyright: National Picture/Hanna McKay. License: CC-BY-NC-ND.

homeless migrants as they try to cover themselves and to protect their few belongings, the viewer is driven towards asking who they are, where they come from, and what they are experiencing. Their mode of existence remains ungraspable for any outsider and more than often one must remain in silence. Despite its universal nature, the sleeping figure is an ultimate embodiment of estrangement. So familiar, yet so difficult to fathom, it reminds us of our alienation even towards ourselves, when we wake up in confusion after incomprehensible and feverish dreams. At the same time, there is an absolute calmness to sleep, the beauty of simply being within and for oneself; unknowing of all worldly worries and concerns. In sleep, even the ones at flight may find tranquility and joy.

Becker, "Aby Warburg's *Pathosformel* as a Methodological Paradigm," *Journal of Art Historiography* 9 (2013): 1.

Conclusions

Multimedia aspects are crucial for an understanding of Michelangelo's *Night*. Poetry and hymns celebrating the figure and the chapel must be considered in order to fully understand her. The poetry itself is simple and conventional, and the hymns are unknown but they represent important intermediate links to specific literary and musical traditions—just as much as to the figure itself. The very existence of poetry and sacred soundscape so close to the figure—and the few words that have been noted down—is enough to redefine the concept of *Night*. It places her in a humanistic or syncretistic context and makes explainable her pose of anguish and evasive gesture. She comes forth as an in-between existence, as a victim of circumstances, and in a tense and difficult dialogue with historical time and cultural shifts, as they have happened to unfold around her. Such aspects fall beyond conventional ideas about intermediality but are conveniently included in intertextual studies. Even though both traditions are concerned with the interpretation of multimedia or multimodal phenomena, an intertextual analysis is richer and more multifaceted.

Intertextuality, finally, comes in many forms. In our case, there seems to be a direct relationship between *Night* and the *Cleopatra* of the Belvedere court, both in media, form and content. Both are celebrities from the East, arriving in Italy in the sixteenth century and praised as mysterious and intriguing figures. There is a certain erotic undertone in how they are celebrated, and there is a sense of amazement and respectfulness as well. It seems that the whole ensemble of "ancient heroes" at the Belvedere court (as Castiglione spoke of them) may have influenced Michelangelo in his work on the Medici chapel. In both cases the statues appear as performative forces at their sites, as foreign elements that have been accidentally brought within an architectural and cultural construct that is not their own—but upon which they have a strong and definite impact. In that sense, the Belvedere court and most of all the so-called *Cleopatra* served as a prototype for Michelangelo's own work. Equally important are the personal, cultural, or political experiences of artists and commissioners. Michelangelo's own experiences of being at flight, as an anonymous overnighter at obscure lodgings, give nerve to the final rendering of this piece of sculpture. Medici considerations of the political wisdom in displaying an interest in Orphic hymns and deities at a public place such as the church of San Lorenzo may have been influential. Such influences are more elusive than the sculptured prototypes, but as productive forces for artistic creativity they must not be underestimated.

Following Kristeva it can be claimed, then, that the artistic work originates in an artistic personality as it is challenged by individual as well as collective experiences and influenced by works of art—in many different media—that the artist is involved with. In this instance, the *Cleopatra* at the Belvedere courtyard, the planned iconography of the Medici chapel and its prominent soundscape, the experiences of being at flight, negotiations with and threats from the commissioners, changed and discarded plans, Orphic or syncretistic ideas as well as the urge to represent and overcome all these difficulties in an artistic work belong to the intertextual network that makes both conceivable and readable Michelangelo's *Night*.

References

Bal, Mieke. "Intercultural Story-Telling." In *Kultur – Wissen – Narration: Perspektiven transdisciplinärer Erzählforschung für die Kulturwissenschaften,* edited by Alexandra Strohmaier, 289–306. Bielefeld: Transcript Verlag, 2013.

Barkan, Leonard. "The Beholder's Tale: Ancient Sculpture, Renaissance Narratives." *Representations* 44 (1993): 133–166.

Barthes, Roland. "De l'oeuvre au texte." *Revue d'esthétique* 3 (1971): 225–232.

Barthes, Roland. "From Work to Text." In *Image–Music–Text*. Selection and translation by Stephen Heath, 155–164. London: Fontana, 1977 [1971].

Becker, Colleen. "Aby Warburg's *Pathosformel* as a Methodological Paradigm." *Journal of Art Historiography* 9 (2013): 1–25.

Benjamin, Walter. *The Origin of German Tragic Drama.* Translated by John Osborne. London: Verso, 1992 [1928].

Boccaccio, Giovanni. *Genealogy of the Pagan Gods.* Translated by Jon Solomon. Cambridge: Harvard University Press, 2011 [1370s].

Bocchi, Francesco. *Le belezze della città di Fiorenza.* Florence, 1677 [1591].

Bocchi, Francesco. *The Beauties of the City of Florence: A Guidebook of 1591.* Translated by Thomas Frangenberg and Robert Williams. London: Harvey Miller, 2006 [1591].

Braun, Joseph. *Der Christliche Altar in seiner geschichtlicher Entwicklung.* Munich: Alte Meister Guenther Koch, 1924.

Condivi, Ascanio. "Life of Michelangelo Buonarroti." In *Michelangelo: Life, Letters and Poetry.* Translated by George Bull, 1–73. Oxford: Oxford University Press, 1987 [1553].

Condivi, Ascanio. *Vita di Michelangelo Buonarroti.* Pisa, 1823 [1553].

Curran, Brian. *The Egyptian Renaissance: The Afterlife of Ancient Egypt in Early Modern Italy.* Chicago: University of Chicago Press, 2007.

Deswarte-Rosa, Sylvie. "Francisco de Holanda el le *Cortile di Belvedere.*" In *Il cortile delle statue: Der Statuenhof del Belvedere im Vatikan,* 389–410. Mainz: von Zabern, 1998.

Ettlinger, L. D. "The Litugical Function of Michelangelo's Medici Chapel." *Mitteilungen des Kunsthistorischen Institutes in Florenz* 22 (1978): 287–304.

Guthrie, William Keith Chambers. *Orpheus and Greek Religion.* Princeton: Princeton University Press, 1993 [1952].

Heraclitus. "Fragments." In *Early Greek Philosophy.* Translated by John Burnet. London: Black, 1912.

Joannides, Paul. "A Newly Unveiled Drawing by Michelangelo and the Early Iconography of the Magnifici Tomb." *Master Drawings* 29:3 (1991): 255–262.

Kristeva, Julia. *Desire in Language: A Semiotic Approach to Literature and Art.* Edited by Leon S. Roudiez, translated by Thomas Gora,

Alice Jardin, and Leon S. Roudiez. New York: Columbia University Press, 1980.

Kristeva, Julia. *La révolution du langage poétique*. Paris: Seuil, 1974.

Kristeva, Julia. "Le mot, le dialogue et le roman." In *Sēmeiōtikē: Recherches pour une sémanalyse*, 143–173. Paris: Seuil, 1969.

Kristeva, Julia. "Le sujet en procès." In *Polylogue*, 55–106. Paris: Seuil, 1977.

Kristeva, Julia. *Revolution in Poetic Language*. Translated by Margaret Waller. New York: Columbia University Press, 1984 [1974].

Kristeva, Julia. "The Subject in Process." In *The Tel Quel Reader*, edited by Patrick Ffrench and Roland-François Lack, 133–178. London: Routledge, 1998 [1977].

Kristeva, Julia. "Word, Dialogue and Novel." In *The Kristeva Reader*, edited by Toril Moi, 34–61. New York: Columbia University Press, 1986 [1969].

Mariotti, Rogers. "Selections from a ledger of Cardinal Giovanni de' Medici, 1512–1513." *Nuovi Studi: Rivista di Arte Antica e Moderna* VI–VII, 2001–2002 (2003): 103–146.

Michelangelo Buonarroti. *The Poetry of Michelangelo*. Translated by James M. Saslow. New Haven: Yale University Press, 1991.

Moreni, Domenico. *Delle tre sontuose cappelle Medicee sitate nell'imp. basilica di S. Lorenzo*. Florence, 1813.

Nagel, Alexander. *Medieval Modern: Art Out of Time*. London: Thames and Hudson, 2012.

Olszewski, Marek Titien. "The Orpheus Funerary Mosaic from Jerusalem in the Archeological Museum at Istanbul." In *11th International Colloquium on Ancient Mosaics 2009*, edited by Mustafa Sahin, 655–662. Istanbul: Zero Books, 2011.

Plutarch. "On Superstition." In *Moralia* II. Translated by F. C. Babbitt, 492–55. Harvard: Loeb Classical Library, 1928.

Robillard, Valerie. "Beyond Definition: A Pragmatic Approach to Intermediality." In *Media Borders, Multimodality and Intermediality*, edited by Lars Elleström, 150–162. Basingstoke: Palgrave Macmillan, 2010.

Rosenberg, Raphael. *Beschreibungen und Nachzeichnungen der Skulpturen Michelangelos: Eine Geschichte der Kunstbetrachtung*. Munich: Deutscher Kunstverlag, 2000.

Vasari, Giorgio. *Le Vite de' più eccellenti pittori, scultori, e architettori*. Florence, 1568.

Vasari, Giorgio. *Lives of the Painters, Sculptors and Architects* I–II. Translated by Gaston du C. de Vere. New York: Everymans Library, 1996 [1568].

Vieillefon, Laurence. *La figure d'Orphée dans l'Antiquité tardive: Les mutations d'un mythe: Du héros païen au chantre chrétien*. Paris: Editions De Boccard, 2003.

Voegelin, Salomé. *Listening to Noise and Silence: Towards a Philosophy of Sound Art*. New York: Continuum, 2010.

Wind, Edgar. *Pagan Mysteries in the Renaissance*. New York: Norton & Co., 1968 [1958].

Wolf, Werner. *The Musicalization of Fiction: A Study in the Theory and History of Intermediality*. Amsterdam: Rodopi, 1999.

The Unlimited Performativity of Instruction Art: *Space Transformer* by Yoko Ono

Magdalena Holdar

Abstract

In 1966 American artist Dick Higgins coined the term *intermedia* as descriptive of contemporary avant-garde art. Building on a system of medial in-betweenness and artistic overlaps, Higgins aimed to show the interconnections between new artistic practices such as mail art, happenings, and action music. This article attempts to read his theory through an artwork whose concept is contemporary to Higgins's intermedia theory but also—through its use of new media—to our time. Yoko Ono's instruction piece *Space Transformer* consists of three elements: a material artefact; an instruction on how to use the artefact; and the execution of the instruction by the interpreter. The article follows the itinerary between them, concluding that the piece's intermedia qualities are crucial for its emancipatory aim and outcome.

A couple of years ago, a friend of mine gave me a small memento from his recent trip to New York. It was a white card, very inconspicuous, with printed text in black, capital letters (Figure 1). From the size it could easily be mistaken for a business card, although the text—and indeed the rather eye-catching size of the print—suggested self-awareness and big dreams that was rather at odds with the subtle format. The text on the card read "SPACE TRANSFORMER"; a simple enough message, but nonetheless possible to interpret in a number of different ways and thereby raising a number of questions.

How to cite this book chapter:
Holdar, Magdalena. "The Unlimited Performativity of Instruction Art: *Space Transformer* by Yoko Ono." In *The Power of the In-Between: Intermediality as a Tool for Aesthetic Analysis and Critical Reflection*, edited by Sonya Petersson, Christer Johansson, Magdalena Holdar, and Sara Callahan, 99–128. Stockholm: Stockholm University Press, 2018. DOI: https://doi.org/10.16993/baq.e. License: CC-BY.

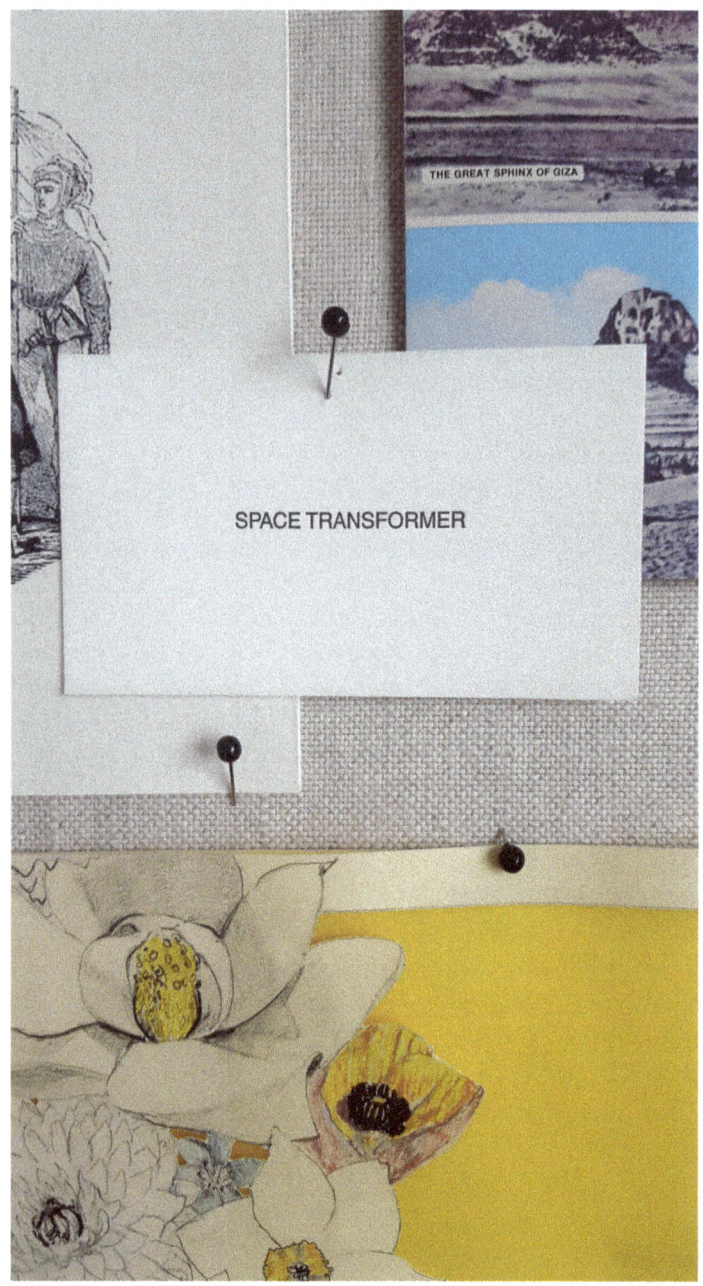

Figure 1. *Space Transformer*. Yoko Ono, c. 2010. Multiple, print on paper, 9×5 cm. Photo: Magdalena Holdar. License: CC-BY-NC-ND.

As the card's format associated to the identity-producing business card, should I understand the text as the title of its holder? If so, it could associate to a Superhero's trademark: the Space Transformer, whose characteristics find a perfect match in the self-affirming, capital letters—perhaps I could even take advantage of the situation and adopt the title for myself. But maybe it wasn't a title after all? Or rather, maybe *Space Transformer* was the title of the card itself, empowering this small object with the agency to act on the same level as me, or my friend; that is, making the card—through the printed text—equivalent to a human actant.[1] Could this *Space Transformer* card, eventually pinned to my office notice board, have the power to make a real difference; to "transform space"?

If adding more context around its conception, I actually think it can rightly claim to do so. It had been handed out at a gallery exhibition with works by Yoko Ono, an artist who since the late 1950s has developed instructions as an artistic tool to empower her audience, making it active participant rather than passive recipient of the presented work. Its common denominator is not so much medium as the art's dependence on the audience's collective realization of it, according to art historian Kevin Concannon. In his analyses of Ono's works he continuously returns to the artist's wish to empower her audience, and to let it take control of the art.[2] Nonetheless: before getting to grips with the superpowers of the *Space Transformer* card, this open-ended piece of paper also needs some theoretical context.

---

[1] For a discussion on the agency of things, see Jane Bennett, *Vibrant Matter: A Political Ecology of Things* (Durham and London: Duke University Press, 2010) and Gabriel Levine, "The Museum of Everyday Life: Objects and Affects of Glorious Obscurity," *Journal of Curatorial Studies*, vol. 4, no. 3 (2015): 364–390.

[2] Kevin Concannon, "Fluxus and Advertising in the 1960s... and Now," *Performance Research* 7:3 (2002): 59, accessed November 17, 2016, DOI: https://doi.org/10.1080/13528165.2002.10871874; Kevin Concannon, "Yoko Ono's Dreams," *Performance Research* 19:2 (2014): 103, accessed November 17, 2016, DOI: https://doi.org/10.1080/13528165.2002.10871874.

A 1966 Intermedia Theory

Despite her background in classical music, Yoko Ono's career from the 1950s onwards has come to encompass almost every artistic expression; from performance and drawing to film, composition, poetry, and billboard advertisements. Throughout the years she has moreover been a prominent producer of events, for example, her collaboration with composer La Monte Young in the seminal Chambers Street Loft Series 1960–61 (a number of experimental concerts and performances, whose explicit purpose was "not entertainment" according to the program[3]), and the administrative and financial support of artist Charlotte Moorman's curatorial work, most notably her annual festival of the avant-garde.[4] Ono's exploration of media and media transgressions is strongly affiliated to the creative milieu in New York and Tokyo that she took part in from the late 1950s, both as artist and producer. On a more general note, Ono's constant movement between and beyond media is in this respect representative for the turn towards performance and technology that we find in North American, European, and Japanese art during this period: the transnational artist network Fluxus, and formations such as Hi Red Center (Tokyo), Experiments in Art and Technology, E.A.T. (New York), and Group Zero (Europe) are but a few examples. It goes without saying that the general modernist art theory and its tendency to stress media separation, objectivity, and detachment to the object of study was too blunt a tool for understanding the new art. However: Ono's artistic activities are like blueprints for the intermedia theory developed by artist Dick Higgins in the mid-1960s, as a means to better catch the specific kind of flux and motion that he saw in the arts at the time. First printed in his publication series *Something Else Newsletter* (1966), Higgins would make sev-

---

[3] Program for "Terry Jennings" from Chambers Street Loft Series, Yoko Ono's Loft, New York 1960. Mimeograph on paper. Accession number 2002.97, Walker Art Center, digitized source material, accessed March 20, 2015, http://www.walkerart.org/collections/artworks/program-for-terry-jennings-from-chambers-street-loft-series-yoko-onos-loft-new-york.

[4] Joan Rothfuss, *Topless Cellist: The Improbable Life of Charlotte Moorman* (Cambridge: MIT Press, 2014), 307.

eral reprints of the essay "Intermedia" over the next decades. The connections between Higgins and Ono are numerous. They knew each other, were part of the same Fluxus circle in New York, and partook in several events together. Nonetheless, they are rarely explicitly connected in the general research on either Ono, Higgins, or Higgins's intermedia theory.[5]

While it is true that theories of art often build on observations, it does not necessarily follow that they are interrelated with the artistic practice *per se*. In terms of Dick Higgins's intermedia theory, however, I claim that the interconnection between his own context and practice, and the theory he produced, are fundamental for comprehending its essential traits. Thus, Higgins's definition of intermedia was formulated through the artistic practices explored by himself and others in the counterculture movement and anti-institutionalism of the 1960s, but he had picked up the term from a lecture by poet Samuel Taylor Coleridge, published as early as 1816.[6] Higgins's "Intermedia" essay was published in 1966, but a 2001 reprint in *Leonardo* also includes a commentary by the author (dated 1981) as well as an intermedia chart (dated 1995, see Figure 2).[7]

Despite the time span between the publications, comments, chart, and other texts of his, Higgins's definition of intermedia seems to remain consistent.[8] However, as intermedia was increasingly

---

[5] A recent dissertation by Gregory Laynor, *The Making of Intermedia: John Cage to Yoko Ono, 1952 to 1972* (PhD diss., University of Washington, 2016) is one of very few research initiatives that more explicitly investigates the publication of Higgins's "Intermedia" article and the artistic practices of its time.

[6] Nicolas Zurbrugg, ed., *Art, Performance, Media: 31 Interviews* (Minneapolis and London: University of Minnesota Press, 2004), 201.

[7] Dick Higgins, "Intermedia," *Something Else Newsletter* 1, no. 1, (New York: Something Else Press, 1966); Dick Higgins, "Intermedia," *Leonardo*, vol. 34, no. 1 (2001).

[8] See for example Dick Higgins, *Horizons: The Poetics and Theory of the Intermedia* (Carbondale: Southern Illinois University Press, 1984); Dick Higgins, "Fluxus: Theory and Reception," *Fluxus Research*, ed. Jean Sellem, vol. 2, no. 2 (1991); Dick Higgins, *Modernism since Postmodernism: Essays on Intermedia* (San Diego: San Diego State University Press, 1997).

Intermedia Chart

Dick Higgins

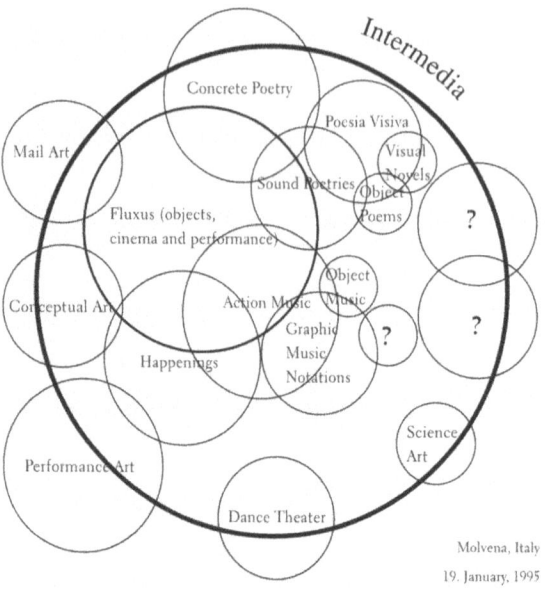

Figure 2. Intermedia chart. Dick Higgins, 1995. Photo: Charles Deering, McCormick Library of Special Collections, Northwestern University Libraries. Copyright: Courtesy of the Estate of Dick Higgins. License: CC-BY-NC-ND.

theorized (albeit not necessarily with reference to Higgins's writings), the 1981 comment includes a clear stance towards the new use of the term. After its 1966 publication, Higgins states,

> The term [intermedia] shortly acquired a life of its own, as I had hoped. [...] It was picked up; used and misused, often by confusion with the term "mixed media." This last is a venerable term from art criticism, which covers works executed in more than one medium [...]. [By] extension it is also appropriate to such forms as the opera, where the music, the libretto, and the mise-en-scène, are quite separate: at no time is the operagoer in doubt as to whether he is seeing the mise-en-scène, the stage spectacle, hearing the music, etc. Many fine works are being done in mixed media: paintings

which incorporate poems in their visual fields, for instance. But one knows which is which.[9]

Intermedia, in Higgins's understanding of the concept, was about the *fusion* of expressions rather than the *layering* of them. His aim was to open the door to something that could appear confusing and incomprehensible: to establish a vocabulary around art that looked, felt, and sounded like nothing you had experienced before.

In the field of Fluxus research, scholars agree that Dick Higgins was indeed imperative for establishing the term *intermedia* as theoretical concept in arts and aesthetics.[10] But the lack of references to Higgins in later research, as corroborated by the above quote, also illustrates how the concept soon moved away from the context for which he had found it so productive. Deeply rooted in artistic practice rather than academic research, *intermedia* was a term with which Higgins hoped to illuminate an aesthetic condition without negotiating art's potential for change. It is clear that his writings have a different agenda from the scholars who have taken the concept further (often without acknowledging his early text).[11] Putting more emphasis on theoretical interconnec-

---

[9] Higgins, "Intermedia" (2001): 52.
[10] Hannah Higgins, "Intermedial Perception or Fluxing Across the Sensory," *Convergence*, vol. 8, no. 4 (2002): 59 and Hannah Higgins, *Fluxus Experience* (Berkeley and Los Angeles: University of California Press, 2002), 91; Elwell J. Sage, "Intermedia: Forty Years On and Beyond," *Afterimage*, vol. 33, issue 5 (Mars/April 2006): 25; Jessica Santone, "Archiving Fluxus Performances in Mieko Shiomi's Spatial Poem," *Across the Great Divide: Modernism's Intermedialities, from Futurism to Fluxus*, eds. Chris Townsend, Alex Trott, and Rhys Davies (Newcastle upon Tyne: Cambridge Scholars Publishing, 2014), 122; Alison Green, "Intermedia, Exile, and Carolee Schneemann," *Across the Great Divide: Modernism's Intermedialities, from Futurism to Fluxus*, eds. Chris Townsend, Alex Trott, and Rhys Davies (Newcastle upon Tyne: Cambridge Scholars Publishing, 2014), 140.
[11] The introductory chapter of this publication provides an overview corroborating this conclusion. It is worth mentioning that one theorist who is a recurring reference in intermedia studies, art historian W. J. T. Mitchell, seems to be more affiliated to Higgins's theoretical writings than other scholars in the field. This might possibly be an effect of Mitchell's repeated emphasis on the artwork's agency. It is also a fact that he and

tions and implications, as customary in many intermedia studies, the concept turns into a tool with which you analyze different materials. To Higgins, on the other hand, intermedia was the effect of the art, rather than an analytical tool. He saw it as the best formulation of what art *did*, and how we could be assisted in understanding art that escaped conventional definitions. Like the art it stemmed from, the concept itself was in constant flux, morphing as the art morphed and eluding fixed definition. The point is the *effect* of the mix of artistic expressions, not its separate ingredients. Nonetheless, irrespective of Higgins's absence from later intermedia theory, it is undoubtedly a well-found and catchy concept. And when his specific, artist-based definition of it is removed, it can suddenly be applied on anything from ekphrasis to new media.[12] As this article argues, his theory placed movement and flux (key elements in artistic practice at the time) at stage center in intermedia art, and similar to Ono, he saw the audience as pivotal for identifying intermedia in an artwork.

In his 1966 article, Higgins describes intermedia as the fusion of artistic expressions, which can illuminate links and relationships that are found, for example, in creative poetry, object music, happenings, and mail art. Moreover, he says, intermedia in fine arts can be apprehended as "more or less universal [...] since continuity rather than categorization is the hallmark of our new mentality".[13] He exemplifies with artist Allan Kaprow's artistic move from painting, to collage, to happening as a form of collage inhabited by people, and composer John Cage's exploration of the intermedia between music and philosophy. Both produced art

---

Higgins were acquainted and that Mitchell eventually would be the advisor for the PhD project of art historian and Fluxus researcher (and Dick Higgins's daughter) Hannah Higgins. Although this may seem trivial, it is in fact symptomatic that the theorist closest to Higgins's thinking is also uncommonly close to artistic practice.

[12] This conclusion does not disregard the fact that Higgins also expressed great interest in the more technological strata of late 1960s thinking. It might be further from his own practice as artist, albeit closer to Ono's, but one can nonetheless note that he for example published several of Marshall McLuhan's theoretical texts through his publishing house, Something Else Press.

[13] Higgins, "Intermedia" (2001): 50.

that clearly moved away from the media specificity characteristic of modernist theory. Indeed, much of the art that emerged on the post-war art scene were articulations that fused media, which had previously been clearly separated or, at least, whose fusions had not been highlighted in cultural theory before. Despite the tendency to stress activities in the US as key to this creative renegotiation within the arts, it was by no means a singularly Western phenomenon. Artistic intermedia investigations occurred simultaneously but independently of each other in different parts of the world, which makes the period an interesting case of global yet autonomous artistic anarchism.

In the first years of the 1960s, Yoko Ono developed the concept of instruction paintings at gallery exhibitions in Tokyo and New York. Instructing the audience to take action in front of a piece like *Painting to be stepped on* ("Leave a piece of canvas or finished painting on the floor or in the street"[14]) or *Painting to see the room* ("Drill a small, almost invisible, hole in the center of the canvas and see the room through it"[15]), the instructions were an act of empowerment and similar to turning the artwork (through the instruction) into a gift to the gallery visitor. She later explained:

> Displaying just the instructions as paintings [...] was pushing visual art to its optimum conceptualism; it would open up a whole new horizon for the visual arts. I was totally excited by the idea and its visual possibilities. To make the point that the instructions were not themselves graphic images, I wanted the instructions to be typed.[16]

With this knowledge regarding Ono's practice in mind, the *Space Transformer* card would definitely aim to entail real change, both through its own agency and through the action of the interpreter. We often tend to discuss the experimentation within, for example, new music, pop art, experimental dance, and performance throughout

---

[14] Yoko Ono, *Grapefruit: A Book of Instructions + Drawings* (New York: Simon and Schuster, 2000 [1964]), unpaginated.
[15] Yoko Ono, *Instruction Paintings* (New York and Tokyo: Weatherhill Inc. 1995), 29.
[16] Ono, *Instruction Paintings*, 5.

the 1960s as strategies to investigate, revise, and reformulate the concept of art. However, it is equally important to recognize the close ties between the counterculture movement's *artistic* and *political* veins.[17] In the transnational network of artists that from 1962 collaborated under the name Fluxus (and which included both Yoko Ono and Dick Higgins), life and art were inseparable. Hence, I would claim that both Ono's empowerment of her audience and Higgins's fusion-oriented intermedia theory suggest a more far-reaching aim, beyond the immediate situation that the meeting with art provides. In different ways, they both worked towards demonstrating real change, in the arts (Higgins) and thereby of the world (Ono). They both exemplify countercultural strategies for imposing radical political difference: Yoko Ono, through a card, provides the opportunity to transform space, and Higgins, through theory, enables us to discover the subversive potential in the creative fusion of artistic expressions.

Instructions for Action

Instruction-based art highlights the route between *thing*, *command*, and *action*. It usually starts off with the material stuff which holds the instruction; a page in a book, a paper nailed to a gallery wall, or a card stuck in your wallet. The material's agency to *do* something—to perform—suggests that we have a thing rather than a passive object at hand. But the agency of the instruction, irrespective of its material form, is of course dependent on the command itself—what the instruction asks us to do. And there is furthermore a massive difference between *receiving* an instruction and *acting* upon it, as a security guard at Seattle Art Museum (SAM) was brutally made aware of when interacting with Yoko Ono's piece *Painting to Hammer a Nail* in 2009. The instruction reads:

---

[17] Timothy Scott Brown, "The Sixties in the City: Avant-gardes and the Urban Rebels in New York, London, and West Berlin," *Journal of Social History* 46:4 (2013): 819, accessed November 17, 2016, DOI: https://doi.org/10.1093/jsh/ sht007.

Hammer a nail into a mirror, a piece of glass, a canvas, wood or metal every morning. Also, pick up a hair that came off when you combed in the morning and tie it around the hammered nail. The painting ends when the surface is covered with nail.[18]

But over the course of a couple of weeks in exhibition, visitors did not stop when the board was covered with nails. Instead, they continued attaching a wide array of bits of paper onto the painting and the wall around it, expanding their interpretation of the instruction so that they could participate in the work by prolonging the timeline of the painting, beyond its end "when the surface is covered with nails." Chewing gum wrappings, receipts, and diverse scraps of found material covered the board and wall.

Ono's artistic demands to the museum stated that things were allowed to be added to the artwork (and thereby overruling the traditional practice of "not touching the artwork"), but not taken away from it. The museum security guard (also an artist), however, decided to clear the painting from the extraneous material, arguing that SAM had "allowed the public to obstruct the artwork."[19] She referred to her action of tidying up the artwork as a performance, but that did not hinder the museum from firing her for intervening with the artistic intention of the piece.

In line with her artistic strategy to hand over her instructions into the hands of others, not meddling with the effects they reach, Ono concluded when informed about the controversy:

> I thought it [i.e. the painting being covered in scraps of paper] was hilarious, and loved it! Then a woman decided that was not good, and tried to put the work back to its original shape. Then the museum decided that the woman should not have done that and fired her. Things keep happening, very much like life itself, with the original instructions being the genesis of it all. Life is beyond criticism, much less mine.[20]

---

[18] Ono, *Grapefruit*, unpaginated.
[19] The cited statement by the security guard/artist is from her blog, here quoted from Rebecca Close, "Yoko Ono Work Controversy," *Art Asia Pacific* (Nov/Dec 2009): unpaginated, accessed September 22, 2016, http://artasiapacific.com/Magazine/66/YokoOnoWorkControversy.
[20] Ono quoted in Close, "Yoko Ono Work Controversy," unpaginated.

The incident goes to show that *thing*, *command*, and *action* can travel in unexpected directions. They might be compared to "creative touchdowns," to use a sports term, or "productive resting points" that are performatively bound together through the work. Each point has a body of its own: the physical body of Ono's instruction for *Painting to Hammer a Nail,* printed and published in many different fora; the performative command as displayed at the museum; the final action of visitors performing the instruction; and that of the security guard, acting on the performance of others. However, they also create a larger, performative body of fusing media, which Dick Higgins would refer to as intermedia.

Higgins and Ono were part of a transnationally spread tendency to expand the formulations of artistic work. Although sometimes disparate in their expressions, the creative activities and cross-references between music, poetry, visual art, etc., which were central for these artists' position *next to* established institutions and traditional definitions of art, had many similarities in attitude and performative agency. Expressively disassociating his theoretical approach from any wish to organize understanding of the arts through marking differences, Higgins explores the similarities and links between different phenomena in order to uncover a wider picture—to bind the pluralistic world together into a more coherent whole. One could connect this to the influence of other contemporary thinking as well, for example John Dewey's significant writings on art as integrated in life. One could also refer to it as art ecology and thereby pronounce the continuity of thought into present day theory. Indeed, if treating all arts as aspects of the same prism, they would communicate the similar interchange of complex phenomena in life too. Also, stressing the fused layers of media as productive and performative, Higgins—through theory—illuminates the continuous exchange between artists acting in the different fields, which possibly was an insight that stemmed from his own artistic practice. But Higgins's concentration on productive fusions pays little attention to the conditions *within* each demarcated practice in his intermedia chart (Figure 2): *how* letters and words are used in concrete poetry, and *how* the postal system is manipulated in mail art. Importantly however, intermedia does not necessarily entail the fusion of art forms only. As Higgins declares, it can also entail "the conceptual fusion of two or more previously defined areas of art or concern," as was the case with Cage's philosophy cum music referred to earlier.[21] This surely brings new and almost unlimited possibilities to the fore, which needs a further investigation. What piece would provide a better case for this task than Yoko Ono's *Space Transformer*, which starts off with an artist's idea and (possibly) ends with global change?

Space Transformer: An Itinerary of Things and Actions

To the interpreter, *Space Transformer* begins with card—a material something that can be handed out, given away, or saved for later. But in order to interpret and perform the card's text, one also needs its instruction, which reads: "Attach a card saying SPACE TRANSFORMER to the room and/or object you wish to transform."[22]

Bordering on trivial in both form and message, the card and instruction are nonetheless the starting point for an almost limitless performativity. In this sense, the piece makes it perfectly clear that its author Yoko Ono has a background in music. Instructions function similarly to a musical score: they present the foundation for action, but in doing so, they simultaneously leave the piece open for the recipient's interpretation. You receive this initial, material origin for an action—the printed card and its instruction having the same function as sheet music—but you also have the possibility to perform it in many different ways. The details of a traditional musical score might produce a certain frame for individual interpretation, letting variations appear in, for example, tempo and articulation, whereas the variations of performances of instructions can be almost unlimited. Ono's friend and colleague La Monte Young wrote a composition with the instruction "Draw a straight line and follow it" (c. 1960/61). When

---

[21] Higgins, *Modernism since Postmodernism*, 93.
[22] Instruction as published on Yoko Ono's Facebook page in October 2011, one of several media for publication: accessed October 18, 2016, https://www.facebook.com/yokoonopage/posts/10150417555695535.

performing Young's piece in 1962, artist and composer Nam June Paik rolled out meters of white paper on the floor, dipped his hair in a bucket containing calligraphy ink and tomato juice, and drew the straight line by pressing his head against the paper and backing down its full length.[23] The example illustrates the possibility of free interpretation of the suggested action, but it is likewise important to stress the commitment that follows from receiving and acting on these instructions. An instruction can be seen as a gift of sorts as the author/composer/artist passes on the piece to an unknown recipient—a gift to take care of and hopefully treasure. If so handled, the piece can live on through different interpretations and by being repeatedly re-enacted, which grants it a lifetime that might very well exceed that of its author. For many artists in Fluxus, authorship was, however, of less importance, and claiming it could even be considered contradictory to the collectiveness of the network. *Space Transformer* is not signed, possibly for the same reason. The piece is now in your hands; the identity of the author is (supposedly) no longer relevant.

In fact, in this particular case it seems that you do not even need access to the prefabricated card in order to perform the piece. I received mine from a friend who had picked it up at a gallery exhibition, but the instruction—separated from my card but retrievable via the internet—suggests that *any* card can do, as long as its text says "Space Transformer." Thus, Ono does not only hand over the *performance* of the piece to an unknown recipient; she also empowers him or her to *produce the actual card* that transforms space. Her role as artist and originator turns into that of a creator of concepts, or of thoughts, rather than creator of objects.

Indeed, realizing the status of the printed card as superfluous for the performance of the action, it seems that my imagined itinerary of the piece (from thing, to command, to action) was a

---

[23] Paik's interpretation was well documented, visually striking, and re-performed several times. It was soon considered a work of its own, *Zen For Head*, but its origin is nevertheless La Monte Young's 1960/61 score.

misconception. *Space Transformer* does not begin with the thing: the card has already been set in motion through Ono's instruction preceding it. The card (prefabricated or DIY) is thereby the performative *means* for the interpreter rather than the *origin* for his or her *Space Transformer* performance. Emancipating the audience is thus also to encourage it to take the matter into common hands, to paraphrase curator Maria Lind's description of collaborative artistic practice.[24] *Space Transformer* makes us co-producers, both through the possibility to create the card ourselves, and through our performance of the instruction "Attach a card saying SPACE TRANSFORMER to the room and/or object you wish to transform." But the instruction does not hint at the outcome of our action. Instead it hooks into someone's general wish to transform and change an everyday situation, thus forcing us to reflect on our desires and everyday life. What do I want to transform? Is it transformable? Do I possess the power to transform it?

The imagined itinerary consequently takes another and unexpected route. When discussing performativity in visual arts, we often acknowledge it as an agency of a material thing (a painting, a sculpture, a stage design, or indeed the body of the artist), acknowledging its power to set off a series of effects through its specific materiality. In a large part of Fluxus's creative corpus, the material artwork was, if not subordinate to so at least equally important as its circulation. George Maciunas, often named "founder" of Fluxus, made distribution and circulation into its own artistic medium. Art historian David Joselit states: "[The] experiential transformation sought by Fluxus must necessarily be tailored to each individual person," meaning that the wish to reach out to many through a system of mass-distribution would need a careful adaptation of the piece in order to create a sense

---

[24] Maria Lind, Johanna Billing, and Lars Nilsson, *Taking the Matter into Common Hands* (London: Black Dog Publishing, 2007). Although the articles in the publication primarily concern contemporary artistic practice, they also trace its predecessors: collaborative artistic work, mainly from the 1960s and '70s that served the goal of expanding the notion of the common.

of urgency for the recipient.[25] Maciunas built a transnational network of artists and in the process he created endless lists of addresses and contacts, distributed charts, magazines, and artworks to order via mail. He created a dense, global, and analogue system for distribution of physical material. Yoko Ono, likewise interested to reach out beyond the limited space of the art world, has from the 1990s taken internet and eventually social media as prime tool for circulating her work. She has thereby enabled an almost infinite engagement in in her participatory work. *Space Transformer* no longer needs her in order to be materialized—once published online, the now-immaterial instruction receives a life of its own, endlessly circulating and endlessly shareable.

As the analysis of *Space Transformer* has shown this far, the piece bears all the traces of a Fluxus work. It is inexpensive, reproducible, easy to distribute, and it encourages the receiver to enact an instruction. Through its materiality and ability to circulate *ad infinitum*, the Fluxus piece navigates away from the conventional art world rounding marks, such as uniqueness, authorship, and authenticity. However, whereas Fluxus instructions are generally acting in a one-on-one situation, offering a subjective and internal interaction with the piece, Ono's online mediation suggests a wish for global transformation. The performativity of *Space Transformer* is thereby of a different sort than most Fluxus works, which also illustrates the more public direction that Ono's artistic work took during the late 1960s, and which has continued since then. Together with John Lennon, she started using media and mass communication as an artistic tool and method to reach a wider audience than the more limited avant-garde circles had allowed.[26] Most explicitly this comes forth in the *War Is Over (if you want it)* campaign that she has kept running through a variety of media since first launching it together with Lennon in 1969:

> The WAR IS OVER! campaign was once a tiny seed, which spread and covered the Earth.

---

[25] David Joselit, "The Readymade Metabolized: Fluxus in Life," *RES: Anthropology and Aesthetics* 63/64 (Spring/Autumn 2013): 1.
[26] Concannon, "Yoko Ono's Dreams," 105–106.

John and I believed it helped many people to stop their wars. Since then, every WAR IS OVER! campaign has impacted the world as powerfully as the first one.

Start yours tomorrow, and you will see that it spreads and covers the world very fast and, meanwhile, makes you a Small Pebble Person.

Small Pebble People are people who know that small pebbles, when they're dropped in the ocean, will immediately affect the ocean of the whole wide world.

Don't throw a big stone. It scares people and creates repercussions.

Just drop a small pebble.

We'll keep doing it. Together.

That's how the world gets changed [...] by Small Pebble People. We change, and the world changes.[27]

Throughout the duration of this project, Ono has continually developed others that in similar ways are "dependent upon a collective realization."[28] Acting on the same line, *Space Transformer* would empower the Small Pebble Person to transform space by sticking a card to an object or space. And with this notion, we move from *thing* and *command* into the third stop of the imagined itinerary: *action*, very possibly the most complex of the three due to its extreme openness. Because given the status of the thing-as-actant and the command that turned out to precede rather than stem from the *Space Transformer* card, we cannot really pin down the performative effect of the performance. Indeed, we cannot even nail *who performs what* in this piece. Is it the card that transforms space or your wish to do so? Is the performative agency inherent in the material thing or in your performance of the instruction? Or is it an iterative performance, produced by the agency of thing and human together? In her attempt to build a theory of vital materialism that empowers both human and non-human actants, Jane Bennett argues for a material theory in which the demystification of the object does not necessarily means privileging one

---

[27] For quote and further exploration of the project, see Yoko Ono's website Imagine Peace, accessed October 7, 2016, http://imaginepeace.com/warisover/.

[28] Concannon, "Yoko Ono's Dreams," 106.

before the other. A major problem in the critical theory that aims at demystifying objects, she finds, is its human-centeredness:

> What demystification uncovers is always something human, for example, the hidden quest for domination on the part of some humans over others, a human desire to deflect responsibility for harms done, or an unjust distribution of (human) power. Demystification tends to screen from view the vitality of matter and to reduce *political* agency to *human* agency.[29]

In Ono's work, it seems that performative agency is placed in equal shares on thing, command, and action. As has become apparent when investigating the nodes that connect the three, there is no given itinerary between them. Agency can move in literally any direction. The *War Is Over!* campaign has spread its focus globally since its inauguration, working with mass media and social media, advertisements, and free downloads of posters from Yoko Ono's website, which—typically—is called Imagine Peace.[30] *Space Transformer,* however, returns to the single, subjective Small Pebble Person: transform what you wish by performing this act.

In the early 2000s, curator Hans Ulrich Obrist performed a series of interviews with Yoko Ono, eventually collected and published in 2009. From some of the sections in the book, it seems however that the conversation almost took the form of performed poetry:

> Hans Ulrich Obrist — What is your favorite sound?
> Yoko Ono — All sounds are beautiful.
> Hans Ulrich Obrist — What is your least favorite sound?
> Yoko Ono — All sounds are beautiful.
> Hans Ulrich Obrist — The moment we are waiting for?
> Yoko Ono — We are not waiting for any moment, we are just living this moment as fully as we can.[31]

Whereas the artist at times seemed spurred to provide long narratives on her work and the contexts in which she has been active,

---

[29] Bennett, *Vibrant Matter*, xv (italics in original).
[30] Ono, Imagine Peace, accessed October 7, 2016, www.imaginepeace.com.
[31] Hans Ulrich Obrist, *Yoko Ono* (Köln: Verlag der Buchhandlung Walther König, 2009), 66.

other questions appear to have generated responses that can be characterized as a choreographed verbal interaction with the interviewer. As shown in the quote above, Ono takes command of the situation by not conforming to a conventional conversation format. She alters the relationship between interviewer and interviewee, destabilizing the power balance in the situation by undercutting Obrist's role as catalyst in command and herself as the responding object of investigation. Thus, Ono takes on the interview format, but simultaneously creates a performative effect by using a strategy that is familiar from her instruction pieces, in which she—then as catalyst in command—hands over the performance proper to someone else.

Consistent with this strategy, Ono communicates her ideas regarding art's relation to life and the individual's ability to create real change through the power of thought and imagination. Indeed, she situates the capacity to *transform space* as a common denominator of many of her works—or, perhaps, as a generative, performative effect of them. In relation to *Grapefruit* (1964/1970), her seminal collection of scores, instructions, and texts, she declares: "*Grapefruit* is a book of instructions and by doing those instructions you become a space transformer, each one of you."[32] The instructions in *Grapefruit* date from the mid 1950s through 1964, although later editions of the publication include works that are more recent.[33] Suggesting that the performance of the instructions make you a space transformer points to the idea that they all have (in one way or other) a consistent approach. They point to the individual performer, instructing (or perhaps encouraging) him or her to *do* something. Moreover, they often want you to do something with *an object* or *a thing*:

> *Lighting piece* (1956)
> Light a match and watch till it goes out.
>
> *Painting to be constructed in your head* (1962)
> Observe three paintings carefully. Mix them well in your head.

---

[32] Obrist, *Yoko Ono*, 67.
[33] The second edition of *Grapefruit* was published in 1970 and has been followed by re-prints and new editions in 1971 and 2000.

The instructions in *Grapefruit*, thus, encourage you to take action, if only in your mind. They rarely ask you to physically destroy or reshape something, but rather to perform the change "in your head"—either explicitly or due to the fact that performing the action in real life would be physically or technically impossible. As consequence, space transforming can be apprehended as a *state of mind* rather than as a condition that stems from bodily action. But although declaring that you become a space transformer by following the instructions in *Grapefruit*, she also states that the same effect can be obtained through interaction with a single work, such as the *White Chess Set* (1966). The *White Chess Set* is a monochrome, constructed from a white chess board and only white pieces. You continue playing for "as long as you can remember where all your pieces are."[34] In her talks with Obrist she elaborates:

> I really think that we are more than 100% space transformers and through being the space transformer, and all of us can be if we believe in it. [...] As space transformers we are going to enter into the most incredible future that we will make together. I believe too, no, I know that we are all here at the beginning of the new age where we are all here to become space transformers.[35]

The space transformer, she seems to claim, is in fact each one of us. And if we want to, each one of us thereby have the power to change the name of the game, and the conditions under which we play it. War is over (if we want it) and if enough people want the same thing, a major transformation is about to happen.[36]

Intermedia in Artistic Practice

From the discussion above, we can conclude that instructions, as for example *Space Transformer*, are artworks in the imperative

---

[34] Tim Stott, *Play and Participation in Contemporary Arts Practices* (London and New York: Routledge, 2015), 28.
[35] Obrist, *Yoko Ono*, 69.
[36] Kevin Concannon has explored this aspect of Ono's creative work, reminding of the continuous presence of faith in wishful thinking in her work. Concannon, "Yoko Ono's Dreams."

mood. They propose potential performance but also inhabit a performative potential, an important distinction that is also stressed by Mieke Bal when she concludes that: "Performance—the unique execution of a work—is of a different order from performativity, an aspect of a word that *does* what it says."[37] Indeed, a central aspect of this distinction is the fact that the inherent performativity of an instruction piece does not necessarily regard its execution or performance. Rather, the work opens up for conceptual awareness and thereby a new space for action: the mind of the receiver. This mind expands in the meeting with the instruction, through the instruction's ability to suggest contradictions, word play, improbabilities, and fantasy, all directed to the individual, subjective reader-receiver. The instruction stresses the one-on-one mode of communication by asking you to perform an action—and in doing so, it simultaneously opens up your individual interpretation of its performative claim. Does the instruction go so far as to abandon the relevance of its own materiality? It has been suggested that the format with instructions and event scores proposes

> [that] the event itself is an articulation between artist and reader, paper and eyes, sound and hearing—it is a kind of secret passed in the operations of artistic practice as it attempts to extend past the object to meet the potential viewer or visitor. It is a verbalization of a possibility that suggests an entire philosophical and ontological shift that necessarily leaves the art object behind.[38]

As a generative effect of its performativity—occupying the receiver's mind as its main platform—the instruction piece moves in a mental sphere, which Dick Higgins would refer to as the "pre-cognitive" level of our perception. This, according to Higgins, is a level of consciousness that deals less with apprehending the basic meaning of statements, but rather relates to language as game-playing through suggesting multiple meanings and

---

[37] Mieke Bal, *Travelling Concepts in the Humanities: A Rough Guide* (Toronto: University of Toronto Press, 2002), 175.
[38] Brandon LaBelle, "Reading Between the Lines: Word as Conceptual Project," *Performance Research* 7:3 (2002): 49–50.

sentiments in the interplay of statement and receiving mind.[39] The pre-cognitive apprehension of art disregards artistic medium or expression, stressing instead the effect art has on the viewer or interpreter. Once again, thus, Higgins creates a theoretical approach to art that shifts focus from the seen to the imagined and from the tangible media to the spaces where expressions merge and reshape. When Dick Higgins discussed the concept intermedia, he generally did so from his position as artist and through his experience from different artistic practices: scores, instructions, mail art, performance, visual poetry, and painting. Intermedia, Higgins argued, had been developed by artists from the 1950s onwards, when moving away from traditional forms of media:

> [The] media have broken down in their traditional forms, and have become merely puristic points of reference. The idea has arisen, as if by spontaneous combustion throughout the entire world, that these points are arbitrary and only useful as critical tools, in saying that such-and-such a work is basically musical, but also poetry. This is the intermedial approach, to emphasize the dialectic between the media.[40]

Thus, intermediality does not appear *within* each category according to Higgins, but is rather an effect of the fusion of different media in one and the same work, as visualized in his chart: visual art merges with poetry in *poesa visiva*, or is a fusion of performance and music in action music.[41] Importantly, this merge does not act at the expense of either medium, but rather boosts the combination to a new expression transgressing its different

---

[39] LaBelle, "Reading Between the Lines," 49.
[40] Dick Higgins, "Statement on Intermedia," originally in *Dé-coll/age: Happenings, Stücke, Partituren*, ed. Wolf Vostell (Frankfurt: Typos Verlag, 1966), here quoted from Kristin Stiles and Peter Selz, *Theories and Documents of Contemporary Art: A Sourcebook of Artists' Writings* (Berkeley: University of California Press, 1996), 729.
[41] For a thorough discussion on Higgins's definition of intermedia as "fusion" and Fluxus's links to postmodern aesthetic theory, see Natilee Harren, "The Crux of Fluxus: Intermedia, Rear-guard," *Art Expanded, 1958–1978* (Minneapolis: Walker Art Center, Living Collections Catalogue vol. 2, 2015), accessed 16 September, 2016, http://www.walkerart.org/collections/publications/art-expanded/crux-of-fluxus/.

parts. As an effect of this, the movement and space in-between become fields for intense action. This space of creative exchange and material transformation is thus where the concept's conceptions appear the most clearly.

Instruction-based art, such as the instruction paintings by Yoko Ono, are however surprisingly seldom discussed in terms of intermedia, despite their undisputable transgression of both conventional media and artistic practices. Building on the structure of the musical score, with its openness towards future performance by someone else but the author, and its acknowledgement of the freedom of interpretation, instructions constituted a core element in Fluxus. The artists used them as base for transnational mail art projects and experimental performances. Like the musical score, instructions are of course not limited to being performed in a particular context. Indeed, if returning to Higgins's intermedia concept, the artistic expressions he refers to in his chart might even be the most innovative when fueled by the space in between—for example, when an instruction is envisioned to be moving between the materiality of the written component and the interpretation and performance of it. Could it in fact be so that motion is a vital element in Higgins's understanding of intermedia? The organization of his 1995 chart (Figure 2) suggests as much. It shows a firm limit for intermedia, but just as importantly it also identifies several overlaps of the 15 named artistic expressions, and moreover lines out empty spaces between them—indeed, there are even overlaps of the empty circles with question marks, bubbles that "may be named by the reader."[42] It is easy to imagine the three-dimensionality of his chart and a constant motion and change in it. Visually, it is similar to a cluster of soap bubbles that could move and merge, expand and contract. I argue that Dick Higgins's chart, thus, illuminates *movement* rather than marks different *ontological entities*, which is something that both corresponds to his own artistic practice and to his theoretical aims at large, that is, the overall wish to take another route in the (at the time) linear visualization of art history.[43] Higgins's writings

---

[42] Higgins, *Modernism since Postmodernism*, 2.
[43] Harren, "The Crux of Fluxus," 1.

suggest a position that is standing athwart modernist art history in both content, interest, and theoretical approach. This includes his Fluxist view on authorship (or rather, his Fluxist disinterest in the same) as expressed in a letter to George Maciunas:

> When the name of the artist determines the market value of a work and not its meaning in our lives—beware! And there again we come to Fluxus. In the early sixties, when the first generation of Fluxus artists were doing and giving away their experiences, it mattered little which of us had done which piece. The spirit was: you've seen it, now—very well, it's yours. Now you are free to make your own version of it if you like, and the piece and the world will be a little richer for all that.[44]

For Higgins, thus, the strategy to hand over the artwork to someone else was a logical effect of art's immaterial value. In addition, the gesture of handing over, or giving away, also meant that you enabled the piece to take on new forms in the hands of others, and in doing so enrich the receiver and the world alike. In a narrative that creates an intricate web of connections between things, people, and situations, Higgins builds a theoretical system that encompasses art and life and in which borders are transgressed when people ("the reader" of his chart; "you" in the letter to Maciunas) are invited to take command of the possibilities that the art offers. Similarly, Yoko Ono's instructions through their online life have come to find an even more limitless implementation than Higgins would have been able to formulate in the decades during which he explored intermedia theory. As mentioned before, the itinerary of *Space Transformer* is not so much decided by the material card as by the performativity—the doing—of the performance, and thereby by the *decision* to make the card and instruction the object that moves from silence to action. Together they open for a complex route as the instruction leaves its site and takes on new, different forms—endless, global, and by design out of the artist's control.

---

[44] Letter from Dick Higgins to George Maciunas, November 19, 1974. Jean Brown papers, Getty Research Institute. Quoted in Natilee Harren, "Fluxus and the Transitional Commodity," *Art Journal*, (Spring 2016): 69, accessed November 17, 2016, DOI: https://doi.org/10.1080/00043249.2016.11715 40.

Unlimited Performance, Unlimited Performativity

My initial aim with this article was to investigate the itinerary between *thing, command,* and *action* in instruction-based art, taking my own *Space Transformer* card as entry point into one of Yoko Ono's emancipation projects. Was it the card that was a potential space transformer, or was it me, who could transform space by enacting the instruction and attaching the card to the room and/or object I wished to transform? But the route of the piece took unexpected turns as the thing was not—as I had imagined—predestined to precede the command, and that the action could follow from a card or piece of paper onto which anyone had written "space transformer." Thus, *Space Transformer* was emancipatory to a degree that opened up for almost total freedom. Ono had turned into disembodied catalyst for the piece: originator perhaps, but likewise important as mediator, through her online arrangement to spread the instruction globally and allow any kind of interpretation of it. Despite the fact that *Space Transformer* in its current form is a relatively recent piece, published online in the early 2000s, she has referred to the conceptual idea with space transformation as going back to her Fluxus years, particularly her book *Grapefruit* and the *White Chess Piece* (1966).[45] And indeed, the format is consistent with Fluxist ideas regarding instructions as gifts to be given away. It also links to Fluxus's active avoidance of art world structures that make the artist more important than the work and that turn the work into a commodity to own and conserve; a material investment whose power lies in cultural capital rather than artwork agency.

Thus, in relation to the artwork as gift and the openness towards the recipient's own interpretation, Ono's instruction works are clearly relating to Fluxus theory. She was a central actor in Fluxus from its first official events in the early 1960s and one whose work Dick Higgins developed his theoretical writings on. But is it possible to disregard Yoko Ono as the originator of *Space Transformer*? When theorizing Fluxus, Higgins made a strong point in putting artwork rather than artist at stage center,

---

[45] Obrist, *Yoko Ono*, 67.

as shown in his letter to George Maciunas quoted earlier. It seems, however, that Ono's strategic work with mass media and mass communication since the late 1960s contradicts the irrelevance of her name in relation to her projects. In fact, are not her name and fame key to the global outreach for her work? Fluxus was a transnational network that enabled artists to collaborate and interact in innumerable constellations. Through its organization, it was like an analogue predecessor to social media: an "eternal network" to use Fluxus artist Robert Filliou's term—a web that lacked a spatial as well as temporal beginning and end. Ono, however, has found a way to merge her use of mass media as creative tool with the networking strategies of Fluxus and thereby developed a firm platform for her collaborative work with audiences around the globe. To her, internet is both the logic continuation of the network idea from Fluxus's early years, as well as in keeping with the activism she partook in together with John Lennon:

> All the stuff we were discussing in the 60s in terms of the global village is actually happening now. [...] It's happening on a conceptual level and it will become very physical one day—in fact, it's becoming physical already. [...]
>
> Many writers kept predicting a doomsday future. John (Lennon) and I kept predicting a very beautiful, open future. [...] At the time we were accused of being naive by other songwriters, artists, and underground political people. We felt we stood alone. I think it is very important to keep the dialogue going and keep our future open, not closed.[46]

Internet, then, has become a platform for her work that is both material and immaterial, and has both instant effect and infinite endurance. Its multiple layers remind us of Ono's partiality for puns, word play, and double meanings in the titles of her work—*Cut Piece*, *Bed Peace*, or indeed *Space Transformer*, which could be read as both noun and merit. For her, internet as medium in combination with her position as a well-known, public person have been tools for outreach. But the emancipatory effect of her

---

[46] Ono quoted in Obrist, *Yoko Ono*, 19. Parentheses in original.

works remains; the act of handing over the artwork and giving the recipients agency to act on it in any way they like. In this sense, *Space Transformer* maintains the political project of the 1960s counterculture, a context that was key also for Dick Higgins's development of his intermedia theory. If Ono took advantage of the network as political strategy, Higgins theorized on the subversive potential in fusing media. He identified a shift in artistic practices, although we (for the past decades) have become so accustomed to the effects of that shift in contemporary art that we barely notice it any more, let alone necessarily see it as politically radical. Nonetheless, by establishing the concept of intermedia, Higgins encouraged a position *next to* modernism's definition of artistic media and thereby opened for a stance that was not rooted in the already known and defined. But he also saw intermedia as elusive and constantly in motion:

> It allows for an ingress to a work which otherwise seems opaque and impenetrable, but once that ingress has been made it is no longer useful to harp upon the intermediality of a work. [...] What was helpful as a beginning would, if maintained, become an obsession which braked the flow into the work and its needs and potentials.[47]

To him, intermedia was a concept that related to reconfigurations and transgressions of the known into something new. It was a fusion of different established media that resulted in novel creative expressions, often unfamiliar to the audience and thereby difficult to immediately take in and understand. Yoko Ono's instruction paintings would thereby be an illustrative example of intermediality, merging painting with poetry in a way that steers our understanding of art's mode of communication down a different route. "It is today [1998], as it was in 1965, a useful way to approach some new work; one can ask oneself, 'what that I know does this new work lie between?'" Higgins explains.[48] Intermedia, thus, appears before the new expression is familiar and rooted in our apprehension of what is art.

---

[47] Higgins, "Intermedia" (2001): 53.
[48] Higgins, "Intermedia" (2001): 53. My brackets.

References

Bal, Mieke. *Travelling Concepts in the Humanities: A Rough Guide*. Toronto: University of Toronto Press, 2002.

Bennett, Jane. *Vibrant Matter: A Political Ecology of Things*. Durham and London: Duke University Press, 2010.

Brown, Carlos Cuellar. "Intermedial Being." *PAJ: A Journal of Performance and Art*, vol. 36, no. 1 (January 2014): 88–93.

Cavell, Richard. *McLuhan in Space: A Cultural Geography*. Toronto: University of Toronto Press, 2002.

Close, Rebecca. "Yoko Ono Work Controversy." *Art Asia Pacific* (Nov/Dec 2009). Accessed September 22, 2016. http://artasiapacific.com/Magazine/66/YokoOnoWorkControversy.

Concannon, Kevin. "Fluxus and Advertising in the 1960s… and Now." *Performance Research* 7:3 (2002): 55–63. Accessed November 17, 2016. DOI: https://doi.org/10.1080/13528165.2002.10871874.

Concannon, Kevin. "Yoko Ono's Dreams." *Performance Research* 19:2 (2014): 103–108. Accessed November 17, 2016. DOI: https://doi.org/10.108 0/13528165.2014.928525.

Green, Alison. "Intermedia, Exile, and Carolee Schneemann." *Across the Great Divide: Modernism's Intermedialities, from Futurism to Fluxus*, edited by Chris Townsend, Alex Trott, and Rhys Davies, 137–157. Newcastle upon Tyne: Cambridge Scholars Publishing, 2014.

Harren, Natilee. "Fluxus and the Transitional Commodity." *Art Journal* (Spring 2016): 44–69. Accessed November 17, 2016. DOI: https://doi.org/10.1080/00043249.2016.1171540.

Harren, Natilee. "The Crux of Fluxus: Intermedia, Rear-guard." *Art Expanded, 1958–1978*. Minneapolis: Walker Art Center, Living Collections Catalogue vol. 2 (2015). Accessed September 16, 2016. http://www.walkerart.org/collections/publications/art-expanded/crux-of-fluxus/.

Higgins, Dick. "Fluxus: Theory and Reception," *Fluxus Research*, edited by Jean Sellem, vol. 2, no. 2 (1991): 25–46.

Higgins, Dick. *Horizons: The Poetics and Theory of the Intermedia*. Carbondale: Southern Illinois University Press, 1984. Digital copy published by Ubu Editions, 2007. Accessed 17 February, 2018. http://www.ubu.com/ubu/higgins_horizons.html.

Higgins, Dick. "Intermedia." *Leonardo*, vol. 34, no. 1 (2001): 49–54. Commented version of 1966 article. Accessed November 17, 2016. DOI: https://doi.org/10.1162/002409401300052514.

Higgins, Dick. "Intermedia." *Something Else Newsletter* 1, no. 1. New York: Something Else Press, 1966.

Higgins, Dick. *Modernism since Postmodernism: Essays on Intermedia*. San Diego: San Diego State University Press, 1997.

Higgins, Dick. "Statement on Intermedia." *Dé-coll/age: Happenings, Stücke, Partituren*, edited by Wolf Vostell. Frankfurt: Typos Verlag, 1966.

Higgins, Hannah. *Fluxus Experience*. Berkeley and Los Angeles: University of California Press, 2002.

Higgins, Hannah. "Intermedial Perception or Fluxing Across the Sensory." *Convergence*, vol. 8, no. 4 (2002): 59–76.

Joselit, David. "The Readymade Metabolized: Fluxus in Life." *RES: Anthropology and Aesthetics* 63/64 (Spring/Autumn 2013): 190–200.

LaBelle, Brandon. "Reading Between the Lines: Word as Conceptual Project." *Performance Research*, 7:3 (2002): 47–53.

Laynor, Gregory. *The Making of Intermedia: John Cage to Yoko Ono, 1952 to 1972*. PhD diss., University of Washington, 2016.

Levine, Gabriel. "The Museum of Everyday Life: Objects and Affects of Glorious Obscurity." *Journal of Curatorial Studies*, vol. 4, no. 3 (2015): 364–390. Accessed November 17, 2016. DOI: https://doi.org/10.1386/jcs.4.3.364_1.

Lind, Maria, Johanna Billing, and Lars Nilsson. *Taking the Matter into Common Hands*. London: Black Dog Publishing, 2007.

Obrist, Hans Ulrich. *Yoko Ono*. Köln: Verlag der Buchhandlung Walther König, 2009.

Ono, Yoko. Facebook page. Accessed October 18, 2016. https://www.facebook.com/yokoonopage/posts/10150417555695535.

Ono, Yoko. *Grapefruit: A Book of Instructions + Drawings by Yoko Ono*. New York: Simon and Schuster, 2000 [1964].

Ono, Yoko. Imagine Peace website. Accessed October 7, 2016. www.imaginepeace.com.

Ono, Yoko. *Instruction Paintings*. New York and Tokyo: Weatherhill Inc., 1995.

Program for "Terry Jennings" from Chambers Street Loft Series, Yoko Ono's Loft, New York 1960. Mimeograph on paper. Accession number 2002.97, Walker Art Center. Digitized source material. Accessed March 20, 2015. http://www.walkerart.org/collections/artworks/program-for-terry-jennings-from-chambers-street-loft-series-yoko-onos-loft-new-york.

"Review: Dick Higgins, Horizons: The Poetics and Theory of the Intermedia." *Poetics Today*, vol. 5, no. 2 (1984): 441.

Rothfuss, Joan. *Topless Cellist: The Improbable Life of Charlotte Moorman*. Cambridge: MIT Press, 2014.

Sage, Elwell J. "Intermedia: Forty Years On and Beyond." *Afterimage*, vol. 33, issue 5 (Mars/April 2006): 25–30.

Santone, Jessica. "Archiving Fluxus Performances in Mieko Shiomi's *Spatial Poem*." *Across the Great Divide: Modernism's Intermedialities, from Futurism to Fluxus*, edited by Chris Townsend, Alex Trott, and Rhys Davies, 120–136. Newcastle upon Tyne: Cambridge Scholars Publishing, 2014.

Scott Brown, Timothy. "The Sixties in the City: Avant-gardes and Urban Rebels in New York, London, and West Berlin." *Journal of Social History*, vol. 46, no. 4 (2013): 817–842. Accessed November 17, 2016. DOI: https://doi.org/10.1093/jsh/shto07.

Stiles, Kristin, and Peter Selz, *Theories and Documents of Contemporary Art: A Sourcebook of Artists' Writings*. Berkeley: University of California Press, 1996.

Stott, Tim. *Play and Participation in Contemporary Arts Practices*. London and New York: Routledge, 2015.

Zurbrugg, Nicholas, ed. *Art, Performance, Media: 31 Interviews*. Minneapolis and London: University of Minnesota Press, 2004.

From Folk Tale to Photomontage: A Transformation through a Stage Performance

Rikard Hoogland

Abstract

A photomontage from 1894–95 with material from the popular and successful theatre production *Ljungby horn* is the artefact in this chapter. The photomontage is connecting with the development of theatre photography, which was governed by the commercial market for visiting cards. The term *remediation* is used to describe a transformation whereby the different sources are, through the use of photography, placed on the same level in the montage. Other intermedial connections discussed here include music, literature, communications, theatre set design, and mass media.

A large photo was found in a file at the National Library of Sweden in Stockholm containing correspondence between Albert Ranft and Frans Hodell (Figure 1),[1] including a letter written by the theatre manager to Hodell, an author, editor-in-chief, and actor. The letter, dated 1884, relates that Ranft has taken over the management of one of Sweden's most prominent touring theatre companies as one of the first steps towards building his large theatre empire. Ranft seems to be asking for some positive news items about the company, probably in the popular illustrated

---

[1] Albert Ranft in a letter to Frans Hodell, Kempes autografsamling (Kempe's collection of autographs) in Kungliga biblioteket (National Library of Sweden), KB1/13.

How to cite this book chapter:
Hoogland, Rikard. "From Folk Tale to Photomontage: A Transformation through a Stage Performance." In *The Power of the In-Between: Intermediality as a Tool for Aesthetic Analysis and Critical Reflection*, edited by Sonya Petersson, Christer Johansson, Magdalena Holdar, and Sara Callahan, 129–147. Stockholm: Stockholm University Press, 2018. DOI: https://doi.org/10.16993/baq.f. License: CC-BY.

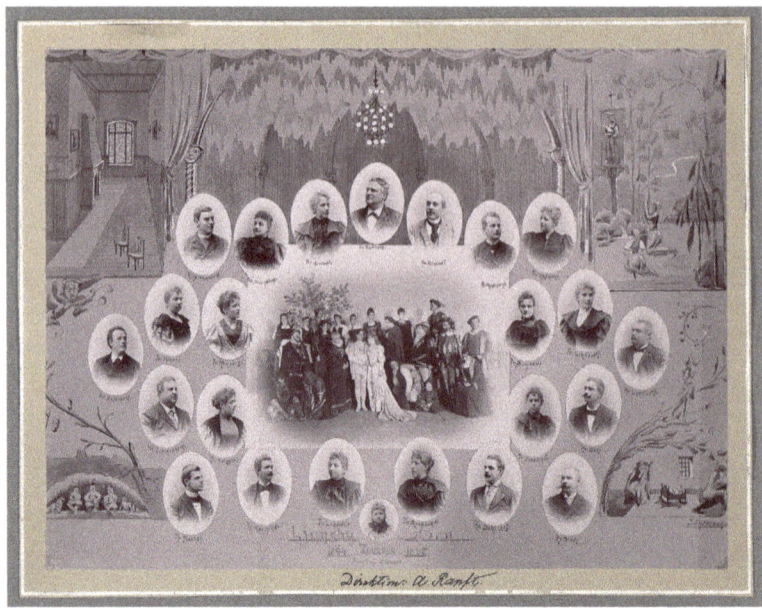

Figure 1. Ljungby horn tournée, 1894–95. Reproduction: National Library of Sweden/Kungliga biblioteket, Stockholm. License: CC-BY-NC-ND.

magazine *Söndags Nisse*, of which Hodell was editor and owner.[2] The photo, however, is from an 1894–95 tour with the melodramatic fairy-tale-based play *Ljungby horn*, so there is no direct connection between the letter and the photo apart from the name Albert Ranft. In this article, I study the picture as an artefact and look not only into its connections to the production but also into connections between media systems of that time and the theatre deriving from this specific photo. The photo can be seen as a form of mediatization of the theatre performance, but may also be used as a link to a performance to which we have no direct connection. In the chapter, the use of theatre photography in the late nineteenth century is described, and the relation between the studio portraits of the actors and the live performance is discussed. I will use the theoretical concept of *remediation* for analyzing the

---

[2] Oscar Wieselgren, "Frans O. L. Hodell," *Svenskt biografiskt lexikon*, accessed October 28, 2016, https://sok.riksarkivet.se/sbl/artikel/13680.

artefact and the different layers in the collage and their relations to the live performance.

The first questions that arise are why the photo was made and what function it could have had. Could it be that the image was sent to the magazine *Söndags Nisse* for publication? The fact that at that time the journal published only sketches and drawings, not reproductions of photos would seem to be evidence against this possibility. Or was it an act of gratitude for the support the magazine had given the production when it ran in Stockholm during the summer of 1894? Or was it a gift that was circulated on a larger scale by Ranft to important individuals in the media industry? The fact that the picture has not yet been found in any other archive would be an argument against this possibility.

The production of the fairy-tale-based play *Ljungby horn* was a big success for Albert Ranft; after a sold-out premiere at Stora Teatern in Gothenburg, it proceeded to Malmö Teater; a special train service was arranged all around Scania and in Stockholm, where it was staged at Djurgårdsteatern. The photomontage is made for the national and Nordic tour that started in the autumn of 1894, following seventy performances in Stockholm. Nearly all of the actors playing the main parts in the play were replaced by new actors for the tour. Even though several popular actors were no longer part of the production, the performances were still successful, and over 300 performances had been given when the tour ended in Trondheim in May 1895.

Photomontage

In taking a closer look at the photograph, one sees that it is clearly a photo of a montage consisting of four different parts. The photo is not large: about 24.7 × 18.6 cm, that is, larger than a postcard but smaller than an ordinary piece of foolscap. It has some resemblance to private albums of the time, with the difference that it is associated with a theatre manager rather than a private person. Anna Dahlgren, in her study of photo albums, has included an example bearing a slight visual resemblance to the *Ljungby horn* example: a collection of photos from visiting cards depicting actors from a production at the Dramatic Theatre in Stockholm

1867. The photos show the actors in their stage costumes, with the individual photos arranged in a semicircle like a fan. Text about the performance of *Min ros i skogen* taken from the theatre's daily poster is pasted in the lower part of the arrangement.[3] Dahlgren's source is the archive of Nordiska museet, but there is no consensus on who was responsible for its composition or whether it is the same person as the unknown owner of the album. However, the composition does not look as if it had been made for a commercial market; rather, it resembles a privately organized album page for remembering a specific theatre evening. Dahlgren also writes about the album as something that might be placed in a private drawing room, where guests could look through it. The album might, in this example, lend the owner cultural value and lead to conversations about the theatre and actors in Stockholm, and the room might be described as a semi-private and public space.[4] The visiting-card photos included in the montage from 1867 demonstrate a more professional touch compared with an amateurish collage, and were clearly made for commercial distribution (I will return later to the question of the market for theatre photographs). There are also other examples from 1860 of montages of actors' visiting-card photos. Mosaic pictures made from visiting-card photos was cut out and pasted in formation on a large piece of paper and afterwards photographed to fit the visiting-card format.[5]

At the time (in either 1894 or 1895) the montage was made for *Ljungby horn*, the development of photography had created new possibilities not yet available in 1867, especially in terms of flash-lighting techniques. There are several photos taken of the actors in their costumes from *Ljungby horn*, and even photos showing two actors. It is uncertain whether the photos were taken in the photographer's studio or on stage. The photos

---

[3] Anna Dahlgren, *Ett medium för visuell bildning: Kulturhistoriska perspektiv på fotoalbum 1850–1950* (Stockholm: Makadam, 2013), 37.
[4] Christopher B. Balme, *The Theatrical Public Sphere* (Cambridge: Cambridge University Press, 2013).
[5] Rolf Söderberg and Pär Rittsel, *Den svenska fotografins historia 1840–1940* (Stockholm: Bonnier Fakta, 1983), 44–45.

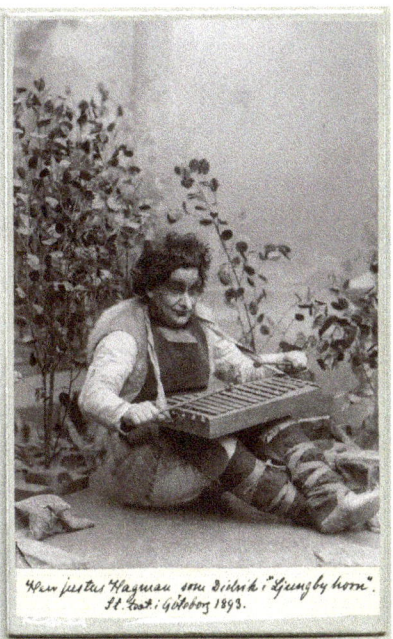

Figure 2. Justus Hagman in *Ljungby horn*, Stora Teatern in Gothenburg 1893, photographed by Alfred Peterson. Permission: Swedish Performing Arts Agency/Statens musikverk, Stockholm. License: CC-PD. Available at Wikimedia Commons: https://commons.wikimedia.org/wiki/File:Justus_Hagman,_rollportr%C3%A4tt_-_SMV_-_H9_188.tif.

taken in Stockholm by Gösta Florman in 1894 were more likely taken in front of the backdrop from the production. Florman, who had moved his atelier from Karlstad to Stockholm, was at that time the most celebrated theatre photographer in Sweden.[6] The photos from Gothenburg 1893 look more like photos taken in the atelier, but the photo of the dwarf and hobgoblin Didrik, played by Justus Hagman, includes props such as bushes and small trees that could have been used in performances (Figure 2). No backdrops or costumes from the production have been preserved. In the archive in Gothenburg, some coloured

---

[6] Söderberg and Rittsel, *Den svenska fotografins historia*, 51.

costume drawings have been collected, showing us the colour scheme of the costumes, which is impossible to guess from the black-and-white photos.[7]

Multilayer

The montage is a collection of several layers from various art forms—ensemble photos, portrait photos, sketches, and handwritten text. The original montage has not been saved; the archival item is a photo of the montage that was pasted onto a carton and thereafter inscribed "Direktion A. Ranft" on the lower part of the carton framing the photo. Albert Ranft was the manager and director, who, with the help of this production, was able to ensure the start of his large theatre company.

I am now going to describe the layers of the montage. In the center is a group portrait of the ensemble in stage dress, surrounded by portraits of the actors in street dress; under the portraits, the actors' family names and civil titles are written. In the outer circle are sketches, probably of the set design and impressions from the stage. There is a signature in the bottom-right corner: "O Anderson," the name of the painter; the owner of the workshop that produced the backdrops for the performance was Carl Grabow of Stockholm. Text in the lower central part reads: "Ljungby Horn, Tournée 1894–1895, (direktion A. Ranft.)." The montage seems to have been arranged on a carton that was then photographed.

Could the original montage been larger than the one found in the archive? This raises questions about the purpose for which such a montage was arranged: was it made for marketing purposes, or as a souvenir? Was the original montage larger, for placement in a display cabinet outside the theatre? I have not seen any examples of such photos being put on display at the theatres at that time.

The relationship between written text and visual pictures during the late nineteenth century has been debated in the field of cultural history. As Aleida Assmann points out, "[t]he textual

---

[7] Costume sketch *Ljungby horn*, Göteborgs stadsmuseum (The Museum of Gothenburg), GTM2120.

tradition was one of clarity and light, and that of pictures and traces was dark and enigmatic [...] The two media were in fact seen as incommensurate, each untranslatable into the other and yet at the same time stimulating acts of translation."[8] Traditionally, written sources have been seen as more reliable than visual; this attitude is still common.

The Play Script

One source that could be combined with visual elements is the play script, a free translation from Danish by the playwright Frans Hedberg. The original, entitled *Et Folkesagn*, was a successful play running at Folketeatret in Copenhagen in the spring of 1893, based on a popular ballet by August Bournonville, which had premiered at the same theatre in 1854.[9] If we can believe his memoirs, Albert Ranft had already pointed out in his commission to Hedberg how the script should be adapted to create a play about the old legend of the Ljungby horn and pipe.[10] Ranft, along with the actor Anders de Wahl, visited Folketeatret in Copenhagen in the course of a stop by the touring company in Malmö in January 1893. Subsequently, de Wahl starred in the performance as the knight Olof. The most important change that had to be made, as far as Ranft was concerned, was that the performance should start with the singing of the popular ballad about the Ljungby horn and pipe.[11] The resemblance to the legend was repeated in reviews and news items, though nobody seemed eager to point out that very few details were in accord with the "original story." Bournonville himself had based his story on a recently published collection of fairy tales collected by Just M. Thieles and on the short story "Everhøj" written by Hans Christian Andersen, so it was a combination of different folk tales that laid the ground for

---

[8] Aleida Assmann, *Cultural Memory and Western Civilization* (Cambridge and New York: Cambridge University Press, 2013), 208.
[9] Knut Arne Jürgensen, *The Bournonville Tradition: The First Fifty Years, 1829-1879* (London: Dance Books, 1997), 167.
[10] Albert Ranft, *Albert Ranfts memoarer: Första delen* (Stockholm: Norstedts, 1928), 134.
[11] Ballad by Frans Friberg and Lorenzo Hammarsköld, 1813.

the production.[12] The re-use of folk tales is a very common phenomenon in the development of popular theatre. As the researcher Joel Schechter states, "[p]opular theatre forms lend themselves to adaption, reinterpretation and changes of content because they originate in unwritten and improvised performance traditions."[13] Bournonville also obtained an agreement to produce the ballet in Stockholm in 1859, but it was never realized.[14] Moreover, the music composed for Bournonville's performance by N. W. Gade and P. E. Hartmann was re-used, not only in the play *Et Folkesagn*, but in other plays and as a popular wedding song as well.

The play runs 243 handwritten pages and places the story in northern Scania around the castle Ljungby at the beginning of the seventeenth century.[15] The main point of the story is that hobgoblins have exchanged children in the cradle. The daughter, Hildur, was replaced in the castle with Birgit, who does not meet feminine norms and who has a bad temper, drinks excessively, and wants to dance at night. It is decided that the "false" daughter should be married to the knight Olof, but he refuses. Hildur, who is held prisoner in the underworld, is to be married to her "brother" Vidrik, who is 300 years older. She escapes with the help of her other "brother," Didrik, and decides to stay in the upper world and finally to marry Olof. When she decides not to return, the underworld collapses and all of its inhabitants have to leave the forest to find a new place to settle. Birgit is married to an old farmer attracted to such dissolute women, and as punishment he is obliged to act as her servant.

---

[12] Svend Kragh-Jacobsen, "August Bournonville og den romantiske ballet," in *Den kongelige danske ballet,* eds. Svend Kragh-Jacobsen and Torben Krogh (Copenhagen: Selskabet till udgivelse af kulturskrifter, 1952), 77.
[13] Joel Schechter, ed., "Back to the Popular Source: Introduction to Part 1," in *Popular Theatre: A Sourcebook* (London and New York: Routledge, 2003), 10.
[14] Jürgensen, *The Bournonville Tradition*, 167.
[15] *Ljungby horn*, play script, Svenska teatern in Helsingfors, Archive of Svenska teatern, Svenska litterära sällskapet (Society of Swedish Literature in Finland), Helsingfors.

Theatre Photographs

The layers of the photo require a more specific description for analysis, starting with the ensemble photo: in the center is the knight Olof, with Hildur, who was saved from the underworld. Their clothing features bright colours which contrast with other, darker colours. On the right side of the photo are men of importance, such as landowners, judges, etc. On the left, next to Hildur, is her mother, who rescued her from being condemned as a witch. Next to her stands Birgit, who had replaced Hildur and who represents a threat to the marriage of Hildur and Olof. In the upper row on the left are women dressed to serve male society as wives or servants. The women to the upper right are probably from the underworld, and at the bottom are gremlins and other dark forces.

In looking through the costume sketches, it becomes clear that the dark colours are red, blue, and green. Also, a hand-coloured photo of Birgit indicates a dark green dress with red puffed sleeves.[16] The dress and her little bag also feature decorations with golden embroidery. The men of importance are variously dressed, with decorations such as chains and multi-coloured costume items. The photo does not depict the entire ensemble, but all of the most important parts are represented. There is also a difference in performative aspects; it is not clear who are in character during the photo session.

This leads to the question of the status of theatre photographs at the end of the nineteenth century. Jens Ruchatz has written in an article about the intermediality of theatre photography, dividing theatre photographs into *pose* and *moment* photos. A *pose* is characterized by lifelessness, whereas a *moment* tries to capture a performative aspect.[17] Laurence Senelick discusses one

---

[16] Constance Gottschalk as Birgit in *Ljungby horn*, hand-coloured photo 1893, Göteborgs stadsmuseum (The Museum of Gothenburg), GTM4743:1.

[17] Jens Rutchatz, "Zeit de Theaters/Zeit der Fotografie: Intermediale verschränkungen" in *Theater und Medien: Grundlagen – Analysen – Perspektiven: Eine Bestandsaufnahme*, eds. Henri Schoenmakers et al. (Bielefeld: Transcript, 2008).

of the first published books (1859) on theatre to be illustrated with photos, about the actress Rachel. The criterion of her acting was her ability to "[fall] into graceful or expressive poses," which was seen as a standard for acting, and the photo book could be used for instruction.[18] But as early as 1865 there were examples of photos that followed an acting sequence using a series of photos. However, all of the examples Senelick cites seem to be atelier photographs, not taken on the stage. He shows that the sequence photographs were widely dispersed in terms of geography, with examples from France, England, and Russia, but he offers no description about how they were received by the market.

Joel Anderson, in his book about theatre photography, comments upon the relation between the studio photo and the stage performance. The action captured on the photos is performed primarily for the photo occasion. "There are connections with actual stage practice: scenery might be sourced from theatre."[19]

The interesting thing in this ensemble photo from *Ljungby horn* is that the actors wear expressions that differ from one another and which relate more or less to their parts. The couple in the central position communicates love and belief, and their eyes are focused exclusively on each other. Almost everyone in the middle row is focusing on the couple. The three nearest all have different attitudes. The judge to the right seems content with rendering a correct judgement so the couple can get married; he holds his hands as if performing a judgement. Hildur's mother, to the left, also seems satisfied and is performing playing a protective mother. Next to her stands the enemy, Birgit, who glares angrily at the couple.

The actors in the upper row are not clearly focusing on the couple, nor is there any contact between them. The gremlins at bottom are performing chiefly for the audience/viewer. Only Justus Hagman, as Didrik, can be recognized.

---

[18] Laurence Senelick, "Early Photographic Attempts to Record Performance Sequence," *Theatre Research International* 22:3 (1997): 256.

[19] Joel Anderson, *Theatre and Photography* (Basingstoke: Palgrave Macmillan, 2015), 43.

The backdrop is partly visible; on the left side, a tree is painted, and at the bottom it is possible to catch a glimpse of a wide landscape. Whether or not the backdrop in the photo was made for the performance is hard to determine, but the floor looks like a stage floor. The decorations made by Carl Grabow, the foremost theatre painter in Sweden, were presented in advertisements and on posters, and a total of six new decorations/set designs were made for the production. Significantly, all of the decorations were freshly made, and no older decorations were re-used.[20] I have not seen any other example from that period where all scenery is listed in advertisements. It is possible that Ranft introduced an international trend here. The critics were astonished by the spectacular quality of the staging and the decorations; they also pointed out the use of effects. After the first night, a reviewer wrote: "No costs have been spared on this new production. Six new decorations, all with a great deal of atmosphere and beauty, painted by Carl Grabow, velvet and silk, beautiful maids and many expensive and peculiar props."[21] He then cites more examples and closes by saying that this exceeds the expectations and fantasies of the readers, who need to go and see it. Grabow's studio in Stockholm was central to Swedish theatre society and produced set designs for all the important theatres.[22] Some of these sets had to be transported to theatres; even Svenska Teatern in Helsinki used Grabow's services. In the case of touring companies, the expanding railway system made it more feasible to tour with several complete productions, thus changing the way the repertoire was put together.[23]

---

[20] Advertisement, *Göteborgs-Posten*, May 11, 1893.
[21] G. B. [signed], "Stora Teatern," *Göteborgs-Posten*, May 11, 1893. My translation.
[22] Gösta M. Bergman, *Den moderna teaterns genombrott 1890–1925* (Stockholm: Bonniers, 1966), 268.
[23] Claes Rosenqvist, *Mittsvenska scener: Härnösand, Sundsvall och det sena 1800-talets landsortsteater* (Umeå: Johan Nordlander-sällskapet, 1998), 233–234.

Flash Lighting

In the ensemble photo the use of the flash light is visible. In Söderberg and Rittsel's book about the Swedish photography's history they take up the development of flash light in the theatre. In 1891 the Swedish journal *Fotografisk tidskrift* informed readers about the possibility of taking indoor photos inside theatres and the same year a theatre in Copenhagen made some photos with actors standing in frozen positions on stage. They have traced a possible first Swedish example to the Royal opera in Stockholm 1894. They used magnesium flash light and the light sources were placed both in the auditorium and on the stage between the flats. During a ten-year period, the photographer Axel Rydin started to make documentations of the theatre performances in Stockholm. The problem with the photos was that they could not capture the theatrical atmosphere in the picture, and they were seen as impersonal.[24] This is obvious when looking at the ensemble picture from *Ljungby horn*, in which parts have been overexposed, the background is not really visible, and the shadows of two of the actors are visible on the backdrop. Probably the photographer experimented with only one strong flash. The photo also lacked a director who might have better integrated the back row into the picture, so that its constituents would not look, as they do now, as though they are gazing indifferently in various directions. But there is no unwanted motion in the picture, so the group must have been disciplined.

The next layer of the montage is a circle with portraits of the actors in street dress, with their family names written under each photo. It is hard to analyze the actors' status in society from their clothing. The family names inform us that there are probably three married couples on tour: the Gistedts, Strandbergs, and Hagmans. All of the other females, except for Mrs Svedberg, bear the title *Miss*. Many of the touring companies fostered theatre families, whose children often travelled with the company. Here as well, a difference could be seen after the implementation of the railway system, making it possible to go away for shorter periods

---

[24] Söderberg and Rittsel, *Den svenska fotografins historia*, 162.

and thus still maintain contact with life in Stockholm.[25] But there were also several actresses who remained unmarried. The theatre was an opportunity for women to earn an income and have an independent life. However, at that time their reputation outside the theatre world was questionable. The overwhelming majority of the pictures are taken partly in profile, and only three photos of the actresses are taken frontally. It is possible to study the difference between the main characters in costume and in street clothes, and to consider the theatre's power to transform.

Illustrative Drawings

Five drawings are placed in a half circle around the private photos. Where the lines in the drawing are covered by a photo, new lines are drawn on the latter. The draughtsman has signed his name (O. Anderson), and the drawings seem to be impressions from the performance. Let us start with the drawing at bottom right, which features a cradle that has no connection to the play, but only to the background story about the children that have been exchanged. At top right is a scene from a holy spring, where Hildur feels that she belongs in the upper world; at top center is a hall where the big wedding party in the underworld is held; at top left is a hall in Ljungby Castle; and at bottom left are a couple of brownies in the underworld. At bottom center is a photo of an unnamed young actress and the handwritten text "Ljungby Horn. Tournee 1894–1895" followed by "(direction A. Ranft.)" repeated twice. The last item might have been written by Ranft himself. In the lower part of the montage are two flower stalks serving as ornaments, with two fairy-tale figures on the top. The drawings were probably of more interest for a person who had seen the production than a person wishing to learn about it. There is no indication that they were in colour in the original version. It seems that the montage was better suited as a souvenir than as a marketing tool. The drawings do not promote the actors; rather, they consist of pictures of the milieu where the play takes place.

---

[25] Rosenqvist, *Mittsvenska scener*, 244.

Remediation

In her book, Anna Dahlgren uses Jay David Bolter and Richard Grusin's concept of *remediation*. A medium is defined by its relations to other techniques for representation, and a medium is defined as "that which remediates […] appropriates the techniques, forms, and social significance of other media." New media remediates old, but old remediates new as well.[26] This concept is useful in analyzing this montage.

Bolter and Grusin's point of departure is contemporary new media, thus they find that it is a "lens through which we can view the history of remediation."[27] Even if it is a new object the "act of remediation, however, ensures that the older medium cannot be entirely effaced; the new medium remains dependent on the older one in acknowledged or unacknowledged ways."[28]

The viewer has to combine three layers, namely, the photo of the ensemble, the single photos of the actors, and the drawings, to obtain a view of the performance. There are also connections to the live performance and to the actors' previous stage appearances. The emblematic figures from the folk-tale tradition are linked to oral history, narration, and singing. The actors in street clothes suggest their potential, as actors, for enacting other parts in new productions. In the example of the montage, the picture over the words *Ljungby horn* can be seen as remediating, whereby old and new forms are joined in a new form, photography, which finally places all the different parts on the same level. The process could be compared with Bolter and Grusin's description about how a viewer of a collage "oscillates between looking at patches of paper and paint on the surface of the work and looking through to the depicted objects as if they occupied a real space beyond the surface."[29] Through the process of remediation, a wholeness stands forward that makes it possible for the viewer to examine the details and to assimilate the whole image. And I would also

---

[26] Dahlgren, *Ett medium för visuell bildning*, 12.
[27] Jay David Bolter and Richard Grusin, *Remediation: Understanding New Media* (Cambridge: MIT Press, 1999), 21.
[28] Bolter and Grusin, *Remediation*, 47.
[29] Bolter and Grusin, *Remediation*, 41.

argue that image could be expand with connections to the viewers' memories from the performance and the actors' previous appearances. The acts of viewing are different if the viewer has seen the performance or not.

Even if the use of this montage and the photo thereof is unknown, it can be seen as a mark of the importance of the production. Theatre's relation to other media is complicated; in the early days of film, actors were often subject to contractual restrictions on their appearance in films. This was probably based on the fear that audiences would be satisfied by seeing the actor on film and thus neglect to visit the theatre.

Theatre photographs of performances did not enjoy a long-term market, but photos of actors attained enormous popularity, based on the development of the production of visiting cards as well as the decreasing cost and increasing professional quality of photographs. Elizabeth Anne McCauley highlights the French photographer Nadar, who, for example, photographed the actress Sarah Bernhardt. However, when he made photos of selected actors and singers from the Comédie Française and the Opera, he did not take role photos, but photographed them in street clothes.[30] Nevertheless, in both France and Sweden the most successful celebrity photos were those of actors in costume, associated with a role. In Paris, successful photographers located their ateliers in the same quarter as the theatre and entertainment district.[31] The process of how and where the photographs were sold in Sweden has not been fully researched, but they were sold by booksellers, art shops, and directly by the photographers' ateliers.[32] Some actors' archives, such as those of Anders de Wahl or Tore Svennberg, include a number of both visiting cards and postcard photos. These were also used for sending messages to admirers, autographed over the lower part of the photo, as well as to theatre managers

---

[30] Elizabeth Anne McCauley, *Industrial Madness: Commercial Photography in Paris 1848-1871* (New Haven and London: Yale University Press, 1994), 146.
[31] McCauley, *Industrial Madness*, 78.
[32] Söderberg and Rittsel, *Den svenska fotografins historia*, 45.

and colleagues.[33] Laurence Senelick points out that the photographs were distributed even among people who never got the chance to see them perform live.[34] Joel Anderson finds that the actor portraits "could circulate beyond the parameters of theatre spectatorship, and become emblems for individual worship: buyable, collectable, ownable images, fostering fascination for the figure of the celebrity actor."[35] Here is a separate media system, a sort of star system that has a number of similarities with the distribution of photo cards featuring Hollywood's movie stars in the twentieth century. The term "parasocial interaction" can be used here when describing the star system of the theatre.[36] In the beginning of the twentieth century, when actors were scheduled to give guest performances, they were often asked to send their photos in advance to be used as marketing tools.[37] A long time passed before theatrical photographs were published in newspapers. The first forms of illustration used along with reviews c.1900 were drawings or satirical sketches, which could be used to emphasize some typical aspect of the actors' style or even the interplay between actors. When photos were first published, they included only separate photos of the actors, often in street clothes.[38]

Conclusion

There is an internal connection between the various layers in the montage that combine to compose the object. Individual elements are connected to the production in different ways, based as well

---

[33] Teatersamlingarna (Theatre collections), Statens musikverk (Swedish Performing Arts Agency), Stockholm.
[34] Senelick, "Early Photographic Attempts," 255.
[35] Anderson, *Theatre and Photography*, 45.
[36] Thomas Baker used the term when studying the nineteenth-century culture of literary celebrities; Andreas Nyblom "Mediernas livrustkammare: Nordiska museet och berömmelsens materialitet" in *1800-talets mediesystem*, eds. Jonas Harvard and Patrik Lundell (Stockholm: Kungliga biblioteket, 2010), 180.
[37] Letter from Nicken Rönngren to Pauline Brunius, August 8, 1919, archive of Svenska Teatern, Svenska litterära sällskapet i Helsingfors.
[38] Curt Isaksson, *Pressen på teatern: Teaterkritik i Stockholms dagspress 1890–1941* (PhD diss., Stockholm: Stiftelsen för utgivning av teatervetenskapliga studier, 1987), 104–109.

on the status of different techniques and developments of that time. Together, they construct, via a remediating process, a wholeness that differs depending whether or not the viewer knows about or has seen the performance. The layers employ different techniques; even the two photo layers differ in terms of technique, costume, and collective and individual objects. The handwritten text items place the montage in conjunction with a specific theatre tour; without the text we should have great difficulty determining the relationship between the layers.

In the montage, several aspects of the production are visible: the original folk tale, the performance, the stage design, and the individual actors, prepared to take part in new productions. Together, they build up an image that functions as a souvenir of the performance.

References

Anderson, Joel. *Theatre and Photography*. Basingstoke: Palgrave Macmillan, 2015.

Assmann, Aleida. *Cultural Memory and Western Civilization*. Cambridge and New York: Cambridge University Press, 2013.

Balme, Christopher B. *The Theatrical Public Sphere*. Cambridge: Cambridge University Press, 2013.

Bergman, Gösta M. *Den moderna teaterns genombrott 1890–1925*. Stockholm: Bonniers, 1966.

Bolter, Jay David, and Richard Grusin. *Remediation: Understanding New Media*. Cambridge: MIT Press, 1999.

Dahlgren, Anna. *Ett medium för visuell bildning: Kulturhistoriska perspektiv på fotoalbum 1850–1950*. Stockholm: Makadam, 2013.

G. B. [signed], "Stora Teatern," *Göteborgs-Posten*, May 11, 1893.

Isaksson, Curt. *Pressen på teatern: Teaterkritik i Stockholms dagspress 1890–1941*. PhD diss., Stockholm: Stiftelsen för utgivning av teatervetenskapliga studier, 1987.

Jürgensen, Knut Arne. *The Bournonville Tradition: The First Fifty Years, 1829–1879*. London: Dance Books, 1997.

Kragh-Jacobsen, Svend. "August Bournonville og den romantiske ballet." In *Den kongelige danske ballet*, edited by Svend Kragh-Jacobsen and Torben Krogh, 193–335. Copenhagen: Selskabet till udgivelse af kulturskrifter, 1952.

McCauley, Elizabeth Anne. *Industrial Madness: Commercial Photography in Paris 1848–1871*. New Haven and London: Yale University Press, 1994.

Nyblom, Andreas. "Mediernas livrustkammare: Nordiska museet och berömmelsens materialitet." In *1800-talets mediesystem*, edited by Jonas Harvard and Patrik Lundell, 177–199. Stockholm: Kungliga biblioteket, 2010.

Ranft, Albert. *Albert Ranfts memoarer: Första delen*. Stockholm: Norstedts, 1928.

Rosenqvist, Claes. *Mittsvenska scener: Härnösand, Sundsvall och det sena 1800-talets landsortsteater*. Umeå: Johan Nordlandersällskapet, 1998.

Rutchatz, Jens. "Zeit de Theaters/Zeit der Fotografie: Intermediale verschränkungen." In *Theater und Medien: Grundlagen – Analysen – Perspektiven: Eine Bestandsaufnahme*, edited by Henri Schoenmakers et al., 109–116. Bielefeld: Transcript, 2008.

Schechter, Joel, ed. "Back to the Popular Source: Introduction to Part 1." In *Popular Theatre: A Sourcebook*, 3–11. London and New York: Routledge, 2003.

Senelick, Laurence. "Early Photographic Attempts to Record Performance Sequence." *Theatre Research International* 22:3 (1997): 255–264.

Söderberg, Rolf, and Pär Rittsel. *Den svenska fotografins historia 1840–1940*. Stockholm: Bonnier Fakta, 1983.

Wieselgren, Oscar. "Frans O. L. Hodell." *Svenskt biografiskt lexicon*. Accessed October 28, 2016. https://sok.riksarkivet.se/sbl/artikel/13680.

Archives

Brevsamlingarna (Collection of letters), Kungliga biblioteket/National Library of Sweden, Stockholm.

Svenska teaterns i Helsingfor arkiv (Archive of Svenska teatern in Helsinki), Svenska litterära sällskapet i Helsinfors/Society of Swedish Literature in Finland, Helsingfors.

Teatersamlingarna (Theatre collections), Göteborgs stadsmuseum/ The Museum of Gothenburg.

Teatersamlingarna (Theatre collections), Statens musikverk/Swedish Performing Arts Agency, Stockholm.

Today's Cake is a Log: Remediating the Intermediality of Hotel Pro Forma's Works in an Exhibition

Daria Skjoldager-Nielsen and Kim Skjoldager-Nielsen

Abstract

This article explores intermediality not only as an aesthetic strategy for theatre itself, but also regarding how this strategy can be remediated and applied to another medium: a performative exhibition. The case explored here is the Danish performance theatre company Hotel Pro Forma and their exhibition *Today's Cake is a Log* (2015), produced for the company's thirtieth anniversary. We argue that the exhibition remediates the company's aesthetical strategy in such a way that it transforms the theatre spectator into a performer, who thereby embodies and assimilates the theatre's aesthetic strategy through performative acts during the visit to the exhibition. The analysis is contextualized: first, by a presentation of intermediality theory developed for theatre and performance; second, by an introduction of Hotel Pro Forma, its artistic project and intermedial aesthetics exemplified through staging devices and performances. Finally the analysis of the performance exhibition through the experience of the visitor is presented.

In this article we explore intermediality not only as an aesthetic strategy for theatre, but also how the aesthetics of theatrical performance, its formal performative logics, may be remediated in order to reflect the original work in an exhibition. Our point of departure is intermediality as it is conceptualized for the theatre.

How to cite this book chapter:
Skjoldager-Nielsen, Daria, and Kim Skjoldager-Nielsen. "*Today's Cake is a Log*: Remediating the Intermediality of Hotel Pro Forma's Works in an Exhibition." In *The Power of the In-Between: Intermediality as a Tool for Aesthetic Analysis and Critical Reflection*, edited by Sonya Petersson, Christer Johansson, Magdalena Holdar, and Sara Callahan, 149–181. Stockholm: Stockholm University Press, 2018. DOI: https://doi.org/10.16993/baq.g. License: CC-BY.

Yet our understanding of performance is also inscribed in the broad-spectrum approach of performance studies, as we extend the intermediality concept to include stagings and performances noncompliant with traditional concepts of theatre.[1] This approach allows us to extend performance analysis to include exhibitions, where the visit may be seen as a performance executed by the attendee—ideally the visitor's realization of the curator's staging or arrangement of exhibits.[2]

As we intend to show, the extended approach to our analytical example is particularly appropriate since it connects the theatre to the exhibition as a locus for literally "(re)visiting" the aesthetics of the theatre company put on display. We pursue the question of how the exhibition may be seen as a remediation of the intermedial strategy found in Hotel Pro Forma's stage works. We propose that the exhibition remediates this aesthetical strategy in a way that transforms the theatre spectator into a performer, who may then embody and assimilate the aesthetic strategy through her performative acts. Here we understand "remediation" in the sense Jay David Bolter and Richard Grusin suggest: as an appropriation of "the techniques, forms, and social significance of other media to [...] refashion them in the name of the real."[3] This remediation may be seen as an alternative to theatre exhibitions that

---

[1] Richard Schechner, "Performance Studies: The Broad Spectrum Approach," in *The Performance Studies Reader*, ed. Henry Bial (New York: Routledge, 2004), 7–9.

[2] Of course, the curator's intentions may not always be realized by the visitor. For a discussion of audience behaviors in exhibitions, see Bruno Ingemann, "Den besøgende: Social identitet, læring og oplevelse – en metodisk diskussion," in *Udstillinger mellem focus & flimmer*, eds. Elisabeth Bodin and Johanna Lassenius (Copenhagen: Multivers, 2006). For a discussion of the exhibition as the curator's indirect staging of the visitor's acts in the exhibition space, see Mieke Bal, "Curatorial Acts," *Journal of Curatorial Studies*, vol. 1, no. 2 (2012): 179–192.

[3] We do not, however, subscribe to Bolter and Grusin's claim that all mediation is remediation; it is rather to be considered a creative strategy, as suggested by the theatre scholar Erik Exe Christoffersen. Cf. Jay David Bolter and Richard Grusin, *Remediation: Understanding New Media*, (Cambridge: MIT Press, 1999), 65; Peripeti, "Remediering mellem film og teater – en kreativ strategi," accessed April 12, 2017, http://www.peripeti.dk/ 2009/06/03/265/.

take a less performative approach to the visitor and remain based on conventional displays and informative documentation of stage artefacts.[4]

Our example is the exhibition *Today's Cake is a Log (Dagens kage er en træstamme)* by the Danish performance theatre company Hotel Pro Forma. The exhibition was shown at the arts venue Gamle Strand in Copenhagen November 6–29, 2015. The exhibition was produced for Hotel Pro Forma's thirtieth anniversary and it was curated by Kirsten Dehlholm, who has served as the artistic director of the company since its establishment in 1985. Given the occasion, the exhibition was a retrospective of the works by Hotel Pro Forma, assembling a selection of artefacts and photo and video material from the company's total of more than fifty large and small productions. Moreover, it staged all in all 130 hours of readings of texts originally used in the performances.[5] Contrary to what one might have expected, this jubilee exhibition did not provide the visitor with a documentary and chronological overview of Hotel Pro Forma's works and history; rather it attempted to facilitate a sensorial, experiential insight into the aesthetic strategy of the company. This emphasis on the

---

[4] To be fair, many theatre museums and museums presenting theatre are following the general curatorial trend of experimenting with different formats and strategies of intermediality in the communication with the visitors. A recent instance of this is the exhibition *Curtain Up: Celebrating 40 Years of Theatre in London and New York*, which ran at the Victoria & Albert Museum in London between February 9 and August 31, 2016. Stage designer Tom Piper and RFK Architects created an exhibition environment that allowed the visitor to immerse herself into the different phases of theatre production through evocative set designs, audio-visual displays, and stage artefacts, representing a selection of historically significant performances from the two cities. "Curtain Up: Celebrating 40 Years of Theatre in London and New York," V&A, accessed April 12, 2017, https://www.vam.ac.uk/exhibitions/curtain-up-celebrating-40-years-of-theatre-in-london-and-new-york.

[5] For an introduction to Hotel Pro Forma, see Erik Exe Christoffersen and Kathrine Winkelhorn, eds., *Skønhedens Hotel: Hotel Pro Forma: Et laboratorium for scenekunst* (Aarhus: Aarhus Universitetsforlag, 2015); (in English) Per Theil, Kirsten Dehlholm, and Lars Qvortrup, *Hotel Pro Forma: The Double Staging: Space and Performance* (Copenhagen: Arkitektens Forlag, 2003).

visitor's experience is why we find the performance approach rewarding in understanding the exhibition's remediation of the theatrical works.

Before we begin analyzing the exhibition we will provide a context. First, we present how we understand the topic of intermediality from a theatre and performance studies perspective, building on a complex of what we see as closely interconnected concepts: hypermediality, intermediality, intermedial experience, performance of perception, and performativity of perception.[6] Besides being our theoretical foundation, the overview contributes to the overall introduction and discussion of intermediality in this anthology. Second, we introduce Hotel Pro Forma, its artistic project and intermedial aesthetics exemplified through staging devices and performances. While the theoretical concepts provide our analytical apparatus, the aesthetic strategy of Hotel Pro Forma supplies the necessary backdrop for understanding the remediation of its theatrical works into the exhibition.

Hyper- and Intermediality in Theatre and Performance

How does intermediality come about? And what does it mean? We assume theatre is a hypermedium that includes all other media as well as the co-present bodies of performers and spectators. As we unpack this assumption it will become clear that hypermediality in theatre is the very basis for its intermediality. The live performer functions as the interconnector between media, and, in turn, between the intermedial stage and the spectator, who ultimately realizes intermediality as experience. Understanding this hyper- and intermediality of theatrical performance is important for our analysis. In the case of *Today's Cake is a Log*, the live performances are remediated through exhibited artefacts, and we propose that the exhibition as remediation allows the visitor to

---

[6] We mainly draw on articles from the seminal works on theatre and intermediality: Freda Chapple and Chiel Kattenbelt, eds., *Intermediality in Theatre and Performance* (Amsterdam and New York: Rodopi, 2006); Sarah Bay-Cheng, Chiel Kattenbelt, Andy Lavender, and Robin Nelson, eds., *Mapping Intermediality in Performance* (Amsterdam: Amsterdam University Press, 2010).

become that interconnector of media, thereby experiencing the intermedial strategy of Hotel Pro Forma through the exhibition. Chiel Kattenbelt explains hypermediality in the theatre simply as its capacity "to incorporate all other arts and media."[7] He elaborates on this concept and points to the fact that theatre's all-inclusiveness towards other art forms and media is founded on it being physical and not virtual.[8] The grounding of theatre in physical space provides a platform where the other arts and media can be staged, or more precisely, become components in the communicative process of a theatrical event, which unfolds here and now in the co-presence of performers and spectators. The spectator perceptually connects to the performer as "the player of the different media who acts in the empty spaces between the media."[9] From the point of view of the spectator, the different media simultaneously retain their own immediately perceivable functions, for example, through the screening of live video or video recordings (pre-recorded), or live imagery (zoom-ins on performers and stage action, etc.), and they undergo a transformation into theatrical signs, that is, signs of signs, to be interpreted in accordance with the dramaturgy and the context of the given performance. Of course, these acts of interconnecting different media may vary depending on the character of the staging, for example, from subtly suggesting connections to the spectator (who perceives and interpret them) to letting the performer physically enact them on stage (practically operating technological devices). But interconnecting media, as Kattenbelt hints at, may also simply mean that

---

[7] Chiel Kattenbelt, "Theatre as the Art of the Performer and the Stage of Intermediality," in *Intermediality in Theatre and Performance,* edited by Freda Chapple and Chiel Kattenbelt (Amsterdam and New York: Rodopi, 2006), 32.

[8] According to Meike Wagner, theatre as a hypermedium becomes "a compromise, which opens up possibilities of connecting to the ancient art form of theatre with contemporary notions of media, without renouncing the claim of corporeal presence in live performance." Meike Wagner, "Of other Bodies: The Intermedial Gaze in Theatre," in Chapple and Kattenbelt, *Intermediality,* 127. See also Chiel Kattenbelt, "Intermediality in Theatre and Performance: Definitions, Perceptions and Medial Relationships," *Culture, Language and Representation,* vol. VI (2008): 23.

[9] Kattenbelt, "Intermediality in Theatre and Performance," 23.

the performer, through her physical artistic acts, combines the medialities of art forms that make up the theatre performance (articulation of words—drama/literature; modulation of voice—opera/music; gesticulation of the body—dance/visual arts), and in doing so provides mediation through her own capacity of physical presence.[10] In this context, it is suggested that in theatre and performance intermediality basically conceptualizes "the process of how something that appears fixed becomes different."[11] This process does not limit itself to the level of the performer; it also takes place on the macro level of performance, that is, in-between types of theatre such as "literary theatre," "music theatre," and "visual theatre," of which each has its own dominant sign system of "word," "sound," and "image."[12] Thus, it becomes evident when it produces hybrid notions, for instance, "visual opera" or—as in our case—a merging of performance and exhibition.

Intermedial Experience (in Post-Dramatic Theatre) and How to Analyze It

We assume that the incorporation of different media in theatre qualifies intermediality as an inherent and therefore ever-present structural feature of theatre, employing the medialities of space, time, image, body, voice, gesture, music, lights, text, costumes, props, and set design. What is of particular interest to the conceptual discussion in this book, however, is that intermediality—in its capacity of media interplay—may be utilized in the staging of a performance as an aesthetic strategy. That is, certain philosophical or political aspirations reflect upon and affect the way we as humans relate to our surroundings, our lifeworld, society, media realities—in particular, how we conceive of different phenomena and epistemological categories.[13] Intermediality as aesthetic strategy aims at creating a certain experience for the spectator, which

---

[10] See Kattenbelt's circular model representing theatre as the art of the performer in Kattenbelt, "Theatre as the Art of the Performer," 33.
[11] Chapple and Kattenbelt, *Intermediality*, 12.
[12] Chapple and Kattenbelt, *Intermediality*, 21.
[13] Chapple and Kattenbelt, *Intermediality*, 24.

we will exemplify later in the introduction to Hotel Pro Forma. We are interested in the notion of an intermedial experience, in order to employ it in our analysis. Lisbeth Groot Nibbelink and Sigrid Merx have made an attempt to conceptualize the typical experience and develop it into a pedagogical and analytical strategy that we find useful.

Following Kattenbelt, Nibbelink and Merx summarise intermediality as "performance and performative practices in which media not only exist next to each other, but through their interplay result in both a redefinition of media and resensibilisation of the senses."[14] They relate the intermedial experience to the way "intermedial performance often plays with or explicitly deconstructs perceptual expectations and produces sensations ranging from subtle experiences of surprise or confusion, to more uncanny experiences of dislocation, displacement or alienation."[15] These are effects that are known to occur with so-called postdramatic theatre, wherein the different media or medialities of the performance are organized not in accordance with the principle of *hypotaxis*, subordination, as one would find in dramatic theatre, where all other media support the text and the narrative, but following the principle of *parataxis*, non-hierarchy. This non-hierarchical ordering of media means they are juxtaposed and operate simultaneously on an equal level as to deliberately challenge the spectator's perception:[16]

> Intermediality in the live performance calls for an active attitude on the part of the spectator that Lehmann describes as "evenly hovering attention" [...]. The spectator has to negotiate the perceptual experiences evoked by the various, simultaneous media relationships. [...] To experience intermediality therefore is an active embodied process of negotiating and shifting between different and conflicting medial realities, moving in and out of perceptual worlds, relating different impressions and signs, looking

---

[14] Lisbeth Groot Nibbelink and Sigrid Merx, "Presence and Perception: Analysing Intermediality in Performance," in *Mapping Intermediality*, 218.
[15] Nibbelink and Merx, "Presence and Perception," 119.
[16] Cf. Hans-Thies Lehmann, *Postdramatic Theatre*, trans. Karen Jürs-Munby (London and New York: Routledge, 2006), 86–88.

for a point of connection that might integrate the confusing and disturbing sensations in a meaningful whole, however unstable and ephemeral this whole may be.[17]

The spectator embodies this process of intermedial experience, and the embodiment has consequences for the analytical approach, as "the intermedial is to be found as much in the structuring of the performance itself, where it manifests itself not as an experience, but as the interplay between different media."[18] As Nibbelink and Merx conclude on the method, "[l]ocating the intermedial both in the body and in the performance requires a perceptual as well as a cognitive awareness."[19]

Nibbelink and Merx suggest a spectator/analyst who is intimately part of the production of intermediality, and who needs to be aware of her own participation. To further grasp how the intermedial experience unfolds, we find it necessary to distinguish between perceptual cause, performance (the staged as well as the perceived event), and perceptual effect, performativity (referring to the event's impact upon the one engaged in perception). In doing so, we first refer to Maaike Bleeker's concept "performance of perception," which connects the theatre performance to the spectator.[20] In her example, the performance still plays itself out before the spectator at a certain distance but the structure of the performance is transmutable to the patterns of the spectator's perception.[21] Hence, in theatre we may think of the spectator as someone who enacts or performs her perception as a bodily performance, which in effect is a reflection of a stage performance.

---

[17] Nibbelink and Merx, "Presence and Perception," 220.
[18] Nibbelink and Merx, "Presence and Perception," 220.
[19] Nibbelink and Merx, "Presence and Perception," 220.
[20] Maaike Bleeker, "Corporeal Literacy: New Modes of Embodied Interaction in Digital Culture," in *Mapping Intermediality*, 38.
[21] Bleeker draws attention to the work of the philosopher Alva Noë, who contends that perception is a mode of action, which not only engages the brain but the whole organism, and that it is an acquired skill. We actively engage in our surroundings through a number of perceptual systems at once, sight, hearing, smelling, touch, proprioception and kinesthesis, and a complete experience of the visible, audible, and tangible environment is created. Alva Noë, *Action in Perception* (Cambridge: MIT Press, 2004), 2.

As it will become evident in our analysis of Hotel Pro Forma's exhibition, the bodily performance of perception is radicalized as the seated theatre spectator is transformed into a moving visitor, engaging with the staged environment of the exhibition instead of a performance on a stage.

Bleeker establishes that both bodily and staged performance of perception are culturally determined but also mutable.[22] This concern with the effects of perception leads Bleeker to introduce her second concept, "performativity of perception": "the intermedial character of the theatre may [...] be used to undermine seemingly self-evident modes of perceiving and to draw attention to the performativity of perception: how perception actually produces what appears as the object of our perception."[23] Kattenbelt, who also concerns himself with "the performativity of intermediality," offers a clarification to what end such a realization about perception in intermedial theatre may serve: "Aesthetic action (in production as well as perception) may be considered a form of exploration and reflection, which reinforces the communicative competence of socialized individuals."[24] Localizing the performativity of perception, Kattenbelt points to the process of the theatrical event, which is not only self-referencing and self-reflecting by itself, but also effectuating similar attitudes of the perceiver who takes the position of the spectator:[25] by watching theatre one becomes aware of oneself watching, and in the end, possibly, of what the process may have effectuated. As we shall see in our analysis of Hotel Pro Forma's exhibition, the performativity of perception may become even more conspicuous to the visitor, who physically enters into the exhibition environment, as cause—performance of perception—and effect—performativity of perception—are closer connected in the self-referential and self-reflexive process of the visitor.

---

[22] Bleeker, "Corporeal Literacy," 38.
[23] Bleeker, "Corporeal Literacy," 38.
[24] Chiel Kattenbelt, "Intermediality in Performance and as a Mode of Performativity," in *Mapping Intermediality*, 34.
[25] Kattenbelt, "Intermediality in Performance and as a Mode of Performativity," 32.

Introducing Hotel Pro Forma

Kattenbelt's concept of intermediality as an aesthetic strategy that develops the audience's sensibility towards the construction of reality, through the bringing together and interplay of different media and medialities on the stage, seems particularly interesting in relation to Hotel Pro Forma's artistic project. In the following, we will give a brief introduction to Hotel Pro Forma's aesthetics and connect it with intermediality by looking into the staging devices employed in their productions. This will then serve as the backdrop for observing the transferal of the aesthetic strategy from stage performance to exhibition.

From the point of view of mainstream, realistic theatre, Hotel Pro Forma (established 1985) is vastly unconventional as it negates all that mainstream theatre represents. The performances are non-dramatic, non-linear, and non-narrative in structure and content. The performers do not employ psychological acting. Instead, the performances are located in the in-between where they constantly contest and redefine what theatre is, through highly conceptual stagings that follow visual-musical scores, often staged in found non-theatre spaces. Actions and scenarios are organized and proceed in accordance with principles and systems that stem from, for example, mathematics, mythology, philosophy, encyclopedia, or the Internet's hypertext. In terms of idiom, Hotel Pro Forma draws on a variety of art forms and formats of staging (visual arts, installation, performance art, appropriation art, pop art, exhibition, opera, dance, musical, theatre, ritual, lecture, multimedia, etc.), as well as art historical movements (modernism, the historical avant-gardes, formalism, minimalism, concretism, etc.). Especially the formalist inspiration seems predominant in the way Hotel Pro Forma challenges our pre-understanding of the theatre and the world.[26] Similar to Victor Shklovsky's defamiliarization or *ostranenie*,[27] this is a staging of the spectator's sensation and

---

[26] Erik Exe Christoffersen, "Den u-selvfølgelige sansning," in *Skønhedens Hotel: Hotel Pro Forma: Et laboratorium for scenekunst*, eds. Erik Exe Christoffersen and Kathrine Winkelhorn (Aarhus: Aarhus Universitetsforlag, 2015).

[27] Lawrence Crawford, "Viktor Shklovskij: Différance in Defamiliarization," *Comparative Literature* 36 (1984): 16.

perception, whose habitual or automatic unfolding is obstructed or disturbed by the staging in an effort to make her take a fresh look at the world. Ultimately, it is the creation of a state where all sorts of phenomena, freed from their conventional context, momentarily will appear in their splendid presence and beauty and rouse curiosity and thought. Hotel Pro Forma's project is a phenomenological one, which basically examines how phenomena appear to our consciousness. But it is also a project critical of the self-evident or intuitive ways with which we relate to our world. Thus, Hotel Pro Forma's project can be understood as emancipatory, reclaiming sensuality as a tool for becoming aware of the world; that is, an approach that not just surrenders to the sensual, but is reflective and thereby discovers new perspectives on already known phenomena.

Hotel Pro Forma has been compared to a laboratory.[28] The investigations that take place as part of the artistic work are not scientific studies in which a hypothesis can be falsified or validated according to truth. On the contrary, they are aesthetic studies that call for decisions based on aesthetic judgment, that is, whether something within the frame of the staging concept is a valid or an invalid expression; whether it works or not. Hotel Pro Forma's process is similar to the operation of a scientific laboratory in that their aesthetic study is subject to systematized development, resulting in new performances, which in turn provides new knowledge about the world. As the director Kirsten Dehlholm puts it: "We are investigating the world and the performance is the investigation. We use the production to make 'a journey' into the world and come back with new knowledge and awareness. This should be clear to the audience, so they become involved in this study."[29]

According to Lars Qvortrup, the aesthetic investigations may be systematized by a categorization through which they unfold in the performances on three different levels (often simultaneously): 1) studies questioning epistemological categories such as space,

---

[28] Lars Qvortrup, "Hotel Pro Forma: Laboratorium for æstetiske undersøgelser," *Peripeti* 25 (2016). See also Katherine Winkelhorn, "Et blik ind i Hotel Pro Formas kunstneriske praksis," in *Skønhedens Hotel*, 224–225.
[29] Cited from Christoffersen, "Den u-selvfølgelige sansning," 25. Translation by the authors.

time, and transcendence, as a basic research of cognitive forms; 2) studies on a number of fundamental phenomena that exist in society, for example war, religion, and education; and 3) studies and challenges of a number of established artistic genres, including text-based theatre, exhibitions, and opera, which serve the development of the performing arts and their conditions, often resulting in hybrids such as visual opera or performative exhibitions.[30]

Just as the premises for a scientific laboratory experiment are known through the experimental setup or design, the constituents of staging are evident to the spectators of a Hotel Pro Forma performance. The performance does not seek to disguise its staging as the naturalistic or realistic theatre attempted through the creation of illusion, as in the drawing-room dramas of Ibsen and Strindberg; instead it exhibits the devices of staging in a way similar to post-dramatic theatre.[31] This blatantly self-referring strategy makes it possible for the spectator to observe the very process of the staging itself as it unfolds in the performance. By installing "an observer, who not just observe the world (as it 'is') but who watches his own observations of the world" our so-called "natural" or self-evident view of objects, that is, a first-order observation is challenged "implying that it could also be observed differently."[32] Through the staging, the spectator makes what is called "a second-order observation."[33] In this sense the performance becomes a medium for the spectator's self-observation and recognition of the premises for the performance's conception of reality. Qvortrup suggests that second-order observation applies as Hotel Pro Forma's aesthetic strategy as it creates "counter-intuitive images of epistemological categories as well as fundamental phenomena and artistic genres."[34]

It is interesting that the second-order observation bears resemblance to the self-reflexivity pointed out by Kattenbelt as a characteristic of the theatrical performance process, and which

---

[30] Qvortrup, "Hotel Pro Forma," 87.
[31] Hans-Thies Lehmann includes Hotel Pro Forma in his list of post-dramatic theatre, see Lehmann, *Postdramatic Theatre*, 24.
[32] Qvortrup, "Hotel Pro Forma," 91–92.
[33] Qvortrup, "Hotel Pro Forma," 91–92.
[34] Qvortrup, "Hotel Pro Forma," 91–92.

is highlighted in contemporary post-dramatic, intermedial theatre. Therefore, we suggest that second-order observation is the perceptual operation the spectator performs in the realization of intermediality, as in Nibbelink and Merx's localization of intermediality in the spectator's body, and Bleeker's concept performance of perception.

At this point, we might ask, what would it be like to attend a Hotel Pro Forma performance? Firstly, Hotel Pro Forma challenges the expectations of conventional realist theatre. Instead, a number of slowly moving and sensuously saturated scenarios are staged that in various ways bring into play basic epistemological categories such as space, time, and transcendence. The staging affects the spectator's sensation and perception through the use of different media and medialities. Often, virtual technologies are involved (projection of digital video, use of audio effects, elaborate light designs), but the intermediality might just rely on the juxtaposition of real components (space/time/body). For example, in *Why Does Night Come, Mother* (1989), the spectators had their attention drawn to space and transcendence as epistemological categories, as they were placed on balconies from which they—with a dizzying feeling in the body—could look straight down at the performers, who were slowly alternating between standing, walking, gesturing, and lying on a floor deep below (Figure 1). This way the spectators were engaged in an optical play between space and surface, between two and three dimensions as the performers in the lying position cancelled out the conventional experience of space and gravity. Seen against the white floor surface, they seemed to be in weightless fall. Hence, through the unconventional spectator perspective, the experience of everyday space was transcended. It created an unreal, dreamlike sensation of looking into eternity. The perceptual interplay of the medialities (space, time, body, and compositional stage image) took on a cognitive dimension as text, and voice added itself to the experience. Poems about longing and loss were sung and recited ceremoniously in the cathedral-like sounding, tall room.

Instead of playing dramatic roles, the performers in a Hotel Pro Forma production perform *functions* in the unfolding of stage images, choreographies, and soundscapes. The functions

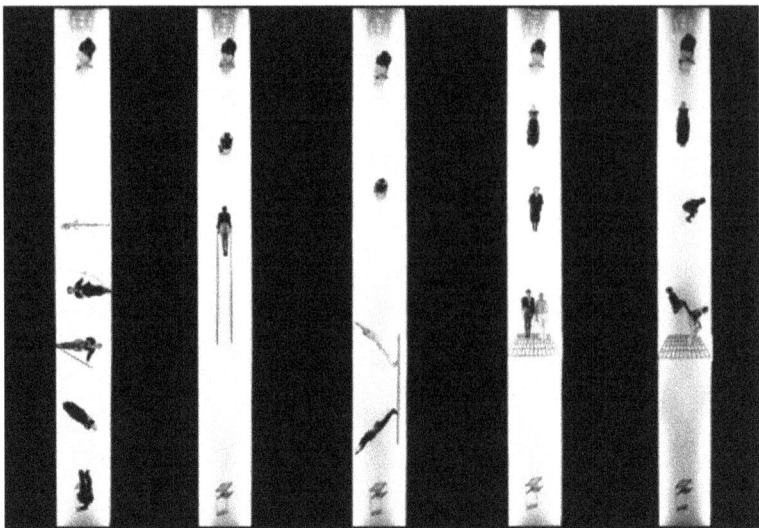

Figure 1. Montage of stage images from *Why Does Night Come, Mother*. Hotel Pro Forma, 1989. Photo: Roberto Fortuna. Copyright: Hotel Pro Forma. License: CC-BY-NC-ND.

focus on their skills, history, or physiognomy, and what they may add to the entirety of the performance. Thus, the rowers' task in *Navigare* (1996) was to row an imaginary long-ship; the author Carsten Jensen's task in *Chinese Compass* (1998) was to recite a text by Carsten Jensen about his travel experiences in China; the task of performers of short stature in *The Picture of Snow White* (1994) was to just be dwarfs surrounding "Snow White" while framed by their own personal stories through a soundtrack. The insistence on presence, precision, and authenticity of the performer causes a reality effect that carries its own credibility.

The staging always refers to a theme, the choice of a fundamental phenomenon, for example, gravity, perspective, or the war, as a meaning-constituting frame for that which is staged. As semiosis the staging instigates an investigative mode, that is, a second-order observation of the theme, whereby loose links between the stage signs and their interpretants are maintained.[35] Assignment of meaning to the signs is disturbed and delayed. The spectator

---

[35] For an explanation of "dynamic interpretant," see Albert Atkin, "Peirce's Theory of Signs," in *The Stanford Encyclopedia of Philosophy*, ed.

not only sees things for what they are, but also *how* they are what they are on stage. This second-order observation may be formulated as some concrete staging devices: ritualization, appropriation, and simple orchestration. These devices allow us to further connect Hotel Pro Forma's aesthetics with intermediality.

Ritualization means, in Max Weber's sense, that an action is no longer an action. The physical phenomenon, the act, has become detached from its intention, and the intention is postponed. In this way, the action is "meaningless" in that it has opened itself to a wealth of interpretations.[36] As pointed out elsewhere, ritualization is also characteristic of the stylized and elevated acts in Hotel Pro Forma's performances.[37] Dehlholm refers to these as "clenched actions." Unlike the ritual to which the myth offers an interpretation that decides the ritual's meaning, a Hotel Pro Forma performance postpones the meaning-making, in order for the spectator to make her own interpretation. A ritual is not performed, but ritualization is a qualitative characteristic of the staging. It means that the representation is an effect of the spectator's perception. For example, depending on the connections that one makes between the medial components space, body, image, and text in *Why Does Night Come, Mother*, it is possible to interpret the performers as dead souls in a white, weightless limbo. Ritualization in the performance reflects or mediates the spectator's process as the co-creator of meaning.[38]

Appropriation is related to ritualization: it also invites the spectator to realize the meaning. Appropriation means that found and non-manipulated materials, artefacts, people, and media

---

Edward N. Zalta (Summer 2013 Edition), accessed March 10, 2017, https://plato.stanford.edu/archives/sum2013/entries/peirce-semiotics/.

[36] Cf. Max Weber, "The Nature of Social Action," in *Weber: Selections in Translation*, ed. W. G. Runciman (Cambridge: Cambridge University Press, 1991). For a definition of ritualization, see Caroline Humphray and James Laidlaw, *The Archetypical Actions of Ritual: A Theory of Ritual Illustrated by the Jain Rite of Worship* (Oxford: Clarendon Press, 1994), 73.

[37] Cf. Kim Skjoldager-Nielsen, "Performance and Congregation: Experiential Metaphysics in Hotel Pro Forma's Operation: Orfeo and jesus_c_odd_size," *Performance Research* 13:3 (2008): 168–169.

[38] Cf. Nibbelink and Merx's definition of intermediality as realized by the spectator. Nibbelink and Merx, "Presence and Perception," 220.

technologies from the outside world are brought inside the frame of staging and made to play in the production of meaning.[39] A sign's immediate interpretant is thereby transformed through a contextual interpretation. Just as Marcel Duchamp's readymades that turned from industrial product to art object, an inflatable plastic chair may be exalted, or the before-mentioned rower's special skill, rowing, is made into an art form, or the real-life dwarf doubles as one of Snow White's companions. Appropriation is generating material for the performance, and it initiates a conceptual reflection or second-order observation of what art and theatre are, how theatre is a hypermedium that may include all media and art forms, and how these potentially can be redefined. For example, opera becomes visual opera by bringing together the media voice, words, body, image, in a way that highlights visual art properties of the performance. When other media and art forms are creatively appropriated for the theatre hypermedium it is "remediation."

Finally, simple orchestration is a staging device that brings together media and art forms in the production of meaning. Components engage temporarily with one another in the unfolding of the performance's scenarios and structure.[40] With Hotel Pro Forma it is montage of different opposable, incongruent or unexpected elements, cf. formalistic de-familiarization (*ostranenie*) or Eisenstein's montage of attraction. The simple orchestration is the device that directly facilitates intermediality. It is obtained by keeping the media and medialities—image, words, sounds, space, time, body, voice—separate from one another rather than letting them enter into a *Gesamtkunstwerk* in which all components are integrated in a homogeneous expression. In the *manga*-opera *War Sum Up* (2011), whose theme is war, large images in Japanese *manga* cartoon style of modern weapons systems, eyes, hands, explosions, etc., are projected on screens in front of and

---

[39] Cf. appropriation art. For definitions of this art form, see Hal Foster, *The Return of the Real* (Cambridge: MIT Press, 1996), 146; Sherri Irvin, "Appropriation and Authorship in Contemporary Art," *British Journal of Aesthetics* 45 (2005): 123–137.

[40] Cf. Ida Krøgholdt, "At blive performer hos Hotel Pro Forma," in *Hotel Pro Forma*, ed. Erik Exe Christoffersen (Aarhus: Klim, 1998), 165.

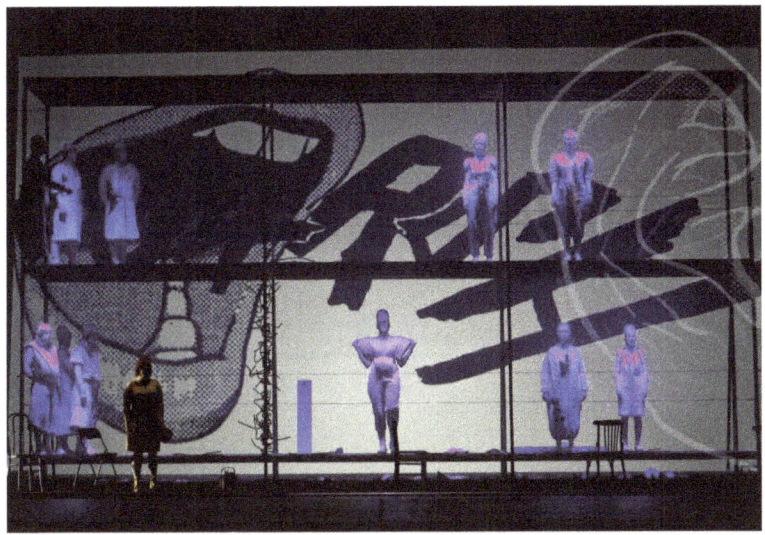

Figure 2. *War Sum Up*. Hotel Pro Forma, 2011. Photo: Roberto Fortuna. Copyright: Hotel Pro Forma. License: CC-BY-NC-ND.

behind the stagnant opera singers posing on a scaffolding or on the proscenium (Figure 2).

The choir on the scaffolding is wearing white costumes, reminiscent of medieval warriors. A solo singer on the proscenium wears a similar but red costume and holds what looks like a spear. Opposite her another woman in a bright yellow modern business dress keeps an eye on what is happening on stage. By keeping the body at rest, focus is shifted to the voices and the song. But sung in Japanese, the words become incomprehensible to most of the audience. However, subtitles displayed on a screen above the stage means that the text's mediality is nonetheless highlighted: it becomes clear that the minimalistic acting on stage and manga images do not directly illustrate the text or vice versa. In fact, the libretto is composed of various texts from the Japanese Noh theatre and merely inspiration for performance's theme. The music, in playback, is stylistically a clash of newly composed symphonic music and what Hotel Pro Forma refers to as chamber- and electro-pop, and it works as affective backdrop for the scenarios. As a meaning-constituting structure, the performance is unfinished.

Rather than exploring a text's dramatic dynamics, subjugating performance elements to the logics of narrative, causality, and psychology, while at the same time reducing the ambiguity of actions and meaning (*hypotaxis*), there is a theatrical dynamics in a Hotel Pro Forma production that correlates media and elements for their equality of signification (*parataxis*). In accordance with Irina Rajewsky, this means "each and every medial form of articulation occurs by right of its own materiality and contributes to the constitution and meaning-making of the entire product in each their individual way. Thus, intermediality is a communicative-semiotic concept based on the combination of at least two medial forms of articulation."[41] At the same time, meaning is contingent, uncertain, or the meaning that the spectator found by making connections between the various media and medialities of the performance could also have been different. Through perception, the spectator realizes a montage of signs and decides on an interpretation of what is seen. This is what simple orchestration as a staging device does to enable intermediality.

Approaching *Today's Cake is a Log*

We will now turn to the analysis of Hotel Pro Forma's exhibition. Before we embarked on our exploration in the first place, we were cued on what to expect and how to relate to the exhibits by Kirsten Dehlholm's presentation on Hotel Pro Forma's website: "*Today's Cake is a Log* is a performance, an exhibition, an attitude."[42] Knowing Hotel Pro Forma's aesthetic strategy, these keywords reinforced our expectations: first, that the exhibition design would emphasize its performative feature—it even has the subtitle "a performative exhibition"; second, that it would mean the realization and affirmation of a certain attitude. What else could this attitude be than an assimilation of Hotel Pro Forma's

---

[41] Irina O. Rajewsky, "Intermediality, Intertextuality, and Remediation: A Literary Perspective on Intermediality," *Intermédialités: Historie et théorie des arts, des lettres et des techniques* 6 (2005): 10.

[42] Hotel Pro Forma, "Today's Cake is a Log," accessed 16 March 2017, http://www.hotelproforma.dk/projects/todays-cake-is-a-log/.

aesthetic strategy of looking at the world anew? As Dehlholm explains: "*Today's Cake is a Log*, the woman announced as she pushed her catering trolley through the Danish State Railways-train. It struck me how easily a few words can completely alter the meaning of everyday phenomena."[43]

These curatorial notes by Dehlholm inspired us to adopt Mieke Bal's thinking on curatorial work for our analytical approach. Bal's concept "curatorial acts" suggests that the acts or performance of a visitor may to some degree be scripted by the curator's organization or staging of the exhibition, the presentation of objects before the gaze of the visitor asserting its influence on her behavior: "Like speech and the speech acts it generates, vision can be performative and produce acts of vision. Not only does looking have a performative potential, but *showing*, the primary act of curating, is specific in its impact upon exhibition visitors."[44] Bal's curatorial acts remind us of Maaike Bleeker's observation that "[t]he theatre presents a staged version of the [spectator's] performance of perception."[45] We suggest that the notion "performance of perception," with its self-reference and self-reflexivity, could serve to expand curatorial acts to include the whole human sensorial and perceptual apparatus, not merely sight, but also hearing, smelling, touch, proprioception, and kinesthesis, and thereby increase its calibration for the performative exhibition analysis. Obviously the exhibition visitor's situation is different from that of the theatre spectator: whereas the visitor is situated inside the exhibition environment and in close proximity to the artefacts, the spectator is (typically) placed outside (in front of and at distance from) the stage; and whereas the visitor is mobile, the spectator is (typically) seated. Compared to the distanced and fixated position of theatre spectator, the exhibition visitor's relative freedom to move about in space and spend time on the various exhibits might heighten her awareness of perception as *performance*, through the ways she navigates the environment, orients herself and relates

---

[43] Hotel Pro Forma, "Today's Cake is a Log," accessed 16 March 2017, http://www.hotelproforma.dk/projects/todays-cake-is-a-log/.
[44] Bal, "Curatorial Acts," 179.
[45] Bleeker, "Corporeal Literacy," 38.

to artefacts, and how she negotiates their different medialities and materialities. Thus, the visitor's performance of perception becomes conspicuous through its structurally related effects. We recall Bleeker's second concept "performance of performativity": "how perception actually produces what appears as the object of our perception."[46]

Our analytical approach is auto-ethnographical in the sense that we base it on our own experience of the exhibition's medialities and materialities. We want to understand the experiential potentiality of the exhibition as it is concretely created through its curation or staging. To paraphrase Nibbelink and Merx, we attempt to locate the intermedial both in the body and in the performance by observing ourselves through perceptual as well as a cognitive awareness.[47] Instead of being spectators watching performers on the intermedial theatre stage, we enter the hypermedial space of the exhibition to become what Kattenbelt called "the player of the different media acting in the empty spaces between the media."[48]

Seeing photographs from the exhibition on the website before our visit, our attention was caught by the incorporation of the different media; video, text, props, set design, installation, as well as performers (image, body, voice) who originate in or refer to the past performances. They appeared to become remediated through the exhibition: a new intermedial feature. This prospect prompted us to formulate a series of analytical questions. How are the media redefined by their new setting? What kind of experiential potential is created by the way these objects are presented and by their different medialities and materialities? How is one addressed by the objects? How may one inspect them? What actions and associations do they prompt? To which extent does prior knowledge about Hotel Pro Forma affect the experience? And finally, does the exhibition succeed in transferring the aesthetic strategy of Hotel Pro Forma?

---

[46] Bleeker, "Corporeal Literacy," 38.
[47] Bleeker, "Corporeal Literacy," 38.
[48] Kattenbelt, "Intermediality in Theatre and Performance," 23.

Performing the Exhibition[49]

At the foot of the staircase to the exhibition halls we pass the wardrobe (Figure 3). We are not invited to leave our coats there, the rag is already full of clothes: shiny, colourful, and metallic— very eye-catching. At closer look, it turns out that the suits are made of wrapping materials, empty candy and sugar packaging with Japanese and Danish characters and logos. This brings to mind the familiarity of everyday objects (suits) but with an unexpected twist (the material they are made of). This is a remediation in the sense Bolter and Grusin suggest, as "that which remediates [...] appropriates the techniques, forms, and social significance of other media to rival or refashion them in the name of the real."[50] In a sense, we are faced with a double remediation that changes the social significance of media: first, the wrapping materials are removed from their social context and redefined in the artistic context of the original performance, reappearing as suits; second, the costumes are removed from the theatre stage to reappear in the performative exhibition. Only *en passant* we notice the discreet text plaque that let us know that Annette Meyer designed the suits for the performance *Monkey Business Class* (1996), suggesting that this information is of lesser importance. Significant, however, are the artefacts in their extraordinary materiality and the perceptual and cognitive engagement they offer. Accessible as the suits are, we are tempted to try them on, but museum etiquette kept us from doing so. Yet, already through the proximity of the artefacts and our self-observation we were implemented as performers in the exhibition.

On the first floor our awareness of being performers is increased as we enter the first exhibition room and are greeted by our own reflections (Figure 4). A large dressing mirror is placed in front of the entrance. On a chair next to the mirror sits a lady, knitting. At first, it is difficult to tell if she is just a museum custodian or

---

[49] Another version of the analysis appeared in Kim Skjoldager-Nielsen and Daria Kubiak, "Hotel Pro Forma. Dagens kage er en træstamme," review of the exhibition, *Peripeti* 25 (2016).
[50] Bolter and Grusin, *Remediation*, 65.

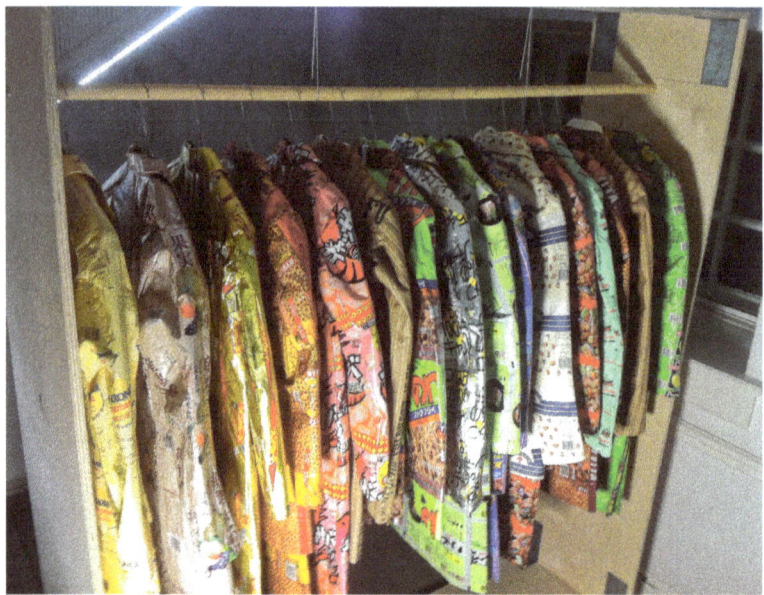

Figure 3. Clothes rag, *Today's Cake is a Log*. Hotel Pro Forma, 2015. Photo: Daria Skjoldager-Nielsen. Copyright: Hotel Pro Forma. License: CC-BY-NC-ND.

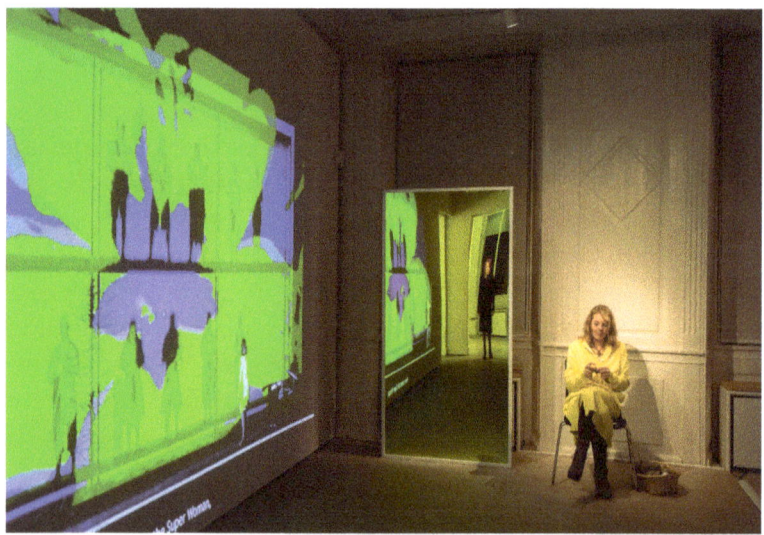

Figure 4. Mirror room, *Today's Cake is a Log*. Hotel Pro Forma, 2015. Photo: Torben Eskerud. Copyright: Hotel Pro Forma. License: CC-BY-NC-ND.

if Dehlholm has placed her there as a performer. She notices our and other visitors' presence in the room. She greets us with a smile and goes back to knitting. Her bright yellow business dress, however, is almost too extraordinary for a museum custodian, and we assume that she is a performer. She sits in between two large screens covering opposite walls. On the screens we see video images of medieval warrior-like figures standing on scaffolding with Japanese *manga*-style backdrops. The small plaque on the wall explains that the video presents the opera *War Sum Up* (2011). There is no sound. To hear what turns out to be opera music and singing, you have to take a seat on the benches in the center of the room and put on headphones. Here the performance's intermediality is subtly mirrored in the exhibit's use of technology initially keeping image, voice, music, and body apart, its simple orchestration only possible for the visitor to realize by sitting down and putting on the headset. The visitor is faced with the choice to literally become the player acting in the empty spaces between media. If she chooses to do so, in a sense, she momentarily reacquires the theatre spectator's position. If she dwells and looks carefully enough, she may notice that the lady sitting on the proscenium in the video is knitting and wearing the exact same yellow dress as the lady in the chair in the exhibition room. The doubling of the lady in the video makes the artwork reach across time and space. The knitting lady is both part of the performance on the screens and the observer of visitors' performance. The visitor is at the same time observing and being observed, thus reaffirmed as a co-performer of the exhibition.

In the next room large white paper rolls of printed text are hanging from the ceiling all-along the wall (Figure 5). The texts are from the performances and are arranged into collages. Through the materiality of the rolls, the words used by Hotel Pro Forma are made tangible (we may actually manipulate the rolls and read more of the texts) and give the impression of a theatre that is not only visual. In a sense, the rolls of text seem to cascade off the wall as a waterfall of words that flows into the room. What is more, you may manipulate the paper and create folds by the way it settles onto the floor. Thereby we play with the texts and make different parts of text come together in the formation of

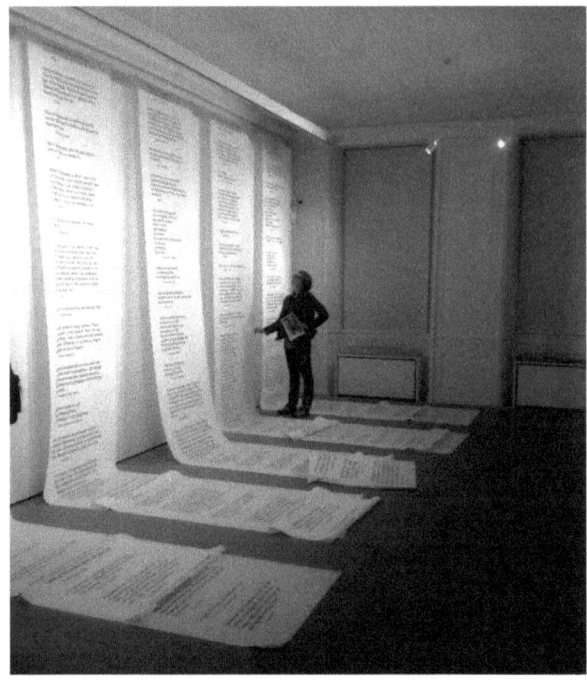

Figure 5. Text collages, *Today's Cake is a Log*. Hotel Pro Forma, 2015. Photo: Kim Skjoldager-Nielsen. Copyright: Hotel Pro Forma. License: CC-BY-NC-ND.

new texts. Our playful displacement of the texts in space enacts once again the staging device of simple orchestration, while at the same time, the text medium of the performances is remediated as a social artefact to engage the visitors.

Another installation in the same room consists of set design that extends through the doorway into the next room. A total overview is impossible. Seen from its end, the series of illuminated Plexiglas plates with coloured motifs seem to depict a continuous landscape. In order to see them all, one has to walk along the installation. If one does that, one will find that the motifs do not constitute one large continuous image, but are composed of individual parts not really matching each other. The installation plays with vision and perspective. It is not important that the set design was used in *I Only Appear to be Dead* (2005) or how it was used there; remediated by the exhibition space, it stages a playing with

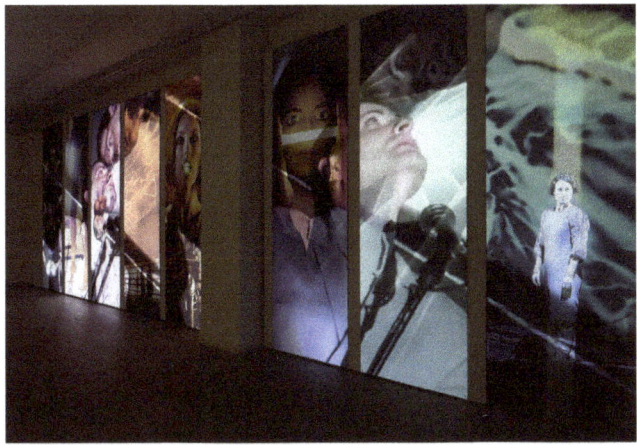

Figure 6. Photo/video montage, *Today's Cake is a Log*. Hotel Pro Forma, 2015. Photo: Torben Eskerud. Copyright: Hotel Pro Forma. License: CC-BY-NC-ND.

the point of view. The contingency of perspective that Hotel Pro Forma explores is hinted at through the embodied perspective of the visitor and her possibility to shift it.

Contingency as an effect is further demonstrated by means of simple orchestration in another installation, which uses images from different performances. Videos are projected onto still photographs in a way that creates unforeseen and unexpected montages of performances and actors (Figure 6). Faces and bodies are distorted and the installation creates deformed or temporal overlapping between different performances. To experience and appreciate this intermediality, you have to watch it for quite a while, pointing to Hotel Pro Forma's investigations of time as an epistemological basic category.

The artefacts activate us through their mediality, materiality, and placement; there are no descriptions of the exhibits and no explanations are provided, as would usually be the case in a museum. We have to behave like explorers, driven by curiosity in order to experience and attribute meaning to the objects—not unlike the engaged spectator in the theatre, except for our mobility. One installation is almost hidden and reveals itself only to the one who delves into the exhibition (Figure 7). Plexiglas covers

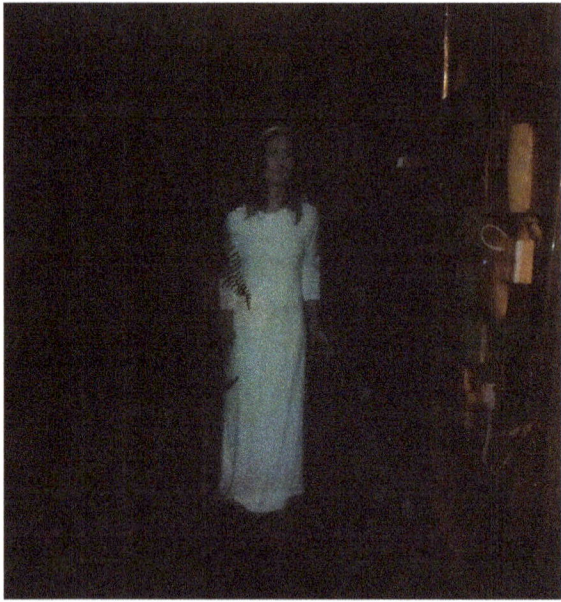

Figure 7. The ghost, *Today's Cake is a Log*. Hotel Pro Forma, 2015. Photo: Daria Skjoldager-Nielsen. Copyright: Hotel Pro Forma. License: CC-BY-NC-ND.

the opening of a narrow crevice in the wall. One of the inside walls is covered by green plants and ferns and the other one by humming machines; medialities of life and lifelessness confronting each other. At first this contrast grabs the attention, but the main clue of the installation is yet to be revealed. A thin woman dressed in white is hidden deep in that space. She stares at us and stretches her hands as if she wanted to be held or rescued from this strange space. She is scarily beautiful and seems very real. Only a close look reveals that she is in fact a video projection on a loose canvas waving in a slight breeze. She is a ghost, caught between life and death. The display has no plaque referring to any performance; but the experience it creates is reminiscent of Hotel Pro Forma's work with visual illusion, whether produced by technology or mere perspective (as in the 1989 *Why Does Night Come, Mother*).

While climbing the stairs to the next floor a voice captures our attention. When we get there we see a young woman with loose,

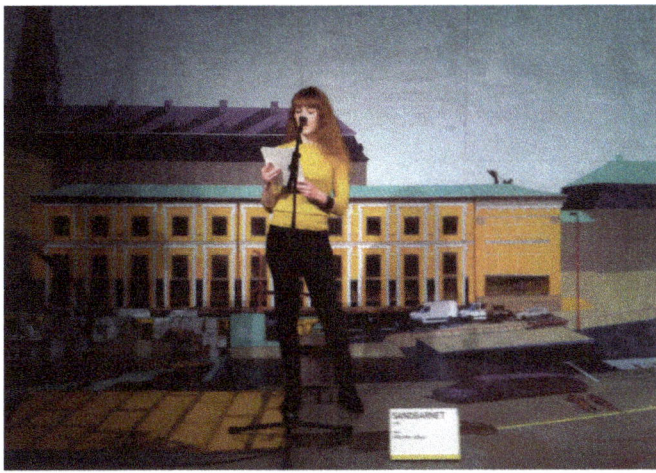

Figure 8. Readhead reader, *Today's Cake is a Log*. Hotel Pro Forma, 2015. Photo: Daria Skjoldager-Nielsen. Copyright: Hotel Pro Forma. License: CC-BY-NC-ND.

flaming red hair (Figure 8). She stands by a microphone against a painted background depicting the cityscape outside, behind the very same wall: the parliament building Christiansborg, the traffic in the street, and the ongoing metro construction. The painting covers the entire wall and part of the floor, suggesting that she belongs to the other world, the world of the artworks. She makes eye contact with us but, busy reading a text, she does not greet us. A sign stands on the floor with the title "The Sand Child / 2007 / Text / Tahar Ben Jelloun" indicating the performance whose text she is reading and the author of that text. She is sharing the story with the listener, but at the same time she is observing the audience sitting and standing in front of her. Dressed in her private clothes, she could be just anyone from the audience, as if anyone could take her place. Only those who know Hotel Pro Forma's works very well will recognize her as one of their performers, but again that is of no real importance. The sense that any of the visitors could replace her is important, as it points to appropriation as a staging device applied to the performers, who often retain an authenticity whether it is through their appearance, skill, or known history.

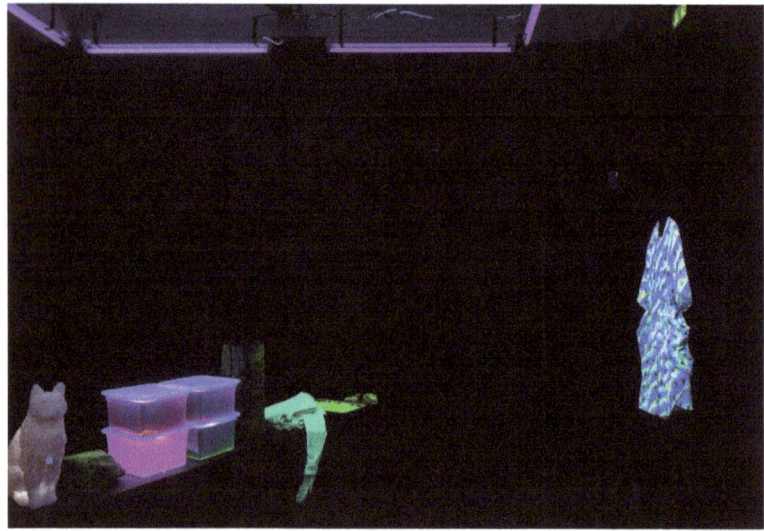

Figure 9. UV room, *Today's Cake is a Log*. Hotel Pro Forma, 2015. Photo: Torben Eskerud. Copyright: Hotel Pro Forma. License: CC-BY-NC-ND.

The final room presents a collection of props from the performance *The One Who Whispers* (2012) (Figure 9). On a table stand, among other things, are semi-transparent plastic boxes, like the ones used at home for storage. They are filled with colourful jelly. Next to them there are some kitschy plastic cats that could have been brought home as souvenirs or given away as hate gifts. They are ordinary found objects, appropriated for the performance/exhibition. A blue-and-green striped dress hangs on the wall, spread out like a fan. Suddenly the light in the room changes to UV light. Everything is transformed: the dress, the cats, and the boxes. They glow as if lit with a fire from within. It works as a kind of remediation using light: the artefacts are the exact same ones but now seen through the medium of UV. The glow affects the visitor in a strange way. Our sensation of the objects is heightened. It is—as the Danish philosopher Dorthe Jørgensen would say—as if one is out of oneself (Greek *ek-stasis*) to truly see the objects, liberated from their everyday intentionality, as if they were ritualized. The objects and the visitor simply co-exist in this moment without any other concern. It is a liberating moment that can bring joy. It is an experience of beauty in that it has no other purpose and carries a value of its own.[51] This part of the exhibition may be recognized as an extract of Hotel Pro Forma's performative aesthetics: to stage the visitor's sensation not merely to titillate but to stimulate reflection on what it means to be in this world—to look at the world anew. A world where nature, the people, the arts, everything, much too often becomes subject to some agenda rather than left to be valued by what they are in themselves.

Conclusion

True to her own project, Kirsten Dehlholm did not celebrate Hotel Pro Forma's thirty years by creating a retrospective with documentation of works ordered in accordance with their place in the company's history. Rather, she created an *insight* into— or metaphorically in line with the title: a *cross-section* of—Hotel Pro Forma's aesthetics in the form of a brand-new exhibition, distributed across, altogether, eight rooms on two floors: a work of works, or rather, a remediation for the exhibition hypermedium of artefacts, texts, fragments of images, video, and audio selected from the performances as well as new staging in the form of live performance readings. In this sense of hypermediacy, by bringing together animate and inanimate material in one and the same space, the exhibition repeats theatre's all-inclusiveness towards other art forms and media defined by Kattenbelt. This hypermediacy is further foregrounded as the visitors enter into the perceptual interplay with both exhibits and the present performers, creating the visitors' conspicuous self-awareness of becoming performers themselves. Navigating through different rooms and exhibits and negotiating their presentation of media and materialities, the visitors create their own narratives and understanding of Hotel Pro Forma's intermedial aesthetics. This aesthetics is transferred from the stage to the exhibition, and realised by the visitor

---

[51] Dorthe Jørgensen, *Skønhed: En engel gik forbi* (Aarhus: Aarhus Universitetsforlag, 2006), 7.

as performer, physically acting the in-between of media and realising the intermediality of the exhibition.

We refer to remediation as a creative strategy as we see the exhibition appropriating "techniques, forms, and social significance of other media to refashion them in the name of the real."[52] Here the aim of the remediation is to transfer the intermedial experience of Hotel Pro Forma's aesthetic strategy, as it was produced in the performances, to the exhibition, and through this experiential paradigm, in a very real sense, transform the theatre spectator into a performer of the exhibition. This is achieved to the extent the visitor's intermedial experience is created through surprises and confusions, the deconstruction of perceptual expectations, as Nibbelink and Merx describe it—the intent here seemingly being the achievement of resensibilization through second-order observation, or awareness of perception.

Only then does it make sense that the exhibition offered no explanations, but left one to one's own senses. No system by which to navigate was presented. The text plaques next to exhibits referred only to title and production year of the performance. The chronology and history were not established and therefore of no importance. Instead our attention was subtly directed to the experiential potential of artefacts/media in their interplay with space and visitor. This seemed the only curatorial concern: to let the visitor engage and reflect on her own, the theme, Hotel Pro Forma's aesthetic strategy, only hinted at by the title *Today's Cake is a Log* and Dehlholm's curatorial notes.

This intention might not have occurred to every visitor. However, what was required was exploration and play with the possibilities offered by medialities and materialities of the exhibits, that is, to become the performer of perception as suggested by the exhibition. Only if one was willing to do so could the experiential transferal, the effect or performativity of perception, succeed.

---

[52] Bolter and Grusin, *Remediation*, 65.

References

Bal, Mieke. "Curatorial Acts." *Journal of Curatorial Studies*, vol. 1, no. 2, (2012): 179–192.

Bay-Cheng, Sarah, Chiel Kattenbelt, Andy Lavender, and Robin Nelson, eds. *Mapping Intermediality in Performance*. Amsterdam: Amsterdam University Press, 2010.

Bolter, Jay David, and Richard Grusin, *Remediation: Understanding New Media*. Cambridge: MIT Press, 1999.

Chapple, Freda, and Chiel Kattenbelt, eds. *Intermediality in Theatre and Performance*. Amsterdam and New York: Rodopi, 2006.

Christoffersen, Erik Exe. "Den u-selvfølgelige sansning." In *Skønhedens Hotel: Hotel Pro Forma: Et laboratorium for scenekunst*, edited by Erik Exe Christoffersen and Kathrine Winkelhorn, 19–45. Aarhus: Aarhus Universitetsforlag, 2015.

Christoffersen, Erik Exe, and Kathrine Winkelhorn, eds. *Skønhedens Hotel: Hotel Pro Forma: Et laboratorium for scenekunst*. Aarhus: Aarhus Universitetforlag, 2015.

Crawford, Lawrence. "Viktor Shklovskij: Différance in Defamiliarization." *Comparative Literature* 36 (1984): 209–219.

Foster, Hal. *The Return of the Real*. Cambridge: MIT Press, 1996.

Humphray, Caroline, and James Laidlaw. *The Archetypical Actions of Ritual: A Theory of Ritual Illustrated by the Jain Rite of Worship*. Oxford: Clarendon Press, 1994.

Ingemann, Bruno, "Den besøgende: Social identitet, læring og oplevelse – en metodisk diskussion." In *Udstillinger mellem focus & flimmer*, edited by Elisabeth Bodin and Johanna Lassenius, 85–109. Copenhagen: Multivers, 2006.

Irvin, Sherri. "Appropriation and Authorship in Contemporary Art." *British Journal of Aesthetics* 45 (2005): 123–137.

Jørgensen, Dorthe. *Skønhed: En engel gik forbi*. Aarhus: Aarhus Universitetsforlag, 2006.

Kattenbelt, Chiel. "Intermediality in Theatre and Performance: Definitions, Perceptions and Medial Relationships." *Culture, Language and Representation*, vol. VI (2008): 19–29.

Kattenbelt, Chiel. "Theatre as the Art of the Performer and the Stage of Intermediality." In *Intermediality in Theatre and Performance*, edited by Freda Chapple and Chiel Kattenbelt, 29–40. Amsterdam and New York: Rodopi, 2006.

Krøgholdt, Ida. "At blive performer hos Hotel Pro Forma." In *Hotel Pro Forma*, edited by Erik Exe Christoffersen, 153–168. Aarhus: Klim, 1998.

Lehmann, Hans-Thies. *Postdramatic Theatre*. Translated by Karen Jürs-Munby. London and New York: Routledge, 2006.

Nibbelink, Lisbeth Groot, and Sigrid Merx. "Presence and Perception: Analysing Intermediality in Performance." In *Mapping Intermediality in Performance*, edited by Sarah Bay-Cheng, Chiel Kattenbelt, Andy Lavender, and Robin Nelson, 218–229. Amsterdam: Amsterdam University Press, 2010.

Noë, Alva. *Action in Perception*. Cambridge: MIT Press, 2004.

Qvortrup, Lars. "Hotel Pro Forma: Laboratorium for æstetiske undersøgelser." *Peripeti* 25 (2016): 84–98.

Rajewsky, Irina O. "Intermediality, Intertextuality, and Remediation: A Literary Perspective on Intermediality." *Intermédialités: Historie et théorie des arts, des lettres et des techniques* 6 (2005): 43–64.

Schechner, Richard. "Performance Studies: The Broad Spectrum Approach." In *The Performance Studies Reader*, edited by Henry Bial, 7–9. New York: Routledge, 2004.

Skjoldager-Nielsen, Kim. "Performance and Congregation: Experiential Metaphysics in Hotel Pro Forma's Operation: Orfeo and jesus_c_odd_size." *Performance Research* 13:3 (2008): 163–175.

Skjoldager-Nielsen, Kim, and Daria Kubiak. "Hotel Pro Forma: Dagens kage er en træstamme." *Peripeti* 25 (2016): 142–146.

Theil, Per, Kirsten Dehlholm, and Lars Qvortrup. *Hotel Pro Forma: The Double Staging: Space and Performance*. Copenhagen: Arkitektens Forlag, 2003.

Wagner, Meike. "Of other Bodies: The Intermedial Gaze in Theatre." In *Intermediality in Theatre and Performance*, edited by Freda Chapple and Chiel Kattenbelt, 125–136. Amsterdam and New York: Rodopi, 2006.

Weber, Max. "The Nature of Social Action." In *Weber: Selections in Translation*, edited by W. G. Runciman, 7–32. Cambridge: Cambridge University Press, 1991.

Winkelhorn, Katherine. "Et blik ind i Hotel Pro Formas kunstneriske praksis." In *Skønhedens Hotel: Hotel Pro Forma: Et laboratorium for scenekunst*, edited by Erik Exe Christoffersen and Kathrine Winkelhorn, 213–225. Aarhus: Aarhus Universitetsforlag, 2015.

Websites

The Stanford Encyclopedia of Philosophy. "Peirce's Theory of Signs." Accessed March 10, 2017. https: //plato.stanford.edu/archives/sum2013/entries/peirce-semiotics/.

Victoria & Albert Museum. "Curtain Up: Celebrating 40 Years of Theatre in London and New York." Accessed April 12, 2017. https://www.vam.ac.uk/exhibitions/curtain-up-celebrating-40-years-of-theatre-in-london-and-new-york.

Peripeti. "Remediering mellem film og teater – en kreativ strategi." Accessed April 12, 2017. http://www.peripeti.dk/2009/06/03/265/.

Hotel Pro Forma. "Today's Cake is a Log." Accessed March 16, 2017. http://www.hotelproforma.dk/projects/todays-cake-is-a-log/.

PART TWO: NETWORKS

Panoramic Visions: Sven Hedin in "Transhimalaya" 1906–1909

Staffan Bergwik

Abstract

This chapter studies the panoramic visions created by Swedish geographer Sven Hedin on a journey to Tibet between 1906 and 1909. It reads Hedin's geographic images and texts through a broader nineteenth-century history of the panorama and indicates how his panoramic visions were part of a broader media culture of the century. Furthermore, the chapter claims that Hedin's geographic images and texts contributed to the shaping of a modern regime of vision where the world in overview was a desirable object. Using intermediality as a method, I display how these visions emerged through a network of media formats, including photographs, hand-drawn panoramas, water-colour sketches, and texts. The article argues that these formats were combined through "descriptive layering." They shared the panorama as a motif, yet they were also layered in a material sense: attached to, and interlaced with, each other. I argue that descriptive layering was a way of handling the vexed relationship between overview and detail, and it allowed the panoramic representations to move between knowledge-based and aesthetic experiences.

In a documentary broadcasted on Swedish television in 1971, historians Hans Villius and Olle Häger described the Swedish geographer Sven Hedin (1865–1952) as "a voice from the past"; a person marked by an era of European imperialism, by a world of "Garibaldi, Bismarck, and Kipling. He never grew out of that

---

How to cite this book chapter:
Bergwik, Staffan. "Panoramic Visions: Sven Hedin in 'Transhimalaya' 1906–1909." In *The Power of the In-Between: Intermediality as a Tool for Aesthetic Analysis and Critical Reflection*, edited by Sonya Petersson, Christer Johansson, Magdalena Holdar, and Sara Callahan, 185–212. Stockholm: Stockholm University Press, 2018. DOI: https://doi.org/10.16993/baq.h. License: CC-BY.

world, even though he lived into our own time."[1] Hedin completed four journeys between 1893 and 1935, traveling in the deserts of inner Asia and the highlands of Tibet. He described the wandering lake Lop-Nor, parts of Himalaya, and the sources of the rivers Brahmaputra and Indus. Books written by the Swede are filled with idealized accounts of journeys and his own manly bravery. Furthermore, Hedin is a notorious character in Swedish history, infamous for his profound conservatism, his Nazi sympathies, and his personal friendship with Adolf Hitler.

His biography, political sensibilities and tales of heroism are well documented. Instead, I explore the *panoramic visions* that Hedin produced in images and texts while traveling in Himalaya between 1906 and 1909. He repeated a European tradition going back to the 1700s, where expeditions were opportunities for data collection and cultural performances. Previous studies of this tradition, and of turn-of-the-twentieth-century geography, have offered fine-grained analyses of how the European discoverer was idealized and of how geography was institutionalized as a scientific discipline.[2] My aim is to contribute to a media history of geography by tying the discipline to the new "modes of perception, sensations and somatic engagement with the world" which widespread nineteenth-century media like photography, telegraphy, the

---

[1] Hans Villius and Olle Häger, "En röst ur det förgångna," svtplay.se, accessed February 8, 2018, https://www.oppetarkiv.se/video/1363736. The quote is translated from Swedish by the author. This study is part of a larger research project financed by Riksbankens jubileumsfond (The Swedish Foundation for Humanities and Social Science). I am indebted to Fredrik Krohn Andersson, Peter Gillgren, Elina Druker, and the editors for valuable comments.

[2] Vanessa Heggie, "Why Isn't Exploration a Science," *Isis* 105, no. 2 (2014); David Livingstone, *The Geographical Tradition: Episodes in the History of a Contested Enterprise* (Oxford: Blackwell, 1992); Simon Naylor and James R. Ryan, "Exploration and the Twentieth Century," in *New Spaces of Exploration: Geographies of Discovery in the Twentieth Century*, ed. Simon Naylor and James R. Ryan (London: Tauris, 2010), 1–22; Marie-Claire Robic, "Geography," in *The Cambridge History of Science: The Modern Social Sciences*, ed. Theodore M. Porter (Cambridge: Cambridge University Press, 2003), 379–390.

telephone, and motion picture produced.[3] More important in this case, the century saw the emergence of "overview media" aimed at seeing the whole world in a bird's eye view. Dioramas, ballooning, and world exhibitions augmented experiences and were considered productive to understand nature and society.[4]

An important example of overview media was the panorama. It became a mass medium in nineteenth-century visual culture and profoundly altered modes of seeing.[5] Scholars like Bernard Comment, Stephan Oetterman, and Erkki Huhtamo have indicated how artists known as "panoramists" carried out meticulous surveys of landscapes, creating "encyclopaedic" documentation.[6] Certainly, as noted by Charlotte Bigg, panoramic descriptions were related to scientific discourse: the panorama was discussed as a tool for research in physical geography throughout the nineteenth century. It opened for realistic renditions, and panorama painting was a "continuation of the topographer's activity."[7]

Yet, panorama historians have not systematically studied how geographers utilized, and contributed to, the panorama as a

[3] Alison Griffiths, "Sensory Media: The World Without and the World Within," in *A Cultural History of the Senses: In the Age of Empire*, ed. Constance Classen (London: Bloomsbury Academic, 2014), 211–234, 211.

[4] Anders Ekström, "Seeing from Above: A Particular History of the General Observer," *Nineteenth-Century Contexts* 31, no. 3 (2009); Charlotte Bigg, "The Panorama, or la Nature a Coup d'Oeil," in *Observing Nature – Representing Experience: The Osmotic Dynamics of Romanticism 1800–1850*, ed. Erna Fiorentini (Berlin: Reimer, 2007), 73–95.

[5] Bernard Comment, *The Panorama* (London: Reaktion, 1999); Stephan Oettermann, *The Panorama: History of a Mass Medium* (New York: Zone Books, 1997); Erkki Huhtamo, *Illusions in Motion: Media Archeology of the Moving Panorama and Related Spectacles* (Cambridge: MIT Press, 2013).

[6] Comment, *The Panorama*, 85–86.

[7] Bigg, "The Panorama, or la Nature a Coup d'Oeil," 74–75. Quote on p. 90. Marie-Clarie Robic has suggested the panorama as one of the ways in which geographers tried to handle the limitations of ground-level photography, although Robic instead focuses on aerial photography: Marie-Claire Robic, "From the Sky to the Ground: The Aerial View and the Ideal of *Vue Raisonée* in Geography during the 1920s," in *Seeing From Above: The Aerial View in Visual Culture*, ed. Mark Dorrian and Frédéric Pousin (London and New York: I. B. Tauris, 2013), 163–187, 164.

knowledge-making practice around 1900. In combining the history of geography with the history of overview media, I want to indicate how Hedin's panoramic representations formed a basis for geographical knowledge making and as an effect, how geography added to the emergence of a "modern and heterogeneous regime of vision."[8] According to Marie-Claire Robic, geographers' main concern was knowing how to look, and through maps and images they communicated their gaze to a larger public.[9] Geographers like Sven Hedin contributed to ongoing "perceptual recalibrations" of the era through technologies of display and projection. There was a keen interest in exploration, and Hedin's books and articles were bestsellers, reaching millions of people. His panoramic visions invited audiences that never traveled to Asia to envision large landscapes and experience remote and inaccessible environs.

The bulk of this chapter will be devoted to indicating how Sven Hedin's panoramic visions emerged through exchanges between media formats—including photography, hand-drawn panoramas, watercolour-sketches, texts, and books—which reinforced each other. My method to unpack the construction and function of panoramic visions is intermediality, which is a concept that allows an understanding of how media technologies strengthen and "remediate" each other.[10] To specify the idea of intermediality, I argue that the formats Hedin utilized formed *descriptive layering*. According to Maria Antonella Pelizzari, descriptive layering indicates how words and images "echo and intensify each other."[11] Hedin's panoramic visions emerged through a network of visual

---

[8] Kathryn Yusoff, "Configuring the Field: Photography in Early Twentieth-century Antarctic Exploration," in *New Spaces of Exploration: Geographies of Discovery in the Twentieth Century*, ed. James R. Ryan and Simon Naylor (London: I. B. Tauris, 2010), 52–77, 56.

[9] Robic, "From the Sky to the Ground," 164–165.

[10] Jay David Bolter and Richard Grusin, *Remediation: Understanding New Media* (Cambridge: MIT Press, 1999); David Thorburn and Henry Jenkins, "Introduction: Toward an Aesthetic of Transition," in *Rethinking Media Change: The Aesthetic of Transition*, eds. David Thorburn and Henry Jenkins (Cambridge: MIT Press, 2003), 1–16.

[11] Maria Antonella Pelizzari, "Retracing the Outlines of Rome: Intertextuality and Imaginative Geographies in Nineteenth-century Photographs," in *Picturing Place: Photography and the Geographical Imagination*, eds. Joan M.

and textual media formats that enhanced and complemented each other. Of particular importance is how traffic between the formats enabled Hedin to determine the meaning of panoramic visions and allow that meaning to vary in the right ways.

Sven Hedin's third expedition took place between 1906 and 1909. He had the ambition to map a section of Himalaya that had not yet been described on European maps. Crossing the mountain range a handful of times, he dubbed the area "Transhimalya." The results from the journey were presented in two major works. The first was *Southern Tibet: Discoveries in Former Times Compared with My Own Researches in 1906–1908*, published in twelve volumes covering the geography, orography, geology, and hydrography of the area as well as the work of previous travelers. A massive work summing up Hedin's results, the volumes contained 552 sketched panoramas, which were collected in a separate volume entitled *Southern Tibet: Atlas of Tibetan Panoramas*. Second, the expedition was presented in the three-volume work *Transhimalaya: Discoveries and Adventures in Tibet*. The volumes were prepared and published once back in Sweden, and on the cover sheet Hedin stated that they contained "544 illustrations from photographs, watercolour-sketches, and drawings by the author."[12] In *Southern Tibet* and *Transhimalaya*, Hedin published visual depictions of the Tibetan landscape as well as intermittently discussing the status and function of panoramic outlooks. The two works share the importance of the panorama, yet they also differ in narrative style. *Southern Tibet* envisions a scholarly audience through its detailed reports of data about geographical features, and Hedin himself described it as "the scientific report" of his journey.[13] *Transhimalaya* is written with a broader audience in mind; the narrative about adventures is central, yet stories of secluded monks, harsh weather, and wild yaks are repeatedly interspersed with visual and textual panoramas.

Schwartz and James R. Ryan (London and New York: I. B. Tauris, 2003), 55–73, 57.

[12] Sven Hedin, *Transhimalaya: Discoveries and Adventures in Tibet*, 3 vols., vol. 2 (New Delhi: Asian Educational Services, 1999 [1909]), cover sheet.

[13] Hedin, *Transhimalaya*, 101.

The Panoramic Genre, Geography, and Imperialism

Both the word "panorama" and the medium it denoted were invented at the turn of the nineteenth century. Originally, it was a "form of landscape painting" which "reproduced a 360-degree view" and was placed in a rotunda.[14] Panoramas became a mass medium in Europe from 1800, with a second boom in the late 1800s. The medium attracted millions of spectators and put the onlooker in places which differed radically from everyday experiences, thus contributing to collective dreams of the distant. The panorama was gradually replaced by new mass media in the late nineteenth century, including magazines and cinema.[15] When Sven Hedin went to Tibet, the medium experienced, in Bernhard Comment's words, "the last gasp of a dying man."[16]

The differences between the panorama as a mass medium and Hedin's panoramic visions should be noted. The images of the Swedish explorer were not displayed in specially built rotundas, nor constructed by specialized artists. Nevertheless, the word "panorama" was transformed during the nineteenth century into a broader concept gesturing at the capacity to display landscapes as a whole. The meaning of the word became metaphorical and "the panoramic view" turned into "a mode of seeing" which denoted overview, a circular vista produced from an elevated point, or survey of a field of knowledge.[17] Indeed, following Erkki Huhtamo, panoramas should be understood beyond a history of the stationary medium; they were an early manifestation of a broader media culture, including a whole landscape of mass spectacle.[18] Hedin's panoramic visions were part of this "panoramic genre": designed in a horizontal, oblong format and with the desire to create an all-encompassing view.[19] Indeed, they were part of the long history

---

[14] Comment, *The Panorama*, 7; Oettermann, *The Panorama*, 5–6.
[15] Comment, *The Panorama*, 66–67, 116–117; Oettermann, *The Panorama*, 4–14; Huhtamo, *Illusions in Motion*, 1–5.
[16] Comment, *The Panorama*, 75.
[17] Oettermann, *The Panorama*, 7, 22.
[18] Huhtamo, *Illusions in Motion*, 5–10.
[19] Comment, *The Panorama*, 83.

of panoramas instructing the audience to see nature in a specific way and became a "pattern for organizing visual experience."[20]

Links between geography and the panoramic genre cannot be fully understood without considering the context of imperialism. Europeans produced new forms of Western power as they mapped areas in Africa, Asia, and the Arctic. Existing research has acknowledged how geography became the "queen of all imperial sciences."[21] A crucial aspect of European imperialism was viewing the world as a unit and the earth as a surface to be mapped and controlled. The panorama furthered colonial gazes aimed at taking possession of landscapes.[22]

Sven Hedin fit in this historical schema, and he represented a world of imperialistic efforts. The individual Western explorer traveling by himself in an unmapped territory with a team of local assistants—presenting his findings in adventure books—was partly outdated even in Hedin's own lifetime. In fact, the Swede himself acknowledged the transition: "The four final decades of the nineteenth century may with justice be called the last phase of the great age of geographical discovery."[23] Nevertheless, he by and large fulfilled the nineteenth-century paradigm of geography and carried an imperialistic world order all the way up to the mountain passes in Tibet. The Swede traveled as a lone European, utilizing local carriers and assistants to form the expedition party with scarce acknowledgment of them as contributors to the scientific results. Filling in the white spots on maps of Himalaya was a paramount driving force for his efforts.[24] Moreover, Hedin picked

---

[20] Oettermann, *The Panorama*, 22.
[21] Michael Heffernan, "Histories of Geography," in *Key Concepts in Geography*, eds. Nicholas Clifford, et al. (London: SAGE, 2009), 3–20: 10. See also Livingstone, *The Geographical Tradition*; Morag Bell, Robin Butlin, and Michael Heffernan, *Geography and Imperialism 1820–1940* (Manchester: Manchester University Press, 1994).
[22] John Zarobell, "Jean-Charles Langlois's Panorama of Algiers (1833) and the Prospective Colonial Landscape," *Art History* 26, no. 5 (2003): 638–668, 640.
[23] Sven Hedin, "The Scientific Results of Dr. Sven Hedin's Last Journey," *The Geographical Journal* 24, no. 5 (1904): 524–545, 524.
[24] Sven Hedin, *My Life as an Explorer* (Washington: National Geographic Adventure Classics, 2003 [1925]), 381, 441.

up the imperialistic tradition to understand the earth as a surface to see at one view, using the technologies of the panoramic genre.

Understanding the Whole Landscape

Sven Hedin described the orography (studies of the topographic relief of mountains) of Tibet and the sources of rivers like Brahamaputra. Panoramic visions were a way to transform massive amounts of data into overviews, or in Hedin's own words "a much clearer idea of the habitus and morphology of the country than any maps or any verbal descriptions could do."[25] Panoramas gave "an idea of the general view," and the distances they sketched were sometimes staggering.[26] Even contours of mountains lying "fully ten days journey" away were occasionally discernible.[27] The effort to understand landscapes as a whole was key in Hedin's geographical endeavors.

His career as a geographer was lined with controversy. Author August Strindberg was one of Hedin's most aggressive critics, and in one of their debates, he claimed that the geographer had merely mapped well-known heaps of sand and rocky knolls.[28] Nevertheless, Strindberg admitted that Hedin's depictions of Tibet allowed an arrangement of details into "a clear vision of the depicted" landscape.[29] The two combatants agreed on this issue, as Hedin himself stated that his drawings and sketches of landscapes "become a series of milestones, giving a vision of the drawn."[30] The ability to see the landscape as a whole was also thought to separate the Western explorer from natives in Tibet. Eric Wennerholm's hagiographic biography of Hedin is telling in the way he distinguishes between the geographer's and the

---

[25] Sven Hedin, *Southern Tibet: Discoveries in Former Times Compared with My Own Researches in 1906–1908*, 9 vols., vol. 4 (Stockholm: Lithographic Institute of the General Staff of the Swedish Army, 1922), 5.
[26] Hedin, *Southern Tibet*, vol. 2, 316.
[27] Hedin, *Transhimalaya*, vol. 3, 35.
[28] Villius and Häger, "En röst ur det förgångna."
[29] Eric Wennerholm, *Sven Hedin: En biografi* (Stockholm, Bonniers, 1978), 184.
[30] Wennerholm, *Sven Hedin*, 184.

Tibetan's perception of the mountains. The "nomads" knew "the narrow valley" where they traveled, yet they lacked "every concept of the scope and structure of the whole land." Indeed, Hedin had "discovered" the country in the sense that he had "measured, mapped, described" the area and "with the right dimensions put it into its larger context."[31] It is not surprising then that Hedin in his description of the mountains claimed that the "Tibetans very seldom give general names for whole ranges."[32]

The ambition to picture a complex mountain landscape in apprehensible overviews had inherent difficulties. From mountain passes at the height of 6,000 meters, Hedin described the country as "a confusion of hills and ridges."[33] To get "a clear idea of the general orographic arrangement" was sometimes difficult or "impossible."[34] All the explorer could see from the pass Shib-La was a "labyrinth of ridges."[35] At several points, the presence of "high mountains" obstructed a "distant view."[36] Moreover, the relationship between details and overview was vexed: the latter potentially eradicating the former. Moving from masses of detailed observations to coherent images threatened to obliterate important data. The "near-far paradigm" had marked nineteenth-century discussions about panoramic representations, indicating the relationship between a distant image enabling landscape to emerge in its totality and a close-up image that left nothing out but restricted itself to fragments.[37] Hopes were tied to the panorama to transcend this potential contradiction, for example, when naturalists portrayed the Alps and wanted to capture both an all-encompassing view and pay attention to detail.[38] Hedin used photographs, hand-drawn panoramas, watercolour sketches, text, and the book itself

---

[31] Wennerholm, *Sven Hedin*, 135.
[32] Hedin, *Southern Tibet*, vol. 2, 299.
[33] Hedin, *Southern Tibet*, vol. 3, 328.
[34] Hedin, *Southern Tibet*, vol. 2, 316. For yet another example, see Hedin, *Transhimalaya*, vol. 2, 100.
[35] Hedin, *Southern Tibet*, vol. 3, 255.
[36] Hedin, *Southern Tibet*, vol. 3, 359. See also 252.
[37] Comment, *The Panorama*, 112.
[38] Bigg, "The Panorama, or la Nature a Coup d'Oeil," 79.

as descriptive layers to create panoramas and steer the onlooker's understanding of both overview and detail.

Photographic Panoramas

Sven Hedin was educated in the German geographical tradition where scientific instruments were emphasized, and he used photographic equipment as a knowledge-making tool to capture geographical phenomena.[39] Research in the history of geography has indicated how the new visual technology increasingly became part of the instrumental arsenal of discovery from the 1850s onwards.[40] Geographers declared the unique potential to objectivity and visual legibility; in the words of Marie-Claire Robic, they were "infatuated with the photographic medium."[41] Considered a tool to achieve objectivity, it had originally promised to clear away individual idiosyncrasies among observers. Following the title of William Henry Fox Talbot's first photographically illustrated book, published between 1844 and 1846, the technique was described as "the pencil of nature." The photograph was interpreted as a surface where the object of the imaging could be read, interpreted, and perceived in new ways.[42] Moreover, the panorama had been tested since in the early stages of photography and used as an instrument to capture the vastness of distant and complex landscapes. It created new criteria for authenticity.[43]

According to some geographers, the photograph had the potential to synthesize details and efficiently present nature's proportions

---

[39] Hedin, *Southern Tibet*, vol. 1, xiii.
[40] Joan M. Schwartz and James R. Ryan, "Introduction: Photography and the Geographical Imagination," in *Picturing Place: Photography and the Geographical Imagination*, eds. Joan M. Schwartz and James R. Ryan (London: Tauris, 2003), 1–18; James R. Ryan, "Photography, Visual Revolutions, and Victorian Geography," in *Geography and Revolution*, eds. David Livingstone and Charles W. Withers (Chicago: University of Chicago Press, 2005), 199–238.
[41] Robic, "From the Sky to the Ground," 164.
[42] Yusoff, "Configuring the Field," 71; Jennifer Tucker, *Nature Exposed: Photography as Eyewitness in Victorian Science* (Baltimore: The Johns Hopkins University Press, 2005), 239.
[43] Comment, *The Panorama*, 8; Huhtamo, *Illusions in Motion*, 274; Rebecca Solnit, *River of Shadows: Eadweard Muybridge and the Technological Wild West* (New York: Penguin Books, 2003), 156–157.

to the observer. Other commentators had doubts, and the reality effects of photographs were increasingly challenged towards the end of the nineteenth century. Applied to geography, critics argued that photographs carried with them too many details. Others argued that the limited and rectangular format was problematic: it could only inadequately capture the wide 360° perspective that met the eye in the field.[44] Albeit Hedin did not partake in these epistemological discussions, he handled the issues in practice. The Swede transported cameras and a large number of glass plates on his travels. Pictures were taken on "Edwards's plates. All the large photographs were taken with a camera by Watson of London, and about a thousand of the small photographs on glass were taken with a Richard's Verascope camera."[45] The importance of taking pictures of the landscape is also illustrated by the large collection of photographs by the Swedish explorer kept in a special section of his personal archive (*Sven Hedins Kartsamling*).

From elevated positions, Hedin utilized opportunities of photographs to picture proportions of the landscape, for instance through taking several pictures "forming a consecutive series."[46] Once developed, the pictures were literally overlapped to shape a wider scope. This practice to measure topographical features was named photogrammetry and had been developed since the mid-nineteenth century. It had been introduced in Swedish natural science in the 1880s.[47] The technique had also been tried by panoramists, projecting several juxtaposed photographs onto a circular canvas and toning down the joins between them.[48]

As figure 1 indicates, Hedin taped photographs together to enable the geographical outlook not to be interrupted by the edges of the pictures. The desired overview could thus be captured. The

---

[44] Yusoff, "Configuring the Field," 63, 71; Naylor and Ryan, "Exploration and the Twentieth Century," 6–7; Magnus Bremmer, *Konsten att tämja en bild: Fotografiet och läsarens uppmärksamhet i 1800-talets Sverige* (Stockholm: Mediehistoriskt arkiv, 2015), 80, 94.
[45] Hedin, "The Scientific Results," 539.
[46] Hedin, *Transhimalaya*, vol. 2, 102.
[47] Bremmer, *Konsten att tämja en bild*, 156.
[48] Comment, *The Panorama*, 76, 86.

196   The Power of the In-Between

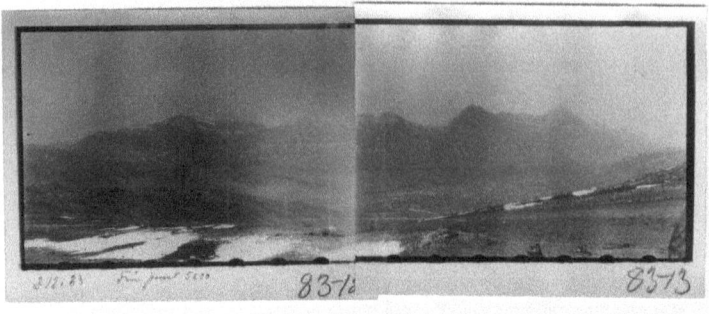

Figure 1. A photographic panorama consisting of interlaced images by Sven Hedin. From *Sven Hedins Kartsamling* (vol. G1 0917-958, no. 720811: 954). Copyright: The Sven Hedin Foundation and National Archive of Sweden/ Sven Hedins stiftelse and Riksarkivet, Stockholm. License: CC-BY-NC-ND.

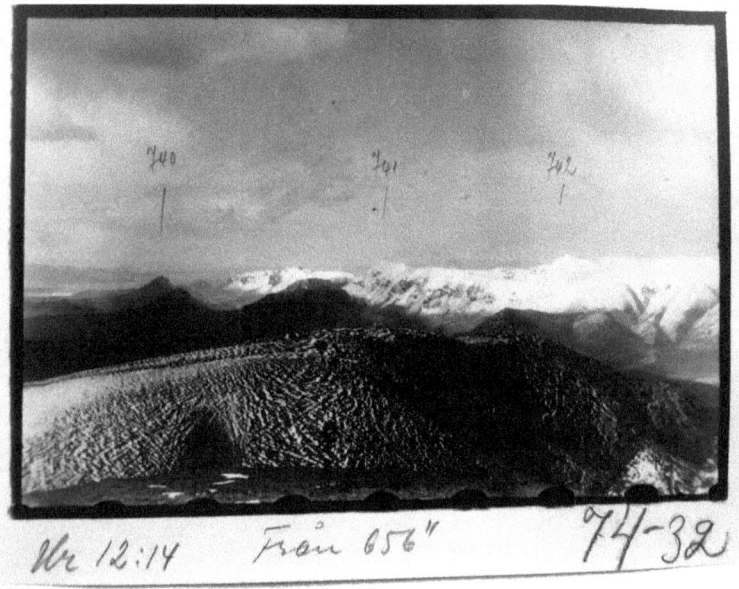

Figure 2. Photograph from Transhimalaya by Sven Hedin. From *Sven Hedins Kartsamling* (vol. G1 0917-958, no. 720811: 945). Copyright: The Sven Hedin Foundation and National Archive of Sweden/Sven Hedins stiftelse and Riksarkivet, Stockholm. License: CC-BY-NC-ND.

practice was repeatedly used, testified to by the presence of at least 50 similar specimens saved in his archive.

In one sense then, the descriptive layering was material as edges of photographs were placed over each other. Yet layers of information were also added to the surface of photographs as data were scribbled down on them. On numerous photographs, the geographer wrote notes to indicate geographically important phenomena. The image displayed in Figure 1 contains a note determining the place where the pictures were taken, ("Från punkt 5200"), as well as the numbers of the photographs to place them correctly in large series of images, "212:83," "83:12" and "83:13."

Yet another example displays even more written information. In this picture from Transhimalaya (Figure 2), Hedin has scribbled down notes indicating his system of determining the location of summits, glaciers, branches of rivers, and other features of the landscape. The notes determined the position where the photograph was taken ("Från 656"), as well as the number on the peaks that it showed (740, 741, 742). Written data transferred features and characteristics in the field into geographically and orographically important data. Indeed, in the examples displayed in Figures 1 and 2, the photograph was a basis for knowledge making rather than a surface of immediate projection. The photograph did not convey robust and unsupported visual information. In both cases, the image was combined or molded to create meaning. Photographic panoramas needed to be supplemented or enhanced to create overview (as in Figure 1) and fixate the very locale being displayed (as in both Figures 1 and 2). They eventually found their way into Hedin's published work, where larger sections of text functioned as supporting layers—an issue to which I will return.

Visual Layers: Photographs, Hand-Drawn Panoramas, and Watercolour Sketches

In a comment on his work published after the trip to Tibet, Hedin described how his published illustrations had been produced through "autotypes" which "consist for the most part of reproductions of my own photographs; in addition to them there are a number of drawings by my own pencil."[49] Prior to the trip, the Swede declared that he had not allowed the camera to make him "unfaithful to the pen and the brush."[50] In the introduction to *Southern Tibet*, Hedin stated that the camera had not been the only tool for mapping, since he was unable to bring "the thousands of photographic plates which would have been necessary" to survey using only the camera. Accordingly, his panoramas were "meant in some measure to compensate for the want of photogrammetric material."[51] Hedin combined photographs with hand-drawn panoramas and watercolour sketches, and the formats were brought together by panoramic visions as a visionary motif in the description of geographical features. Furthermore, the combination of formats offered aesthetic as well as scientific experiences.

Picturing landscapes was part of the Swedish geographer's everyday routine in Tibet. He produced hundreds of handmade panoramas from the mountains in Transhimalaya, often as high up as 5000 meters.[52] Indeed, at "almost every camp [...] I drew a panorama of the surroundings and tried sometimes to paint small water-colour drawings."[53] Repeatedly, he stopped to make panoramic sketches of mountain pass.[54] The readers of his work *Southern Tibet* were informed how "I made it a rule to draw a panorama of the whole region, within my horizon, from each camp and from each dominating pass."[55] Sketched panoramas were produced in the same setting as photographs, both part of grinding scientific work.[56] "I sit at the fire, drawing and making

---

[49] Hedin, "The Scientific Results," 539.
[50] Sven Hedin, *En levnads teckning* (Stockholm: Albert Bonniers förlag, 1920), 100. Quote translated by the author.
[51] Hedin, *Southern Tibet*, vol. 1, xvi.
[52] Hedin, *Southern Tibet*, vol. 2, 261.
[53] Hedin, *Transhimalaya*, vol. 2, 261–262.
[54] See for instance Hedin, *Transhimalaya*, vol. 2, 100; Sven Hedin, "Journeys in Tibet 1906–1908," *The Geographical Journal* 33, no. 4 (1909): 353–392, 361.
[55] Hedin, *Southern Tibet*, vol. 1, xv.
[56] Hedin, *My Life as an Explorer*, 339.

Panoramic Visions 199

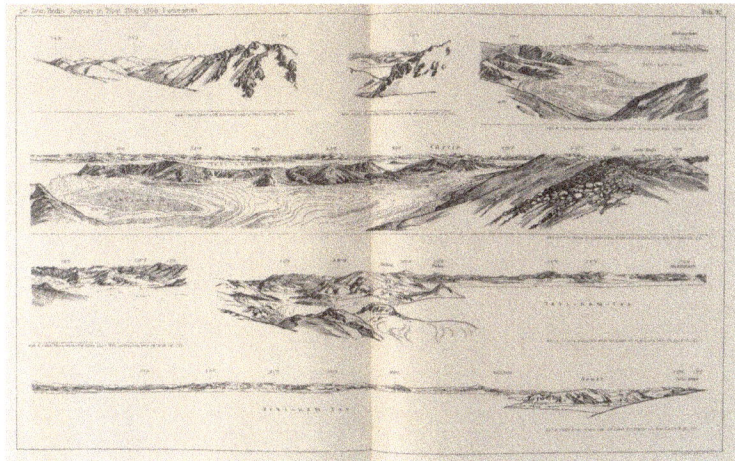

Figure 3. Hand-drawn panorama by Sven Hedin. From *Southern Tibet: Atlas of Tibetan Panoramas* (illustrations 494–497). Reproduction: National Library of Sweden/Kungliga biblioteket, Stockholm. License: CC-BY-NC-ND.

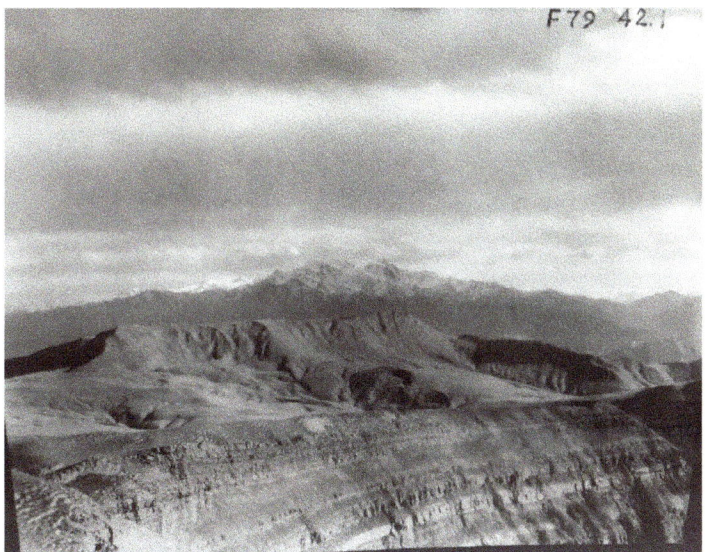

Figure 4. Panoramic photograph by Sven Hedin. From *Sven Hedins Kartsamling* (vol. G1 0917-958, no. 720811: 931). Copyright: The Sven Hedin Foundation and National Archive of Sweden/Sven Hedins stiftelse and Riksarkivet, Stockholm. License: CC-BY-NC-ND.

observations as on all the passes."[57] In *Transhimalaya*, Hedin explicated how he at one point first took several photographs and immediately afterward "sat for nearly four hours drawing a panorama which embraced the whole horizon."[58]

Intermittently, Hedin also emphasized the scientific value of both sketches and photographs. To the reader of *Southern Tibet* he argued: "The several panoramas and the photos I took at different places will, together with my map, give a clearer view of the situation than any description in words."[59] Moreover, the panorama could give "the spectator an idea of the layout" of the mountains.[60] The "panoramas I have sketched and the photographs I have taken," he argued, would even "give an idea" of sections of the landscape he had not been able to traverse.[61] In commenting on the separate volume *Southern Tibet: Atlas of Tibetan Panoramas*, he suggested that the many sketches secured a "richer" and "more systematic" illustration compared to previous publications.[62] The hand-drawn panoramas were not to be considered "little works of art to be put behind glass and frame on the wall"; instead, their purpose was topographical.

The particular quality of the panorama was the fact that it offered a horizontal view to complement the vertical, and much reduced overview offered by maps in very high resolution. They displayed the landscape "horizontally and the mountains from the side."[63] Each panorama was provided with notes defining the point from where it was made, and "from which sheet of the map its projection is to be found. Thus it will be possible, in each separate case, to compare the horizontal view with the vertical one."[64] The panoramas, stated Hedin, "embraces the whole horizon," and they could be compared with the vertical outlook of maps, and in

---

[57] Hedin, *Transhimalaya*, vol. 3, 35. See also 51.
[58] Hedin, *Transhimalaya*, vol. 2, 102. See also 33.
[59] Hedin, *Southern Tibet*, vol. 2, 260.
[60] Hedin, *En levnads teckning*, 101. Quote translated by the author.
[61] Hedin, *Southern Tibet*, vol. 3, 284.
[62] Hedin, *Southern Tibet*, vol. 4, 4–5; Sven Hedin, *Southern Tibet: Atlas of Tibetan Panoramas* (Stockholm: Lithographic Institute of the General Staff of the Swedish Army, 1917).
[63] Hedin, *En levnads teckning*, 101. Quote translated by the author.
[64] Hedin, *Southern Tibet*, vol. 1, xvi.

combining them, the observer could "recognize all the topographical details. One has only to remember the laws of perspective."⁶⁵ Other geographers besides Hedin argued the scientific value of panoramas along the same lines: they complemented the vertical projection of maps with a horizontal projection.⁶⁶

The combination of media formats also meant that Hedin's production of images was developed on the border between science and art. He repeatedly painted "watercolours representing Tibetan landscapes."⁶⁷ Exchanges between science and art, for example between landscape painting and photography, were commonplace in the nineteenth century. Several scientists borrowed visual motifs from artists, and the language of naturalism shaped discourses of scientific images.⁶⁸ As noted by Charlotte Bigg, science and art were combined in panoramic descriptions among naturalists in the Alps already in the early nineteenth century.⁶⁹

Hedin repeated this tradition, sometimes explicitly arguing that the sceneries in Asia would have been perfect objects for landscape painters.⁷⁰ The importance of his watercolour sketches and drawings is indicated by the fact that he became acknowledged as an able geographical artist. On several occasions, his visual works were displayed to the public. In 1920 an exhibition was arranged in Stockholm, and according to one of Hedin's biographers, the quality of his sketches and paintings surprised the art critics. Several commentators agreed that Hedin was "absolutely an artist," indeed an important sketcher in "black and white."⁷¹ The exhibition also resulted in the book *En levnads teckning*, republished in an abbreviated version as *Sven Hedin as Artist*.⁷²

---

⁶⁵ Hedin, *Southern Tibet*, vol. 4, 5.
⁶⁶ Oettermann, *The Panorama*, 38.
⁶⁷ Hedin, *Southern Tibet*, vol. 1, xiii.
⁶⁸ Solnit, *River of Shadows*, 42; Tucker, *Nature Exposed*, 125–126.
⁶⁹ Bigg, "The Panorama, or la Nature a Coup d'Oeil," 79–80.
⁷⁰ Hedin, *En levnads teckning*, 106.
⁷¹ Wennerholm, *Sven Hedin*, 185, 291.
⁷² Hedin, *En levnads teckning*; Gösta Montell, *Sven Hedin as Artist: For the Centenary of Sven Hedin's Birthday* (Stockholm: Bonniers, 1964).

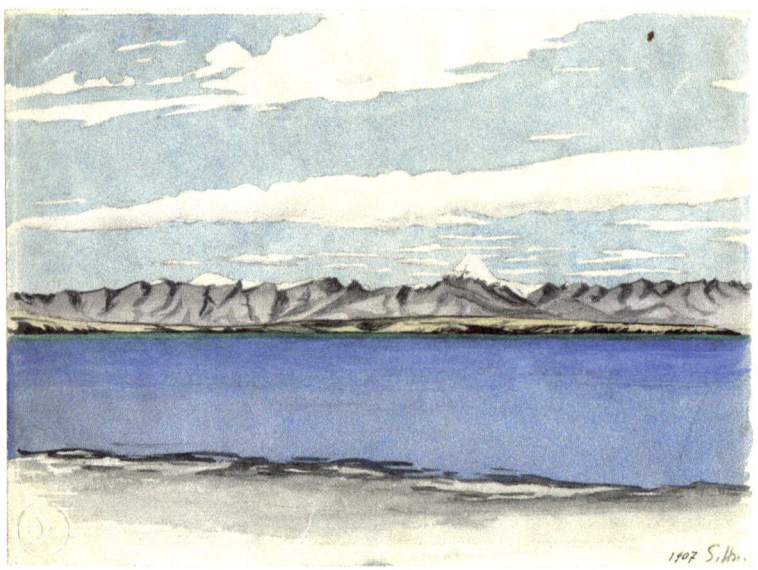

Figure 5. Watercolour sketch by Sven Hedin. Copyright: The Sven Hedin Foundation and National Archive of Sweden/Sven Hedins stiftelse and Riksarkivet, Stockholm. License: CC-BY-NC-ND.

The watercolour sketches were mainly integrated in books like *Transhimalaya* with a wider audience in mind. Figure 5 gives an example of a watercolour-sketch drawing that portrayed "The holy lake Manasarowar from Tugu-gompa." In a comment, Hedin added, "On August 10 I sat in my tent door and painted Kailas in different lights (Illust. 260)."[73] The image is not directly surrounded by scientific discourse as was the case with drawings and photographs. Instead, Hedin described the beauty and sublime nature of the surroundings. The "white summit" of the mountain Kailas "stood out cold and bare against a bright blue cloudless sky, and the lake was of a deep, dazzling ultramarine."[74] Nevertheless, the image is placed in a textual flow in *Transhimalaya* where Hedin discussed his efforts to sound the depth of the lake Manasarowar. Albeit sensitive to the religious status of the place, and taken by its beauty, the lake was a scientific project for the Western explorer:

---

[73] Hedin, *Transhimalaya*, vol. 2, 153.
[74] Hedin, *Transhimalaya*, vol. 2, 153. For another example of watercolour sketches by Hedin see illustrations 301–305.

"the lake had never been sounded—I would sink my lead to the bottom and make a map of its bed."[75]

In sum, photographs, hand-drawn panoramas, and watercolour-sketch drawings were descriptive layers rather than isolated genres. The panorama was a theme binding these media formats together, and as in other instances of the history of the panorama, sketches, and paintings were combined with photographs in a "hybrid process" to create and explain panoramas.[76] The descriptive layering enabled Sven Hedin to produce a vision of the Tibetan landscape where room was made for both overview and detail. Moreover, geographical knowledge was combined with artistic expressions with an appeal beyond the limited circle of geographical peers.

Anchoring Meaning: Texts as Steering Device

In *Southern Tibet* and *Transhimalaya*, visual panoramas were complemented with texts anchoring the meaning of the pictures. A repeated issue in the history of nineteenth-century scientific photography was how to make the observer able to distinguish vital elements in images and the object that they were meant to convey.[77] The same concern surfaced in Hedin's books, and the solution was to design sections of text, captions, and the very layout of the book as descriptive layers which steered the reader's gaze and clarified the geographically valuable insights.

Sections of text in Hedin's books had a visionary quality and produced an image before the eyes of the reader. In these passages, Hedin textually described a 360° panorama and the narrative became a tool to place the reader in the location where he had been standing. The Swede repeatedly described the height of his camps, for example, "Camp 188" at a "height of 4.590 m. (15.055 feet)."[78] In his narrative—as well as in his actual travel—Hedin paused in the high places to gaze the surroundings: such

---

[75] Hedin, *Transhimalaya*, vol. 2, 111.
[76] Huhtamo, *Illusions in Motion*, 274–275.
[77] Tucker, *Nature Exposed*, 80, 94.
[78] Hedin, *Southern Tibet*, vol. 2, 322. See also 326, 327.

locations gave "a very extensive and most instructive view."[79] In *Southern Tibet* the audience was invited to experience the landscape: "Quite a new panorama now opens up to the west, with a mighty part of the Himalaya called Mogum-gangri."[80] The geographer turned to "the south" where "the view is surprising" as mountains which had been very distant before, now presents "every detail of their wild, black, rugged peaks, the *nevees* in the background, and the mighty glaciers between the rocks."[81] From another location Hedin told his readers:

> The Dongdong massive appears to the S. 50° W.; to the right of it is a glacier, and W.S.W the wild peaks of Chemayundung-pu. Due west is another glacier, which must also send a brook to the Chemayundung-chu. To the N. 78° W. is a snow-covered group with an abrupt promontory N. 10° W., called Dugmo-kar. N. 68° W. the country looks rather open. N. 55° W. the mountains which belong to the Transhimalaya are visible. N. 35° W. is a violet-coloured conical peak in our neighbourhood.[82]

Several passages in Hedin's books defined the ideal consumption of image and text in combination, thus creating and amplifying panoramic visions. In *Southern Tibet*, he found it "suitable to say a few words" of the panorama as "a way of illustrating the journey." Even though the visual techniques were important, Hedin also pointed out the necessity of a combined reading. "The text in the following chapters will be much better understood if the corresponding panoramas are studied simultaneously. Text and illustrations have to follow each other."[83] Also in *Transhimalaya* the geographer explicitly commented on the relation between image and text, in this case focusing on the site in the mountains

---

[79] Hedin, *Southern Tibet*, vol. 2, 256. For a related example see Hedin, *Transhimalaya*, vol. 2, 95.
[80] Hedin, *Southern Tibet*, vol. 2, 321. For a related example see Hedin, *Transhimalaya*, vol. 2, 92 and 256.
[81] Hedin, *Southern Tibet*, vol. 2, 256.
[82] Hedin, *Southern Tibet*, vol. 2, 263. For more examples see also 317, 321, 322; Hedin, *Transhimalaya*, vol. 2, 102.
[83] Hedin, *Southern Tibet*, vol. 4, 4–5.

where he argued that the river Brahamaputra had its source: "In order to give the reader a notion of the scene I here reproduce a part of the panorama embracing the Kubi-gangri."[84] Immediately following the comment, Hedin went on to textually describe the geographical features visible in the panorama, including peaks and glaciers.[85]

Captions are yet another example of how image and text could, and should, be experienced in tandem. Hedin's publications were part of the emergence of the photo-illustrated book as a media format. Photographs were only slowly integrated in books—and in scientific prints more specifically—thus expanding the visual potential of the page. A recurring feature in photographically illustrated publications in the late nineteenth century was the effort to instruct the viewer on how to perceive the images. Accordingly, captions became a genre to regulate or enhance the content of images.[86]

Hedin published his travel narratives accompanied by auto-typified photographs, and he used new opportunities with the halftone technique.[87] Captions explained the content of images; in *Transhimalaya* Hedin explained pictures displaying a view "from Singrul, looking towards the pass Chang-La" or the "View from Sultak."[88] In several instances, captions also conveyed more geographically dense messages, highlighting what phenomena the reader was seeing. Sketched panoramas were accompanied by explanatory information about geographical features, for example, the "Chomo-uchong group from the Kinchen-La, May 23, 1907."[89] Or even more informative: "Kubi-Gangri from camp 201. S 19° E., Ngomo-dingding (1), with the Ngomo-dingding glacier below. S. 2° W., Absi (2), with the Absi glacier. S.21°-35° W., the massive of Mukchung-simo (3)."[90]

---

[84] Hedin, *Transhimalaya*, vol. 2, 102.
[85] Hedin, *Transhimalaya*, vol. 2, 102 and illustration 242.
[86] Bremmer, *Konsten att tämja en bild*, 12–18, 150, 196–198.
[87] Hedin, *Southern Tibet*, vol. 1, xiii.
[88] Hedin, *Transhimalaya*, vol. 1, illustration 42.
[89] Hedin, *Transhimalaya*, vol. 2, illustration 199.
[90] Hedin, *Transhimalaya*, vol. 2, illustration 197.

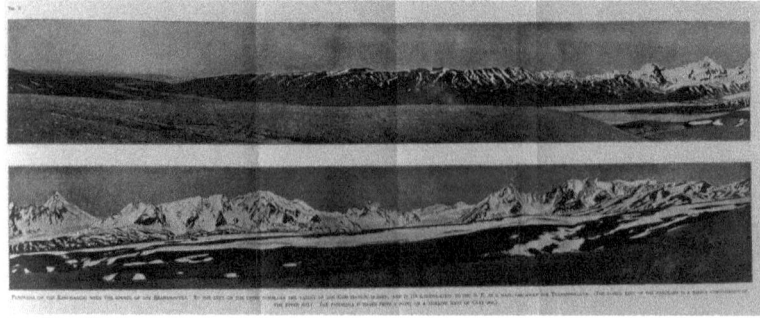

Figure 6. Unfolded panoramic image where the lower section is a continuation of the upper, together forming a 360° panorama, by Sven Hedin. From *Southern Tibet: Discoveries in Former Times Compared with My Own Researches in 1906–1908*, vol. 2. Reproduction: National Library of Sweden/Kungliga biblioteket, Stockholm. License: CC-BY-NC-ND.

A related technique was to photograph a 360° panorama which was then printed as two separate sections onto the book page. A caption explained how the image was to be interpreted. As Figure 6 indicates, in *Southern Tibet*, Hedin offered the reader such a panorama which was folded into the book. The instructive caption reads: "The lower part of the panorama is a direct continuation of the upper part."[91]

Furthermore, Hedin used the potential of the book medium to place explanatory text adjacent to illustrations, making the book spread into an entity. In *Transhimalaya*, he repeatedly placed text which described experiences of the landscape on the left page while a visual panorama in the form of photograph, hand-drawn image, or watercolour sketch was placed on the right page. For example, a hand-drawn panorama could be accompanied by text stating that the "view is marvelous," and that "peaks of the Himalaya rise like islands above the sea of clouds."[92] In certain places, crucial geographical features like the source of the river

---

[91] Hedin, *Southern Tibet*, vol. 2, 262. See also x.
[92] See for example Hedin, *Transhimalaya*, vol. 2, 78 and illustration 233. See also 26.

Brahmaputra was described, and the reader could fold out the right page and see a visual display of the area.⁹³

Conclusion: Descriptive Layers and a Network of Media Formats

I have suggested the importance of a media history of geographical knowledge making, and the perspective of intermediality has functioned as a method to indicate how Sven Hedin's panoramic visions were constructed. Photographs, hand-drawn panoramas, watercolour sketches, and texts contributed to the emergence of these visions, while also making them intelligible and meaningful. I have argued that the panoramic visions should be considered a network of media formats, and to define their intermedial relations, I have discussed them as descriptive layers. The concept highlights how images and texts were joined together thematically—sharing the panorama as a motif—as well as concretely: text written onto photographs or images attached to each other. Ultimately, they allowed Hedin to present and understand landscapes scientifically.

To see in overview was a recurring desire, yet fraught with tensions. Descriptive layers addressed the inherent problems of media formats: none of them could both create overview and capture enough details. When the formats complemented each other, however, these inherent difficulties could be addressed. Moreover, through descriptive layers, the narrative about Tibet could move between the knowledge making carried by photographs and meticulously hand-drawn panoramas and the artwork presented in watercolour sketches. This offered opportunities to shift the meaning of panoramic visions; combined, the media formats allowed the meaning of panoramic visions to vary in productive ways. Watercolour sketches opened for a story about the sublime nature of the landscape, while as a geographer Hedin could simultaneously present the scientific results by way of related imagery. In this regard, the book page became crucial by bringing together image and text, illustrations, and captions, and knowledge and

⁹³ Hedin, *Transhimalaya*, vol. 2, 102 and illustration 242.

aesthetics. The book was part of the network of media formats, and in highlighting it, I have followed Elisabeth Baigent's suggestion that a history of geography at the turn of the twentieth century must include a "history of the book."[94]

The perspective of intermediality suggests a dismantling of boundaries between media technologies like photography, art, or the book. The idea also illustrates the fact that Hedin's panoramic visions were part of a broader nineteenth-century history of the panorama as a motif and practice (rather than isolated medium) in the media culture of the late nineteenth century. Erkki Huhtamo has indicated how the panorama in this broader sense crisscrossed mediated experiences. With Hedin as an example of an influential geographer around 1900, the lines between the history of panoramic experiences and the history of geography emerge.

There are important lessons to be learned from panorama historians. Huhtamo, for example, clearly indicates how panoramic viewpoints massively shaped nineteenth-century outlooks on the world, indeed he argues that the panorama dissolved the boundary between "local existence and global vision."[95] The same claim can be made about Hedin's panoramic visions: they made it possible to experience the inaccessible. Most people at the time never traveled to the mountainous regions in Asia. To see coherence in chaotic mountain landscapes demanded a transformation of what did not emerge to the naked eye into something comprehensible. In that sense, Hedin contributed to a regime of vision where visual and textual portraits of the earth "instituted a globalised time of landscape—as a telepresent terrain—where even the 'ends of the earth' could be made available to vision."[96]

Even though Sven Hedin was a voice from the past—and even though the imperial European vision of the world was decidedly changed after the heyday of colonialism around 1900—his

---

[94] Elisabeth Baigent, "Deeds not Words? Life Writing and Early Twentieth-century British Polar Exploration," in *New Spaces of Exploration: Geographies of Discovery in the Twentieth Century*, eds. Simon Naylor and James R. Ryan (London: I. B. Tauris, 2010), 23–51, 24.
[95] Huhtamo, *Illusions in Motion*, 5.
[96] Yusoff, "Configuring the Field," 71. See also Bigg, "The Panorama, or la Nature a Coup d'Oeil," 86.

panoramic visions indicate historical trajectories and forms of intermediality with an impact on late modern experiences of larger patterns in nature and culture. After the Second World War, the ability to see the earth in overview was invested with new meaning as technologies developed into photographs from space shuttles and satellites. In the 1960s, such images were interpreted in a context of a growing environmental movement and a gradually developing discourse about globalization. The geographic knowledge that Hedin and other imperialistic adventurers circulated through interconnected forms of media later fed into technologies which have made possible what literary scholar Ursula Heise has labeled "a sense of planet."[97]

References

Baigent, Elisabeth. "Deeds not Words? Life Writing and Early Twentieth-century British Polar Exploration." In *New Spaces of Exploration: Geographies of Discovery in the Twentieth Century*, edited by Simon Naylor and James R. Ryan, 32–51. London: I. B. Tauris, 2010.

Bell, Morag, Robin Butlin, and Michael Heffernan. *Geography and Imperialism 1820-1940*. Manchester: Manchester University Press, 1994.

Bigg, Charlotte. "The Panorama, or La Nature a Coup d'Oeil." In *Observing Nature – Representing Experience: The Osmotic Dynamics of Romanticism 1800–1850*, edited by Erna Fiorentini, 73–95. Berlin: Reimer, 2007.

Bolter, Jay David, and Richard Grusin. *Remediation: Understanding New Media*. Cambridge: MIT Press, 1999.

Bremmer, Magnus. *Konsten att tämja en bild: Fotografiet och läsarens uppmärksamhet i 1800-talets Sverige*. Stockholm: Mediehistoriskt arkiv, 2015.

Comment, Bernard. *The Panorama*. London: Reaktion, 1999.

---

[97] Ursula K. Heise, *Sense of Place and Sense of Planet: The Environmental Imagination of the Global* (Oxford: Oxford University Press, 2008).

Ekström, Anders. "Seeing from Above: A Particular History of the General Observer." *Nineteenth-Century Contexts* 31, no. 3 (2009): 185–207.

Griffiths, Alison. "Sensory Media: The World Without and the World Within." In *A Cultural History of the Senses: In the Age of Empire*, edited by Constance Classen, 211–234. London: Bloomsbury Academic, 2014.

Hedin, Sven. *En levnads teckning*. Stockholm: Albert Bonniers förlag, 1920.

Hedin, Sven. "Journeys in Tibet 1906–1908: General Narrative." *The Geographical Journal* 33, no. 4 (1909): 353–392.

Hedin, Sven. *My Life as an Explorer*. Washington: National Geographic Adventure Classics, 2003 [1925].

Hedin, Sven. *Southern Tibet: Atlas of Tibetan Panoramas*. Stockholm: Lithographic Institute of the General Staff of the Swedish Army, 1917.

Hedin, Sven. *Southern Tibet: Discoveries in Former Times Compared with My Own Researches in 1906–1908*. 9 vols., vol. 1. Stockholm: Lithographic Institute of the General Staff of the Swedish Army, 1917.

Hedin, Sven. *Southern Tibet: Discoveries in Former Times Compared with My Own Researches in 1906–1908*. 9 vols., vol. 2. Stockholm: Lithographic Institute of the General Staff of the Swedish Army, 1917.

Hedin, Sven. *Southern Tibet: Discoveries in Former Times Compared with My Own Researches in 1906–1908*. 9 vols., vol. 3. Stockholm: Lithographic Institute of the General Staff of the Swedish Army, 1917.

Hedin, Sven. *Southern Tibet: Discoveries in Former Times Compared with My Own Researches in 1906–1908*. 9 vols., vol. 4. Stockholm: Lithographic Institute of the General Staff of the Swedish Army, 1922.

Hedin, Sven. "The Scientific Results of Dr. Sven Hedin's Last Journey." *The Geographical Journal* 24, no. 5 (1904): 524–45.

Hedin, Sven. *Transhimalaya: Discoveries and Adventures in Tibet*. 3 vols., New Delhi: Asian Educational Services, 1999 [1909].

Heffernan, Michael. "Histories of Geography." In *Key Concepts in Geography*, edited by Nicholas Clifford, Sarah Holloway, Stephen P. Rice, and Valentine Gill, 3–20. London: SAGE, 2009.

Heggie, Vanessa. "Why Isn't Exploration a Science?" *Isis* 105, no. 2 (2014): 318–334.

Heise, Ursula K. *Sense of Place and Sense of Planet: The Environmental Imagination of the Global.* Oxford: Oxford University Press, 2008.

Huhtamo, Erkki. *Illusions in Motion: Media Archeology of the Moving Panorama and Related Spectacles.* Cambridge: MIT Press, 2013.

Livingstone, David. *The Geographical Tradition: Episodes in the History of a Contested Enterprise.* Oxford: Blackwell, 1992.

Montell, Gösta. *Sven Hedin as Artist: For the Centenary of Sven Hedin's Birthday.* Stockholm: Bonniers, 1964.

Naylor, Simon, and James R. Ryan. "Exploration and the Twentieth Century." In *New Spaces of Exploration: Geographies of Discovery in the Twentieth Century*, 1–22. London: Tauris, 2010.

Oettermann, Stephan. *The Panorama: History of a Mass Medium.* New York: Zone Books, 1997.

Pelizzari, Maria Antonella. "Retracing the Outlines of Rome: Intertextuality and Imaginative Geographies in Nineteenth-century Photographs." In *Picturing Place: Photography and the Geographical Imagination*, edited by Joan M. Schwartz and James R. Ryan, 55–73. London and New York: I. B. Tauris, 2003.

Robic, Marie-Claire. "From the Sky to the Ground: The Aerial View and the Ideal of *Vue Raisonée* in Geography during the 1920s." In *Seeing From Above: The Aerial View in Visual Culture*, edited by Mark Dorrian and Frédéric Pousin, 163–187. London and New York: I. B. Tauris, 2013.

Robic, Marie-Claire. "Geography." In *The Cambridge History of Science: The Modern Social Sciences*, edited by Theodore M. Porter, 379–390. Cambridge: Cambridge University Press, 2003.

Ryan, James R. "Photography, Visual Revolutions, and Victorian Geography." In *Geography and Revolution*, edited by David

Livingstone and Charles W. Withers, 199–238. Chicago: University of Chicago Press, 2005.

Schwartz, Joan M., and James R. Ryan. "Introduction: Photography and the Geographical Imagination." In *Picturing Place: Photography and the Geographical Imagination*, edited by Joan M. Schwartz and James R. Ryan, 1–18. London: Tauris, 2003.

Solnit, Rebecca. *River of Shadows: Eadweard Muybridge and the Technological Wild West*. New York: Penguin Books, 2003.

Thorburn, David, and Henry Jenkins. "Introduction: Toward an Aesthetic of Transition." In *Rethinking Media Change: The Aesthetic of Transition*, edited by David Thorburn and Henry Jenkins, 1–16. Cambridge: MIT Press, 2003.

Tucker, Jennifer. *Nature Exposed: Photography as Eyewitness in Victorian Science*. Baltimore: The Johns Hopkins University Press, 2005.

Wennerholm, Eric. *Sven Hedin: En biografi*. Stockholm: Bonniers, 1978.

Yusoff, Kathryn. "Configuring the Field: Photography in Early Twentieth-century Antarctic Exploration." In *New Spaces of Exploration: Geographies of Discovery in the Twentieth Century*, edited by James R. Ryan and Simon Naylor, 52–77. London: I. B. Tauris, 2010.

Zarobell, John. "Jean-Charles Langlois's Panorama of Algiers (1833) and the Prospective Colonial Landscape," *Art History* 26, no. 5 (2003): 638–668.

The Lithographic Album 1873: Reproductive Media and Visual Art in the Age of Lithographic Reproduction
Anna Dahlgren

Abstract

This chapter merges media studies with art history or visual studies, as it combines an attentiveness to aesthetics and the materiality of images with an interest in their medium and mediation. It thereby seeks to bridge the alleged gulf between the hermeneutic traditions of art history and the focus on medium and techniques of media studies in general and of media archaeology in particular. As a case study and in focus for the analysis is the Swedish publication *Lithographic Album: Portfolio for the Parlour Table*, published in Stockholm 1873. This 21-page publication includes lithographic reproductions of photographs, oil paintings, and sculptures adjoined by explanatory texts. In focus is how the combination of texts and images convey how the artworks should be interpreted. Moreover, the texts display contrasting understandings of different artistic mediums, how they should be perceived and their ability to advance certain contents. Taken together, it is evident that the *Lithographic Album* is tinged by a photographic paradigm of truth and immediacy both in the cases where it describes paintings as documents and when it urges the reader to see the artworks with their own eyes.

The late eighteen century and early nineteenth century saw a number of new techniques for reproducing images like xylography

---

How to cite this book chapter:
Dahlgren, Anna. "The Lithographic Album 1873: Reproductive Media and Visual Art in the Age of Lithographic Reproduction." In *The Power of the In-Between: Intermediality as a Tool for Aesthetic Analysis and Critical Reflection*, edited by Sonya Petersson, Christer Johansson, Magdalena Holdar, and Sara Callahan, 213–237. Stockholm: Stockholm University Press, 2018. DOI: https://doi.org/10.16993/baq.i. License: CC-BY.

or wood engraving, lithography, steel print, and photography.[1] During the following decades there was in turn an immense production of illustrated books, often labeled "albums," which typically collected portraits, views or reproductions of artworks.[2] The latter, the reproductions of artworks, had a two-part audience at the time. First, they were tools for practicing artists and in art education, where the work of copying old masters was a core feature in the curriculum.[3] Second, they were aimed at the general public, primarily the bourgeoisie, who sought to educate themselves in the visual art. This chapter considers an example of the latter, the Swedish publication *Lithographic Album: Portfolio for the Parlour Table* (*Litografisk album: Portfölj för salongsbordet*) published in Stockholm in 1873 (Figure 1).[4]

Lithographic Album comprises twenty-one pages, which includes twelve images and some explanatory text. The images are reproductions of photographs, oil paintings, and sculptures. In total it holds reproductions of three photographs, five oil paintings, three sculptures, and an image of unknown medium. The original images and artworks were contemporary and depicted living celebrities of the period, paintings made by Swedish and Danish artists between 1854 and 1872, and statues which had recently been produced and stood in Stockholm at the time. Although the title of the publication indicates that it contains lithographs, it may also include wood engravings. In fact, the term "lithography" was extensively used in the nineteenth century and did not always refer to the stone-based printing method, but rather to printed

---

[1] The xylographic method/wood engraving was invented by Thomas Bewick in 1777, lithography by Alois Senefelder in 1798, steel print by Jacob Perkins in 1820 and photography by several persons in the 1820s and 1830s. See for example Gerald W. R. Ward, *The Grove Encyclopedia of Materials and Techniques in Art* (Oxford: Oxford University Press, 2008), 347–350, 484–485, 781–782; Jane Turner, ed., *The Dictionary of Art*, vol. 10 (London: MacMillan Publishers Ltd, 1996), 394–396; Per Bjurström, *Gamla grafiska blad* (Västerås: ICA-förlaget, 1974).

[2] Anna Dahlgren, *Ett medium för visuell bildning: Kulturhistoriska perspektiv på fotoalbum 1850–1950* (Stockholm: Makadam, 2013).

[3] Turner, *The Dictionary of Art*, vol. 7, 830–831.

[4] *Litografiskt album: Portfölj för salongsbordet*, Stockholm Artistiska Litografiska Anstalt (Stockholm: J. W. Svenssons Boktryckeri, 1873).

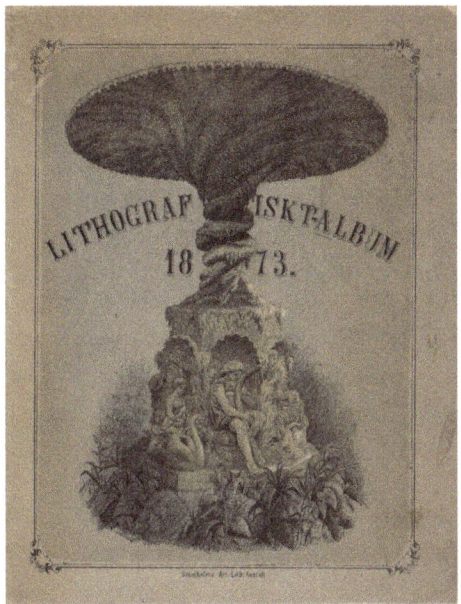

Figure 1. The cover of *Lithographic Album*, 1873. Reproduction: National Library of Sweden/Kungliga biblioteket, Stockholm. License: CC-BY-NC-ND.

images in general. However lithography was highly popular in the period as is could resemble pen, wash, or crayon drawing as well as engravings.[5]

The *Lithographic Album* opens with a table of contents, just like a book, where the twelve pictures are listed and labeled. They are:

> H. M. The King, H.R.H. Prince August, Earl Grefve von Rosen, The Beggar Boy (with text), Danish soldier (with text), Hjalmar den Hugfulle (with text), the convalescent (with text), Bellman's statue (with text), The fisherman boy (with text), Molin's fountain (with text), Scanian landscape (with text), and Ruin.

---

[5] Lithographic prints are made through drawings on stone while xylographic prints are made through engraving in end wood. The latter rather look like line drawings and are similar to steel print. For an overview of different printing techniques see references in note 1.

Thus eight of the images are adjoined by explanatory text, which follows immediately after the table of contents. The shortest are only one paragraph of six lines, while the most extensive is a just over two full pages long. This is in turn followed by twelve spreads displaying one lithographic print each.

In this chapter, I seek to discuss how the combination of texts and images convey how the images should be interpreted and perceived. Moreover the texts display contrasting understandings of different artistic mediums and their ability to advance certain contents or messages. In the following, I will pay particular attention to the wordings and concepts used to describe how the artworks convey meaning and how they are to be perceived literally and figuratively. It is evident that some images' techniques required extensive explanation while they were superfluous is some cases and even detrimental in others.

Art, Image, and Media Studies

The present chapter ties into recent developments of images studies, which recognize that "the physical properties of images are as important as their social function."[6] As such, it is informed by media studies on the one hand, and art history, *Bildwissenschaft*, and visual studies on the other. It thereby seeks to bridge the alleged gulf between the hermeneutic traditions of art history and the focus on medium/techniques of media studies in general and of media archaeology in particular. It thus combines what Wolfgang Ernst has argued are two incompatible methods: the technological considerations from media archaeology with attentiveness to visual details and aesthetics common to art historical analysis.[7] The latter includes a consideration of form, colour, image technique, perspective, and content of the images. Accordingly, the following case study includes close formal and content analyses of particu-

---

[6] Keith Moxey, "Visual Studies and the Iconic Turn," *Journal of Visual Culture* 7:2 (2008): 131–146, 132.
[7] Wolfgang Ernst, "Let There Be Irony: Cultural History and Media Archeology in Parallel Lines," *Art History* 28:5 (2005): 582–603.

lar pictures common to art historical studies with a simultaneous consideration of the materiality of the medium and the system in which this mediating apparatuses appear and function, which are common to media studies. By using the word media system, I seek to acknowledge that artefacts like the *Lithographic Album* act as components in a historically situated system of distribution and circulation of different media, which also then per default have intermedial relations, thus both within itself and in relation to other media. The term *media system* refers to the networking character of media and acknowledges the relations between the whole media system and its constituted parts. Consequently, this perspective directs the attention to intermedial relations in which technical, social, economic aspects, and I would add aesthetic aspects, are taken into consideration.[8]

The overall aim is to disclose the general implications of acknowledging images as mediated and the further implications of these mediations. Moreover, this combination of media history and art history uncover the entangled history of mass media and art in modernity. As pointed out by Hans Belting, there is a need for a dialogue between art history and media studies because of the "coexistence of art and non-art images even in historical times."[9] As the following analysis will uncover, a media perspective on the art field and an artefact like the *Lithographic Album* has a number of implications. First, a media perspective acknowledges the multi-modality of this object, being a combination of different media, texts, and lithographic images, which in turn remediate other image media. Thus there are intermedial relations within the album itself and yet also between the album and that which it

---

[8] Jonas Harvard and Patrik Lundell, eds., *1800-talets mediesystem* (Stockholm: Kungliga biblioteket, 2010), 7–9. See also Lisa Gitelman and Geoffrey B. Pingree, eds., *New Media 1740–1915* (Cambridge: MIT Press, 2003); Erkki Huhtamo and Jussi Parikka, eds., *Media Archaeology: Approaches, Applications and Implications* (Berkley: University of California Press, 2011); Sunil Manghani, *Image Studies* (London: Routledge, 2013), 26–27.

[9] Hans Belting, *Art History after Modernism* (Chicago: University of Chicago Press, 2003), 163.

seeks to represent.[10] Second, the *Lithographic Album* is a medium in the sense that it is a conveyer for interpersonal information. It has a sender and audience, and in this analysis I will also study how this composite medium addresses its audience.

The present case study is also informed by the notions of mediatization. It is an example of what Jürgen Wilke has defined as the "dissemination of art by secondary media," that is mediation and dissemination of art via mass media.[11] Indeed printed books like the album in focus in this chapter could be understood as pre-modern mass media, which assumed the same functions as did later film and television as a conveyer of art to the large public. However, I do not only consider this print media as a neutral conveyor for different cultural contents, but rather this case displays that print media has played a decisive role in the construction of art and the understanding of different artistic mediums, not only through writings on art but in addition also in the way art has been reproduced via printed media. This includes an attentiveness to form, colour, perspective, and content.

Typically writings on the mediatization in society consider the contemporary early twenty-first century, sometimes the period of high modernity but seldom earlier historical periods.[12] It is indeed true that the processes of mediatization are progressive. Yet I argue that media has not only left its mark on the everyday life in high modernity and contemporary times but also in earlier historical periods. If by media convergence we mean "flow of content across multiple media platforms," this has been going on well before the contemporary age of digital dissemination.[13] This is particularly

---

[10] Hans Lund, *Intermedialitet: Ord, bild och ton i samspel* (Lund: Studentlitteratur, 2002).

[11] Jürgen Wilke, "Art: Multiplied Mediatization," in *Mediatization of Communication*, ed. Knut Lundby (Berlin: De Gruyter Mouton, 2014), 465–482.

[12] See for example Andreas Hepp, *Cultures of Mediatization* (Cambridge: Polity, 2012); Stig Hjarvard, *The Mediatization of Culture and Society* (London: Routledge, 2013), 6–7; Lundby, ed., *Mediatization of Communication*.

[13] Henry Jenkins, *Convergence Culture: Where Old and New Media Collide* (New York: New York University Press, 2006). See also Hepp, *Cultures of Mediatization*, 26.

true within the art field where the practices of making replicas, pastiches, and paraphrases has a long tradition. An important starting point for this chapter is thus to acknowledge images as embedded, networked, and mediated. While this is a default stance in scholarly work on imagery of journalism and media, it is not always highlighted in studies on visual art. However, visual art is, and has historically always been, mediated and entangled in media systems, be it the illustrated handbooks of art history, lithographic and photographic reproductions of artworks, or the gallery or museum itself.[14] Simultaneously the majority of media-historical studies focuses on text and not images, and accordingly, the present study stands out in its focus on images.[15]

Photographs

The first three images in the *Lithographic Album* are portraits of the King of Sweden Oscar II (1829–1907), his brother Prince August (1831–1873), and Georg von Rosen (1843–1923). The latter is presented as Earl in the table of contents and as a history painter below the image itself. Von Rosen was at the time a member of the Art Academy in Stockholm and was later appointed professor at the Royal Academy of Arts. These three portraits are made from photographic originals, although this is not stated anywhere in the album. The King's portrait was made by the photographers Eurenius & Quist while Prince August's and Rosen's were made by the photographer Gösta Florman.[16] This could not only be deduced from the treatment of light and

---

[14] For examples of such studies, despite they are not presented as "media studies," see Dan Karlholm, *Art of Illusion: The Representation of Art History in Nineteenth-century Germany and Beyond* (Bern: Peter Lang, 2004); Thomas. W. Gaehtgens and Louis Marchesano, *Display and Art History: The Düsseldorf Gallery and Its Catalogue* (Los Angeles: Getty Research Institute, 2011).

[15] This is for example pointed out by James Mussell, *The Nineteenth-Century Press in the Digital Age* (Basingstoke: Palgrave Macmillan, 2012), 69–113. For examples of studies on visual aspects of media see Vanessa R. Schwartz and Jeannene M. Przyblyski, eds., *The Nineteenth-century Visual Culture Reader* (New York: Routledge, 2004).

[16] Eurenius & Quist's and Gösta Florman's photographic portraits are, for

shadows in the images themselves, but also in how they are combined with text in the printed album.[17] None of the portraits have any adjoining separate descriptive text, and in none of the cases is the photographer's name written out. The lack of explanatory text might indicate that the portrayed people were already well-known to the intended audience, and no further information or explanations were necessary. However, this lack of textual information may also indicate how the medium of photography was perceived at the time. While there is no lengthier explanatory text, the images themselves are adjoined by the name of the sitters. The latter's, that is von Rosen's portrait, is adjoined by his name in printed letters. The portraits of the Royals are on the contrary adjoined by their signatures, which consist of their surnames (Figures 2 and 3).

To combine reproductions of photographs with the portrayed person's signature was a very common practice in contemporary press and illustrated books in the second half of the nineteenth century. This did obviously enhance the indexicality of the image. Adding one's signature on photographic portraits was also common practice in the period. Obviously this made the "having been there" effect of the photographic image stronger. Just as the light that had touched the body of the portrayed person had touched the photographic plate and print, the hands of the portrayed person had touched the photographic print while signing the picture. Subsequently, when lithographic reproductions of photographic portraits of contemporary celebrities were published in the illustrated press and albums of portraits, they were often adjoined by the sitters' autograph and not their name in printed letters. Indeed this was a visual strategy for enhancing the photographicality of the xylographic or lithographic prints. Yet the lack of textual information on the medium or technique of the original images and the omission of the producers', that is, the photographers', names

---

example, held in the collection of The National Library of Sweden (Fa3 and Fa14c) and in the Royal Collection, Bernadottebiblioteket (PR A Kq 1).

[17] For an extensive analysis on how the photographic aesthetic influenced the production of portraits in other images techniques see Solfrid Söderlind, *Porträttbruk i Sverige 1840–1865: En funktions- och interaktionsstudie* (Stockholm: Carlsson, 1993), 237–244.

The Lithographic Album 1873   221

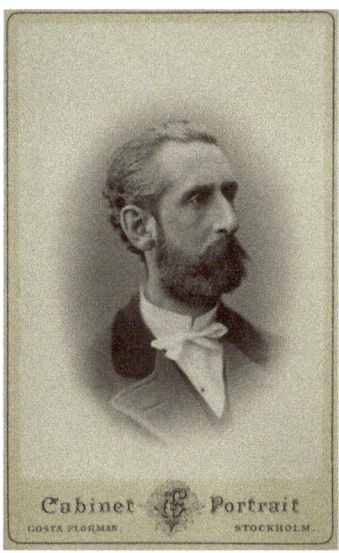

Figure 2. Cabinet portrait of Prince August by Gösta Florman. Photo: Lisa Raihle Rehbäck. Copyright: Swedish Royal Court/Kungl. Hovstaterna, Stockholm. License: CC-BY-NC-ND.

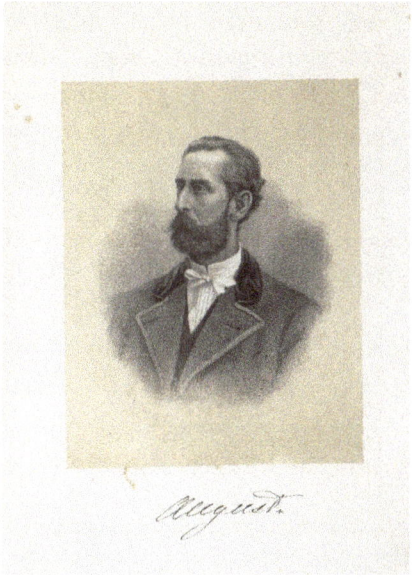

Figure 3. Lithographic reproduction of Florman's photograph of Prince August. *Lithographic Album*, 1873. Reproduction: National Library of Sweden/Kungliga biblioteket, Stockholm. License: CC-BY-NC-ND.

may also indicate an understanding of photography as transparent in another sense. These invisibilities emphasize the view that photographs were mechanically produced images without aesthetic considerations and not influenced by the producers', that is, the photographers', personal styles.

Paintings

The album contains five lithographic reproductions of oil paintings, all of which were produced by Swedish or Danish artists around the mid-nineteenth century. Four of these depict historical or contemporary motifs with edifying content, while one is an image of a rural landscape from the south of Sweden.[18]

Two of the reproduced paintings depict wounded soldiers and in the adjoining text the viewer is encouraged to compare these two images. The full name of the artists and the titles of the paintings are not spelled out in the adjoining text, only the initials and family names of the artists. This might suggest that both artists and these particular paintings were well-known to the intended audience. Hence the reproductions of the artworks that they might already be familiar with through textual sources provided an opportunity to the large public to see the artworks with their own eyes, albeit through a lithographic reproduction. The first painting is presented as *Hjalmar the Brave* (Hjalmar den Hugfulle) in the table of contents and as *Hjalmar's Farewell* printed below the lithographic reproduction in the album (Figure 5). This was a large-format oil painting by the Swedish artist Mårten Eskil Winge (1825–1896) produced in 1866 (Figure 4). The adjoining text points out both its considerable size and image technique by informing the readers

---

[18] The paintings reproduced in the album were made after Carl Henning Lutzow d'Unker's (1828–1866) oil painting *The Beggar Boy* from 1854, Mårten Eskil Winge's (1825–1896) *Hjalmar's Farewell* from 1866, Anna Maria Elisabeth Lisinska Jerichau-Baumann's (1819–1881) *A Wounded Danish Soldier* from 1865, Ferdinand Fagerlin's (1825–1907) *The Convalescence* from 1867 and an undated *Scanian Landscape* most probably by Gustaf Rydberg (1835–1933). The album also includes a reproduction of an unidentified image of Berry Pommery Castle in Devonshire, however, only labeled *A Ruin*.

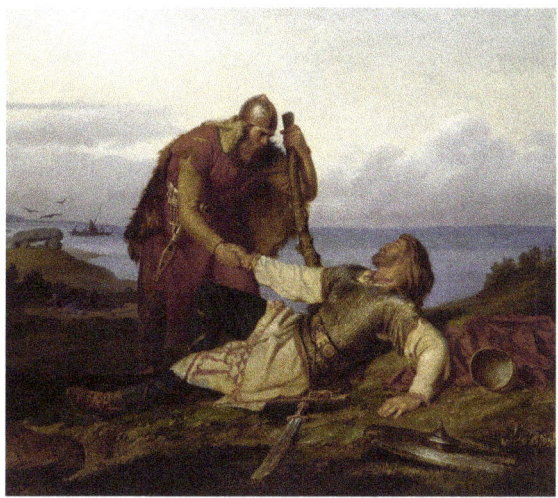

Figure 4. *Hjalmar's Farewell*. Mårten Eskil Winge, 1866. Oil on canvas. Reproduction and permission: Nationalmuseum/Nationalmuseum, Stockholm. License: CC-PD. Available at Wikimedia Commons: https://commons.wikimedia.org/wiki/File:Hjalmars_avsked_av_Orvar_Odd_efter_striden_på_Samsö.jpg.

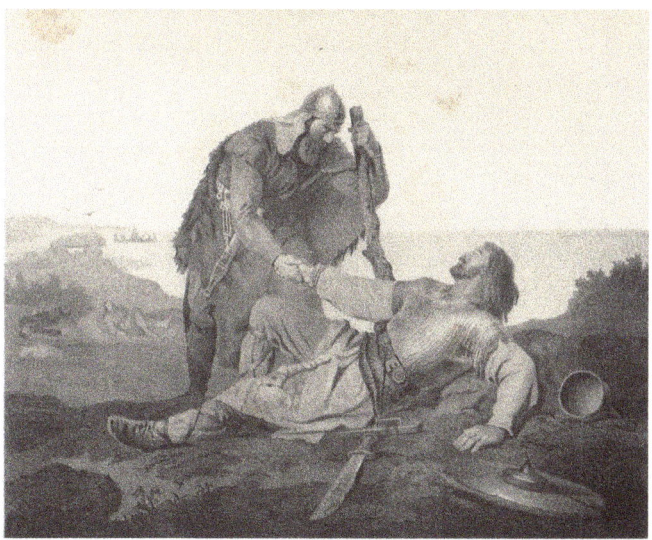

Figure 5. *Hjalmar the Brave*. Lithographic reproduction of Mårten Eskil Winge's oil painting. *Lithographic Album*, 1873. Reproduction: National Library of Sweden/Kungliga biblioteket, Stockholm. License: CC-BY-NC-ND.

that the images have been "taken from Winge's magnificent oil painting."[19] At the time of publication, the painting had recently been bequeathed by the former King Carl XV to the Swedish Nationalmuseum, where it is still part of the collection, now catalogued as *Hjalmars Farewell to Orvar Odd after the Battle at Samsö*.[20] The painting depicts the ancient Nordic saga where the Viking Hjalmar is dying after a battle. It is the dramatic end of the battle, the death moment of the hero, that is depicted.

In the album, Winge's painting was compared to the painting *A Wounded Danish Soldier* (En såret dansk kriger) by the Polish-Danish artist Anna Maria Elisabeth Lisinska Jerichau-Baumann (1819–1881) from 1865 (Figures 6 and 7). At the time of publication it was in the possession of the National Gallery of Denmark.[21] This painting is said to depict a wounded soldier from the nineteenth century. In contrast to the first, the second painting is clearly displaying human fragility and the physical pains of war. The adjoining text invites the readers to compare the two images. Despite that they depict very different types of soldiers, they are said to portray the pains of war and the love of the nation. Their differences are, according to the text, not so much a question of different artistic styles. Rather they depict very different attitudes and characters of the Ancient Nordic times and the contemporary period.[22] Accordingly, the soldiers are said to have the same courage and will to fight for the nation, yet in "physical strength" today's men are "inferior," a conclusion that obviously ties into the contemporary vivid debate about the degeneration of the population in the Western, industrialized world. Indeed, these lithographic reproductions of oil paintings induce comparisons. They

---

[19] The original text reads: "tagen efter Winges präktiga oljemålning."
[20] Nationalmuseum, no. 1248, *Hjalmars avsked av Orvar Odd efter striden på Samsö*, 169 × 208 cm. Oil painting. Donation through testament 1872 by Carl XV.
[21] National Gallery of Denmark/Statens museum for Kunst, *En såret dansk kriger*, 1865, 107 × 142.5 cm. Oil painting, KMS852. Bought by National Gallery in 1866.
[22] The original text reads: "lätt iaktaga hvilka olika typer af krigare, som icke mycket artisten, som icke mer de olika århundradena, framställa för oss."

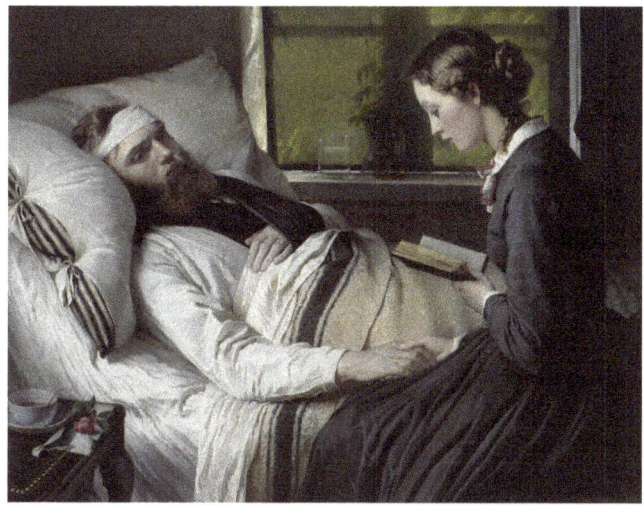

Figure 6. *A Wounded Danish Soldier.* Maria Elisabeth Lisinska Jerichau-Baumann, 1865. Oil on canvas. Photo and copyright: National Gallery of Denmark/Statens Museum for Kunst, Copenhagen. License: CC-BY-NC-ND.

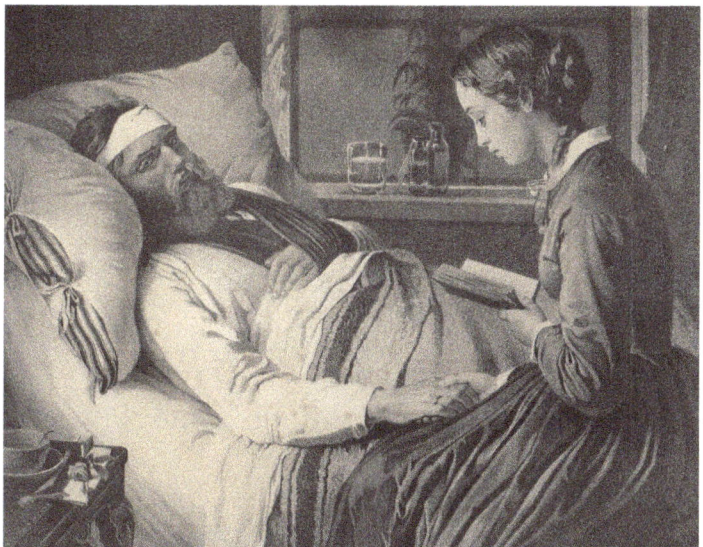

Figure 7. *A Wounded Danish Soldier.* Lithographic reproduction of Anna Maria Elisabeth Lisinska Jerichau-Baumann's oil painting. *Lithographic Album*, 1873. Reproduction: National Library of Sweden/Kungliga biblioteket, Stockholm. License: CC-BY-NC-ND.

make the artworks more similar, as they not only transform the images from colour to monochrome, but also make artworks of very different sizes equally large. Thus lithographic reproduction enhances a focus on content before execution, individual artistic style, or periodical style and material features.

A third painting depicts a female convalescent. The picture is not attributed to any artist in the explanatory text or under the image itself. However, the name "Ferd. Fagerlin" and "1867" can be discerned faintly in the lithographic reproduction itself. It appears that this is a painting by the Swedish painter Ferdinand Fagerlin (1825–1907), which was also part of the former King Carl XV's donation to Nationalmuseum in 1872.[23]

Also in this case, the lithographic reproduction is adjoined by a morally edifying text, which points out that "not before we are ill we learn to appreciate the value of health." The picture, however, displays the important turning point "when the strength and hope returns and the convalescent praises God." According to the explanatory text, it is this "solemn moment" that the "artist has so truthfully depicted."[24] Thus, just as in Winge's painting, it is the peripeteia, the decisive turning point of the story, or the decisive moment using a photographically charged term, which is being depicted.

Taken together, the texts accompanying the reproduction of these paintings have all a more or less clear moral and edifying function, and they evidently tie into contemporary political and ideological discourses such as nationalism, Christian religiosity, and humility and gratitude for good health and life. The text also focuses on facial expressions, which is typical for the time. Phrenology and physiognomy were well-established sciences in the nineteenth century, and the practice of looking at faces to deduce character, abilities, and intention was common practice in science as well as in popular culture in the 1870s.[25] The interest in

---

[23] *Den tillfrisknande*, 45 × 51 cm, Ferdinand Fagerlin, NM 1204. Donation through testament 1872 by Carl XV.
[24] The original text reads: "som artisten så sant tecknat."
[25] See for example Peter Hamilton and Roger Hargreaves, *The Beautiful and the Damned: The Creation of Identity in Nineteenth Century Photography* (London: National Portrait Gallery, 2001).

or focus on the decisive moments in the depicted oil paintings may also be described as a photographically charged interest typical of the time. For a contemporary viewer, this is particularly conspicuous in the adjoining texts describing images that are not visually of decisive moments, at least not as this visual theme or content has been formulated within the photographic discourse since the twentieth century.[26]

While not spoken, there is an underlying assumption that the oil paintings, reproduced through print, are transparent in the sense that they are not influenced by the artist's personal style or periodical style. On the contrary, these paintings are described as literal windows to the world, both into historical and contemporary periods. Thus there is a strong impetus to perceive the paintings as photographic images in the sense "from life," without any distortions. They are described as authentic or true and as the interpretations made in the text are "easy to observe." The interpretations focus on the emotions of the depicted humans, and as these are clearly displayed visually to its readers, they should in turn experience or ponder the same feelings.[27] There is an obvious drive to make the paintings "alive," which connects the medium of the illustrated printed album with other contemporary animating techniques like the tableaux vivant, wax cabinets, and museums, which at the time also reproduced popular oil paintings.[28] The scarcity of information on the artists—in some cases not even their names are spelled out—also emphasizes this will or assumption of transparency.

Statues

Finally the album includes three lithographic depictions of statues. The first is G. Alfred Nyström's (1844–1897) statue of the Swedish public poet Carl Michael Bellman (Figure 8).

---

[26] Henri Cartier-Bresson, *The Decisive Moment* (New York: Simon and Schuster, 1952).
[27] See quote in note 22 above.
[28] Hans Medelius, Bengt Nyström, and Elisabet Stavenow-Hidemark, *Nordiska museet under 125 år* (Stockholm: Nordiska museets förlag, 1998), 277.

Besides presenting Bellman's life and work in eighteenth-century Stockholm, the explanatory text largely dwells on the prehistory and installation of the statue at Djurgården in outskirts of the capital. Not only are the readers informed that the statue was unveiled on August 16, 1872, they also learn that the artist is a pupil of professor Molin and that the pedestal is made with "much taste and care" by the stonecutter Lemon after a design by architect Åbom.[29] In this paragraph as in the others on paintings and sculptures, the majority of the artists are presented only with their family name, which might indicate that they were well-known to the audience.

While the presentation of the Bellman statue rendered a full page of explanatory text, the second statue depicted is briefly described in one paragraph. It is said to be a Neapolitan fisher boy (Neapolitansk fiskargosse) made by Carl Gustaf Qvarnström (1810–1867). According to the text, the statue portrays the young man when he contentedly has finished his fishing and "with his eyes to the sky, through a cheerful song, expresses the vivacious feelings of his heart."[30] The statue in question was produced in marble in 1852 and was bought and hence part of the collection at the Nationalmuseum since 1860. Parian versions of the statue were in production between 1868 and 1925 at the porcelain factory Gustavsberg AB in Sweden. Thus this particular statue appears to have been widely circulated and highly appreciated by the large public in decades to come.[31]

The third statue depicted in lithographic print in the album is only presented as "Molin's fountain" in the table of contents (Figure 9). There is no text beside the lithographic print, and the short explanatory text in the beginning of the album does not give any contextual information on the artist and the artwork. This appears to be the masterpiece of the album as it also adorns the

---

[29] This refers to the architect Johan Fredrik Åbom (1817–1900), artist Johan Peter Molin (1814–1873), and stonecutter F. A. Lemon in Stockholm.

[30] The original text reads: "med blicken emot höjden, utrycker han i en munter sång, sitt hjertas lefnadsfriska känslor."

[31] Both the original and an example of the mass-produced parian versions are today part of the collection at Nationalmuseum. NMSk 397. Marble, height 103 cm; NMGu 24063. Parian, 49.5 × 34.5 × 26.5 cm.

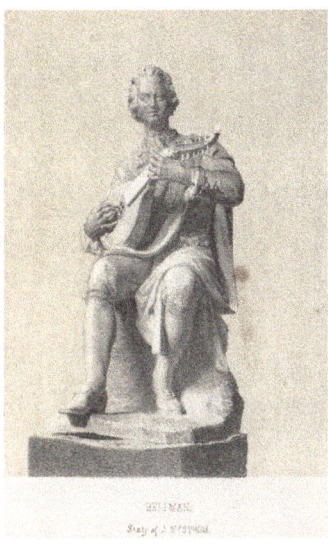

Figure 8. Lithographic depiction of Bellman statue by G. Alfred Nyström, erected in Stockholm 1872. *Lithographic Album*, 1873. Reproduction: National Library of Sweden/Kungliga biblioteket, Stockholm. License: CC-BY-NC-ND.

cover. Depicted is, however, the fountain initially created by Johan Peter Molin (1814–1873) for the Stockholm exhibition in 1866. The white plaster fountain was the centrepiece at the exhibition and was reproduced in several photographic images from the exhibition area.[32] It later became such a success that national fundraising was initiated to make a bronze version of the statue, which eventually was placed in the public garden Kungsträdgården in central Stockholm. The statue depicts characters from Nordic mythology, such as the water nymph Näcken, the sea giant Ägir, and his wife Ran and their daughters, Kolga, Hrönn, Himingläva, Unn, Duva, Blodughadda, Bylgja, Båra, and Hefring. The statue

---

[32] Johannes Jaeger's photograph of the inaguration of the exhibition, where the fontain is in the centre is alleged to be the first press photograph produced in Sweden. Rolf Söderberg and Pär Rittsel, *Den svenska fotografins historia: 1840–1940* (Stockholm: Bonnier Fakta, 1983), 85.

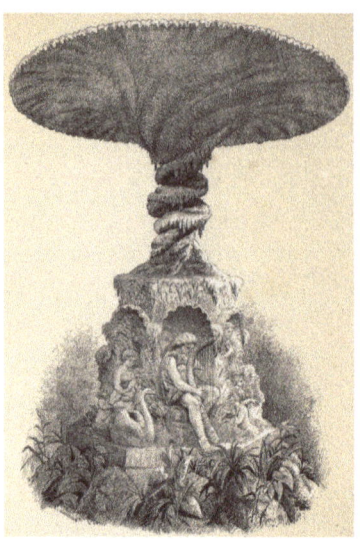

Figure 9. Lithographic depiction of Molin's fountain, erected in Stockholm 1873. In *Lithographic Album*, 1873. Reproduction: National Library of Sweden/Kungliga biblioteket, Stockholm. License: CC-BY-NC-ND.

was veiled on September 25, 1873, most possibly just before the publication of the *Lithographic Album*.[33]

The text adjoining this reproduction differs from all others in the album. It does not acknowledge the content of the artwork at all, and thus it functions as a relay and not an anchor in relation to the image, using the concepts of Roland Barthes.[34] Instead, the text argues that some artworks may not be explained in words. The text reads:

> There are artworks whose poetical content can hardly be reproduced, artworks in which the brush and the chisel express thought, which the eye more easily may apprehend than the pencil may illustrate. And among these phenomena, Molin's fountain is one which

---

[33] Adverts for the *Lithograhic Album* appeared in the daily papers in December 1873. See *Blekingeposten* December 16, 1873; *Kalmar* December 19, 1873; *Barometern* December 23, 1873.

[34] Roland Barthes, "Rhetoric of the Image," in *Image, Music, Text* (London: Fontana Press, 1977 [1964]), 40–41.

has to be seen to be perceived. A description of it would never be able to reproduce the right and original idea of this masterpiece. We limit ourselves therefore to exhibit this plate of the fountain, but eagerly invite every admirer of our melancholy stories about Ägir and his daughters, every lover of the in seaweed-covered "Näckens polka," to with their own eyes behold these romantic fairytale creatures rendered in bronze with poetic warmth.[35]

On the one hand, the lack of text beneath the image and the lack of descriptive text about the artist downplays the fact that this is a two-dimensional reproduction via print. Simultaneously, the text extrapolates that no reproduction could do justice to the original artwork. It has to be viewed in real life. This is for some reason not written out in connection to the other reproductions, while one could argue that this holds true for any reproductions of artworks independent of their medium. For one, all colours in the oil paintings have disappeared in the transformation to lithographic prints, as have their magnificent size. Indeed, it could also be argued that a two-dimensional image never could represent a three-dimensional statue. Consequently, this would hold not only for the Molin's statues, but also for the statues of Bellman and the fisher boy depicted in the album.

Transparency, Media Specificity, and Print Culture

At the time of publication the *Lithographic Album* certainly had news value. If nothing else, the cover of the album displays a topical news event—the fountain by Johan Peter Molin had been unveiled the same year, shortly after the artist's death. The other

---

[35] The original text reads: "Det finns konstverk, hvilkas poetiska innehåll kritiken har svårt att återgifva; konstverk i hvilka penseln eller mejseln, uttrycka tankar, som ögat lättare uppfattar än pennan kan åskådliggöra med ord. Och ibland dessa företeelser, är Molins fontän ett som måste ses, för att uppfattas. En beskrifning af densamma skulle aldrig kunna återgifva mästerverkets rätta och originela idé. Vi inskränkta oss derföre att hänvisa till vår plansch öfver fontänen; men uppmana ännu ifrigare hvarje beundrare af våra vemodsfulla sagor om Ägir och hans döttrar, hvarje älskare af den tongfulla 'Näckens polska,' att med egna ögon skåda dessa romantiska sagoväsenden återgifna i brons med poetisk värme."

paintings and statues reproduced in the album could likewise be considered as news. Four of the oil paintings and one of the sculptures had recently been acquired by Nationalmuseum and were hence incorporated in the Swedish art historical heritage. In addition, the paintings where inscribed, through the suggested interpretations in the adjoining texts, in contemporary political and ideological debates and thus transformed into relevant societal and political issues. Thus the texts raised the value of the artworks beyond their artistic or aesthetic value and hence the album can be said to mix art, news, and political and ideological issues of the day.

There are two understandings of transparency with regard to art and visual expressions in the album. For one, the interpretations and suggestions on how the images should be understood in the adjoining text do not acknowledge that the images are reproductions. First, the reproductive technique of lithography and its inherent media-specific features are not spelled out. Second, the two-dimensional representations are rather treated as they are real events and individuals. The anachronism is particularly poignant in the case of Winge's painting, which is taken as evidence that men endured pain and hardship much better in the Viking Age than in the nineteenth century. It appears as the oil paintings are apprehended as transparent containers of content. The fact that they are painted by a certain individual, in a certain period and geographical place, and that these paintings in turn have been reproduced through the technique of lithography is not spelled out and acknowledged. This focus on the story and downplay of the artist's work or style can be described as an expression of a photographic paradigm. Put differently, it displays a kind of photographic belief in the images. This, in turn, also implies that these artworks do not need to be viewed in reality and that their media-specific features do not have to be accounted for. Their main purpose is, on the contrary, to convey a visual message, mainly of inducing the right feelings and beliefs in the audience.

Secondly, the adjoining text of Molin's fountain displays another notion of transparency. In this case, the text urges the readers to see the fountain with their own eyes. Underlying this emphasis lies an idea of aesthetic experience, which cannot be reached through reproductions. The artwork has to be seen in real life, without any intermediaries, or its value cannot be perceived. Accordingly, this kind of artwork is not presented as a conveyer for a certain ideological, political topic or issue, but should be perceived as a media-specific aesthetic object. Yet this sculpture is a very time-typical expression of national romanticism with its characters from Nordic folklore. However, this single artwork in the album portends the notion of media specificity that has permeated the discourse on the perception of art in the twentieth century. Although not spelled out, this urge to see the artwork in place and not through a reproduction can be linked to its three-dimensional form.

In general, the medium of the original as well as the implications for transforming and representing it in two-dimensional prints is not spelled out in the *Lithographic Album*. The reader is informed that one original is an oil painting while the other two-dimensional images are only labelled "picture" (tavla, stycke). In the case of the photographs, nothing is mentioned on their original technique. The sculptures are, however, presented as sculptures and their material, such as stone and copper, are hinted at in the texts. In the case of Molin's fountain, there was, however, a veritable incentive of studying the sculpture in real life. While the sculptures on Bellman and the fisher boy had a clear "front" and "back," the Molin's fountain had vital ornaments and details all around. To see the fountain, one had to move in a circle around it, which other publications on this statue remedied by including images from four different viewpoints.[36] Such re-mediations, that is, representations of one medium through another medium, emphasize the spatially determined media specificity of the medium of sculpture.[37] Despite the fact that the concept of media specificity

---

[36] *Molins fontän i fotografi af Johannes Jaeger* (Stockholm, 1866). See also Magnus Bremmer, *Konsten att tämja en bild: Fotografiet och läsarens uppmärksamhet i 1800-talets Sverige* (Lund: Mediehistoriskt arkiv, 2015), 87–139.
[37] The term "remediation," suggested by media scholars David Jay Bolter and Richard Grusin, implies that every medium is defined as "that which remediates [...] which appropriates the techniques, forms, and social significance of other media." Jay David Bolter and Richard Grusin,

is primarily related to later periods, the high modernist art theory and critique of the mid-twentieth century, the interest and sensitivity to the particularity of different artistic mediums emerged much earlier, in art theoretical writings and, as this example evidently displays, in popular discourse on art.[38]

All but one of the adjoining texts in the *Lithographic Album* present the images as conveyer of a certain issue. Moreover, the texts emphasize that these insights could indeed be "seen" in the images. Thus this publication displays a belief typical of the time that the eye could be trained and edified and thereby used as an important tool for increasing one's knowledge. This held for contemporary scientists as well as for the public at large. In 1861, the Swedish pedagogue and researcher Per Adam Siljeström published an essay on the education of the eye, in which he argued for the importance of exercising one's eyes. He concluded that

> If anyone wants to learn to view the beauty in art he must diligently look at beautiful pictures and accustom and sharpen the eye to the right perception of beauty. Collections of paintings, statues etcetera, and in addition nature itself, are schools that one cannot neglect to visit [...]. To read gives only half the knowledge. Primarily it is about *seeing* what you read about.[39]

Remediation: Understanding New Media (Cambridge: MIT Press, 1999), 44–65.

[38] The concept of media specificity was popularized by art critic Clement Greenberg in the mid-twentieth century. See, e.g., his essays "Towards a Newer Laocoön," *Partisan Review* VII, no. 4 (July/August 1940): 296–310, and "Modernist Painting" (1961) in *Voice of America Forum Lectures* (Washington: U. S. Information Agency, 1965), 105–111. The issue was, however, adressed much earlier by Gotthold Ephraim Lessing in *Laocoön*, trans. Edward Allen McCormick (Baltimore: Johns Hopkins University Press, 1984 [1766]).

[39] Per Adam Siljeström, "Ögats uppfostran," *Läsning vid husliga härden* (1861): 170–180. The original text reads: "Vill någon lära sig att se det sköna i konsten så måste han flitigt se sköna bilder för att vänja och skärpa ögat till en rätt uppfattning af skönhetsdragen. Samlingar af taflor, statyer, o.s.v., och slutligen naturen sjelf äro skolor, som han icke får underlåta att flitigt besöka [...]. Att läsa ger blott half kunskap. Det gäller framför allt att *se* vad man läser om."

Although this text was published some ten years before, it is clear that the *Lithographic Album* combines a traditional and more modern view on what visual art might bring and how it should be perceived. It ties into the more traditional views on art as conveyer of edifying contents. Moreover, it displays some awareness of the medium of the artwork. This holds true for the oil paintings and sculptures, but not for the photographs and the reproductive techniques of lithography. From a media-historical perspective, it is evident that the *Lithographic Album* seeks to provide immediacy, which has tinged many later media, like film, television, and virtual reality, particularly in their introductory phase. What is furthermore interesting from a media-historical perspective is that a photographic paradigm colours this album in its ambition to convey stories and experiences visually, and this is done irrespective of medium used. This album thus displays mediations of different media before the advent of media specificity, which prevailed in the twentieth century.

References

Barthes, Roland. "Rhetoric of the Image." In *Image, Music, Text*. Translated by Stephen Heath. London: Fontana Press, 1977 [1964].

Belting, Hans. *Art History after Modernism*. Chicago: University of Chicago Press, 2003.

Bjurström, Per. *Gamla grafiska blad*. Västerås: ICA-förlaget, 1974.

Bolter, Jay David, and Richard Grusin. *Remediation: Understanding New Media*. Cambridge: MIT Press, 1999.

Bremmer, Magnus. *Konsten att tämja en bild: Fotografiet och läsarens uppmärksamhet i 1800-talets Sverige*. Lund: Mediehistoriskt arkiv, 2015.

Cartier-Bresson, Henri. *The Decisive Moment*. New York: Simon and Schuster, 1952.

Dahlgren, Anna. *Ett medium för visuell bildning: Kulturhistoriska perspektiv på fotoalbum 1850–1950*. Stockholm: Makadam, 2013.

Ernst, Wolfgang. "Let There Be Irony: Cultural History and Media Archeology in Parallel Lines." *Art History* 28:5 (2005): 582–603.

Gaehtgens, Thomas W., and Louis Marchesano. *Display and Art History: The Düsseldorf Gallery and Its Catalogue*. Los Angeles: Getty Research Institute, 2011.

Gitelman, Lisa, and Geoffrey B. Pingree, eds. *New Media, 1740–1915*. Cambridge: MIT Press, 2003.

Greenberg, Clement. "Modernist Painting." In *Voice of America Forum Lectures*. Washington: U. S. Information Agency, 1965.

Greenberg, Clement. "Towards a Newer Laocoön." *Partisan Review* VII, no. 4 (July/August, 1940): 296–310.

Hamilton, Peter, and Roger Hargreaves. *The Beautiful and the Damned: The Creation of Identity in Nineteenth Century Photography*. London, National Portrait Gallery, 2001.

Harvard, Jonas, and Patrik Lundell, eds. *1800-talets mediesystem*. Stockholm: Kungliga biblioteket, 2010.

Hepp, Andreas. *Cultures of Mediatization*. Cambridge: Polity, 2012.

Hjarvard, Stig. *The Mediatization of Culture and Society*. London: Routledge, 2013.

Huhtamo, Erkki, and Jussi Parikka, eds. *Media Archaeology: Approaches, Applications, and Implications*. Berkley and Los Angeles: University of California Press, 2011.

Jenkins, Henry. *Convergence Culture: Where Old and New Media Collide*. New York: New York University Press, 2006.

Karlholm, Dan. *Art of Illusion: The Representation of Art History in Nineteenth-century Germany and Beyond*. Bern: Peter Lang, 2004.

Lessing, Gotthold Ephraim. *Laocoön*. Translated by Edward Allen McCormick. Baltimore: Johns Hopkins University Press, 1984 [1766].

Litografiskt album: Portfölj för salongsbordet, Stockholm Artistiska Litografiska Anstalt. Stockholm: J. W. Svenssons Boktryckeri, 1873.

Lund, Hans. *Intermedialitet: Ord, bild och ton i samspel*. Lund: Studentlitteratur, 2002.

Lundby, Knut, ed. *Mediatization of Communication*. Berlin: De Gruyter Mouton, 2014.

Manghani, Sunil. *Image Studies*. London: Routledge, 2013.

Medelius, Hans, Bengt Nyström, and Elisabet Stavenow-Hidemark. *Nordiska museet under 125 år*. Stockholm: Nordiska museets förlag, 1998.

Molins fontän i fotografi af Johannes Jaeger. Stockholm: 1866.

Moxey, Keith. "Visual Studies and the Iconic Turn." *Journal of Visual Culture* 7:2 (2008): 131–146.

Mussell, James. *The Nineteenth-Century Press in the Digital Age*. Basingstoke: Palgrave Macmillan, 2012.

Schwartz, Vanessa R., and Jeannene M. Przyblyski, eds. *The Nineteenth-century Visual Culture Reader*. New York: Routledge, 2004.

Siljeström, Per Adam. "Ögats uppfostran," *Läsning vid husliga härden* (1861): 170–180.

Söderberg, Rolf, and Pär Rittsel. *Den svenska fotografins historia: 1840–1940*. Stockholm: Bonnier Fakta, 1983.

Söderlind, Solfrid. *Porträttbruk i Sverige 1840–1865: En funktions- och interaktionsstudie*. Stockholm: Carlsson, 1993.

Turner, Jane, ed. *The Dictionary of Art*. London: MacMillan Publishers Ltd, 1996.

Ward, Gerald W. R. *The Grove Encyclopedia of Materials and Techniques in Art*. Oxford: Oxford University Press, 2008.

Wilke, Jürgen. "Art: Multiplied Mediatization." In *Mediatization of Communication*, edited by Knut Lundby, 465–482. Berlin: De Gruyter Mouton, 2014.

Stages of Consumerism: Mass Advertising and Children's Literature in Early Twentieth-Century Sweden
Elina Druker

Abstract

This chapter discusses the motif of the sentient product in advertising during the 1930s and 1940s. The studied corpus consists of advertising that specifically targets children and adolescents but also short advertising films aimed at a wider audience. As a theoretical standpoint for my discussion, I apply Jean Baudrillard's theories about advertising and mass media and Nathalie op de Beeck's studies on the modern picture book of the interwar era and its connections to both the avant-garde and mass culture. The chapter proposes that children are to an increasing degree viewed as future members of the society but also as future consumers. The new ideas and marketing strategies expressed in the material also coincide with fundamental social changes in Swedish society resulting from modernity and new technologies. Consumption in general is described as an essential part of the modern, urban experience and the aesthetics used to describe this experience fluctuate between popular culture and experimental arts.

In the black-and-white advertising film from 1938, *The Pastille Dance* (*Pastilldansen*) by Marabou, it is the commodities that take center stage (Figure 1). In the film, the product is used to form the bodies of a female and male figure, which are constructed with round, white and black cough pastilles "Tenor" and "Figaro." The film depicts the inanimate products as dynamic and vivacious. They court each other, dance, whirl, and sing together,

---

How to cite this book chapter:
Druker, Elina. "Stages of Consumerism: Mass Advertising and Children's Literature in Early Twentieth-Century Sweden." In *The Power of the In-Between: Intermediality as a Tool for Aesthetic Analysis and Critical Reflection*, edited by Sonya Petersson, Christer Johansson, Magdalena Holdar, and Sara Callahan, 239–260. Stockholm: Stockholm University Press, 2018. DOI: https://doi.org/10.16993/baq.j. License: CC-BY.

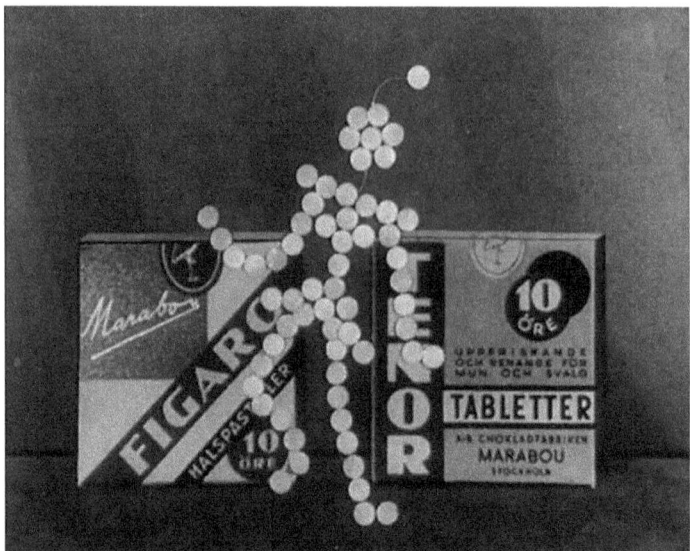

Figure 1. Advertising short film *The Pastille Dance*. Produced by Marabou, 1938. Permission: Swedish Film Institute/Svenska Filminstitutet, Stockholm. License: CC-PD. Available at http://www.filmarkivet.se/movies/marabou-pastilldansen/.

accompanied by jazz music. The short sixty-second film then concludes with a voice-over that informs the audience of the popularity and price of the products (10 öre) while the trademarks and the candy boxes are carefully presented in a final shot.[1]

The film is one of many examples of 35 mm black-and-white advertising short films from the interwar era, shown in movie theatres prior to the main film, and most likely aimed at both children and adults. The motif of the anthropomorphic figures, as well as the dual target audience of the film, points at interesting connections to children's literature, where anthropomorphized characters and animals are a well-established motif from

---

[1] Advertising short film *Pastilldansen* by Marabou 35 mm (length 1.37:1) black-and-white film, optic mono (1938). Available at the Film Archive of the Swedish Film Institute and National Library of Sweden, accessed April 10, 2017, http://www.filmarkivet.se/movies/marabou-pastilldansen/.

ancient fables to modern-day stuffed bears, toy rabbits, and dolls. However, the choice of using the products as the main characters in *The Pastille Dance* seems to reflect a general change of attitude in relation to how the emerging product world is demonstrated in advertising, literature, and art. This change is expressed through an increased fascination with sentient machines, mechanical bodies, and hybrids between human and machine. A similar interest is conveyed even in children's books. As Nathalie op de Beeck notes in her study of the modernist picture book, "independent-minded machines became a trendy topic in children's literature in the late 1920s and 1930s."[2]

In this chapter, I will discuss how the motif of the sentient product is used in early advertising aimed to children. I will study so-called branded picture books published for children in the 1930s and 1940s as well as contemporary advertising short films, with a slightly ambiguous target group. In my discussion, I will apply Jean Baudrillard's theories about advertising and mass media and Nathalie op de Beeck's research on children's literature of the interwar era, pointing at connections to both the avant-garde and mass culture. My aim is to study how different kinds of media that address both adults and children during this time period were constructed and to discuss what kind of message was conveyed to the future consumers—children.

Product Placement in Picture Books

"Look at us! We are of the best quality—KF-shoes—but we must say that it is the polish—KF's shoe polish—we have to thank for our radiant appearance."

"Now that is not quite true," said the shoe polish. "I am quite modest, if I must say, and fair's fair. Not even I could have helped you when it is so dirty outside, had you not used Gislaved's galoshes and overshoes. It is thanks to them that you can stay so

---

[2] Nathalie op de Beeck, "'The First Picture Book for Modern Children': Mary Liddell's 'Little Machinery' and the Fairy Tale of Modernity," *Children's Literature* 32 (2004): 79.

clean. For the shoes', the floor's and health's sake: use Gislaved's outdoor shoes."

Per and Lisa's Christmas Kitchen, Cooperative Union (1935)[3]

In the opening scene of *Per and Lisa's Christmas Kitchen* (*Per och Lisas julkök*, 1935) two children wake up in the middle of the night and realize that all the kitchen utensils and food products have come alive (Figure 2). The story consists of a dialogue between the two children and different kinds of products, who proudly describe their qualities and repeatedly mention their trademarks. The book is representative of publications that incorporate trademarks and products in the narratives, produced by a range of Swedish companies from the 1920s on. Some of the manufacturers that can be mentioned are candy producers Mazetti and Cloetta; others are the soap company Barnängen, the manufacturer Volvo, or the pharmaceutical company Ferrosan.[4] The largest producer of this kind of branded publication was, however, the Cooperative Union.

Branded publications were usually free of charge, and some of them were printed in very large editions (up to 250,000 copies) and were often written and illustrated by established authors and

---

[3] *Per och Lisas julkök* (Stockholm: Kooperativa förbundet, 1935). "Se på oss! Bästa kvalitet—KF-skor— men vi måste säga att det är krämen— KFs skokräm—som vi har att tacka för vårt strålande yttre." /"Det är nu inte alldeles riktigt," sa skokrämen. "Jag är blygsamheten själv och rätt skall vara rätt. Inte ens jag skulle kunna hjälpa er så smutsigt som det är ute nu, om ni inte hade använt Gislaveds galoscher och bottiner. Det är deras förtjänst att ni håller Er så fina. För skornas, golvets och hälsans skull: använd Gislaveds ytterskor."

[4] See, e.g.: Bo Beskow, *Sagan om den snälla Björnen* (Stockholm: Barnängen, 1921); *Stinas märkliga födelsedagsresa*, unknown author and illustrator (Malmö: Mazetti, 1928); Harry Molin, *Sverige runt på 8 dagar – med Örnen: En skildring av vårt lands natur och näringsliv m.m. tillägnad skolungdomen* (Stockholm: Cloetta, 1945); Astrid Lindgren and Ingrid Vang Nyman, *Pippi Långstrump delar ut solkulor* (n.p.: Ferrosan, undated, most likely 1949); *Ville Volvo vinner världen och prinsessan: Modern saga*, unknown author and illustrator (Göteborg: Volvo, 1952). For presentation and further discussion of the genre, see Elina Druker, *Eva Billow: Bilderbokskonstnär och författare* (Göteborg: Makadam, 2014), 167–180.

Stages of Consumerism 243

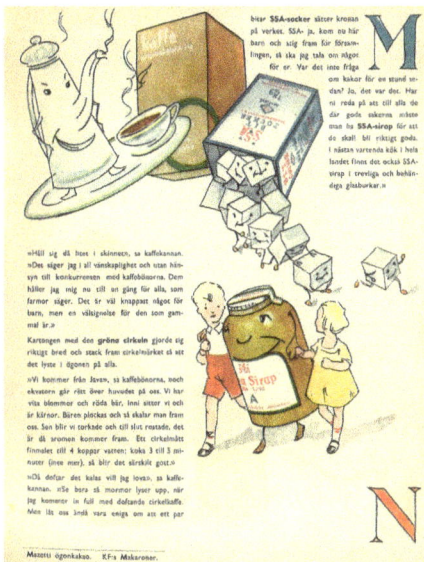

Figure 2. Anthropomorphized consumer articles in the children's picture book *Per och Lisas julkök*. Unknown illustrator, most likely Marie Walle. Produced by Atelier E.O., Kooperativa förbundet, 1935. Reproduction: Swedish Children's Literature Institute/Svenska Barnboksinstitutet, Stockholm. License: CC-BY-NC-ND. Location of rights holder for this work has been unsuccessful after a diligent search. Copyright claims to this work are welcomed.

illustrators.[5] The stories combine traditional rhymes, fairy tales, and adventure stories with advertising slogans. Product placement was implemented by including different products in the illustrations and by explicitly naming the brands in the text. Many of the books are illustrated with traditional illustration techniques, but quite often photo lithography is used and photographic reproductions of the products are included in the illustrations, creating collage-like aesthetics.[6] The reader is introduced to a range of anthropomorphized consumer articles like living food items,

---

[5] Elina Druker, "ABC for Father and Mother and Me: Representations of Children as Consumers in the Picturebook of the Interwar Period," *Issues in Early Education* 33:4 (2016): 33.

[6] Kristin Hallberg, *Den svenska bilderboken och modernismens folkhem*, (lic. diss., Stockholm University, 1996), 51.

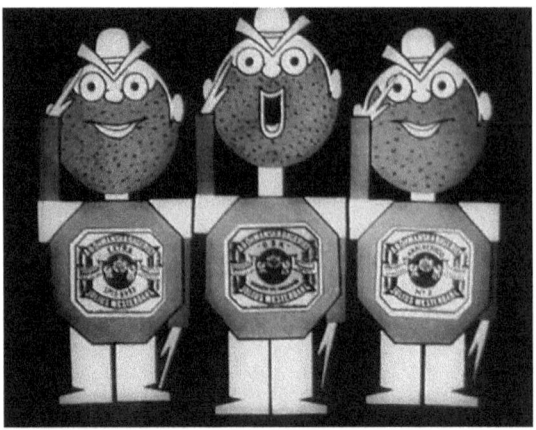

Figure 3. Advertising short film *Crisp Bread Parade*. Produced by Öhmans Spisbrödfabrik, 1933. Permission: Swedish Film Institute/Svenska Filminstitutet, Stockholm. License: CC-PD. Available at http://www.filmarkivet.se/movies/ohmans-spisbrodsfabrik-knackebrodsparaden/.

talking light bulbs or singing coffee pots. By including the animated objects as characters in the stories, with their own characteristics, feelings and voices—and quite often as companions to the children—the advertising concept is taken beyond product placement.

The Sentient Machine

Even the advertising short film *Crisp Bread Parade* (*Knäckebrödsparaden*, 1933) depicts animated and lively consumer products with human traits (Figure 3). In this black-and-white, drawn animated film promoting the Öhman Bread Factory, three packages of crisp bread, accompanied by brisk march music, stride forward. Their faces are shaped with round pieces of crisp bread, and their bodies formed with the bread packages.[7] During the song the characters' bodies are converted

---

[7] Advertising film "Öhmans Spisbrödfabrik – Knäckebrödsparaden" (1933). Music "March of the Björneborgers," unknown eighteenth-century composer. 35 mm (length 1.19:1) black-and-white film, optic mono. Available at the Film Archive of the Swedish Film Institute and National

from boxes to human-like bodies before folding down and becoming packages again, with their brand clearly visualized. They show dynamic facial expressions and move to the music with a strong regular rhythm. The tempo matches the pace of the characters, who walk side by side in step, as if marching. With their gazes aimed toward the audience, they sing: "We are Öhman's crisp bread / from the mountains of Lapland, the hills of Småland, the plains of Skåne / you will find us."[8] They also call for other "victorious" crisp breads to step forward. The march music and the vocabulary, with names of Swedish landscapes and expressions like "victorious," strengthen the military feel.[9]

The line between the animate and inanimate is called into question in the transformations taking place in both *The Pastille Dance* and the *Crisp Bread Parade*. While the products are depicted as lively, dynamic and human-like, the actual packages and their trademarks are carefully presented to the viewer, to ensure that the merchandise and brand are easily recognizable. As Anna Dahlgren points out in her article about marketing and the visual culture of window displays, brand-name packaged goods were a relatively new medium in retail stores during the 1930s.[10] By repeatedly highlighting the package in various ways in different forms of advertising, the consumer was made familiar with the brand.

Library of Sweden, accessed January 16, 2017, http://www.filmarkivet.se/movies/ohmans-spisbrodsfabrik-knackebrodsparaden/.

[8] Öhmans Spisbrödsfabrik – Knäckebrödsparaden, "Vi är Öhmans knäckebröd / Bland Lapplands fjäll, Smålands kullar, Skåneslätten finner ni oss / över allting tränga fram / Ett härligt bröd, en läckerbit för frejdad stam / Stig fram du segerrika kaka / avvisa alla livets [be]kymmerfulla dar / Att sorgen liten var. Så länge som det finnes Öhmans Spisbröd kvar."

[9] Öhmans Spisbrödsfabrik – Knäckebrödsparaden. Although "March of the Björneborgers" is a Finnish honorary march with lyrics by Johan Ludvig Runeberg, the mentioning of the Swedish landscapes can be seen in relation to the original text, which mentions several battlefields: "Söner av ett folk, som blött / På Narvas hed, på Polens sand, på Leipzigs slätter, Lützens kullar."

[10] Anna Dahlgren, "Butiken som ansikte: Skyltning som visuell kultur" in *Burkar, påsar och paket: Förpackningarnas historia i vardagens konsumtionskulturer*, eds. Ulrika Torell, Roger Qvarsell, and Jenny Lee (Stockholm: Nordiska museets förlag, 2010), 146.

In the material studied here, the products are also associated with and represent different qualities and connotations. While the bonbons in the *Pastille Dance* are accompanied by lighthearted jazz music, which provides rhythmic support to their movements, the sturdy crisp breads march to Nordic military music that could be described as patriotic. In both these examples, however, the binary of the human and the machine is constantly explored through humanization of commodities and through bodily transformations. The crisp bread packages' transformations are depicted using machine-like, non-stop, rhythmic movements. Together with the text, they are associated with qualities such as vigor, strength, and resourcefulness.

Even in the branded children's books products are given different features and characteristics, depending on the item for consumption. While cleaning products and shoe polish remind the reader of the importance of hygiene and cleanliness, it is the exotic origins of items like coffee or cacao that are emphasized. The scent of Mazetti's popular Ögon-cacao is described as "tropical loveliness" and the taste of Indian Blend tea by the Cooperative Union is said to originate "from the wonderful gardens of the orient."[11]

Even the short film *The Ideal Baking Powder* (*Marabou bakpulver – den idealiska burken*), by Marabou (1945) emphasizes machine-like but dynamic movements (Figure 4). The black-and-white stop motion film depicts three jars of baking powder, with arms and feet. The audience is first presented with two older products and then with a more recent version of the same brand. The new product greets his older relatives:

> Hello guys! Today, I am looking so fine that you should tip your hats to me. But since your hats are so hard to get off, you don't have to bother. Instead, I would like to bow to the audience and introduce my new bayonet mount, which opens instantly. It prevents

---

[11] *Per och Lisas julkök*. "KF-teet India-Blend, för det riktigt ångar av Österns underbara trädgårdar" […] "Är det inte som om alla tropikens härligheter uppenbarade sig i doften av Mazettis Ögon-kakao?"

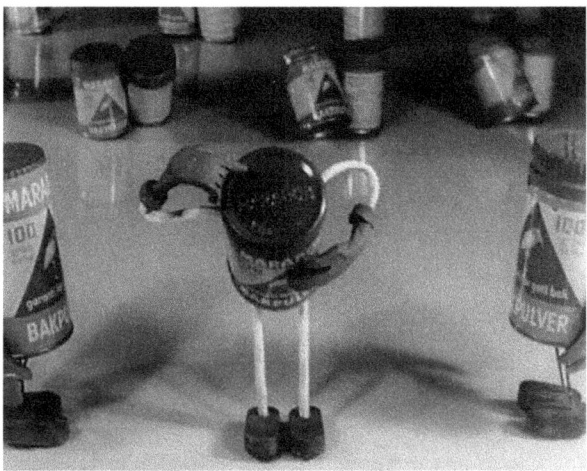

Figure 4. Advertising short film *The Ideal Baking Powder*. Produced by Marabou, 1945. Permission: Swedish Film Institute/Svenska Filminstitutet, Stockholm. License: CC-PD. Available at http://www.filmarkivet.se/movies/marabou-bakpulver-den-idealiska-burken/.

spillage and protects against moisture. An ideal jar for the ideal baking powder.[12]

The new jar steps forward and bows to the audience, lifting his hat/lid and presenting the new lid with its enhanced fastening mechanism. Unlike the pastilles and the crisp bread, it is not the merchandise itself—baking powder—but its advanced packaging to which attention is called. Behind the three main characters, other jars of the same brand are depicted, engaged in a rotating, enthusiastic dance accompanied by accordion music in the French café style. They are less anthropomorphic and are depicted

---

[12] Advertising film "Marabou bakpulver – den idealiska burken," (1945), 35 mm (length 1.37:1) black-and-white film, optic mono. "Hejsan grabbar! I dag är jag så fin så ni får lyfta på hatten för mig. Men ni har ju så svårt att få av den så ni slipper. I stället ska jag be att få bocka mig för publiken och presentera mitt nya lock med bajonettfattning, öppnas i en handvändning. Förhindrar allt spill, skyddar mot fukt, en idealisk burk för ett idealiskt bakpulver." Available at the Film Archive of the Swedish Film Institute and National Library of Sweden, accessed January 16, 2017, http://www.filmarkivet.se/movies/marabou-bakpulver-den-idealiska-burken/.

without arms and legs. In the dialogue between the characters, the juxtaposition of old and new technologies and products is emphasized, demonstrated through the meeting of the older generation and the younger, but also through the energetic movements of the dancing products and the highlighting of new technologies, represented by the novel, improved product packaging. While one of the older baking powder jars mentions that he has recently provided baking powder for a sponge cake (spilling some due to his old fashioned lid), it is noteworthy that even here, human beings are excluded entirely and the focus lies on the commodities and their interactions with each other.

An interesting characteristic in the advertising films is that the characters perform their number as actors on a stage, as if there is a live audience watching. They look directly into the camera, present themselves and the merchandise they are representing, and describe the product and its benefits. The stage-like composition can be compared to contemporary ideas about marketing and window displays. The idea of the window display as a stage was widespread during the 1920s and 1930s, shop windows were designed in a more theatrical way, with dramatic lighting that drew attention to the display, and products arranged in a narrative where they play their specific roles.[13]

This kind of use of stage-like compositions is also connected to the choice of music in the advertising films. The music is not in any way related to the products in the studied examples, but is used to convey different associations. A sense of temporariness, trendiness, and lightheartedness is created when using French café style music or jazz music, and a feeling of sturdiness and robustness is generated through march music. In his study about branding, Kevin Keller emphasizes the choice of music as a crucial part of the mental concepts or "imagery" associated with brands and brand marketing.[14] In the case of these early advertising films the

---

[13] See, e.g., Louise Nilsson, *Färger, former, ljus: Svensk reklam och reklampsykologi, 1900–1930* (PhD Diss., Uppsala: Acta Universitatis Upsaliensis, 2010), 142–147. Dahlgren, "Butiken som ansikte," 147.

[14] Kevin Lane Keller, *Strategic Brand Management: Building, Measuring, and Managing Brand Equity* (New York City: Pearson, 2013). See also

use of music is connected to popular culture, to dance troupes and films. Studying advertising jingles, David Huron proposes that use of music in advertising can serve the overall promotional goal in several capacities, to target a wanted demographical audience, to enhance an ad's credibility and to create memorability, to mention some of the most central objectives.[15] According to Huron, one of the most significant capacities is, however, the entertainment value of music. Advertising that is experienced as entertaining and engaging is seen as the most straightforward way of achieving the audience's attention.[16] Associations with contemporary popular music, with music industry, dance troupes, and musicals in the advertising films can thus be seen as attempts to create an imagery that links the product with innovation and trendiness, but also with a sense of entertainment, even though the marketed commodities are everyday items like cough pastilles or baking products.

The interest in the modernist's fetishized thing, already introduced in avant-garde cinema and photography, is apparent in both the advertising short films and the branded picture books. They represent a mixture of the real—everyday products—and the fantastic. Aesthetically, several of the films demonstrate the influence of contemporary, experimental film. In fact, the rotating and swirling images, repetitive movements, quick cuts, and dramatic graphic forms are reminiscent of the experimental Dadaist and Surrealist cinema of the 1920s, which frequently use rhythmic, machine-like effects and movements.[17] Both *The Pastille Dance* and a following short film by the same company, *Tenor & Figaro* from 1939, play with the figurative and abstract, employing geometric figures in motion, organized into two-dimensional forms

---

Nicolai Jørgensgaard Graakjær, "The Bonding of a Band and a Brand: On Music Placement in Television Commercials from a Text Analytical Perspective," *Journal of Popular Music and Society*, vol. 37, issue 5 (2014): 517–537.
[15] David Huron, "Music in Advertising: An Analytic Paradigm," *Musical Quarterly*, vol. 73, no. 4 (1989): 557–574.
[16] Huron, "Music in Advertising," 562.
[17] See, e.g., Malcolm Turvey, *The Filming of Modern Life: European Avant-garde Film of the 1920s* (Cambridge: MIT Press, 2011).

and patterns. In the latter film, the product is not used to form anthropomorphic figures, but, instead, the film plays with the spatial illusionism that derives from the dynamic interplay of contrasting round forms in black and white, formed by the pastilles. This means of expression bears a resemblance with Hans Richter's abstract films from the early 1920s or Oskar Fischinger's abstract colour film *Optical Poem* (1938), where colourful circles move rhythmically across the screen.

It appears that these early advertising films borrowed stylistic expressions and narrative techniques from both the avant-garde experimental films and the buoyant, rapidly growing mass-market entertainment. This kind of influence of the avant-garde can be seen in all fields of mass-media advertising. Inspired by both futurist and constructivist aesthetics, arrangements with consumer articles were used to form strongly stylized shapes like circles, arcs, squares, and semicircles in both posters and window displays.[18] Even the functionalist ideas often emphasized repetition and machine-like aesthetics. In her description of the Cooperative Movement exhibition *Without Borders* in 1957, Helena Mattsson writes that using a repetitive technique of presentation of the exhibited products "was a way to de-emphasise the uniqueness of each item, and to highlight their communal quality."[19] The method of repetition of identical, mass-produced products is applied in a similar manner in the advertising short films, where the goods are used to create ornamental, rhythmic compositions. Another parallel, which is probably most obvious in *The Pastille Dance*, is found in the music and dance industry during the 1930s and 1940s, with its hugely popular dance troupes and dance films. Even here, a fascination for figures in motion is essential, with dancers, singers, or even synchronized swimmers forming rotating, rhythmic arrangements and geometric figures.

How, then, should we evaluate the transmediations and aesthetic experiments taking place in these advertising short films?

---

[18] Dahlgren, "Butiken som ansikte," 150.
[19] Helena Mattsson, "Designing the Reasonable Consumer: Standardisation and Personalisation in Swedish Functionalism," in *Swedish Modernism: Architecture, Consumption and the Wellfare State*, eds. Helena Mattsson and Sven-Olov Wallenstein (London: Black Dog, 2010), 90.

According to Jean Baudrillard, advertising, marketing strategies, mass media and culture, as well as the increasing proliferation of products during this era, multiplied the quantity of signs and spectacles, and created a proliferation of sign-value. Products cannot consequently merely be characterized by their use-value and exchange value, but also by their sign-value.[20] The term thus describes the value given to an object because of what it communicates, rather than the material value and function derived from the use of the object. For example, the advertising film *The Ideal Baking Powder* not only promotes baking powder, but the product also *signifies* knowledge of new, modern kitchen equipment and consumer articles and, in general, a modern, up-to-date lifestyle.

At the beginning of the previous century, both the magazine and advertising industries were quick to borrow visual mannerisms from modernist art movements such as Art Nouveau or Art Deco, and later, from avant-garde movements such as Surrealism. Innovative style, speed and energy, as well as associations with new techniques and media, are an important part of the "imagery," to use Kelly's term, that is associated with the products. This means that products like baking powder or cough pastilles are promoted using mental concepts that are associated with connotations outside the product's function. The kind of stylistic imitation that is expressed in advertising could be described as a market-driven aesthetics that makes use of associations with the avant-garde—its innovation and novelty as a sign-value—and transfers these associations to the product.

Designing Consumers

Both the advertising books and the advertising short films demonstrate an interesting and dynamic meeting of commercial entertainment and artistic innovation, of oppositional and marginalized strands of art, advertisement, and culture. On one hand, repeating certain products and trademarks in different forms of advertising

---

[20] Jean Baudrillard, *Selected Writings*, ed. Mark Posner (Stanford: Stanford University Press, 1988), 42.

for children, the child—a future consumer—is made familiar with certain brands and trademarks. On the other hand, seen in the context of children's culture and literature, the mixed-media aesthetics applied in the commercial books, as well as the focus on machines and anthropomorphic consumer articles, means that new motifs were introduced to children. The expressions and the narrative techniques used in children's literature during this time were thus broadened.

The sentient product, both in the children's books and in the advertising films, offers an early example of media cross-over. In both these cases, objects obtain a voice and an independent agency—even though they are at the same time depicted as mass-market commodities, produced in large quantities, and identical to other similar products. The motif with the animated, sentient consumer item reflects a general commercialization of children's daily life in the Western world that took place during the first four decades of the twentieth century, as shown by previous researchers like Viviane Zelizer or Daniel Thomas Cook.[21] The development is similar in Sweden, where children were increasingly often treated as consumers in different forms of advertisement starting in the 1930s.[22] This coincides with a time period in Sweden where the consumer became of central concern in a wider design discourse.[23] Both governmental and private actors began gradually creating consumer policies and marketing strategies in order to construct a welfare state consumer.

The idea that children's culture and literature bears ideological traces of the culture that produces them is possibly self-evident. As

---

[21] Daniel Thomas Cook, *The Commodification of Childhood: The Children's Clothing Industry and the Rise of the Child Consumer* (Durham: Duke University Press, 2004); Viviana A. Rotman Zelizer, *Pricing the Priceless Child: The Changing Social Value of Children* (New York: Basic Books, 1985).

[22] Viveka Berggren Torell and Helene Brembeck, eds., *Det konsumerande barnet: Representationer av barn och konsumtion i svensk dags- och veckopress under 1900-talet med utgångspunkt i reklamannonser* (Gothenburg: Gothenburg University, 2001).

[23] Helena Mattsson, "Designing the 'Consumer in Infinity': The Swedish Co-operative Union's New Consumer Policy, c. 1970," in *Scandinavian Design: Alternative Histories*, ed. Fallan Kjetil (London: Berg, 2012), 67.

Nathalie op de Beeck writes in her study of the American picture book of the interwar period, *Suspended Animation: Children's Picture Books and the Fairy Tale of Modernity*, "[t]he picture book developed at a time when avant-garde art movements, sociopolitical climates, and changing technologies called for shifts in perceptions."[24] In her study, Op de Beeck points briefly at connections between the development of the animated film and children's literature, although she doesn't discuss advertising aimed at children. She argues that while the moving images of a film and the sequential still images in a picture book "stand in different relations to time" (since the reading of a picture book is a process that can be halted, hastened, or even reversed), the early animation and picture books share similar subject matters and are strongly based on a sequentiality.[25] Both animation and children's books from the interwar era also share a fascination with the mechanized body, as Op de Beeck suggests.

How should we then understand the lively, anthropomorphic products appearing in both the advertising books for children and in the short films? It is quite clear that new motifs are introduced to the child audience in the studied corpus, motifs that to some extent differ from children's literature published via traditional publishing houses. While the majority of children's literature during the interwar era still expresses strong interest in idyllic settings and fairy tales, many of the branded picture books portray new technologies through a general affirmation of speed and movement, modern means of transportation, urban environments, and technical innovations.[26] The children are depicted traveling to other countries, communicating with sentient machines, flying airplanes or even space ships. The publications with embedded marketing express a general optimism and confidence in the child's capacity to cope with the urban consumer society and its new technologies and media.

---

[24] Nathalie op de Beeck, *Suspended Animation: Children's Picture Books and the Fairy Tale of Modernity* (Minneapolis: University of Minnesota Press, 2010), xvi.
[25] Op de Beeck, *Suspended Animation*, 142.
[26] Elina Druker, "ABC for Father and Mother and Me."

Apart from the commercial objectives expressed in the studied material, the motif of the sentient commodity can be seen as a way of addressing the urban child's increasing alienation from the means of production, instead placing the child as a consumer and an actor in a mass-market society. The fundamental changes taking place in the society meant that machines and commercially manufactured things were now becoming an increasingly important part of people's lives, including children. Personifying the machines and products can be seen as a way of establishing positive relationships between children and the changes shaped by such items and devices. Taking part in consumer information and advertisement, recognizing and relating to consumer articles, as well as responsible consumer behavior were seen as qualities that the modern child had to acquire. The branded picture books can thus be seen as a way to prepare children for future life in a consumer society.

Some of the branded books published for children also described how and where the articles were produced and include illustrations of the manufacturing plants in the stories. This is the case in, for instance, *Stina's Peculiar Birthday Journey* (*Stinas märkliga födelsedagsresa*, 1928), which describes how cocoa is produced and transported to Sweden.[27] The illustrations in this simple book can be described as conventional, but the concept of describing the manufacturing and transport of the product in stories for children can be seen in relation to "factual books" or "production books," which describe modern industry and technology in the young reader's modern context.[28] These notions are consistent with some of the ideas about "modern" children's books that emerge during the 1920s in America, Europe and Soviet Russia. An influential work in this context is Lucy Sprague Mitchell's *Here and Now Story Book* (1921), in which the author applies a "here and now" methodology. This involves children learning

---

[27] *Stinas märkliga födelsedagsresa* (Malmö: Mazetti, 1928).
[28] Evgeny Steiner, "Mirror Images: On Soviet-Western Reflections in Children's Books of the 1920s and 1930s," in *Children's Literature and the Avant-garde*, eds. Elina Druker and Bettina Kümmerling-Meibauer (Amsterdam: John Benjamins Publishing Company, 2015), 201.

about the world by studying their surrounding reality, especially modern technical things, machines, and urban life.[29] Op de Beeck describes the tendency as follows: "Children were to be armed with practical understandings of the modern world so that they might become active engineers of the future, as opposed to passive victims of industry."[30] This would mean that even advertising aimed at children could be seen as a way to offer practical understanding of the modern world and the consumer society and thus change the child audience's awareness of themselves.

In a Swedish context it is also significant that the most comprehensive and large-scale marketing strategy targeting the child audience was that of the Cooperative Union, which for several decades was a significant actor in the Swedish commercial and political landscape. The organization had a vast influence on consumer policies but also on marketing, design, and advertising, and became an important participant in the development of the Swedish welfare state.[31] Through its advertising agency Svea, the Cooperative Union developed marketing techniques that combined advertising, design, art, film, and different informational campaigns.[32] Even here, the idea of repetitive marketing in different forms of advertising and media is seen as the most effective strategy.

How, then, are ideas of modernity, welfare ideology, and early consumerism connected in the studied material? According to Baudrillard, rather than promoting a specific product with the purpose of selling, advertising promotes the entire social system. In other words, advertising could be considered more as a way of signifying a way of life than an economic practice. "The fundamental, unconscious, and automatic choice of the consumer is to accept the life-style of a particular society (no longer is there a real choice: the theory of the autonomy and sovereignty of the consumer is thus refuted)," Baudrillard states in "Consumer

---

[29] Lucy Sprague Mitchell, *Here and Now Story Book: Two- to Seven-year-olds* (New York: Dutton, 1921).
[30] Op de Beeck, *Suspended Animation*, 129.
[31] Mattsson, "Designing the 'Consumer in Infinity,'" 65.
[32] Mattsson, "Designing the 'Consumer in Infinity,'" 70.

Society."[33] He argues that rather than focusing on the functional properties of the advertised goods, advertising articulates their emotional or symbolic properties, thereby unleashing an endless process of consumption that has lost its connection to exchange and only reflects a symbolic system which classifies goods into different categories. Applying Baudrillard's interpretation of the idea of the spectacle, Op de Beeck claims that the picture book of the interwar era "signals a change in reading subjects' awareness of themselves as spectators and as parts of the grand modern spectacle."[34] The advertising books and short films can thus be seen as two examples among many types of stories and images that were used in an attempt to reach the child consumer and, furthermore, with the goal of creating modern, competent consumer subjects who could function in the emerging welfare society.

Conclusion

In this chapter I have studied advertising that targets children and adolescents and demonstrates some of the wide-ranging changes taking place in Sweden during the first half of the twentieth century. Both the short advertising films and the branded publications for children are part of new commercial platforms that emerged in the beginning of the twentieth century. The occurrence of speaking, singing, and dancing anthropomorphic products in the studied corpus points at a shift during this era where children were viewed to an increasing degree as future members of the society but also as consumers. The sentient products presented in the material were used to attract both child and adult consumers and to create brand awareness among them, but they can also be seen as a way of addressing a general, increasing interaction between children, different commodities, and the consumer society.

It is apparent that already during the 1930s the advertising industry is intentionally and strategically using different fields of marketing and various media, even when targeting the child

---

[33] Baudrillard, *Selected Writings*, 37.
[34] Op de Beeck, *Suspended Animation*, 162.

consumer. Consumption is described as an essential part of the modern, urban experience and children are included here as both competent child consumers and as implied future (grown-up) consumers. The same products, and their brand-named packages, are presented in a range of media, from posters and window displays to short films and picture books for children. What we see is a network of media where advertising that targets children is constantly formed in connection to children's culture, media, consumerism, and art, a system of relations that swings between high arts, avant-garde, and mass culture.

When describing the quickly developing commercial market during the inter-war era in Sweden, relations between media become not only illustrative but fundamental for the media-historical changes taking place. The networks of influences and stimuli between different media also raises theoretical and methodological questions about the study of children's literature and culture and stresses the fruitfulness of taking a larger media-historical context in to consideration when studying media or literature targeted to children. Transmediation, in this case understood as movement of products, subject matters, and aesthetic strategies between different media, is central in the all-embracing marketing strategies applied. The depictions of the sentient products in the studied material are characterized by energetic and lively movement as well as innovative, rhythmic visual effects. The commodities convey a general sense of innovation and modernity but are also described with human-like behavior and emotions; they take center stage, not only in the advertisements, but in the modern consumer society in general.

References

Baudrillard, Jean. *Selected Writings*. Edited by Mark Posner. Stanford: Stanford University Press, 1988.

Berggren Torell, Viveka, and Helene Brembeck, eds. *Det konsumerande barnet: Representationer av barn och konsumtion i svensk dags- och veckopress under 1900-talet med utgångspunkt i reklamannonser*. Gothenburg: Gothenburg University, 2001.

Beskow, Bo. *Sagan om den snälla björnen*. Stockholm: Barnängen, 1921.

Cook, Daniel Thomas. *The Commodification of Childhood: The Children's Clothing Industry and the Rise of the Child Consumer*. Durham: Duke University Press, 2004.

Dahlgren, Anna. "Butiken som ansikte: Skyltning som visuell kultur." In *Burkar, påsar och paket: Förpackningarnas historia i vardagens konsumtionskulturer*, edited by Ulrika Torell, Roger Qvarsell, and Jenny Lee, 143–161. Stockholm: Nordiska museets förlag, 2010.

Druker, Elina. "ABC for Father and Mother and Me: Representations of Children as Consumers in the Picturebook of the Interwar Period." *Issues in Early Education* 3:34 (2016): 22–35.

Druker, Elina. *Eva Billow: Bilderbokskonstnär och författare*. Göteborg: Makadam, 2014.

Jørgensgaard Graakjær, Nicolai. "The Bonding of a Band and a Brand: On Music Placement in Television Commercials from a Text Analytical Perspective." *Journal of Popular Music and Society*, vol. 37, issue 5 (2014): 517–537.

Hallberg, Kristin. *Den svenska bilderboken och modernismens folkhem*. Lic. diss., Stockholm University, 1996.

Huron, David. "Music in Advertising: An Analytic Paradigm." *Musical Quarterly*, vol. 73, no. 4 (1989): 557–574.

Keller, Kevin Lane. *Strategic Brand Management: Building, Measuring, and Managing Brand Equity*. New York City: Pearson, 2013.

Lindgren, Astrid, and Ingrid Vang Nyman. *Pippi Långstrump delar ut solkulor*. N.p.: Ferrosan, 1949 (?).

Mattsson, Helena. "Designing the 'Consumer in Infinity': The Swedish Co-operative Union's New Consumer Policy, c. 1970." In *Scandinavian Design: Alternative Histories*, edited by Kjetil Fallan, 65–82. London: Berg, 2012.

Mattsson, Helena. "Designing the Reasonable Consumer: Standardisation and Personalisation in Swedish Functionalism." In *Swedish Modernism: Architecture, Consumption and the Welfare*

State, edited by Helena Mattsson and Sven-Olov Wallenstein, 74–99. London: Black Dog, 2010.

Mitchell, Lucy Sprague. *Here and Now Story Book. Two- to Seven-year-olds.* New York: Dutton, 1921.

Nilsson, Louise. *Färger, former, ljus: Svensk reklam och reklampsykologi, 1900–1930.* PhD. Diss., Uppsala: Acta Universitatis Upsaliensis, 2010.

Molin, Harry. *Sverige runt på 8 dagar – med Örnen: En skildring av vårt lands natur och näringsliv m.m. tillägnad skolungdomen.* Stockholm: Cloetta, 1945.

Op de Beeck, Nathalie. "'The First Picture Book for Modern Children': Mary Liddell's 'Little machinery' and the Fairy Tale of Modernity." *Children's Literature* 32 (2004): 41–83.

Op de Beeck, Nathalie. *Suspended Animation: Children's Picture Books and the Fairy Tale of Modernity.* Minneapolis: University of Minnesota Press, 2010.

Per och Lisas julkök. Stockholm: Kooperativa förbundet, 1935.

Steiner, Evgeny. "Mirror Images: On Soviet-Western Reflections in Children's Books of the 1920s and 1930s." In *Children's Literature and the Avant-garde,* edited by Elina Druker and Bettina Kümmerling-Meibauer, 189–213. Amsterdam: John Benjamins Publishing Company, 2015.

Stinas märkliga födelsedagsresa. Malmö: Mazetti, 1928.

Turvey, Malcolm. *The Filming of Modern Life: European Avant-garde Film of the 1920s.* Cambridge: MIT Press, 2011.

Ville Volvo vinner världen och prinsessan: Modern saga. Göteborg: Volvo, 1952.

Zelizer, Viviana A. Rotman. *Pricing the Priceless Child: The Changing Social Value of Children.* New York: Basic Books, 1985.

Films

Marabou bakpulver – den idealiska burken, Marabou, 1945. Available at the Film Archive of the Swedish Film Institute and

National Library of Sweden. Accessed April 10, 2017. http://www.filmarkivet.se/movies/marabou-bakpulver-den-idealiska-burken/.

Pastilldansen. Stockholm: Marabou, 1938. Available at the Film Archive of the Swedish Film Institute and National Library of Sweden. Accessed April 10, 2017. http://www.filmarkivet.se/movies/marabou-pastilldansen/.

Öhmans Spisbrödfabrik – Knäckebrödsparaden, 1933. Available at the Film Archive of the Swedish Film Institute and National Library of Sweden. Accessed April 10, 2017. http://www.filmarkivet.se/movies/ohmans-spisbrodsfabrik-knackebrodsparaden/.

Mediating Public Cultural Policy: Buildings, Bills, and Films as Governmentality

Fredrik Krohn Andersson

Abstract

This article examines how the supposedly new public cultural policy in Sweden during the 1960 and 1970s was mediated and materialized in a number of forms. The cultural policy encompassed both a contradiction between the emphasis on a broadened concept of culture and a more narrow understanding of cultural practices, as well as a conflict between elements of power and control in policymaking, and assertions on the necessarily free character of the cultural domain. Departing from three cases, in form of the government committee report *Ny kulturpolitik* 1972 and the government bill on cultural policy 1974, the building Kulturhuset in Stockholm 1974, and the information film *Jämlikhet – för handikappade?* 1973, an approach of governmentality is in conjunction with perspectives of inter- and transmediality implemented in order to analyze how the potentially inherent conflicts and contradictions of the cultural policy were enacted in these various mediated forms.

Introduction

A radical change in the understanding of the concept of culture and the role of culture in society occurred in Sweden, as well as

---

How to cite this book chapter:
Krohn Andersson, Fredrik. "Mediating Public Cultural Policy: Buildings, Bills, and Films as Governmentality." In *The Power of the In-Between: Intermediality as a Tool for Aesthetic Analysis and Critical Reflection*, edited by Sonya Petersson, Christer Johansson, Magdalena Holdar, and Sara Callahan, 261–283. Stockholm: Stockholm University Press, 2018. DOI: https://doi.org/10.16993/baq.k. License: CC-BY.

in many other countries, during the post-war period.[1] In Sweden, from the very late 1950s onwards, an actual cultural policy began to take shape, epitomized in the 1974 government bill of cultural policy. Parallel to this change a physical infrastructure was constructed in the form of "kulturhus," that is, cultural centers or, literary, "culture houses." The culture houses were buildings that during the time were described as being "the jewel in the crown" of the Swedish welfare state construction, and the field of culture as the last major reform area in society.

The aim of this article is to examine a number of mediations of the "new" Swedish cultural policy. The mediating materials and cases that I will focus on are the government committee report *Ny kulturpolitik* (*New cultural policy*) from 1972 and the government bill on cultural policy from 1974, the Kulturhuset (*Culture house*) building in Stockholm built between 1968 and 1974, and an information film called *Jämlikhet – för handikappade?* (*Equality – for the Handicapped?*) concerning the possibilities for disabled to take part in public cultural activities, from 1973.

In this article a basic intermedial approach is proposed. This approach enables a flattened view on the studied materials, a view that serves to destabilize and de-hierarchize some of the previous ways of reading and interpreting them. The purpose of the approach is twofold: first that it disentangles the given order of reading between the materials where notions of supposedly original meaning and source is suspended, and secondly that it makes possible a more distanced and non-teleological approach to the realizations, by not necessarily privileging certain formerly handed down utterances of established and canonized author functions. What is of interest here is how a common content, the new cultural policy, is realized, transformed, and scrutinized in a number of medial and material forms that also in different respects remediate each other.

In their influential work *Remediation*, Bolter and Grusin contend rather straightforwardly that a medium is that which

---

[1] This work was supported by generous grants from the Åke Wiberg foundation, the Birgit and Gad Rausing foundation, and the Brandförsäkringsverket research foundation.

remediates.² As Lars Elleström has pointed out, there is a vagueness to this conceptualization of mediation, in that everything indiscriminately can mediate and remediate everything else.³ Following Elleström, a basic differentiation and qualification of relations of mediations and remediations, in Elleström's words "media border crossings," is applied. These concern, on one hand, medial relations as combination and integration, in other words intermediality, and, on the other hand, relations as mediation and transformation, in other words, transmediality.⁴ Drawing upon the work of Jørgen Bruhn, who has elaborated on this distinction, I will focus on different types of mediating relations between my different cases.⁵ Regarding the relations between the report, the bill, and the building I will do so primarily in terms of transmediality, that is, highlighting the processes of the transferring of certain aspects between the mediations, and consequently, not of others.⁶ To some extent I will also pay attention to relations of combination and integration, and then mainly in the case of the film and its relations to the other two cases.

It is essential to underscore that these intermedial and transmedial relations are seen as dimensions of the mediations and not constitutive features. The mediations are not integrating or transferring in and out of themselves but rather points to one aspect of them. On a basic level it would be possible to see how the committee report, with its printed text and reproduced photographs, and the building, incorporating a vast number of materializations including books in the library section, exhibit combinatory qualities or mixed elements, but those relations are not necessarily highlighted.

---

² Jay David Bolter and Richard Grusin, *Remediation: Understanding New Media* (Cambridge: MIT Press, 1999), 65.
³ Lars Elleström, "The Modalities of Media: A Model for Understanding Intermedial Relations," in *Media Borders, Multimodality and Intermediality*, ed. Lars Elleström (Basingstoke: Palgrave Macmillan, 2010), 47, note 53.
⁴ Elleström, "Modalities of Media," 28.
⁵ Jørgen Bruhn, *The Intermediality of Narrative Literature: Medialities Matter* (Palgrave Macmillan: London, 2016).
⁶ Bruhn, *Intermediality of Narrative Literature*, 26.

In line with Bolter and Grusin, I regard the studied mediations, and especially the juxtaposition of the relations between them, as potentially constituting a network.[7] How temporary and contingent the fixation of this network may be, it is as a network that the "new" cultural policy is being produced, thus also underscoring the implications of the mediations as parts of wider technical, social, and economic circumstances.

Concerning the content of the mediations, there are two central issues that I particularly want to focus on. Firstly, it involves a possible contradiction between the emphasis on a broadened concept of culture in the discourse of cultural policy, and what seems to be an actually more narrow understanding of culture in the mediated cultural practices. Secondly, it concerns the conflict between, on the one hand, the obvious and inevitable element of enactment of power, control, and governance in cultural policymaking, and, on the other hand, the strong assertions in the cultural policy discourse on the necessary and unconditional character of freedom in and of the cultural domain. The aim is to analyze if and, in that case, how these inherent conflicts and contradictions were enacted in these various mediated forms. Do they support or challenge each other? What do they tell us, and how do they tell us, about the potential or limits of the new cultural policy, and what kind of understanding of culture did these mediations produce?

Previous Studies

There has not been any shortage of studies concerning cultural policy in Sweden and elsewhere, and its development and effects during the second half of the twentieth century.[8] Neither has there been any shortage of studies of culture houses, or rather,

---

[7] Bolter and Grusin, *Remediation*, 65–67.
[8] See, e.g., Anders Frenander, *Debattens vågor: Om politisk-ideologiska frågor i efterkrigstidens svenska kulturdebatt* (PhD diss., University of Gothenburg, 1999); Anders Frenander, *Kulturen som kulturpolitikens stora problem: Diskussionen om svensk kulturpolitik under 1900-talet* (Hedemora: Gidlund, 2005); Anders Frenander, "Svensk kulturpolitik under 1900-talet," *Tijdschrift voor Skandinavistiek* 22, no. 1 (2001); Tobias Harding, *Nationalising Culture: The Reorganisation of National Culture in Swedish Cultural Policy 1970–2002* (PhD diss., University of

specifically the Culture house or Cultural center in Stockholm. The perspective in which the Culture house in Stockholm has been framed has almost exclusively been from the side of the creator of the building, the architect Peter Celsing. This previous research follows a standardized art and architectural historical modus, producing an author-creator function, and relating it to other even more established author-creator functions in the pantheon of, in this case, architectural history. Wilfried Wang, for example, relates Celsing to Lois Kahn, Le Corbusier, Louis Sullivan, and Ludwig Mies van der Rohe; Daniel Fernández-Carracedo relates Celsing to Mies van der Rohe and Le Corbusier, and, in the case of the Swedish central bank building, which was a part of the total Culture house programme, to Palladio, Borromini, and Nicodemus Tessin the Elder; Lars Olof Larson relates Celsing to Le Corbusier, Adolf Loos, Claude-Nicolas Ledoux, and Giovanni Battista Piranesi; and Johan Örn relates Celsing to Carlo Scarpa and Alvar Aalto.[9]

Studies of the relations between cultural policy and buildings for cultural activities and culture houses are scarcer, but the phenomenon have been briefly touched upon by literary historian and cultural policy researcher Sven Nilsson.[10] Nilsson builds an argument on the premises that the idea and concept of culture houses was at best an expression of utopianism and at worst

---

Linköping, 2007); My Klockar Linder, *Kulturpolitik: Formeringen av en modern kategori* (PhD diss., Uppsala University, 2014).

[9] Wilfried Wang, "An Architecture of Inclusive Purity," in *The Architecture of Peter Celsing*, ed. Olof Hultin (Stockholm: Arkitektur förlag, 1996); Daniel Fernández-Carracedo, *Peter Celsing en el complejo de Sergels Torg: La Casa de la Cultura de Estocolmo* (PhD diss., Technical University Madrid, 2015); Daniel Fernández-Carracedo, "Celsings bärande idé," *Arkitektur: Swedish Architectural Review*, no. 5 (2012); Daniel Fernández-Carracedo, "Confluences of Two Worlds in Peter Celsing's Architecture. Outside & Inside – West & East," *Esempi di Architettura* 3, no. 1 (2016); Lars Olof Larsson, "Peter Celsings arkitektur," in *Peter Celsing: En bok om en arkitekt och hans verk*, eds. Lars Olof Larsson et al. (Stockholm: Liber förlag/Arkitekturmuseet, 1980); Johan Örn, *I rummets kraftfält: Om arkitektur och offentlig inredning i Sverige 1935–1975* (PhD diss., Swedish Royal Institute of Technology, 2007).

[10] Sven Nilsson, "När kulturen satte bo," *Arkitektur: Swedish Architectural Review*, no. 5 (2003).

authoritarian totalitarianism and dictatorship. Moreover, Nilsson contends that the Swedish and social democratic context has been anti-utopian and, implicitly, also anti-authoritarian, and consequently concludes that the idea of culture houses has not been particularly viable in Sweden. Where they do exist, they are interpreted entirely against a background of the French initiative of *Maisons de la culture* under the French ministry of culture of André Malraux. According to Nilsson, the concept of culture houses is not consistent with what he calls the Swedish cultural situation, which he describes as low-key, intimate, and home-like. Consequently, this then stands in conflict with the integrated, centralized, and multi-functional character of the culture house. Despite Nilsson's skepticism about the strength and power of the culture house idea, a number of culture houses were built in Sweden during the period when public cultural policy began to take shape, of which the Culture house in Stockholm was perhaps one of the most striking and, at the time, discussed, but far from only, example.

Points of Departure

Departing from the aforementioned conflicts and contradictions between concepts of culture and between freedom and governance I will draw upon Michel Foucault's conceptualization of biopolitics and governmentality.[11]

Within an architectural theoretical and historical context there has been a frequent reference to the idea of the Panopticon that Foucault analyzed in *Discipline and Punish*.[12] The main focus in these cases has been the production of docile bodies, on discipline

---

[11] This approach is indebted to Sven-Olov Wallenstein and his work on architecture, biopolitics, and governmentality, see Sven-Olov Wallenstein, *Biopolitics and the Emergence of Modern Architecture* (New York: Princeton Architectural Press, 2009); and Sven-Olov Wallenstein, "A Family Affair: Swedish Modernism and the Administering of Life," in *Swedish Modernism: Architecture, Consumption and the Welfare State*, eds. Helena Mattsson and Sven-Olov Wallenstein (London: Black Dog Publishing, 2010).

[12] Michel Foucault, *Discipline and Punish: The Birth of the Prison* (Harmondsworth: Penguin, 1979).

and the internalization of discipline by those being monitored, and the classic examples have been the prison, the barracks, and the clinic.[13]

In the cases studied here, the apparent and explicit disciplination seems to be less prominent. In many ways, it rather seems to concern quite the opposite through the claims and strong emphasis on freedom, participation, and democracy in the cultural policy discourse. This actualizes the idea of governance without governing that Foucault develops in the later lectures on governmentality and biopolitics.[14] I will also draw upon the elaboration of the concept of governmentality by Nikolas Rose and Peter Miller, where they formulate this mode as a "governing at a distance" and as to act "at a distance."[15]

The emerging cultural policy discourse can, admittedly, be seen as a way to discipline, administer, and explicitly control both individuals and the population through the establishment of an actual political field or domain, which is linked to specific physical institutions and associated with specific practices. However, at the same time, a non-intervening feature is strongly present in this discourse, for example through notions of "arm's length principle" and the vivid articulations on culture's, by necessity, free and independent character, and assertions that culture, paradoxically, must not, and even cannot, be neither governed nor regulated.

The concept of governmentality has often been used to describe and analyze neoliberal forms of governing and power, and as such in contrast of welfarism, which this study, with its focus on the Swedish political context during the 1960s and early 1970s seems

---

[13] See, e.g., Kim Dovey, *Framing Places: Mediating Power in Built Form* (London and New York: Routledge, 1999); Thomas A. Markus, *Buildings and Power: Freedom and Control in the Origin of Modern Building Types* (London and New York: Routledge, 1993).

[14] Michel Foucault, *Security, Territory, Population: Lectures at the Collège de France, 1977–1978*, ed. Michel Senellart (Basingstoke: Palgrave Macmillan, 2007); Michel Foucault, *The Birth of Biopolitics: Lectures at the Collége de France, 1978–1979*, ed. Michel Senellart (Basingstoke: Palgrave Macmillan, 2008).

[15] Nikolas Rose and Peter Miller, "Political Power beyond the State: Problematics of Government," *The British Journal of Sociology* 43, no. 2 (June 1992).

to be an example of. However, I will argue that a number of features of governmentality are especially apt for analyzing and understanding the specificities concerning the cultural policy and its mediations during this period.

In the lectures of 1978 Foucault outlines a kind of, decisively not a succession, but a series of changes in the dominant characteristic of forms or, rather, technologies of governing, and how they are exercised, from sovereignty, over discipline, to what he calls the apparatus or *dispositif* of security.[16]

In short, the apparatuses of security refer to technologies of governing that differs from sovereignty, which is exercised within the borders of a territory, and discipline, which is exercised on the individual bodies, in that security rather is exercised over a population.[17] Security then, is concerned with the "probable" or "probabilities," rather than the "permitted" or the "prohibited."[18] In contrast to security, discipline, by definition according to Foucault, regulates everything and, as he says, "allows nothing to escape."[19] Nothing is too small or too insignificant to be left unattended.

It is in this perspective that an initiative of the Swedish minister of ecclesiastical affairs, Ragnar Edenman, in 1959 becomes interesting. Not that Edenman would claim that the sphere or issue of culture was small or insignificant, but the real problem seems in Edenman's view to be that it was an unpoliced area.[20] This, I mean, marks a difference in relation to the later discussions on the "New cultural policy" of the late 1960s and early 1970s, which rather than being a continuation and maturation of the Edenman initiative, forms a new mode of governing characterized

---

[16] Foucault, *Security, Territory, Population*, 4–10.
[17] Foucault, *Security, Territory, Population*, 11.
[18] Foucault, *Security, Territory, Population*, 6.
[19] Foucault, *Security, Territory, Population*, 45.
[20] Ragnar Edenman, "Konst i offentlig miljö: Föredrag av statsrådet Ragnar Edenman vid kulturkonferensen i Eskilstuna," *Svenska Stadsförbundets tidskrift*, no. 9 (1959): 256: "A large and wide area is however in essential respects yet unproven as a field of reform, namely the free sector of cultural life." ("Ett stort och vidsträckt område är emellertid ännu i väsentliga hänseenden oprövat som reformfält, nämligen kulturlivets fria sektor.")

by security, a mode seemingly more-open ended and loose. The attention is not on the minute detail, on the contrary,"[t]he apparatus of security, by contrast [...] 'lets things happen.'"[21]

This discontinuity also actualizes one of the spatial ways in which Foucault describes the difference between discipline and security. Discipline, he argues, is essentially centripetal in that it isolates, focuses, and encloses a space. This is what can be seen in the example of Edenman where a disciplinary mode actually establishes a space "in which its power and the mechanisms of its power will function fully and without limit."[22] Security, on the other hand, is centrifugal; it is constantly expanding, subduing, and swallowing more and more. According to Foucault, new elements are constantly being integrated, which, as we will see in the case of the new cultural policy, means that culture can seem to encompass just about everything, even if it actually does not.

However, the specific case of the Culture house in Stockholm would then in some respect also be an instance of the disciplinary centripetality since it obviously encloses and circumscribes a space. But as Foucault also argues, the different systems or mechanisms of government should not be seen as a successive order of "ages" where one follows the other and subsequently replaces it.[23] Instead, they can be present in parts of each other, and for example, as in this case, disciplinary elements can be redeployed within the specific tactic of a technology of security.[24] We now have the prerequisites for looking more closely at the actual cases and the way in which they work.

Documents of Cultural Policy

The actual committee report *Ny kulturpolitik* (*New Cultural Policy*) by Kulturrådet (The culture council) is a very comprehensive

---

[21] Foucault, *Security, Territory, Population*, 45.
[22] Foucault, *Security, Territory, Population*, 45.
[23] Foucault, *Security, Territory, Population*, 8.
[24] Foucault, *Security, Territory, Population*, 8–10.

product. It amounts to 577 very densely printed pages.[25] It was furthermore transformed and distributed in a supposedly more accessible form, as a kind of summary, in 112 pages, which must be regarded as an indication of the intention of how the ideas of the policy should be more widely accessible.[26] The summary also incorporated illustrations in the form of reproduced photographs, which in themselves actualizes an interesting feature since they are visual representations of what culture and cultural policy refers to.

What is primarily important to observe in this context is the non-detailed way in which the policy in the report, and later in the government bill, seems to be cast.

The central characteristic of the report and later the government bill was that the policy was specified in a number of goals or objectives. On the surface of it, this can of course be seen as way of in detail regulating how to govern. Significantly, however, it was a question precisely of goals, and not of the ways in which these were to be achieved. Looking specifically at them and the way in which they are formulated, this is striking, especially in the case of the government bill.

The committee report comprised seven goals: the goal of decentralization, the goal of coordination and differentiation, the goal of community and activity, the goal of freedom of speech, the goal of renewal, the goal of preservation, and the goal of responsibility.[27] In the government bill, these goals were somewhat modified and transformed, and one of the goals was also split up in two. What is conspicuous with these goals is not only their meaning and content, but as just said, the way in which they are formulated. According to the government bill, cultural policy "should contribute to," "should give [...] opportunities for," "should promote," "should to an increased extent be formed with consideration to," and "should enable" the actual goals.[28]

---

[25] *Ny kulturpolitik: Nuläge och förslag,* Betänkande av Kulturrådet, SOU 1972:66 (Stockholm: Utbildningsdepartementet, 1972).
[26] *Ny kulturpolitik: Del 2: Sammanfattning,* Betänkande av Kulturrådet, SOU 1972:67 (Stockholm: Utbildningsdepartement, 1972).
[27] *Ny kulturpolitik,* SOU 1972:66, 171–188.
[28] *Proposition 1974:28 angående den statliga kulturpolitiken* (1974): 295. This is also observed by Frenander, see Frenander, "Svensk kulturpolitik under 1900-talet," 68.

What is also striking in this context is that the Culture council in the committee report does not want to define or delimit the concept of "culture."[29] Moreover, the cultural policy, the council explain, should be regarded as a part of the larger environmental-political commitment (both in social as well as in physical respect) of society, which then clearly meshes in with the physical framework of the culture houses.[30]

A Building for Culture

As was noted earlier, Nilsson expressed a skepticism concerning the viability and success of the concept of the culture house in Sweden. Still, a number of culture houses or cultural centers were built in Sweden during the period when public cultural policy began to emerge. Moreover, there was also a more or less discursive boom regarding culture houses and buildings for cultural activities in, for example, architectural journals during this time.[31]

Concerning the Culture house in Stockholm specifically, there is yet another aspect of it that in Nilsson's argument appears as a failure. According to Nilsson, the original plan for the Culture house in Stockholm was to move the Museum of modern art there, an at the time highly profiled institution. However, this eventually did not become the case and the Culture house did not get what Nilsson calls the "powerful engine" that would have brought life to the building.[32] Nilsson contends that both the City and the State disapproved of the ideas of the director of the Museum of modern art Pontus Hultén regarding the multifunctional and integrative notion of "all-activity," and that Hultén instead went on to

---

[29] *Ny kulturpolitik*, SOU 1972:66, 169.
[30] *Ny kulturpolitik*, SOU 1972:66, 168.
[31] See, e.g., the entire issues of *Arkitektur*, no. 7 (1967); *Arkitektur*, no. 7 (1970); *Arkitektur*, no. 11 (1970); *Arkitektur*, no. 5 (1971); *Arkitektur*, no. 6 (1971); *Arkitektur*, no. 3 (1977); *Arkitekttävlingar*, no. 3 (1968), and apart from these issues many separate articles, as well as an entire book on the subject 1970 by the architect of the Culture house in the municipality of Skövde and member of Culture council Hans-Erland Heineman. See Hans-Erland Heineman, *Rum för kulturen?* (Stockholm: Rabén & Sjögren and Föreningarna Nordens Förbund, 1970).
[32] Nilsson, "När kulturen satte bo," 9–10.

Centre Pompidou in Paris where the plans were implemented.[33] In this perspective, the Culture house does seem as a failure.

However, the original plans for the Culture house did not include a move of the Museum of modern art there. Nor was the reason for not moving the museum the City's or the State's disapproval of Hultén's ideas.[34] Instead, what the discussions concerning a move indicate and put into focus, because such discussions did take place, is rather the initially radically open, undecided, and seemingly ungoverned character of the space.

The short history of the Culture house project is as follows: In June 1965 a Nordic architectural competition was announced by the City of Stockholm in collaboration with the Swedish central bank, and implicitly the Swedish state.[35] The competition concerned one of the last major parts of the extensive remodeling of the Stockholm inner city, of which, for example, the Sergel square and the high-rise buildings of the Hötorg city was some of the planned or already completed parts.

The competition brief consisted of providing buildings for, on one hand, the Swedish central bank and, on the other hand, buildings for cultural activities, a theatre, and a hotel. According to the brief, the intention with the competition was to balance the north side of the Sergel square, which was wholly characterized by commerce, with "a flexible culture house" along the south side

---

[33] Nilsson, "När kulturen satte bo," 10.
[34] The concept of "all-activity" was widespread and discussed in the committee report, in architectural journals, see, e.g., *Arkitekttävlingar*, no. 3 (1968) and *Arkitektur*, no. 7 (1970), and also thoroughly elaborated on in Heineman's *Rum för kulturen?* (1970), as well as a recurrent feature in the conceptualizations on culture houses in many European countries on both sides of the Iron Curtain; see Kenny Cupers, "The Cultural Center: Architecture as Cultural Policy in Postwar Europe," *Journal of the Society of Architectural Historians* 74, no. 4 (December 2015). If there was a disapproval of Hultén's ideas it concerned rather the perceived unifunctional or one-activity character of the museum.
[35] "Tävlingar: Sergels torg," *Arkitekten: SAR:s medlemsblad*, no. 13 (1965); "Nordisk idétävling om bebyggelse vid Sergels torg i Stockholm," *SAR:s tävlingsblad*, no. 4 (1966); *Nordisk idé-tävling om bebyggelse inom kvarteren Fyrmörsaren, Skansen och Frigga söder om Sergels torg i Stockholm*, Stadskollegiets utlåtanden och memorial, bihang, 1966, no. 105 (1966).

of the square.³⁶ And this flexible culture house was according to the brief, "without an actual building program."³⁷

So this planned uncertainty and relying on probability is, rather than the governing of details, in other words inscribed right from the beginning, and not a misfortune along the way. Rather than seeing this as a lack of planning it can be regarded from a governmentality perspective as letting things run their course, to let "things happen."³⁸

It was the architect Peter Celsing and his office that won the competition that was settled in June 1966.³⁹ Celsing's proposal was an open-shelf system with a wide stretched transparent glass façade along the entire south side of the Sergel square (Figure 1), demarcated and separated from the theatre building and hotel and Central bank building by a huge concrete wall. The shelf system, hanging on the back wall, enabled an extreme flexibility, precisely as prescribed in the brief. In a memorandum by Celsing in 1968, the Museum of modern art surfaces in this context. Here Celsing describes the formerly very general space for cultural activities or exhibitions in terms of "museum activity" and proposes a use of the spaces in the same "broadened" manner and in the same way as had been done at the Museum of modern art since 1958.⁴⁰

A specific Culture house committee was formed in February 1968 by the city of Stockholm, and in November 1968 the committee appointed an expert group that consisted of, among others, the director of the Museum of modern art, Pontus Hultén.⁴¹ A first

---

36 Trans. of "[…] ett flexibelt kulturhus." "Nordisk idétävling om bebyggelse vid Sergels torg i Stockholm," *SAR:s tävlingsblad*, no. 4 (1966): 84.
37 Wang interprets this in a totally opposing way, and regard the unspecificity of the brief as a deficiency, cf. Wang, "An Architecture of Inclusive Purity," 64.
38 Foucault, *Security, Territory, Population*, 45.
39 "Nordisk idétävling om bebyggelse vid Sergels torg i Stockholm," *SAR:s tävlingsblad*, no. 4 (1966): 98.
40 "Kulturhus och teaterhus på Sergels torgs södra sida. PM angående organisatoriska och arkitektoniska frågor," Bil. 2, *Kulturlokalerna vid Sergels torg: Kulturhuskommitténs slutrapport*, Kommunstyrelsens utlåtanden och memorial, bihang, no. 49 (1971): 49–50.
41 "Kulturhuskommittén," *Kulturlokalerna vid Sergels torg: Kulturhuskommitténs slutrapport*, Kommunstyrelsens utlåtanden och memorial, bihang, no. 49 (1971): 18.

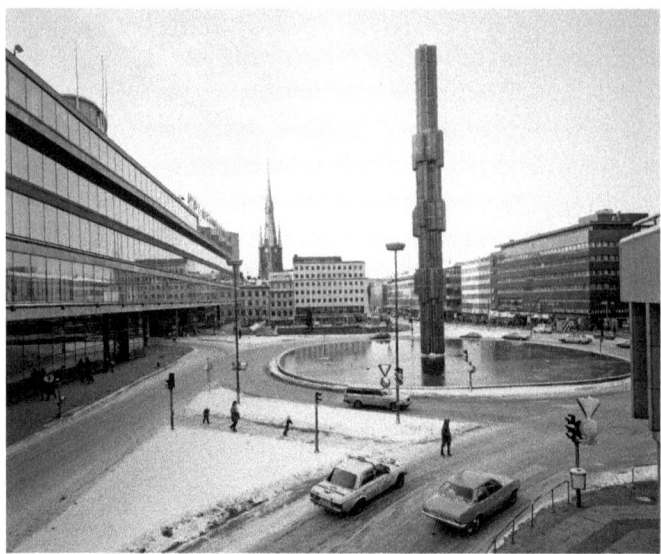

Figure 1. View of Sergel square, Stockholm, with the northern façade of the Culture house to the left. Sune Sundahl, 1985. Permission: Swedish National Centre for Architecture and Design/Statens centrum för arkitektur och design, Stockholm (ARKM 1988-111-SX2423-4). License: CC-BY. Available at DigitaltMuseum: https://digitaltmuseum.org/011015021173/ kulturhuset-och-sergelstorg-stockholm-vinterbild-exterior.

official contact between the State and the City regarding a localization of the Museum of modern art to the Culture house was made on November 7, 1968. However, an aggravating circumstance had shown up. During the time of planning the Culture house, it had been decided that the old Swedish parliament building was to be rebuilt and restored, in order to facilitate the transformation of the Swedish political system from bicameralism to a one-chamber parliament. The State and the City had therefore reached an agreement to let the Parliament use a large part of the culture house as a provisional parliament building.[42] Hultén and the expert group concluded that the Museum of modern art would need to use virtually all the existing space of the Culture

---

[42] "Riksdagshusprovisoriet," *Arkitektur: Swedish Architectural Review*, no. 6 (1971).

house not occupied by the Parliament.[43] The Culture house committee did not accept this demand and a decision was taken in February 1970 not to proceed with the plans.[44] Instead of the localization of the Museum of modern art, the Culture house came to encompass spaces for the City library including reading and study rooms and spaces for children, restaurants and cafés, spaces for temporary exhibitions, the City's information committee, and smaller stages while the designated theatre building of the complex was to house the heart of the democratic state, the plenary chamber and offices of the Parliament.[45]

The western part of the complex was taken in service to house the Parliament in January 1971 and the eastern part incorporating the bulk of the actual cultural services and activities was inaugurated in October 1974. The Central bank building was finished in 1976.

Collapsing Representations

How then did the cultural policy function in the complex at the Sergel square? In the committee report of the Culture council, the overarching goal of the cultural policy was stated as to contribute to the creation of a better social environment and to equality.[46] Neither this overarching goal nor the sub-goals discussed earlier were particularly detailed. Neither were the spaces of the Culture house particularly programmatically defined. Considering this non-detailed character, was it then possible for everything and anything to happen?

---

[43] "Skrivelse från expertgruppen den 5 januari 1969," Bil. 3, *Kulturlokalerna vid Sergels torg: Kulturhuskommitténs slutrapport*, Kommunstyrelsens utlåtanden och memorial, bihang, no. 49 (1971): 51.
[44] "Förhandlingar med staten angående Moderna museets eventuella förflyttning till Sergels torg," *Kulturlokalerna vid Sergels torg: Kulturhuskommitténs slutrapport*, Kommunstyrelsens utlåtanden och memorial, bihang, no. 49 (1971): 32.
[45] "Riksdagshusprovisoriet," *Arkitektur: Swedish Architectural Review*, no. 6 (1971): 6–11.
[46] *Ny kulturpolitik*, SOU 1972:66, 172.

In order to see if this could be the case we need to pay attention to an information film produced on behalf of the Information committee of the municipality council of Stockholm in 1973. The title of the film was *Jämlikhet – för handikappade (Equality – for the Handicapped?)*.[47] On a very general level, the film concerned the possibilities for disabled people to take part in public activities, and in particular cultural activities, which was the focus of the main part of the film. One obvious point of studying this film is that it depicts and represents the Culture house in Stockholm, fully built but not yet inaugurated by late 1973. The film is consequently interesting, since it can be regarded as a representation of the cultural policy, via the representations of the Culture house and the government committee report and government bill, respectively.

In short, the events of the film are ordered in the following way. It starts with an establishing shot of a room with young—and modern—girls. We can deduce that they are modern because they are, for example, listening to modern popular music and they are wearing what seems as fashionable clothes. They start talking of problems of disability—for example allergic reactions—amongst their friends. One of the girls says that she has read in the papers that the possibilities for the disabled to visit the cinemas and theatres have much improved. Then follows the real starting point in the form of a classical diegesis where one of the girls, who becomes our interlocutor, says: "Then, let me tell you," and as we can infer, a story.

She tells her friends, and us, that her father has a friend with the name of Manne, who is disabled. He had read in the newspaper that it was so easy to visit the new city theatre in the Culture house even if you were disabled. "What happened?" asks one of the other girls. "Take it easy," says our interlocutor, "I will tell you." "They have a taxi entrance under the building, you just

---

[47] *Jämlikhet – för handikappade?*, Information committee of the Stockholm municipality council, produced by Tetavision, 14 min., MPEG video, archive no. ZA_FI08-0439, undated [1973], Swedish Royal Library, audio-visual collection. Also accessible via the archives of the Swedish Film Institute: http://www.filmarkivet.se/movies/jamlikhet-for-handikappade/.

drive down to the underground to reach the theatre entrance." As these words are uttered we are shown the entrance to underground system called "Brunkebergsfaret," actually located one block away from the Culture house. Then a cut to the opening credits and a zoom out and pan over the Culture house and the traffic from the north. Cut again and shot from the underground system up towards the car entrance where a car starts its engine and starts to drive down towards us.

Then a new narrator, a man's voice, speaks up in a voice over:

> When the Culture house was built there were big ambitions of creating a decent standard also for the disabled. The "Brunkebergsfaret" was supposed to serve them who arrived in their own cars. You were supposed to just drive down into the underground and from there reach the different spaces of the Culture house.

The tone so far is highly optimistic. The camera tracks down the underground road system, passing road signs saying "Entrance Parliament" and "Entrance Culture house." A man in wheelchair, which could be inferred as being Manne, rolls of towards an entrance and pushes the entryphone. He waits a little while, look at his watch, and then start to speak: "I am in a wheelchair. I would like to get into the theatre." A voice from the entryphone answers him: "Well, that will be fine, I will push the button here and let you in."

We see a sign of what the theatre is showing this day, and we can thereby figure out that Manne this evening has planned to see *Dödsdansen* (*The Dance of Death*), part I, by August Strindberg, directed by Johan Bergenstråhle and with Allan Edwall in the role of captain Edgar. Manne opens the door and we hear the voice of the narrator again: "The builders have tried to act in accordance with the law," and he continues to explain how the law stipulates that public space should be designed in order to make it possible for everyone to use it, even if they are disabled. The narrator continues: "Manne has accepted his situation, and his optimism of a better society has increased." So far everything uttered still seems positive.

But in an interesting way a discrepancy here emerges between what is told and what is shown. Throughout the film we are shown how Manne has to go up and down in elevators and ramps and pass through locked or blocked doors several times to get to the right place, as if in a Piranesian nightmare. Crosscut with Manne's arduous journey, but verbally uncommented by the narrator, are shots showing people hurrying down the steep stairs leading from the street level down to the foyer of the theater, effectively communicating how hard that would be for a person using a wheelchair. It is as if the film makes a visual metacommentary of the goal of cultural policy that stipulated that the policy ought to be formed with consideration to the needs and experiences of disadvantaged groups.

Manne has now reached the entrance to the theatre. The doorman asks him: "Do you have a car? How are you supposed to get away later, they close at half past eight." Here the story changes and the visual commentary starts to invade also the story verbally told. Manne replies: "But then this is pointless, my evening is ruined." And he wheels away.

So this narrative ends in a total failure. It collapses the narrative logic of the entire story. It started with how we were to hear about how much better it had become for the disabled, and it ends with nothing of the kind. With the words of Northrop Frey, this is an instance of irony with little satire, as Frey puts it "the non-heroic residue of tragedy, centering on a theme of puzzled defeat."[48]

The collapse also *en passant* relates to other goals of the cultural policy mentioned above. The play Manne was supposed to see was, as we saw, a play by the national hero Strindberg. And the Culture house in itself points to a centralizing rather than decentralizing notion of culture, and even more so in regard to the co-localization of Parliament and Culture house denoted by the road signs.[49] The film then manages to represent and re-enact the inherent conflicts in the cultural policy: centrality, not decen-

---

[48] Northrop Frye, *The Anatomy of Criticism: Four Essays* (Princeton: Princeton University Press, 1957), 224.
[49] What further multiplies this quirk is that the Information committee of the Stockholm municipality council itself was located in the Culture house building.

trality, elite art and not all life as culture, art for the privileged and not for everyone. It subverts both the goals of the cultural policy as well as the asserted aims of the Culture house.

Conclusion

I have studied, in different respects, three cases of mediations of public cultural policy in Sweden during the 1960s and 1970s. All of these cases were realizations of initiatives of some sort of governing body that ordered them, being it the state, the government, or local authority. The result of the over layering of the cases are how they both strengthened and, in quiet unforeseen ways, challenged each other.

On the face of it, all of the three cases seem to indicate a movement towards a broadened and more open concept of culture, with emphasis on notions of freedom, democratization, and inclusivity. However, from a perspective of governmentality— and the implications of the perspective becomes even more clear when the cases are transmedially and intermedially related to each other and seen as constituting the network of the "new" cultural policy—we can see how these media realizations, in decisive ways, concern not necessarily less governing but rather another mode of governing, a mode that in some respects encompasses the redeployment of disciplinary elements, but in important respects does not, instead relying on a planned uncertainty in order to act or govern at a distance.

The question is then not whether the concept of culture houses was an expression of authoritarianism and totalitarianism, or if the cultural situation was low-key, intimate and home-like, or if the Culture house in this specific instance then stands in opposition to this. What rather seems to be the issue is that in this case the Culture house mediating cultural policy was not disciplinary enough. It is this openness and uncertainty that the film enacts and unsuccessfully is trying to get a grip on. The film in this way becomes an enactment of the tensions within the discourse of cultural policy in this specific historical context.

References

Arkitekttävlingar, no. 3 (1968).

Arkitektur: Swedish Architectural Review, no. 7 (1967).

Arkitektur: Swedish Architectural Review, no. 7 (1970).

Arkitektur: Swedish Architectural Review, no. 11 (1970).

Arkitektur: Swedish Architectural Review, no. 5 (1971).

Arkitektur: Swedish Architectural Review, no. 6 (1971).

Arkitektur: Swedish Architectural Review, no. 3 (1977).

Bolter, Jay David, and Richard Grusin. *Remediation: Understanding New Media*. Cambridge: MIT Press, 1999.

Bruhn, Jørgen. *The Intermediality of Narrative Literature: Medialities Matter*. Palgrave Macmillan: London, 2016.

Cupers, Kenny. "The Cultural Center: Architecture as Cultural Policy in Postwar Europe." *Journal of the Society of Architectural Historians* 74, no. 4 (December 2015): 464–484.

Dovey, Kim. *Framing Places: Mediating Power in Built Form*. London and New York: Routledge, 1999.

Edenman, Ragnar. "Konst i offentlig miljö: Föredrag av statsrådet Ragnar Edenman vid kulturkonferensen i Eskilstuna." *Svenska Stadsförbundets tidskrift*, no. 9 (1959): 256–260.

Elleström, Lars. "The Modalities of Media: A Model for Understanding Intermedial Relations." In *Media Borders, Multimodality and Intermediality*, edited by Lars Elleström, 11–48. Basingstoke: Palgrave Macmillan, 2010.

Fernández-Carracedo, Daniel. "Celsings bärande idé." *Arkitektur: Swedish Architectural Review*, no. 5 (2012): 46–51.

Fernández-Carracedo, Daniel. "Confluences of Two Worlds in Peter Celsing's Architecture. Outside & Inside – West & East," *Esempi di Architettura* 3, no. 1 (2016): 71–81.

Fernández-Carracedo, Daniel. *Peter Celsing en el complejo de Sergels Torg: La Casa de la Cultura de Estocolmo*. PhD diss., Technical University Madrid, 2015.

Foucault, Michel. *The Birth of Biopolitics: Lectures at the Collège de France, 1978–1979*. Edited by Michel Senellart. Basingstoke: Palgrave Macmillan, 2008.

Foucault, Michel. *Discipline and Punish: The Birth of the Prison*. Harmondsworth: Penguin, 1979.

Foucault, Michel. *Security, Territory, Population: Lectures at the Collège de France, 1977–1978*. Edited by Michel Senellart. Basingstoke: Palgrave Macmillan, 2007.

Frenander, Anders. *Debattens vågor: Om politisk-ideologiska frågor i efterkrigstidens svenska kulturdebatt*. PhD diss., University of Gothenburg, 1999.

Frenander, Anders. *Kulturen som kulturpolitikens stora problem: Diskussionen om svensk kulturpolitik under 1900-talet*. Hedemora: Gidlund, 2005.

Frenander, Anders. "Svensk kulturpolitik under 1900-talet." *Tijdschrift voor Skandinavistiek* 22, no. 1 (2001): 63–88.

Frye, Northrop. *The Anatomy of Criticism: Four Essays*. Princeton: Princeton University Press, 1957.

Harding, Tobias. *Nationalising Culture: The Reorganisation of National Culture in Swedish Cultural Policy 1970–2002*. PhD diss., University of Linköping, 2007.

Heineman, Hans-Erland. *Rum för kulturen?*. Stockholm: Rabén & Sjögren and Föreningarna Nordens Förbund, 1970.

Jämlikhet – för handikappade?, Information committee of the Stockholm municipality council, produced by Tetavision, 14 min., MPEG video, archive no. ZA_FI08-0439, undated [1973]. Swedish Royal Library, audio-visual collection. Also accessible via the archives of the Swedish Film Institute: http://www.filmarkivet.se/movies/jamlikhet-for-handikappade/.

Klockar Linder, My. *Kulturpolitik: Formeringen av en modern kategori*. PhD diss., Uppsala University, 2014.

Kulturlokalerna vid Sergels torg: Kulturhuskommitténs slutrapport. Kommunstyrelsens utlåtanden och memorial, bihang, 1971, no. 49 (1971).

Larsson, Lars Olof. "Peter Celsings Arkitektur." In *Peter Celsing: En bok om en arkitekt och hans verk*, edited by Lars Olof Larsson, Anne-Marie Ericsson, and Henrik O. Andersson, 37–53. Stockholm: Liber förlag and Arkitekturmuseet, 1980.

Markus, Thomas A. *Buildings and Power: Freedom and Control in the Origin of Modern Building Types*. London and New York: Routledge, 1993.

Nilsson, Sven. "När kulturen satte bo." *Arkitektur: Swedish Architectural Review*, no. 5 (2003): 3–11.

Nordisk idé-tävling om bebyggelse inom kvarteren Fyrmörsaren, Skansen och Frigga söder om Sergels torg i Stockholm. Stadskollegiets utlåtanden och memorial, bihang, 1966, no. 105 (1966).

"Nordisk idétävling om bebyggelse vid Sergels torg i Stockholm." *SAR:s tävlingsblad*, no. 4 (1966).

Ny kulturpolitik: Nuläge och förslag. Betänkande av Kulturrådet, SOU 1972:66. Stockholm: Utbildningsdepartement, 1972.

Ny kulturpolitik: Del 2: Sammanfattning. Betänkande av Kulturrådet, SOU 1972:67. Stockholm: Utbildningsdepartement, 1972.

Örn, Johan. *I rummets kraftfält: Om arkitektur och offentlig inredning i Sverige 1935–1975*. PhD diss., Swedish Royal Institute of Technology, 2007.

Proposition 1974:28 angående den statliga kulturpolitiken (1974).

"Riksdagshusprovisoriet." *Arkitektur: Swedish Architectural Review*, no. 6 (1971): 2–21.

Rose, Nikolas, and Peter Miller. "Political Power beyond the State: Problematics of Government." *The British Journal of Sociology* 43, no. 2 (June 1992): 173–205.

"Tävlingar: Sergels torg." *Arkitekten: SAR:s medlemsblad*, no. 13 (1965): 250.

Wallenstein, Sven-Olov. *Biopolitics and the Emergence of Modern Architecture*. New York: Princeton Architectural Press, 2009.

Wallenstein, Sven-Olov. "A Family Affair: Swedish Modernism and the Administering of Life." In *Swedish Modernism: Architecture,*

Consumption and the Welfare State, edited by Helena Mattsson and Sven-Olov Wallenstein, 188–199. London: Black Dog Publishing, 2010.

Wang, Wilfried. "An Architecture of Inclusive Purity." In *The Architecture of Peter Celsing*, edited by Olof Hultin, 9–81. Stockholm: Arkitektur förlag, 1996.

PART THREE: CONCEPTS

"The Analogue": Conceptual Connotations of a Historical Medium
Sara Callahan

Abstract

This essay considers how a number of artworks mobilize what is tentatively termed "the analogue." "The analogue" highlights artistic practices that implicitly or explicitly evoke themes and concepts associated with analogue photography. The essay argues that the so-called digital turn opens the possibility of tapping into analogue photography as a conceptual and cultural sensitivity distinguishable from the technique. It is the discourse of analogue photography that is key, not the technological process itself—therefore "the analogue" can be evoked also in works that are produced digitally. The essay explores how "the analogue" can be a productive way of analyzing specific artworks by artists such as Lotta Antonsson, Brian Ganter, Joachim Koester, Zoe Leonard, Vera Lutter, Joel Sternfeld, and Akram Zaatari. Contemporary artworks located within a postconceptual tradition can be said to have a built-in self-reflexive relationship to medium whereby the method and technique of production are always intimately intertwined with the artwork's content and meaning. With that in mind, this paper shows how the selected artworks can be analyzed precisely in terms of this interplay between medium as technique and medium as concept and content. The essay adapts and modifies the analytical tools of intermediality to fit the specific conditions of contemporary photographic practices among artists, and shows that the artists considered in the text evoke both the documentary, evidentiary connotations of the medium and the more associative,

---

How to cite this book chapter:
Callahan, Sara. "'The Analogue': Conceptual Connotations of a Historical Medium." In *The Power of the In-Between: Intermediality as a Tool for Aesthetic Analysis and Critical Reflection*, edited by Sonya Petersson, Christer Johansson, Magdalena Holdar, and Sara Callahan, 287–319. Stockholm: Stockholm University Press, 2018. DOI: https://doi.org/10.16993/baq.l. License: CC-BY.

material, and mystical implications. The essay is a first attempt to put "the analogue" to work as an intermedial concept to analyze how meaning is generated in a specific subset of photographic practices among contemporary artists.

Damaged Negatives: Scratched Portrait of Mrs. Baqari (1959/2012), by Akram Zaatari, shows a young woman posing self-confidently in a photographer's studio in 1950s Lebanon (Figure 1).[1] The accompanying text provides the back story of the picture: the depicted woman's habit of visiting Hashem El Madani's studio in Saida stopped when she got married, and her jealous husband insisted that all negatives of her be destroyed.[2] El Madani refused; they were part of rolls of 35 mm film, and removing them would affect adjacent negatives. A compromise was reached whereby the woman's face was scratched with a pin—preserving the negatives yet making them unusable as a source for future copies. A few years later the husband returned to El Madani's studio asking for prints to be made from the damaged negatives; his wife had by then taken her own life, presumably because of his abusive behavior.

This essay considers a number of artworks that mobilize what I tentatively call "the analogue." With this term I wish to highlight artistic practices that implicitly or explicitly evoke themes and concepts associated with analogue photography. A basic assumption is that the focus on a number of thematic concerns that are at the heart of "the analogue" only becomes possible when these bump up against, or are perceived to be challenged by, digital photography.[3] This essay specifically pinpoints artistic concerns

---

[1] I wish to thank the participants of the workshop held at Stockholm University on November 10–11, 2016 for valuable comments on an earlier version of this text.

[2] Moderna Museet, *Akram Zaatari Unfolding* (Moderna Museet Exhibition Folder, 2015), 4.

[3] The argument is that the notion of analogue only comes to the fore after the advent of digital media, prior to this, analogue photography was simply "photography." However, it is worth bearing in mind that this pre-digital photography consisted of a whole range of different techniques and was far from a homogenous medium either. See for instance Geoffrey Batchen, *Burning with Desire: The Conception of Photography* (Cambridge: MIT

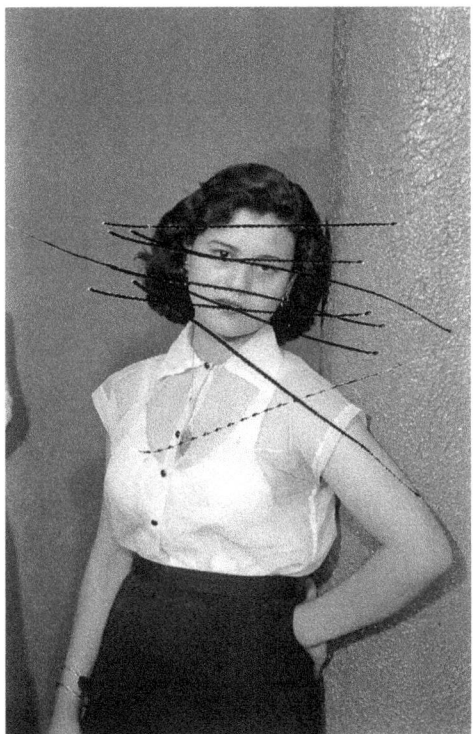

Figure 1. *Damaged Negatives: Scratched Portrait of Mrs. Baqari*. Akram Zaatari, 2012. Inkjet print, framed. Made from 35 mm scratched negative from the Hashem el Madani archive. Copyright: Akram Zaatari. Courtesy of Thomas Dane Gallery, London. License: CC-BY-NC-ND.

with material fragility and decay; temporal layering; reproduction, originality, and manipulation; issues relating to vision and (in)visibility; and the death of the medium itself. Zaatari's *Damaged Negatives: Scratched Portrait of Mrs. Baqari* can be considered in terms of all of these thematic associations of "the analogue."

It is important to stress that although the thematic cluster of "the analogue" is far from independent of technique, nor is it entirely constrained by it. It is the discourse of analogue photography that is key, not the technological process itself—in fact, I suggest that

---

Press, 1999), 50ff; Kaja Silverman, *The Miracle of Analogy, Or, the History of Photography* (Stanford: Stanford University Press, 2015), 13ff, 39ff.

"the analogue" can be evoked also in works that are produced digitally.

The essay focuses on contemporary artistic uses of photography. Meaning is generated in specific ways in these works; ways that differ from other photographic practices because of the self-reflexive, conceptual basis of post-1960s art production. An important question is thus whether intermedial analysis can be adapted to these particular meaning-generating conditions, and if so how? The current essay answers the first question in the affirmative and, via a number of case studies, shows how these practices can be analyzed in terms of a particular notion of intermedial juxtaposition and movement. The notion of "the analogue" allows for disassociating the medium from its technical considerations and instead considering it in terms of its thematic associations. The artistic practices examined here can be termed postconceptual or neoconceptual art, which points to the way they operate within a logic of a discursive art notion.[4] In line with this, "the analogue" as an instance of intermediality is approached as a *conceptual* tool.

The essay is divided into two main parts. The first discusses how "the analogue" as a conceptual category can be considered in relation to the photographic medium and the wider context of intermedial analysis. It also outlines some perceived characteristics of analogue photography as it is contrasted with digital. In

---

[4] In *Anywhere or Not at All: Philosophy of Contemporary Art,* Peter Osborne suggested that "contemporary art is postconceptual art." What he means by "postconceptual art" is specified as "a critical category that is constituted at the level of the historical ontology of the artwork; it is not a traditional art-historical or art-critical concept at the level of medium, form, or style". Peter Osborne, *Anywhere Or Not At All: Philosophy of Contemporary Art* (London and New York: Verso, 2013), 3, 48.
For a discussion of some issues with the prefix "post" in this context, see Dan Karlholm, "After Contemporary Art: Actualization and Anachrony," *The Nordic Journal of Aesthetics*, no. 51 (2016): 35–54. See also James Meyer, "Nostalgia and Memory: Legacies of the 1960s in Recent Work," in *Painting, Object, Film, Concept: Works from the Herbig Collection*, ed. Scott Burton (New York: Christie's, 1998), 30; and Terry Smith, "One and Three Ideas: Conceptualism Before, During and After Conceptual Art," *e-flux journal* #29 (November 2011): unpaginated.

the second part, "the analogue" as a conceptual category is put to work. Here, five thematic concerns that stem from the perceived difference between analogue and digital photography are fleshed out and considered in relation to particular artistic practices.

"The Analogue," Intermediality, and the Perceived Characteristics of Digital and Analogue Media

Postconceptual Art and Photography as Medium

It hardly needs stating that all media come with a set of connotations, and that the medium used in an artwork affects how it is interpreted.[5] What I propose here is to open up the heuristic potential of intermediality by analyzing the perceived characteristics of a given medium, detachable from the technical specificities of this medium.

Before doing so, however, it is important to clarify the meaning of the term *medium* itself. In media theory, the notion is broken down in a number of different ways: Lars Elleström makes the distinction between *technical, basic* and *qualified media*, the latter being socially shaped media like art forms that are dependent on "ever-shifting qualifying aspects."[6] The qualifying aspects can be further divided into two main categories: the *contextual qualifying aspect,* including origin and use of media in specific historical, cultural, and social circumstances; and the *operational qualifying*

---

[5] The term "connotation" that appears in the title and throughout this essay is not used in a strict linguistic or semiotic sense but rather in a more colloquial one, roughly synonymous with "association." This colloquial use of connotation is defined by *The Oxford Encyclopedic English Dictionary* as: "that which is implied by a word etc. in addition to its literal or primary meaning." Joyce Hawkins and R. E. Allen, eds., *The Oxford Encyclopedic English Dictionary* (Oxford and New York: Oxford University Press, 1991), 309.

[6] Basic media for example would be visual still images, technical media are what mediate, or display, the content of media products such as screens or book pages. Lars Elleström, "Photography and Intermediality: Analytical Perspectives on Notions Referred to by the Term 'Photography,'" *Semiotica* 197 (2013): 160.

aspect, including aesthetic and communicative characteristics.[7] According to Elleström, photography has been qualified operationally in two main ways: photography as documentation, tied to indexicality, and photography as art, which "foregrounds how photographs look rather than how they were created."[8] Elleström's distinction between documentary/aesthetic, epistemological/visual is useful for the analysis of many photographic documents. It is useful too when considering contemporary artistic use of photography, precicely because here the distinction breaks down, and it therefore clarifies a number of issues about how these works generate meaning. The works considered in this essay are all steeped in what may be termed a postconceptual tradition whereby an artwork is defined discursively, and the medium in these works is therefore both the medium of photography in a technical-material sense, and photography theorized in a particular way.[9] Irina O. Rajewsky points out that we never encounter "the medium" (photography) as such, only specific instances of it (individual photographs), and she refers to the latter by the term "medial configurations." Rajewsky argues that referring to "a medium" or "individual media" ultimately refers to a theoretical construct. It is therefore important to stress that this essay operates with different levels of media: the photographic practices that I analyze are "medial configurations," and I posit "the analogue" as a medium in the sense of a theoretical construct that is mobilized as conceptual content in the artworks. What is of key importance here is the relationship between these different levels, or types of media notions, and that concept and meaning in postconceptual art are necessarily intertwined with process, technique, and material.[10]

---

[7] Elleström, "Photography and Intermediality," 160, 164.
[8] Elleström, "Photography and Intermediality," 166.
[9] For more on contemporary art as postconceptual art, see Osborne, *Anywhere Or Not At All*, 48.
[10] Irina O. Rajewsky, "Border Talks: The Problematic Status of Media Borders in the Current Debate about Intermediality," in *Media Borders, Multimodality and Intermediality*, ed. Lars Elleström (Basingstoke: Palgrave Macmillan, 2010), 53–54.

The Use of Intermediality as an Analytic Tool

My proposal is that intermediality can be used to serve different heuristic purposes when it is used to analyze these postconceptual photographic artworks.[11] Whereas textbook trans- and intermedial analyses highlight the way a phenomenon or image moves between media or exists across different media (such as opera combining music and literature, or a movie adapted from a novel) my concern is rather with the way qualities associated with the material and technical specificities of one medium (chemical photography) are migrating not to other media but to the content of the artwork.[12] In the case of "the analogue" it makes no sense to speak of one medium referring to another medium, but rather that an artwork done in one kind of "technical medium" (to use Elleström's term) references medium understood as a set of associations. My suggestion is thus that the notion of "the analogue" offers a useful way of thinking about media in terms of ontological and conceptual possibilities, by focusing not on what it means to shift from one medium to another, but what it means to evoke a medium as conceptual content.[13] If intermedial analysis

---

[11] Irina O. Rajewsky, "Intermediality, Intertextuality, and Remediation: A Literary Perspective on Intermediality," *Intermédialités* 6 (Automne 2005): 47.

[12] Rajewsky for instance defines intermediality as "relations between media, to medial interactions and interferences" and states that the term can be applied to any phenomenon that involves more than one medium or that takes place between media. Rajewsky, "Border Talks," 51–52.

[13] Johanna Zylinska writes of a distinction between "affect" and "technology" in her discussion of digitization, and this distinction overlaps somewhat with what I discuss here. The difference between her argument and mine hinges on the crucial element of relating a photographic work to the discursive system of contemporary art where theory and text are integral parts of the artwork. The current text does not provide me with an opportunity to develop this further, suffice to note that W. J. T. Mitchell's discussion of artworks as always in some ways text-based is relevant in the way I consider conceptual and postconceptual use of photography as highly contingent not just on photography theory but also on the institutional theory of art. I thus suggest that "the analogue" can be a tool to understand the special case of intermediality at work in these kinds of photographic practices. Joanna Zylinska, "On Bad Archives, Unruly Snappers and Liquid Photographs," *Photographies* 3, no. 2 (September

is the method of analyzing relations between media, the mode proposed here does not just consider the relation between old and new media, but specifically the way these are used as already theorized media-conceptual clusters in a specific set of photographic practices at the turn of the twenty-first century.

The Analogue/Digital Binary

So, what are the perceived differences between analogue and digital photography that are mobilized in "the analogue"? Martin Lister summarizes the distinction between analogue and digital media via four binaries.[14] Analogue media can be said to store information through a *transcription* where one physical material is configured into an analogous arrangement in another material—a human face is transcribed to lines on a paper in a drawing, or by chemical transcription onto the photographic emulsion of the prepared photographic surface. Digital media on the other hand, *converts* the physical properties of the portrayed face into a numerical code of zeros and ones. In analogue media, representation occurs through variations in a *continuous* field whereas in digital media this is *unitized*; that is to say, divided into discrete, measurable and exactly reproducible elements. Furthermore, if analogue media record via *material inscription* where signs are inseparable from the surface that carries them, digital media is made up of *abstract signals* in a way that makes the numbers or electronic pulses detachable from the material source on which they are stored. This digital conversion of an object or event into zeroes and ones means that the digital medium can be used and

---

2010); 140. W. J. T. Mitchell, "There Are No Visual Media," *Journal of Visual Culture* 4, no. 2 (2005): 257–266.

[14] The outline of these binaries is taken directly from Lister's text. Martin Lister, "Photography in the Age of Electronic Imaging," in *Photography: A Critical Introduction*, ed. Liz Wells (London: Routledge, 2009), 314ff. See also Martin Lister, ed., *The Photographic Image in Digital Culture*, (London; New York: Routledge, 1995). For a discussion of the terminology of the analogue, see also Jonathan Sterne, "Analog," in *Digital Keywords: A Vocabulary of Information Society and Culture*, ed. Benjamin Peters, (Princeton: Princeton University Press, 2016), 31–44.

reused in a range of different formats, it is *generic* rather than *medium-specific* and can travel freely between different platforms. For instance, a music file can generate a graphic visual pattern and vice versa.[15] Lev Manovich rightly points out that in daily use we do not approach digital photography in a significantly different way than we do analogue.[16] My focus here, however, is not on the way we use digital photography in our daily lives, but rather how artists use photography in conceptually deliberate ways.

Truth Claims

Writing by Roland Barthes, Susan Sontag, and Rosalind Krauss are key entries in what has been termed the "narrow bibliographies" of contemporary photography theorists, and have contributed to make indexicality a perceived key feature of how photography operates.[17] The notion is grounded in the evocation of semiotician C. S. Peirce who wrote of photographs: "in certain respects they are exactly like the objects they represent" because they are "physically forced to correspond point by point to nature."[18] This

---

[15] Worth noting too, is that digital is not homogenous grouping either but rather historically changeable: what it connotes is very different today than in the 1990s. For a discussion of the problems with a simplified understanding of digital media, see for instance, Marlene Manoff, "The Materiality of Digital Collections: Theoretical and Historical Perspectives," *Libraries and the Academy* 6, no. 3 (July 2006): 311–325; Marlene Manoff, "Unintended Consequences: New Materialist Perspectives on Library Technologies and the Digital Record," *Libraries and the Academy* 13, no. 3 (July 2013): 273–282.

[16] "Lev Manovich I Essays : The Paradoxes of Digital Photography," accessed September 13, 2012, http://www.manovich.net/TEXT/digital_photo.html.

[17] This notion of "narrow bibliographies" is taken from Jan Baetens, who suggest that "we all quote the same authors." James Elkins, ed., "The Art Seminar," in *Photography Theory*, The Art Seminar 2 (New York: Routledge, 2007), 172. One can argue that the round-table discussion where this is said has now itself become part of a slightly more extended bibliography, as this text is frequently referenced in newer texts on photographic theory. See for instance Nina Lager Vestberg, "Archival Value," *Photographies* 1, no. 1 (2008): 53.

[18] Quoted in Daniel Chandler, *Semiotics: The Basics* (London: Routledge, 2003), 42.

is taken to mean that the negative simply cannot help but capture what is in front of the camera; an idea that is echoed in Barthes' formulation that "in Photography, I can never deny that the thing has been there" and in Sontag's understanding of the photograph as a trace directly stenciled off reality like a footprint or a death mask.[19] A wide range of objections can be made against the strict indexical identification of the photograph. Peirce himself stressed that all signs are mixed and include elements of index, icon, and symbol; and many have pointed out that there is as much convention involved in creating photographic images as there are in other forms of representation.[20] In fact, some have argued that the notion of index was not conceptually attached to early photographic practices, but rather gains traction via art-historical discussions of photography in a postmodern context.[21] Despite this, it has, as James Elkins points out, proved very hard indeed to "cut off all the heads of the hydra of indexicality."[22] Elkins has also convincingly argued that the art-historical use of Peirce

---

[19] Roland Barthes, *Camera Lucida: Reflections on Photography* (London: Vintage, 2000), 76. Susan Sontag, "The Image-World," in *On Photography* (New York: Dell Pub. Co., 1977), 154.

[20] Photographer Garry Winogrand suggests as much in his often-cited explanation for why he takes pictures: "I photograph to find out what something will look like photographed." Cited in Michael Fried, *Why Photography Matters as Art as Never Before* (New Haven: Yale University Press, 2008), 272.

[21] Kaja Silverman argues that index is not key to early photography at all, see Silverman, *The Miracle of Analogy*. Margaret Iversen suggests that the discussion of the index arises in a specific art-historical context that is concerned with the simulacrum. In the same round-table discussion, Jan Baetens attempts to historicize the discourse on indexicality and suggests that the focus on index is a specifically *art-historical* obsession. Jan Baetens et al., "The Art Seminar," in *Photography Theory*, ed. James Elkins, The Art Seminar 2 (New York and London: Routledge, 2007), 132, 143, 173. Similarly Kate Palmer Albers, among others, highlights Rosalind Krauss as the instigator of this art-historical interest in the index. Kate Palmer Albers, *Uncertain Histories: Accumulation, Inaccessibility, and Doubt in Contemporary Photography* (Oakland: University of California Press, 2015), 115–116.

[22] Baetens et al., "The Art Seminar," 146. Nina Lager Vestberg points out that "The Art Seminar itself dedicates more than a third of its transcribed discussion to the index. Lager Vestberg, "Archival Value," 53.

is superficial at best and at worst misleading, as it is based on reflexive references to the same few lines—the ones that I cited above—thereby isolating a small portion of Peirce's complex system of thought.[23] Again, what is important here is not whether the photograph is an indexical sign or not, only that it has persistently been theorized as such and that indexicality is considered stronger in analogue than in digitally produced image—mainly because of the way the former contain a material trace of the depicted subject in its chemical emulsion.[24]

The notion of photographic indexicality is strongly connected to the perceived truth claims of the photographic image. Geoffrey Batchen wrote in 1994 about "two related anxieties" that plagued discussions of photography at that time. The first relates specifically to the way digital images can be passed off as real photographs, and the fear that this will lead to doubt in "photography's ability to deliver objective truth."[25] Although manipulation is in no way alien to analogue photography, the digital medium enables a kind of re-touching perceived as traceless as pixels can simply be added or removed directly in the digital file.[26] I will outline Batchen's second anxiety shortly, but let me first consider the mystical and temporal structures and implications of the photographic document.

---

[23] James Elkins, "What Does Peirce's Sign Theory Have to Say to Art History?," *Culture, Theory & Critique* 44, no. 1 (2003): 5–22.

[24] I am deliberately leaving aside the fact that digital photography is also materially based in the sense of being captured by cameras, and that the conversion of the image into zeroes and ones takes place on physical circuit boards. See Manoff, "The Materiality of Digital Collections: Theoretical and Historical Perspectives." However, although digital media are not in any real sense immaterial, the image is not materially inscribed in the same way that it is in an analogue photograph.

[25] Geoffrey Batchen, "Phantasm: Digital Imaging and the Death of Photography," *Aperture* 136 (1994): 47.

[26] Batchen writes that with the advent of digital imagery photography is openly and overtly fictional: "digitization abandons even the rhetoric of truth" present in the language of analogue photography. Batchen, "Phantasm," 48.

The Unphotographable

Barthes' notion of *punctum* is arguably the most persistent trope of photography after that of the index. Barthes himself explains the difference between the two elements of a photograph by stating that *studium* is ultimately always coded, whereas *punctum* is not.[27] Using the example of an 1865 photograph of a young man about to be executed, he explains that the quality of the photograph and the handsomeness of the boy is the photograph's *studium*, whereas "the *punctum* is: *he is going to die.*"[28] Photographers since the medium's earliest history have been concerned not only with capturing the visible world but also that which is not so readily seen, such as thought, time, ghosts, and dreams.[29] Photography is thus frequently concerned with photographing the "unphotographable," and a 2013 exhibition with that title included images ranging from mysterious double-exposures to photographs of shadows, auras, a levitating table, an empty mirror, mental pictures, photographs of photographic film, and much more.[30] The photographic image is perceived of as a stencil and identical copy of the visible world (a truthful witness), yet it is also considered capable of showing that which is beyond the visible. Although a digital photograph can also capture the invisible, several differences between analogue and digital media contribute to the former being more closely associated with mystical elements. First of all, the chemical process of analogue photography has been discussed as "alive" in a way that invites these kinds of associations. Barthes writes: "the loved body is immortalized by the mediation of a precious metal, silver (monument and luxury); to which we might add the notion

---

[27] Barthes, *Camera Lucida*, 51.
[28] Barthes, *Camera Lucida*, 96.
[29] Jeffrey Fraenkel and Frish Brandt, eds., *The Unphotographable* (San Francisco and New York: Fraenkel Gallery: Distributed Art Publishers, 2013): unpaginated. W. J. T. Mitchell also writes about how photography shows us what we cannot see with the naked eye. Mitchell, "There Are No Visual Media," 260.
[30] Fraenkel and Brandt, *The Unphotographable*. The interest in the invisible or mystical that I am getting at here is a great deal wider than Barthes' notion of *punctum*, although connects to it in numerous ways. Barthes points to it being beyond the visible by referring it as a "blind field." Barthes, *Camera Lucida*, 57.

that this metal, like all the metals of Alchemy, is alive." What is alive is unpredictable in a way that mathematically based digital photography is not.[31] Another but related reason has to do with the time it takes to reveal the analogue photograph compared to the instantly viewed digital image on the camera's built-in LCD screen. This temporal gap means that the photographer is arguably more likely to discover something captured on the negative other than what was intended at the moment of shooting it.

Original and Copies

Analogue and digital media are also perceived to differ in the relationship between original and copies. The second anxiety mentioned by Geoffrey Batchen is grounded in "the pervasive suspicion that we are entering a time when it is no longer possible to tell *any* instance of reality from its simulations."[32] Bringing in the distinction between token and type, Timothy Binkley suggests that each copy of a digital photograph relates to the "original" file more like the same numbers relate to one another than the way a copy of an analogue image relates to the original negative.[33] Walter Benjamin's argument about copies and originals in his 1936 essay, "The Work of Art in the Age of Mechanical Reproduction"— another entry in the "narrow bibliography" of photography theory—today seems to fit more closely with the way digital photography is discussed than the chemical photographic practices that Benjamin in fact refers to.[34] When contrasted with digital photography, each analogue print created by mechanical reproduction no longer seems identical to one another, and because

---

[31] Notably, however, there are digital photographic practices that attempt to add elements of unpredictability to images, see for instance Vendela Grundell, *Flow and Friction: On the Tactical Potential of Interfacing with Glitch Art* (PhD diss., Stockholm: Art and Theory, 2016).
[32] Batchen, "Phantasm," 47. Italics in the original.
[33] Timothy Binkley, "Refiguring Culture," in *Future in Visions: New Technologies of the Screen*, eds. Philip Hayward and Tana Wollen (London: BFI, 1993), 79–80, 97.
[34] Walter Benjamin, "The Work of Art in the Age of Mechanical Reproduction," in *Illuminations*, ed. Hannah Arendt, trans. Harry Zohn (New York: Schocken Books, 1968), 217–251.

of this shift analogue photography may be particularly suited to themes of uniqueness and authenticity.[35] It is worth noting that Batchen's two anxieties are brought up in relation to the notion that photography is dead or dying because of the advent of digital photography. Batchen himself relates this to the way painting was considered to be moribund with the advent of analogue photography in the mid-nineteenth century, and when compared to painting the new medium seemed un-auratic. Meditation on the implications of the death of the medium of analogue photography is, I argue, itself part of "the analogue."

"The Analogue"

"The analogue" as outlined here is a conceptually dense set of connotations that come to be sharpened in the mid-1990s with the proliferation of digital media. Lisa Gitelman describes how one of the chapters in her 2014 book *Paper Knowledge* attempts to answer the question "[w]hat did photocopied documents mean— on their own terms—before the digital media that now frames them as old or analog?"[36] The notion of "the analogue" is intended to do the opposite of Gitelman's endeavor: to consider what analogue photography comes to mean precisely when it *is* framed by digital photography. Mark Godfrey in his 2007 article "The Artist as Historian" acknowledges that digital media may indeed impact the themes taken on by contemporary photographers, and

---

[35] Claire Bishop suggests that the artistic focus on analogue media is potentially detrimental to the relevance of visual art in the future, because it is motivated by the commercial viability of the unique art object, as challenged by infinitely reproducible digital images. See Claire Bishop, "Digital Divide: Contemporary Art and New Media," *Artforum* 51, no. 1 (September 2012): 441. I am not denying that commercial reasons may be part of the clinging to analogue media in some cases, my focus in this paper however, is on the function of "the analogue" as a conceptual category, and how its heuristic potential can be understood.

[36] Lisa Gitelman, *Paper Knowledge: Toward a Media History of Documents* (Durham: Duke University Press, 2014), 15. Here the different spellings of the term analogue stand out sharply; I have throughout this essay opted to use the British English spelling "analogue," rather than the US spelling "analog."

that "perhaps it is the approaching digitalization of all photographic mediums that sensitizes artists to the way in which such mediums used to serve as records of the past—and this sensitivity provokes artists to make work *about* the past."[37] Godfrey's idea of artists being "sensitized" to certain thematic concerns because of the advent of digital media is close to the argument I develop in this essay. I highlight specific elements of the interests artists are concerned with when engaging with "the analogue," and these include, but are not strictly limited to, making work that thematically references the past. In her 2012 essay "Digital Divide: Contemporary Art and New Media," Claire Bishop approaches the issue from a different set of questions, and she expresses surprise that contemporary artists do not deeply engage with digital technology, noting that the most prevalent trends in contemporary art since the late '90s all eschew the digital and the virtual.[38] For Bishop it is clear, however, that the "operational logic" of these practices is tied to digital technology as "the shaping condition," the "structuring paradox" and a "subterranean presence" that determine artistic decisions to work with certain formats and media.[39] Although my essay is less interested in answering the question why digital media is *not* thematized in contemporary art and more focused on considering the *ways in which* the analogue *is*, Bishop's suggestion that the digital is the shaping condition of these practices resonates strongly. The current text can be said to begin in the same observation as Bishop's but attempts to investigate the phenomenon from a different angle.

The "hydra of indexicality" runs through the notion of "the analogue" but rather than fully identifying it with the somewhat blunt notion of the index, I wish instead to focus on five specific thematic clusters that a number of artworks appear to be mobilizing, and it is to these that I now turn.

---

[37] Mark Godfrey, "The Artist as Historian," *October* 120 (Spring 2007): 146. Italics in the original.
[38] Bishop, "Digital Divide."
[39] Bishop, "Digital Divide," 436.

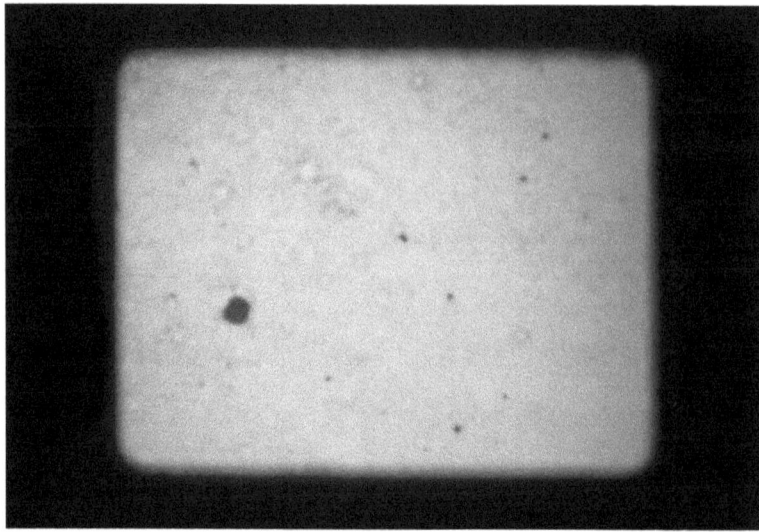

Figure 2. *Message from Andrée*. Joachim Koester, 2005. 16 mm film animation. Copyright: Jocahim Koester. Courtesy of Jan Mot, Brussels and Gallery Nicolai Wallner, Copenhagen. License: CC-BY-NC-ND.

"The Analogue" Put to Work

The Materiality of "the Analogue" and Its Associations to the Human Body

Artists point to the underlying material processes beneath the photographic image in a number of ways; in what follows I focus specifically on the way the fragility of the material substrate makes it analogous to the human body.[40]

The unfixed photograph and associations to the death of the human body is brought up by Brian Ganter's series *Kiss, Stroke, Grip* (2016) that consists of 16 photographic portraits of young men who died prematurely of AIDS. The photographs are stilled

---

[40] In an article of this scope I obviously can only hope to point out some elements of "the analogue." Other aspects of theorizing materiality could be discussed, for instance the tactility of photographic prints as well as the references to dust and hair and other material particles in photographic prints and slide projections.

frames from pornographic movies, showing the men looking directly at the camera or absorbed in a moment of sexual ecstasy.[41] Printed on stained glass and then hidden underneath a coating of thermochromic pigment that appears black at room temperature, the photographs only become visible with the introduction of heat.[42] Bodies that are no longer alive are made to emerge by the heat emitted from a living body, showing the photographic chemical process to be alive yet mortal. Roland Barthes writes about the material mortality of the photograph: "like a living organism, it is born on the level of the sprouting silver grains, it flourishes a moment, then ages."[43] *Kiss, Stroke, Grip* points to the chemical instability of photographic images and makes a conceptual analogy with the ephemerality of the human bodies depicted, fading and partly inaccessible behind the glass.

A different kind of fragility is that in Joachim Koester's *Message from Andrée* (2005) where the focus is on the physical destruction of photographic negatives over an extended period of time (Figure 2). Koester uses images from the ill-fated 1897 Andrée expedition that were found in 1930 together with the bodies of the explorers on their last campsite on White Island in the Arctic Sea. After having been partially buried in the ice for thirty-three years, most of the five rolls of exposed film showed no recognizable imagery at all, only spots and scratches caused by the damaged emulsion. These images can be said to exemplify the materiality of the analogue photographic technique; although non-decipherable as imagery, what they show and bear witness to is the passage of time and the decay and loss resulting thereof. Digital files can be said to age and decay because the fast-changing technological development makes older file-formats illegible. This however, is not a material decay in the same way, but rather an issue of translation and thus has less obvious analogies to the human body.

---

[41] TransformerStation, *Brian Ganter*, 2016, accessed April 17, 2017, https://www.youtube.com/watch?v=wWSoQLXEILU.
[42] Brian Ganter, "Kiss, Stroke, Grip," *Brianganter.com*, accessed April 17, 2017, https://www.brianganter.com/kiss-stroke-grip/.
[43] Barthes, *Camera Lucida*, 93.

Damaged Negatives: Scratched Portrait of Mrs. Baqari by Akram Zaatari also centers around the physical fragility of the photograph and how this is connected to the destruction of the body. Let me cite the way El Madani himself describes the back story of the image, as his choice of words and detail raise a number of interesting issues:

> In the end we agreed that I would scratch the negatives of his wife with a pin, and I did it in front of him. Years later, after she burned herself to death to escape her misery, he came back to me asking for enlargements of those photographs, or other photographs she might have taken without his knowledge. A few years later, he lost one of his eyes in an accident.[44]

Here the destruction of the negative points to a quite literal destruction of the woman depicted. The idea, older than photography itself, is that harming an image is somehow tantamount to harming the person depicted, and that being photographed somehow puts one in harm's way as it entails that one is somehow "exposed" to danger.[45] Margaret Iversen discusses *punctum* in relation to Benjamin's notion of the *optical unconscious*, and the way Benjamin brings up the double portrait of Dauthendey and his wife in "A Short History of Photography."[46] Mrs. Dauthendey, similarly to Mrs Baqari, committed suicide a few years after the photograph was taken, and Iversen describes how knowing this fact makes the contemporary viewer search the picture to find the flaw or trauma of this future event in the woman's face: trying to discover that "which the camera so to speak could not censor, could not *not* see."[47] The portraits of Mrs Baqari and

---

[44] The quote by Hashem el Madani is based on interviews by Akram Zaatari according to the brochure accompanying the exhibition *Akram Zaatari Unfolding* at Moderna Museet, Stockholm, March 7–August 16, 2015. See note 2.

[45] This theme can be seen to be at work in all the works mentioned so far.

[46] Iversen refers to Benjamin's text as "Little History of Photography," but the essay is commonly translated as "A Short History of Photography." Baetens et al., "The Art Seminar," 157–158.

[47] Baetens et al., "The Art Seminar," 157. Italics in the original. Kaja Silverman also mentions this text and the fate of Mrs Dauthendey, see Silverman, *The Miracle of Analogy*, 144 ff.

Mrs Dauthendey are thus overlaid with their subsequent fate—what happens to them later is somehow taken to be visible in the photograph when viewed in the present.[48] In the case of Zaatari's image, another layering is at work as well; the way Mrs Baqari's domestic life, via the photography studio, intersects with wider structural violence and notions of gender at a particular time and place. Notably, the title of the work is *Damaged Negatives: Scratched Portrait of Mrs. Baqari* although according to El Madani's narrative, it is not clear that she was in fact married when the image was taken, only when it was scratched and later reproduced in its damaged condition—what is shown here is as much the later events (destruction) as the moment of the portrayal itself.

Photographing the Invisible

A striking aspect of the statement by El Madani cited above is the way he ties the loss of the husband's eye to the destruction of the negative, as well as to his dramatic lack of knowledge and his desire to bear witness: "I did it in front of him" and "without his knowledge." Blindness can be connected to analogue photography in a number of ways. Archivist and theorist Verne Harris notes that the photographer at the moment of capture is literally blinded—it is only for a brief moment, but it is of course *the* critical moment for the photograph.[49] Harris' text is based on Jacques Derrida's discussion of drawing and blindness where he writes: "how can one claim to look at both a model and the lines [*traits*] that one jealously dedicates with one's own hand to the thing itself? Doesn't one have to be blind to one or the

---

[48] Another possible trajectory to discuss here would be the significance of "burning" and its association to light burning into the chemical emulsion, but also memory burned into one's mind, etc.

[49] Harris even refers to the photograph as "the archive of the invisible." Verne Harris, "Blindness and the Archive: An Exergue," in *Orality, Memory, and the Past: Listening to the Voices of Black Clergy under Colonialism and Apartheid*, ed. Philippe Denis (Pietermaritzburg: Cluster Publications, 2000), 117.

other?"⁵⁰ That is to say, at the moment of drawing, one is either blind to the thing which one depicts, or to the drawing itself. The key point here in terms of "the analogue," is the way blindness is conceptually connected to the photograph by the mechanical camera (one is not similarly blinded when photographing digitally), and that this in turn can be associated with the analogue medium of drawing.

Blindness or invisibility is also brought up in a statement by Joachim Koester who writes the following about his decision to focus on the most damaged negatives from the Andrée expedition: "If language defines our world, the black dots and light streaks on the photographs can be seen as bordering on the invisible, or marking the edge of the unknown. Pointing to the twilight zone of what can be told and what cannot be told, document and mistake."⁵¹ Here the illegible dots and scratches are signs that point beyond language as they have one foot in the evidentiary and the other in the mystical. In the binary division between digital and analogue, the former can be said to represent the rational, measurable, and coherent; while the latter associates to the natural, unpredictable, and unique. A digital photograph breaks up in a different way when enlarged; instead of blurring in continuous tones or graininess, the pixelated image is broken up into equally sized units, equally spaced and regular. Daniel Chandler connects this to other "analogical signs" such as visual images, gestures, textures, tastes, and smells that involve graded relationships on a continuum, and he points out that therefore these cannot be comprehensively catalogued.⁵² Artists that wish to thematize this kind of graded complexity, subtleties, and that

---

[50] Jacques Derrida, *Memoirs of the Blind: The Self-Portrait and Other Ruins*, trans. Pascale-Anne Brault and Michael Naas (Chicago: University of Chicago Press, 1993), 36.

[51] Joachim Koester et al., *Joachim Koester Of Spirits and Empty Spaces* (Villeurbanne: Institut d'art contemporain, Villeurbanne/Rhône-Alpes, 2014), 178.

[52] Chandler, *Semiotics*, 46. The term "analogue" or "analogical" as used by Chandler is broader than merely the technical binary between digital and analogue media. His suggestion that what characterize the "analogical" sign are the subtleties, gradations, and intangibility is highly relevant for the current discussion of "the analogue."

which lies beyond words, may thus do so by mobilizing "the analogue" as a conceptual thematic cluster. When using photography in this way, the evidentiary truth of the medium is stressed as well as its intuitive and associative qualities: "the analogue" captures both of these seemingly contradictory elements, and can be said to operate in the tension between them. It highlights a firm material tie between the event and the image, but also a mystical complex set of connotations that stem from its material substrate.

Temporality and History

A frequently evoked symbol of the photographic process is that of freezing a moment, and therefore the photograph is thought to be a stark reminder of the inevitability of time passing. Vera Lutter's negative images of buildings and cityscapes are made using the camera obscura technique. Her long exposures (often hours, sometimes days and even weeks) create the effect of cities inhabited by shadowy presences as cars and humans generally go by too fast to stick to the photosensitive paper. In her first series of images using a shipping container as a camera obscura, Lutter placed it inside a hangar where a zeppelin was being built (Figure 3). This work can be discussed in terms of an interest in old technology, but another striking temporal aspect is also at work here.[53] After some experimenting, Lutter figured out that the exposure time needed to capture the zeppelin was four days. She explains what happens next:

> The zeppelin was still being tested and corrected, and one day, during my exposure, the company decided to pull it out for a test flight. During the four days of exposure, the zeppelin was flying for two days and for two days it was parked in front of my camera. When the zeppelin was gone, whatever was behind and around

---

[53] The mobilization of "the analogue" can be said to be part of a larger trend to go back to old technology, seen in the development of media archaeology in the academy and interest in camera obscura and other old techniques in art production. There is, however, a difference between using old technology and what I am discussing here as referencing the conceptual connotations of this technology. See also Bishop, "Digital Divide," 436. Baetens et al., "The Art Seminar," 166–167.

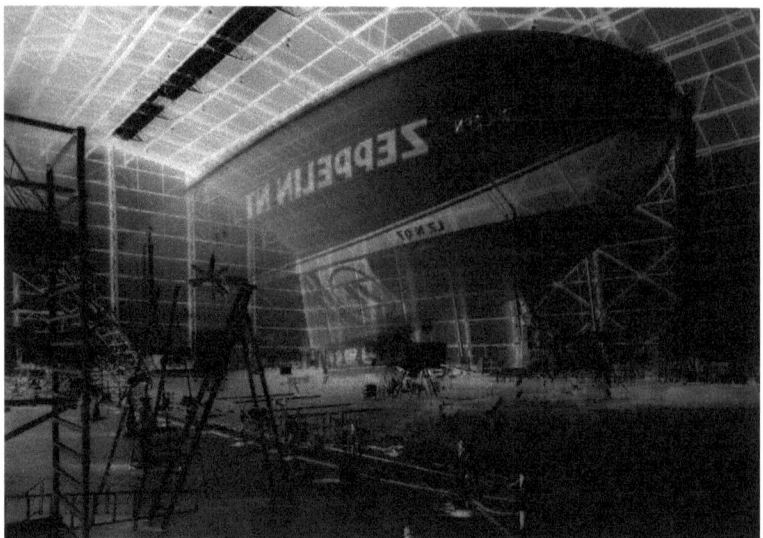

Figure 3. *Zeppelin, Friedrichshafen, I: August 10–13, 1999*. Vera Lutter, 1999. Unique, silver gelatin print. Copyright: Vera Lutter/Bildupphovsrätt 2018. License: CC-BY-NC-ND.

it inscribed itself onto the photograph, but when it was placed inside the hangar, the outline of the zeppelin imprinted itself. It was rather dark inside the hangar, so things inscribed themselves very slowly. The result was this incredible image of a translucent zeppelin, which was half hangar and half zeppelin.[54]

What is captured here is the juxtaposition of several temporalities shown as a gradation of visibility of the zeppelin—it is not a question of a binary visible-or-invisible, but a gradual absence of the zeppelin, visible as a presence in the image. Similarly, *Message from Andrée* can be discussed in terms of capturing time on film, but here with some added layers of temporal references. The work is an animation of still images, and thus it captures the long duration of the negatives being buried under the ice but also the shift from still photography to the extended duration of the animated film.

---

[54] Peter Wollen, "Vera Lutter by Peter Wollen," *BOMB* # 85 (Fall 2003), accessed April 17, 2017, http://bombmagazine.org/article/2584/vera-lutter.

Another way temporality is thematized in contemporary photographic artworks is Godfrey's above-cited suggestion that the artist's work references that of the historian, making work *about* the past. Here the photographic document is treated as a historical trace capable of reconnecting to events in a historical or extended timeframe. *On This Site: Landscape in Memoriam* (1993–1996) is a series where Joel Sternfeld travelled around the United States and documented fifty-two sites of violence including the sites of the 1955 killing of Emmett Till, the 1978 assassination of Harvey Milk, the 1995 Oklahoma City bombing, and the 1991 beating of Rodney King in Los Angeles.[55] The series can be said to use the photographic document as a conceptual index, walking in footprints several decades old. Kate Palmer Albers discusses Sternfeld as one of several examples of a shift in photography from being considered as a record of the past to looking at it "as an object that will activate a relationship with a future audience," that is to say, a way of "rethinking photographic indexicality in terms of the performative."[56] Sternfeld uses the idea of the photograph as capable of connecting materially to the past (index) while simultaneously showing this to be elusive and uncertain. Index is mobilized in interpretations of this work without relying too heavily on Peirce and the materiality of the index as a stencil or proof, but rather as an indication, pointing out, drawing attention to, an event or person.[57]

Copy, Original, and Reproduction

The status of copies and reproductions becomes a key concern with the advent of digital media. It is when analogue photography is contrasted with digital that the former is seen to have a more

---

[55] Albers, *Uncertain Histories*, 111.
[56] Albers, *Uncertain Histories*, 115.
[57] Similarly, David Green and Joanna Lowry distinguish between two types of indexicality where one is connected to loss and the other to the perfomative. David Green and Joanna Lowry, "From Presence to the Performative: Rethinking Photographic Indexicality," in *Where Is the Photograph?*, ed. David Green (Maidstone: Photoworks, Photoforum, 2003), 47–60.

clear-cut relationship between original and copy than the latter where copy and original are largely non-distinguishable. Zaatari's scratched portrait of Mrs Baqari mobilizes this aspect of "the analogue" in the way the husband is described as returing to El Madani's studio and asks for copies to be made from the damaged negatives—damaged because of his own previous insistence that no such copies should be possible. What is accessible at that point is only an image based on a new original in which the damage is inexorably inscribed; the link to the past is intact, but the violence done to the image is part of the modified original and is impossible to bypass. It is notable that the scratch, when enlarged, is seen to go through one of Mrs. Baqari's eyes, blinding also her.

Lotta Antonsson's installations reference the material process of analogue photography directly by placing silver, mirrors, sand on pedestals, thereby pointing to the way photography is never a transparent view of reality, but is already filtered through a material process. Instead of discussing Antonsson in terms of this materiality, however, I wish to focus on another related aspect of her work by considering the diptych *Sans Titre (hommage á B. Lategan)* (2008) and its references to reproduction and post-production manipulation (Figure 4). Based on a found image, the work consists of two seemingly identical images of a woman's face with a large tear in one of her eyes. At closer inspection it is clear that the two prints are developed with slight but clear differences; one is more diffused, the other more high contrast, showing the texture of the woman's skin. The tear, adding dramatic narrative to the picture, has in fact been added by the artist manually during post-production.

Antonsson has a long-standing interest in identity, and she has in several works photographed adolescent girls at the cusp of adulthood. This interest can be related to her focus on the photographic process itself, and post-production as something that is clearly and unambiguously "after" the initial image.[58]

---

[58] With digital photography one can do many alterations such as brighten, get rid of red-eye, and overlay different kinds of filters and effects right in the digital camera. Also, there is no diminishing quality, no sense that the altered copy is less or even hierarchically dependent on the original in the same way as in analogue media.

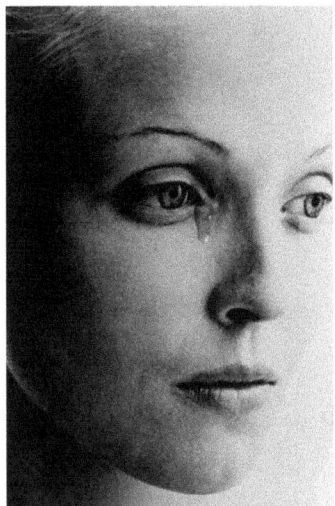 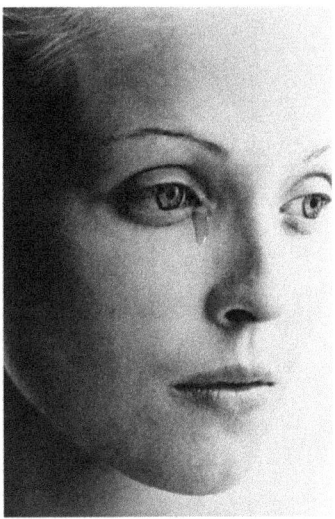

Figure 4. *Sans Titre (hommage á B. Lategan)*. Lotta Antonsson, 2008. Silvergelatin photography, collage. Copyright: Lotta Antonsson. License: CC-BY-NC-ND.

The process of becoming a fully-formed adult is analogous to the process of becoming that is inherent to the analogue photographic process. The seeds of the image are held in the negative, and the image is gently prodded and coaxed, manipulated and forced to appear by the photographer in the darkroom. In that sense, both nurture and nature are needed to create and form the finished image, there is an element of inevitability, yet, as we have seen, also a great deal of unpredictability and room for manipulation. Antonsson's continued use of the analogue mode of working, even after digital technology has become the norm, is deliberate and comes at a cost (time and money). Still, it appears that she is using the specific associations of "the analogue" in order to further the theme of becoming explored in her larger oeuvre as well as the photograph's ability to manipulate the viewer's emotional response by subtle means. Similar to what was brought up in the discussion of Zaatari's work, the eye and vision is the focus here too.

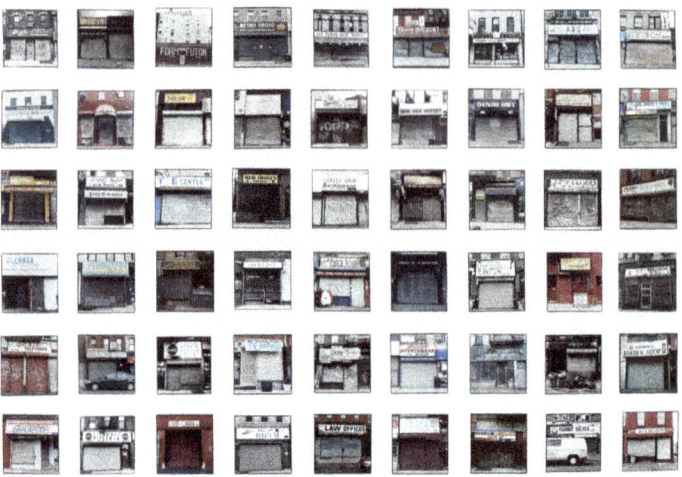

Figure 5. *Selection from the Analogue Portfolio.* Zoe Leonard, 1998/2009. Dye transfer prints, 20 × 16 inches each/50.8 × 40.64 cm each. Copyright: Zoe Leonard. Courtesy of the artist, Hauser & Wirth, New York and Galerie Gisela Capitain, Cologne. License: CC-BY-NC-ND.

Death of a Medium

My final example is Zoe Leonard's photographic series with the fitting title *Analogue* (1998–2009) that works with direct references to the moribund medium (Figure 5). The project began close to the artist's home on Manhattan's Lower East Side and Brooklyn, but it has since expanded in scope to include images from Mexico City, Kampala, Warsaw, and East Jerusalem. Tightly framed views of small photography stores, electronic repair shops, clothing stores, and Coca-Cola stalls, Leonard's series is a systematic documentation of a world on the verge of becoming extinct due to technological development, urban gentrification, and changing structures in the global economy.

On one level, Leonard's title directly refers to the medium she uses: shot on a vintage Rolleiflex camera, the images are always shown with the frame of the negative clearly visible—proving that the photographs have not been cropped but are authentic documents. On another level, the key aspect of the work is that the medium mirrors the subject matter: the storefronts are just as "analogue" as the photographic technique that captures them. Let us here recall Martin Lister's differentiation between digital and analogue media and consider it in relation to Leonard's series. Digital media, characterized by conversion of physical properties into an arbitrary numerical code, is contrasted in analogue media by a process in which one set of physical properties are transferred into another, analogous set; and represents via continuous variations of tone instead of dividing the image into measurable and exactly reproducible elements. Thus by highlighting her work as specifically "analogue," Leonard points to the way these stores are specific, rooted in their local urban materiality, in contrast with the infinitely reproducible chain-stores and multi-national corporations that replace them. Another *analogous* relationship between the medium and the subject matter is that both are about to be made obsolete.[59] Not long ago, it seemed that these kinds of storefronts would always be around, there was nothing remarkable about them, in a similar way that photography was thought to be inseparable from its chemical base. Leonard's photographs are in this sense documents that preserve for posterity that which is lagging behind in a fast-changing world, but the very medium by which these documents are created is also about to disappear. Leonard's motifs are depicted precisely because they are in the "wrong" time; they are in the present, but belong to the past.[60] They look like old photographs, yet their aesthetic is also

---

[59] The term "analgoue" and its etymological closeness to terms like "analogous" or "analogy" is interesting in its own right and could be added to the discussion of the meaning associated with the medium. However, the scope of the current paper does not allow for such an excursion.

[60] Mark Godfrey writes in response to a questionnaire on "The Contemporary" that many artists exhibit an ambivalence to the contemporary, that they are not feeling at home in their own time. This is seen, according to Godfrey, in the way they are resistant to economic, sociological, and political conditions of the present moment, but also in the way they are "not particularly attracted to the conditions or opportunities of the present," Godfrey goes on to contrast Zoe Leonard and Tacita Dean with Dada artists of the 1920s who were willing to use new technologies to respond critically to the 1920s. "Questionnaire on 'The Contemporary,'" *October* 130 (2009): 31.

hyper-contemporary since apps like Instagram mimic the look of these media. The temporal layerings here are multiple: the photographs point back to a past about to be extinct, but also to a future (from the point of view of 1998) when this aesthetic is vernacular again, albeit via digital rather than analogue photographic technique.

Akram Zaatari's *Damaged Negatives: Scratched Portrait of Mrs. Baqari* can also be considered in terms of a moribund medium. Zaatari is the co-founder of the Arab Image Foundation that collects and archives photographic prints and negatives from around the Middle East.[61] The impetus behind the AIF was the disappearance of studios like El Madani's that were enmeshed in the social fabric of a particular community, and the resulting loss of old photographic prints and negatives. *Scratched Portrait of Mrs Baqari* is the result of Zaatari's archaeological excavation of El Madani's studio and is part of a larger installation including super-8 movies, archive cabinets, and several films and photographs showing the material inventory of the studio: pens, rulers, cameras, film, props, highlighting the way the studio is considered as a historical site.

Concluding Remarks

This essay has suggested that the so-called digital turn opens the possibility of tapping into analogue photography as a conceptual and cultural sensitivity distinguishable from the technique, and that this can be productively used in the analysis of specific artworks.

Let me, by way of rounding off, return to Lars Ellestrőm's two dichotomies: that between the contextual and the operational qualifying aspects of photography, and the further sub-division of the latter into photography as document and photography as art. I have already stated that the differentiation between documentary and artistic aspects breaks down in the kind of artworks discussed in this essay, and the reasons for this—that they mobilize notions of photography as document precisely as the conceptual

---

[61] See Arab Image Foundation, accessed April 17, 2017, http://www.fai.org.lb.

and aesthetic content of the artworks—should hopefully be clear by now. Similarly, the distinction Elleström makes between contextual and operational qualifying aspects breaks down in the case of the artworks discussed here via "the analogue" because the contextual—a photographic practice located within a postconceptual art context—is an integral part of the operational logic of these artworks. I want to stress that I am not bringing up Elleström here merely to challenge his distinctions—in fact, he is very clear that these categories do not necessarily operate in opposition to one another—but rather to point out their usefulness in clarifying postconceptual photography as a special case that requires adapted intermedial tools. The intermedial analysis carried out on the previous pages has attempted to dissect relations between media on a number of different levels: relations between old and new media, but more specifically, relations between operational and contextual aspects of analogue photography, as well as that between different kinds of operational qualifying aspects. The artists working with photography in this postconceptual mode mobilize the notion of the photograph as objective, truth-telling, non-auratic document that the conceptual artists in the 1960s and '70s were concerned with—practices where the documentary aspect Elleström highlights became an aesthetic trope and something stressed in various texts surrounding the artworks. However, when contemporary artists mobilize what I have referred to as "the analogue" in their practices, they are simultaneously challenging the way conceptual artists used photography by highlighting material, auratic, and mystical elements of analogue photography, but at the same time that they are operating within the discursive tradition that established photography as a conceptual artistic medium. Put slightly differently, "the analogue" can be understood in terms of image/text as discussed by W. J. T. Mitchell.[62] In a similar way that Mitchell offers "the figure

---

[62] "The image/text problem is not just something constructed 'between' the arts, the media, or different forms of representation, but an unavoidable issue *within* the individual art and media. In short, all arts are 'composite' arts (both text and image); all media are mixed media combining different codes, discursive conventions, channels, sensory and cognitive

of the image/text as a wedge to pry open the heterogeneity of media and of specific representations," "the analogue" is a tool that can pry open different kinds of medial relations in the postconceptual photographic practices under consideration in this essay.[63] When using photography as an artistic medium within a context of a discursive theorization of art, the operational and contextual qualifying aspects inevitably merge, and "the analogue" thus functions both as a reference to a historical discourse as well as a methodological category. The terminologoy of intermeidality can be defined as a movement or space in between or across different media. In this essay, an intermedial analysis has been carried out on the particular case of contemporary photographic practices among artists where the artists' self-reflexivity necessitates a processing of media as non-transparent and with no absolute separation between content and form. The in-betweenness at work here is thus one between medium-as-technique and medium-as-conceptual-connotation. This text has been a first attempt to use the notion of "the analogue" as an intermedial concept to analyze how meaning is generated in a specific subset of photographic practices among contemporary artists, and as such it will no doubt need to be developed further in future studies.

References

Arab Image Foundation. Accessed April 17, 2017. http://www.fai.org.lb.

Albers, Kate Palmer. *Uncertain Histories: Accumulation, Inaccessibility, and Doubt in Contemporary Photography*. Oakland: University of California Press, 2015.

Baetens, Jan, Diarmuid Costello, James Elkins, Jonathan Friday, Margaret Iversen, Sabine Kribel, Margaret Olin, Graham Smith, and Joel Snyder. "The Art Seminar." In *Photography Theory*, edited by James Elkins, 129–201. The Art Seminar 2. New York and London: Routledge, 2007.

---

modes." W. J. T. Mitchell, *Picture Theory: Essays on Verbal and Visual Representation* (Chicago: University of Chicago Press, 1994), 94–95.
[63] Mitchell, *Picture Theory*, 100.

Barthes, Roland. *Camera Lucida: Reflections on Photography*. London: Vintage, 2000.

Batchen, Geoffrey. *Burning with Desire: The Conception of Photography*. Cambridge: MIT Press, 1999.

Batchen, Geoffrey. "Phantasm: Digital Imaging and the Death of Photography." *Aperture* 136 (1994): 47–50.

Benjamin, Walter. "The Work of Art in the Age of Mechanical Reproduction." In *Illuminations*. Edited by Hannah Arendt, translated by Harry Zohn, 217–251. New York: Schocken Books, 1968.

Binkley, Timothy. "Refiguring Culture." In *Future in Visions: New Technologies of the Screen*, edited by Philip Hayward and Tana Wollen, 90–122. London: BFI, 1993.

Bishop, Claire. "Digital Divide: Contemporary Art and New Media." *Artforum* 51, no. 1 (September 2012): 434–441.

Chandler, Daniel. *Semiotics: The Basics*. London: Routledge, 2003.

Derrida, Jacques. *Memoirs of the Blind: The Self-Portrait and Other Ruins*. Translated by Pascale-Anne Brault and Michael Naas. Chicago: University of Chicago Press, 1993.

Elkins, James, ed. "The Art Seminar." In *Photography Theory*, 129–203. The Art Seminar 2. New York: Routledge, 2007.

Elkins, James. "What Does Peirce's Sign Theory Have to Say to Art History?" *Culture, Theory & Critique* 44, no. 1 (2003): 5–22.

Elleström, Lars. "Photography and Intermediality: Analytical Perspectives on Notions Referred to by the Term 'Photography.'" *Semiotica* 197 (2013): 153–69.

Fraenkel, Jeffrey, and Frish Brandt, eds. *The Unphotographable*. San Francisco and New York: Fraenkel Gallery: Distributed Art Publishers, 2013.

Fried, Michael. *Why Photography Matters as Art as Never Before*. New Haven: Yale University Press, 2008.

Ganter, Brian. "Kiss, Stroke, Grip." *Brianganter.com*. Accessed April 17, 2017. https://www.brianganter.com/kiss-stroke-grip/.

Gitelman, Lisa. *Paper Knowledge: Toward a Media History of Documents*. Durham: Duke University Press, 2014.

Godfrey, Mark. "The Artist as Historian." *October* 120 (Spring 2007): 140–172.

Green, David, and Joanna Lowry. "From Presence to the Performative: Rethinking Photographic Indexicality." In *Where Is the Photograph?*, edited by David Green, 47–60. Maidstone: Photoworks, Photoforum, 2003.

Grundell, Vendela. *Flow and Friction: On the Tactical Potential of Interfacing with Glitch Art*. PhD diss. Stockholm: Art and Theory, 2016.

Harris, Verne. "Blindness and the Archive: An Exergue." In *Orality, Memory, and the Past: Listening to the Voices of Black Clergy under Colonialism and Apartheid*, edited by Philippe Denis, 112–123. Pietermaritzburg: Cluster Publications, 2000.

Hawkins, Joyce, and R. E. Allen, eds. *The Oxford Encyclopedic English Dictionary*. Oxford and New York: Oxford University Press, 1991.

Karlholm, Dan. "After Contemporary Art: Actualization and Anachrony." *The Nordic Journal of Aesthetics*, no. 51 (2016): 35–54.

Koester, Joachim, Thomas Caron, Philippe-Alain Michaud, Christopher Pinney, and Clara Schulmann. *Joachim Koester Of Spirits and Empty Spaces*. Villeurbanne: Institut d'art contemporain, Villeurbanne/Rhône-Alpes, 2014.

Lager Vestberg, Nina. "Archival Value." *Photographies* 1, no. 1 (2008): 49–65.

"Lev Manovich | Essays : The Paradoxes of Digital Photography." Accessed September 13, 2012. http://www.manovich.net/TEXT/digital_photo.html.

Lister, Martin. "Photography in the Age of Electronic Imaging." In *Photography: A Critical Introduction*, edited by Liz Wells, 311–344. London: Routledge, 2009.

Lister, Martin. ed. *The Photographic Image in Digital Culture*. London and New York: Routledge, 1995.

Manoff, Marlene. "The Materiality of Digital Collections: Theoretical and Historical Perspectives." *Libraries and the Academy* 6, no. 3 (July 2006): 311–325.

Manoff, Marlene. "Unintended Consequences: New Materialist Perspectives on Library Technologies and the Digital Record." *Libraries and the Academy* 13, no. 3 (July 2013): 273–282.

Meyer, James. "Nostalgia and Memory: Legacies of the 1960s in Recent Work." In *Painting, Object, Film, Concept: Works from the Herbig Collection*, edited by Scott Burton, 26–35. New York: Christie's, 1998.

Mitchell, W. J. T. *Picture Theory: Essays on Verbal and Visual Representation*. Chicago: University of Chicago Press, 1994.

Mitchell, W. J. T. "There Are No Visual Media." *Journal of Visual Culture* 4, no. 2 (2005): 257–266.

Moderna Museet. *Akram Zaatari Unfolding*. Moderna Museet Exhibition Folder, 2015.

Osborne, Peter. *Anywhere Or Not At All: Philosophy of Contemporary Art*. London and New York: Verso, 2013.

"Questionnaire on 'The Contemporary.'" *October* 130 (2009): 3–124.

Rajewsky, Irina O. "Border Talks: The Problematic Status of Media Borders in the Current Debate about Intermediality." In *Media Borders, Multimodality and Intermediality*, edited by Lars Elleström, 51–68. Basingstoke: Palgrave Macmillan, 2010.

Rajewsky, Irina O. "Intermediality, Intertextuality, and Remediation: A Literary Perspective on Intermediality." *Intermédialités* 6 (Automne 2005): 43–64.

Silverman, Kaja. *The Miracle of Analogy, Or, the History of Photography*. Stanford: Stanford University Press, 2015.

Smith, Terry. "One and Three Ideas: Conceptualism Before, During and After Conceptual Art." *E-Flux Journal* 29 (November 2011): unpaginated.

Sontag, Susan. "The Image-World." In *On Photography*. New York: Dell Pub. Co., 1977.

Sterne, Jonathan. "Analog." In *Digital Keywords: A Vocabulary of Information Society and Culture*, edited by Benjamin Peters, 31–44. Princeton: Princeton University Press, 2016.

TransformerStation. *Brian Ganter*, 2016. Accessed April 17, 2017. https://www.youtube.com/watch?v=wWSoQLXEILU.

Wollen, Peter. "Vera Lutter by Peter Wollen." *BOMB # 85* (Fall 2003). Accessed April 17, 2017. http://bombmagazine.org/article/2584/vera-lutter.

Zylinska, Joanna. "On Bad Archives, Unruly Snappers and Liquid Photographs." *Photographies* 3, no. 2 (September 2010): 139–153.

Unfixing the Concept of Illustration: Its Historiographical Ambivalence and Analytical Potential

Sonya Petersson

Abstract

Intermediality enters this study through the concept of illustration. The study's twofold objective is to analyse the concept of illustration historiographically and operationally. The leading questions concern how the concept of illustration has been verbalized and negotiated in both textual and pictorial media, and how it can be further used as an analytical tool in studying illustrations. On the one hand, "illustration" is examined as a genre of pictures, whose characteristic trait is the combined mediality of textual and pictorial elements being both materially present in the same object. On the other hand, it is examined as a genre of pictures also bearing upon/being modelled by past and present meta concepts, such as "illustration." The study makes two claims: one historiographical and one operational. The first is underbuilt by juxtaposing a concept of illustration derived from analysis of historiographic texts with a pictorial instance of the genre of illustration. Here, the outcome of analysis is to stress the historiographic concept of illustration as marked by the ambivalence of conflicting hierarchies and values. The second claim is conditioned by allowing the pictorial example to confront its meta concept. Here, the outcome of analysis is to demonstrate how the two functions of illustrated and illustrating are unfixed from their conventional ties to a textual source and pictorial target. Rather, the insight of study is that the functions of illustrated and illustrating are mutually reversible.

How to cite this book chapter:
Petersson, Sonya. "Unfixing the Concept of Illustration: Its Historiographical Ambivalence and Analytical Potential." In *The Power of the In-Between: Intermediality as a Tool for Aesthetic Analysis and Critical Reflection*, edited by Sonya Petersson, Christer Johansson, Magdalena Holdar, and Sara Callahan, 321–347. Stockholm: Stockholm University Press, 2018. DOI: https://doi.org/10.16993/baq.m. License: CC-BY.

The "same" object could through the serial course of an analysis occupy them both.

In lexical entries "illustration" is generally made synonymous with the function of making clear, evident, and lucid—an abstract definition also generally concretized with the example of a picture clarifying a textual source. The standard lexical entry thus touches upon two core aspects of the concept of illustration. Firstly, its characterization falls within the broad scope of intermedial terminology, since it concerns relations between textual and pictorial media.[1] Secondly, it makes the assumption that the relations between the media involved are asymmetric. The illustration is conventionally understood as conditioned by the object being illustrated. With this said, it is of foremost importance and the very impetus of the present study, to recognize that the lexical definition does not need to correspond neatly to other possible definitions or give an apt description of the pictorial genre sharing its name.

The study's twofold objective is to analyse the concept of illustration historiographically and operationally. On the one hand, this includes disassociating the concept of illustration from a set of powerful assumptions within the post-eighteenth-century field of illustration studies. The leading question here concerns how the concept of illustration implicitly and explicitly has been verbalized and negotiated—in both textual and pictorial media. To meet this end, the study juxtaposes definitions of illustration with an actual illustration, a picture taken from the nineteenth-century illustrated press, which is asked to be self-referential or demanded to illustrate itself as an instance of its own media genre. On the other hand, I also aim to let the analysis of the concept of

---

[1] In the terminology elaborated by Irina O. Rajewsky, "illustration" both falls within intermediality in the "broad sense" of an umbrella term for relations between different media or rather phenomena taking place between media, and intermediality in the "narrower sense" of "media combinations," where text and picture are both materially present in the same media product. Irina O. Rajewsky, "Intermediality, Intertextuality, and Remediation: A Literary Perspective on Intermediality," *Intermediality: History and Theory of the Arts, Literature and Technologies*, no. 6 (2005): 46, 51–53.

illustration serve as a case for discussing how illustrations illustrate, which "texts" they illustrate, and how the objects involved confront and/or bear upon each other.

If the first aspect has historiographic and media-historical relevance, the second has analytical relevance also for studies without an interest in the pictorial genre of illustration. Behind this claim lies the insight that once *any* picture—belonging to the genre of illustration or not—is made into an object of analysis and verbalized in the written representation of a study, it also comes to illustrate the arguments being made, whatever else it has been understood to illustrate in its different sites of reception, past and present. The reason to engage with the *particular* genre of illustration is that it especially presses the case, in being a type of picture conventionally expected to illustrate—but how, exactly? Neither the particular time and media of the later nineteenth century are accidental, but motivated by the period's extraordinary proliferation of illustrations in new media of pictorial reproduction (in xylography, lithography, steel print, autotype, phototype to name but a few), which in its turn were related to a corresponding proliferation of words on illustration.[2] The later part of the nineteenth century and its illustrated print media are decisive in the media history of the genre and the concept's modern historiography.

In other words, there has, since the nineteenth century, existed a corpus of writings that can be named illustration studies,[3] or a discourse that provides a metalanguage on the pictorial genre

---

[2] For the production, publishing, and aesthetics of the genre of illustration in the nineteenth century, see, e.g., Andrea Korda, *Printing and Painting the News in Victorian London:* The Graphic *and Social Realism* (Burlington: Ashgate, 2015); Keri Yousif, *Balzac, Grandville, and the Rise of Book Illustration* (Burlington: Ashgate, 2012); Lorraine Janzen Kooistra, *Poetry, Pictures, and Popular Publishing: The Illustrated Gift Book and Victorian Visual Culture 1855–1875* (Athens: Ohio University Press, 2011); Gerard Curtis, *Visual Words: Art and the Material Book in Victorian England* (Aldershot: Ashgate, 2002).

[3] This naming is actually at odds with the self-proclamation of the field in the launching number of *Journal of Illustration Studies*, cf. "Editorial," *Journal of Illustration Studies* (December 2007), accessed August 18, 2015, http://jois.uia.no/articles.php?article=42.

of illustration, which in the following will be exemplified by Henry Blackburn's *The Art of Illustration* (1896 [1894]) and Walter Crane's *Of the Decorative Illustration of Books Old and New* (1896).[4] This is a field characterized by taking the illustration as an object of study to be discussed and theorized in its own right, including the selection of contemporary and historical examples and the delimitation of its "proper" qualities. What I above called "powerful assumptions" is to be found in the discourse of illustration studies and can—as a tentative start—be formulated as three normative criteria (henceforth called the conventional concept of illustration), that have had currency in the historiography of illustration studies in the nineteenth and the twentieth centuries: 1) That the illustration should follow a textual source and that the paradigmatic case of the latter is delimited to the contents of a literary work; 2) That the illustration should illustrate "significant" aspects of the text as intended by the author; 3) That it is relevant to distinguish between artistic illustrations belonging to major literary genres like poetry and novels and non-artistic illustrations in other texts.[5] These criteria have, not surprisingly, more recently been both contested and problematized.[6] And if so, why are they relevant for the present study? It has to be stressed that my intention is not to take issue with what they are "saying."

---

[4] Henry Blackburn, *The Art of Illustration* (London, 1896 [1894]); Walter Crane, *Of the Decorative Illustration of Books Old and New* (London, 1896).

[5] See for example David Bland, *A History of Book Illustration: The Illuminated Manuscript and the Printed Book* (London: Faber and Faber Limited, 1958), 17–19; Edward Hodnett, *Image & Text: Studies in the Illustration of English Literature* (London: Scolar Press, 1982), 1–24 and esp. 13, from where the quotation is drawn.

[6] An older example is Meyer Schapiro, *Words and Pictures: On the Literal and the Symbolic in the Illustration of a Text* (The Hague: De Gruyer Mouton, 1973) and a more recent is Hans Lund, *Mötesplatser: Ord och bild i samverkan* (Lund: Intermedia Studies Press, 2013), 57–69. Lund offers the concept of "antiphonic" illustration for pictures that add to rather than in any direct way "translates" the textual source, or, as Lund describes it, continues the production of meaning where the text pauses. Lund's concept can further be compared with what Roland Barthes calls the "function of relay" and contrasts to textual "anchorage" in *Image Music Text*, trans. Stephen Heat (London: Fontana, 1977), 38–41.

As obsolete today, it would miss the point. By enumerating them as normative clauses, I wish, on the one hand, to note the defining force that historiographically has been assigned to them, and, on the other, provide for readings of nineteenth-century texts that seek to unfix the already established convention from within its own discourse. This ambition involves reading strategies that are not so much seeking for deliberate propositions as for tensions and inconsistencies within them. Consequently, the conventional concept of illustration is not brought into the study as an object of analysis, but more as a condition.

The study builds on an operational definition of illustration that both takes account of and moves beyond its existence as a combined medium. The latter concerns the illustration's appearance in a conventionally text-based medium like a book or a magazine, where text and picture are present in their own materiality and approached as interrelated and meaning productive.[7] Especially characteristic for the nineteenth-century illustrated press is not only the juxtaposition of pictures with whole blocks of texts but likewise with captions, titles, and inscriptions.

In addition to the combined media-approach, two further aspects are conditioning. The first relies on W. J. T. Mitchell's "imagetext," which is a concept of media hybridity.[8] Even without captions etc., illustrations are never purely pictorial. Besides the often-recognized narrative aspects of motifs, they are also subject to encounter the words of a past or present metalanguage, or concepts like, for example, "illustration." The crucial task is, however, to understand how various textual elements enter the pictorial genre and how the latter resists or accommodates them: Is it by titles and inscriptions? By an imposed metalanguage? By the content of the motif? My aim to use this study as a case for examining the analytical potential of the concept of illustration (as opera-

---

[7] Rajewsky, "Intermediality, Intertextuality, and Remediation," 52.
[8] W. J. T. Mitchell, *Picture Theory: Essays on Verbal and Visual Representation* (Chicago: University of Chicago Press, 1994), 89, 95–99. See also W. J. T. Mitchell, *Image Science: Iconology, Visual Culture, and Media Aesthetics* (Chicago: University of Chicago Press, 2015), 38–47, where the previous concepts of "imagetext," "image-text," and "image/text" are further elaborated and fused into "imageXtext."

tionally defined here) also calls for a preliminary account of what it means to say that something illustrates something else. The answer involves the relations between the positions of "illustrated" and "illustrating" and is implied in the dual option of "resists or accommodates" above. It is a point of departure comparable to what Mieke Bal argues for when she describes "images as texts" in the sense of semiotic entities with "referential recourse to words," and the ability to propose a "counter reading" to those words they in the first instance were "read" in the light of.[9] Following Bal, I understand the possible resistance of the illustrating object as entailing an analytical change of positions, or that the object previously used as illustrating is turned into the object illustrated the moment it is allowed to give rise to a "counter reading."[10] But as much as possible, I will avoid the terms illustrating and illustrated, especially since the latter's passive form does not match the activity of providing the light on and possibly give rise to changes in a juxtaposed counterpart.

The first aspect of my operational definition thus regards the various ways in which illustrations and words intersect. The second aspect is a special case of the metalanguage included in the first, namely the concept of "new media," which I draw partly from Lisa Gitelman and partly from Bolter and Grusin.[11] This perspective recognizes the genre of illustration within a cultural continuum of, and with referential relation to, other old and new media genres, and most importantly the new media of pictorial reproduction mentioned above. The "newness" of illustration

---

[9] Mieke Bal, *Reading "Rembrandt": Beyond the Word-Image Opposition* (Cambridge: Cambridge University Press, 1991), 35–39.

[10] Cf. the reversible and mutually re-modelling positions of (theoretical) concept and object in Mieke Bal, *Travelling Concepts in the Humanities: A Rough Guide* (Toronto: University of Toronto Press, 2002), 42–45, 61.

[11] Lisa Gitelman, *Always Already New: Media, History, and the Data of Culture* (Cambridge: MIT Press, 2006), 1–22; Lisa Gitelman and Geoffrey B. Pingree, eds., *New Media, 1740–1915* (Cambridge: MIT Press, 2003), xi–xxii; Jay David Bolter and Richard Grusin, *Remediation: Understanding New Media* (Cambridge: MIT Press, 1999), see note 37 for further comments on my use of Bolter and Grusin's theory.

in the particular case of the nineteenth-century illustrated press should however be separated both from its containing media (the magazine) and the combination of text and picture, which of course has a long history. Rather, it is the pictorial surface (not the surface of the page) that can be assigned the status of new media, building on the assumption that the visibility of the surface is due to media novelty or the reverse of media being so naturalized by age and habit that it has turned into a transparent package of content.

The study will unfold like this: In the first section I will deal with the concept of illustration as a historiographic entity and offer readings of Crane's and Blackburn's aforementioned texts. The overarching concern is to end up with a concept to bring to the next section, where it will confront an illustration taken from the Swedish nineteenth-century magazine *Ny Illustrerad Tidning*. The concept that is brought on is not a definition of the lexical kind. It is not even a concept of illustration, but a concept expressing what I will argue is a trait of the modern concept of illustration historiographically conceived, or a sort of tension. The latter is thus, together with some other meta concepts, made into a parameter for the illustration in the second section to further negotiate. In the course of analysis, I will have transferred a concept abstracted from historiographic readings to a picture representing the genre of illustration, and then, in reverse direction, bring qualities from the illustration to counter the concept. The overarching move is thereby more diachronic and transmedial than is suggested by the synchrony of the combined media approach.[12] Lastly and in conclusion, I will reflect on the concept of illustration as an analytical tool.

---

[12] About the division of the field of intermedia studies according to the parameters of synchronic and diachronic approaches and their function as analytical perspectives, see Lars Elleström, *Media Transformation: The Transfer of Media Characteristics Among Media* (Basingstoke: Palgrave Macmillan, 2014), 3–4, 7.

The Ambivalence of the Modern Concept of Illustration

On the face of it, the definition of illustration offered by Henry Blackburn in *The Art of Illustration* relies on a double demand and a straightforward hierarchy:

> The first object of an illustration, the principal part, is obviously, *to illustrate and to elucidate the text*—a matter often lost sight of. The second is to be artistic, and includes works of the imagination, decoration, ornament, style.[13]

The first demand places the illustration in the position of a follower, in the normative sense that it should be led by something already present in "the text," which is also underlined by the subordinate clause criticizing much of the illustrated work of the present.[14] Within the field of illustration studies, the first demand belongs to a model of definition that is production and author centred. In two well referred-to studies, David Bland and Edward Hodnett both emphasize the dependent role of the illustrative picture. In Bland, the dependence is measured against the relative autonomy of the text as the product of the author and the medium that comes first in the order of production.[15] In Hodnett, it is assumed that "[t]he best illustrators have the ability to understand the author's intention and to imagine what legitimately can be visualized beyond the words he[!] has used."[16] From the historiographic point of view, it is therefore easy to detect the same hierarchy in Blackburn's definition. But of greater importance is that it is actually paired with an opposite tendency that renders the dependent position of the

---

[13] Blackburn, *Art of Illustration*, 15. Italics in the original.

[14] The first demand has also been noted as well-rehearsed in the literary criticism of the time, where illustrations were judged after how well they adhered to the intentions of the author or qualities first to be found in the literary work. This is exactly Nicholas Frankel's point when he contrasts the concept of illustration in the contemporary reception of the illustrator Aubrey Beardsley with an oppositional concept derived from Beardsley's drawings. Nicholas Frankel, *Masking the Text: Essays on Literature & Mediation in the 1890s* (High Wycombe: The Rivendale Press, 2009), 154–157, 160, 180.

[15] Bland, *History of Book Illustration*, 19.

[16] Hodnett, *Image & Text*, 17.

illustration more complicated. At the same time as the illustration is described as a follower, it is demanded to "elucidate" or expose something that is deviant from its textual source, which is also echoing in the duality signaled by Hodnett's "beyond." Later on, when Blackburn makes a retrospective outlook to the "very earliest days of book illustration," he makes the comment that then

> [t]he illustration was an illustration in the true sense of the word. It interpreted something to the reader that words were incapable of doing [...].[17]

Although the objects referred to are particular historical examples, the statement is principal. It makes claims for what a "true" illustration does, which is to bring something new to the text that the words could not by themselves bring forth, and which depends on the mediation of "the reader." In other words, the conventional concept of illustration as a follower that is only allowed to reproduce what is already in the text, is simultaneously paralleled by a notion of illustration as additional to the text. This doubleness makes the first demand of the definition less straightforward than its propositional content suggests.

These two, both complementary and inconsistent, notions of illustration are connected by supplementary logic the way Derrida has explained the "supplement" as an exterior addition with the ambiguous function of being both superfluous (additional, exterior, extra) and necessary. The supplement adds to something that is supposed to be complete in itself. But as soon as the supplement is called in, that plenitude is threatened, or, as soon as the supplement is needed, it is reached out for to compensate for what Derrida calls an "anterior default" in the supposedly self-sufficient entity represented by the supplement.[18] This supplementary function is further encountered when the concept of the "shorthand of pictorial art" is introduced in Blackburn's text. The latter designates the communicative advantages of the genre of

---

[17] Blackburn, *Art of Illustration*, 184.
[18] Jacques Derrida, *Of Grammatology*, trans. Gayatri Chakravorty Spivak (Baltimore: Johns Hopkins University Press, 1997 [1967]), 141–164, quote 145.

illustration compared to what is described as its textual other.[19] When the illustration—the follower—adds to its textual source, it is argued to do so in order to compensate for a deficiency in the textual medium that is also and paradoxically asserted to take the lead and supposed to be sufficient by itself (since the illustration should follow it or make no addition to it). The lack or deficiency the illustration is called in to "heal" is repeatedly described as the textual burden of un-perspicuity or its cumbersomeness, compared to the instantaneousness of pictorial representation. This is Blackburn's very point in enthusiastically promoting the "shorthand of pictorial art" and its ability to expose a piece of information by pictorial means—information that was not to be gained from the text that was expected to transmit it in the first place.[20] Taken as information, the illustration is aimed at transmitting knowledge or a "content" that is not materially present. It is thereby assigned the task of working in the service of the words that the written text failed to bring forth, which is again an endorsement of the hierarchy of the first demand. But by the illustration's pictorial means, it serves as a necessary substitute to the deficient realization of meaning in writing. With the aid of the "shorthand of pictorial art," Blackburn assures that "our complicated language [will] be rescued from many obscurities,"[21] just as well as it will minimize the risk of misinterpretation or of conjuring up the "wrong" mental image.[22]

Another feature of the concept of illustration in Blackburn's treatise is that it is repeatedly used in conjunction with terms referring to the receiver as a part in the production of meaning. The success and "true" sense of illustration (the second quote above) is judged after how well it "interpreted something to the reader." Its truthfulness is not in the first place measured against different stages in the line of production (conventionally taken as the author's conception followed by an illustrator's interpretation in drawing), but with recourse to the receiver as interpreter—at

---

[19] Blackburn, *Art of Illustration*, 18–39, the concept is termed on p. 26.
[20] Blackburn, *Art of Illustration*, 26–27.
[21] Blackburn, *Art of Illustration*, 29.
[22] Blackburn, *Art of Illustration*, 34–36.

the same time as the first demand adheres to the well-known paradigm of meaning where the textual source is equivalent to authorial intentions. Therefore it is noteworthy that the turn to the receiver is also present and given a determining role in Walter Crane's *Of the Decorative Illustration of Books Old and New*. For example in the passage below, which is preceded by a reference to the evolutionary theory of Herbert Spencer and explicitly regards the development of writing. But notably, it ends by referring to a generalized experience of book illustrations. Like in Blackburn, the speaking voice is in the concluding clause external. It is not the voice of the receiver in the form of an I-speaker that comes forth, but rather attention to the receiver as a factor in meaning production.

> We know that the letters of our alphabet were once pictures, symbols, or abstract signs of entities and actions, and grew more and more abstract until they became arbitrary marks—the familiar characters that we know. Letters formed into words; words increased and multiplied with ideas and their interchange; ideas and words growing more and more abstract until the point is reached when the jaded intellect would fain return again to picture-writing, and welcomes the decorator and the illustrator to relieve the desert wastes of words marshalled in interminable columns on the printed page.[23]

The object spoken about seamlessly changes from an abstracted history of production or the order in which the different types of signs have evolved, to a statement on the experience of reading and viewing them, which cannot but make claims to an extended present tense. This generalized reader/viewer is furthermore granted freedom of interpretation. The reader/viewer may or may not interpret the illustrations in the light of the page's "interminable columns":

> In the journey through a book it is pleasant to reach the oasis of a picture or an ornament, to sit awhile under the palms, to let our thoughts unburdened stray, to drink of other intellectual waters,

---

[23] Crane, *Decorative Illustration*, 5–6.

and to see the ideas we have been pursuing, perchance, reflected in them. Thus we end as we begin, with images.[24]

Both the turn to the receiver and Crane's oasis metaphor entail a view on the relationship between illustration and text as flexible. The picture is recognized as possibly deviating from the "ideas pursued," which is however a deviation that also holds for the latter. As in Blackburn, ideas are referred to as derivative entities that are possibly not grasped in their written form. And even though this quote, like the rest of the text, makes use of recurring contrasts between the pictorial and the other textual medium, they are also recognized as alike. The mind's experience of illustrations is, like reading, an intellectual activity (cf. "other intellectual waters"), although more open-ended in the sense of being the object of a generalized mind that "perchance" lets them reflect the text. The meeting with the illustration is further proposed as a necessary pause that compensates for the exhaustion of the "interminable columns," by the visualization of it as an oasis with vegetation and water in the middle of a barren land. If this, on the one hand, could be understood as a plain case of a series of dichotomies, where the image (illustration, ornament) is placed on the side of fertility, oasis, and seeing, and the words on the side of desert, chase after absent ideas, and reading, it is also plain that seeing the illustration is accounted for as alike reading in the sense of being something both sensory and cognitive, which thus indicates a model that is not mutually exclusive.[25] From the

---

[24] Crane, *Decorative Illustration*, 6.

[25] This is comparable to the way J. Hillis Miller, in his more recent theory of illustration, on the one hand explores the differences between textual and pictorial media and between the meaning and materiality of the sign in any media, and, on the other, still acknowledges the bridge between media that brackets the differences: "After all, both text and image are something seen with the eyes and made sense of as a sign." Also the semiotic perspective on the continuity between media recalls the texts treated of here. Although the accounts of Crane, Blackburn, and Hillis Miller do not share the same category of sign (which is based on different conceptions of what the sign ultimately refers to), they all give expression to the idea that the point of coherence in textual and pictorial media is the meaning productive mediation of the receiver. Cf. J. Hillis Miller, *Illustration* (London: Reaktion Books, 1992), 73.

acknowledgement of the receiver thus follows the notion that the interpretation of the illustration may or may not be bound by the text. And in extension, this view also entails the recognition of the illustration as a possible starting point for other ideas than those expressed in writing, which is historiographically important exactly for the reason that it is the order of production that conventionally has been embraced in illustration studies and converted into a model of analysis.[26] Put differently, the order of production is a model of meaning production partly rejected by the texts of Blackburn and Crane.

So far, I have demonstrated that the modern concept of illustration, represented by the quoted texts, refers to elements of the conventional concept, but is completely different from it. It is better characterized as thoroughly marked by the *ambivalence* of conflicting and intersecting propositions in the same texts. I have, on the one hand, pointed to a hierarchical organization where the illustration is taking the place of a passive follower, and, on the other, a notion of illustration as a necessary and compensatory healer of deficiencies in writing. And more, on the one hand, a correspondence with the paradigm of authorial intentions as the parameter of meaning, and, on the other, a privileging of the receiver as interpreter. The point is not at all to restore any one aspect of the concept of illustration as a historiographic entity, but to stress ambivalence as a pertinent factor of it.

Illustrating Ambivalence and the Ambivalence of Illustration

The concept of ambivalence that has been derived from the historiographic readings will now serve as a guide for my further analysis. But it does not occupy that position alone. In this section, the concept of new media, or the second aspect of my operational

---

[26] One exception is the semiotic paradigm represented by, e.g., Hillis Miller in note 25. Otherwise, Bland is an example of using the model of production as the logic by which illustrations with added texts are treated as deviations from illustration proper. Bland, *History of Book Illustration*, 253, 257.

definition of illustration, will be especially activated. Some points from previous sections first need to be rehearsed and briefly expanded on.

The conventional concept of illustration can be said to refer to a double separation or a double hierarchy: between text and illustration and between illustration as art and as something else. The latter could certainly be almost anything, but in the particular time and media landscape it amounts to the media-historical divide between art and new media of pictorial reproduction. The second demand in Blackburn's definition of illustration actually seems to presuppose the divide, since it singles out "artistic" as a category of its own. And if this marks a separation within the genre of illustration as "merely" reproductive (material and artistic) or as art, it also corresponds well to the division of content in Blackburn's book, where the chapter on "Elementary Illustration" is separated from the chapter on "Artistic Illustration." In its turn, this divide corresponds to the distinction between "useful" and "aesthetic" drawing in Philip Gilbert Hamerton's at the time well-known treatise *The Graphic Arts* (1882), which is also one of Blackburn's references.[27] In both texts, the crucial points are that pictorial print media is multipliable and that the genre of illustration was intimately bound to print media in general and the new media of pictorial reproduction in particular.[28] Hamerton finds reason to deplore the present multiplication of xylography as "an adjunct to journalism" and, together with lithography, blame its "abuse in commerce."[29] Within the discipline of art history, this (purported) split has lately been researched as a product of the rise of the concept of "original print" and associated with the texts and interests of etcher's organizations and graphic art theorists like Hamerton.[30] In a broader perspective, it can be thought

---

[27] Philip Gilbert Hamerton, *The Graphic Arts: A Treatise on the Varieties of Drawing, Painting, and Engraving in Comparison with Each Other and with Nature* (Boston, 1882), 8–48.
[28] See also the definition of illustration in Joseph Pennell, *Modern Illustration: Its Methods and Present Conditions* (London, 1898), 1–8.
[29] Hamerton, *Graphic Arts*, xiv.
[30] Cf. Jan af Burén, *Det mångfaldigade originalet: Studier i originalgrafikbegreppets uppkomst, teori och användning* (PhD diss., Stockholm:

of as underpinned by the romantic and autonomous concept of art or the notion informing the doubly derogative sense of the new media of illustration as "an adjunct to journalism": with a reproduced materiality, in the service of a particular textual source, and lacking original artistic intention. But for the reasons discussed above, my objective is not to search for further signs of the separation that already has the status of convention, but rather to study it in the light of ambivalence, as neither fixed nor especially pure. To that end I now turn to the front page of *Ny Illustrerad Tidning* (Figure 1).

Pictured on the front page is a model of *continuity* rather than divide between media that have been categorized either as art or as reproductive. In other words, it is a model transgressing the boundaries of the (assumed) split within the genre of illustration. The front page shows a montage of reproduced works by the German artist Gustav Richter. Its title at the bottom of the page is non-medium specific; it mentions "Some pictures by [...]." Importantly, the "pictures" are not named paintings, since it is lithographs, a medium on a paper surface that was closely associated with colour reproductions of oil paintings. Seven lithographs are shown mounted on top of each other and pinned to a wooden board. This is a description of the motif suggested by the title, and it involves the respective medium of oil painting (by allusion: the motifs in the motif are attached to an idea of a painted original) and lithography (by depiction). The latter is, however, not the sole media of pictorial reproduction re/presented on the front page. The pictorial surface presents—not represents—the medium of xylography, characterized by its overall parallel strokes and cross-hatchings and still in the 1880s associated with the illustrations of the popular press. The reference to lithography is therefore doubled: it is made both by the imitation of its tonal style in xylographic strokes and cross-hatchings, and by the depiction of the nailed up prints. Another manifest sign of pictorial reproduction is the inscription on the pictorial surface in the left corner—*on* the

---

Carlssons, 1992); Elizabeth Helsinger et al., *The "Writing" of Modern Life: The Etching Revival in France, Britain, and the U.S., 1850–1940*, exh. cat., Smart Museum of Art (Chicago: University of Chicago, 2008).

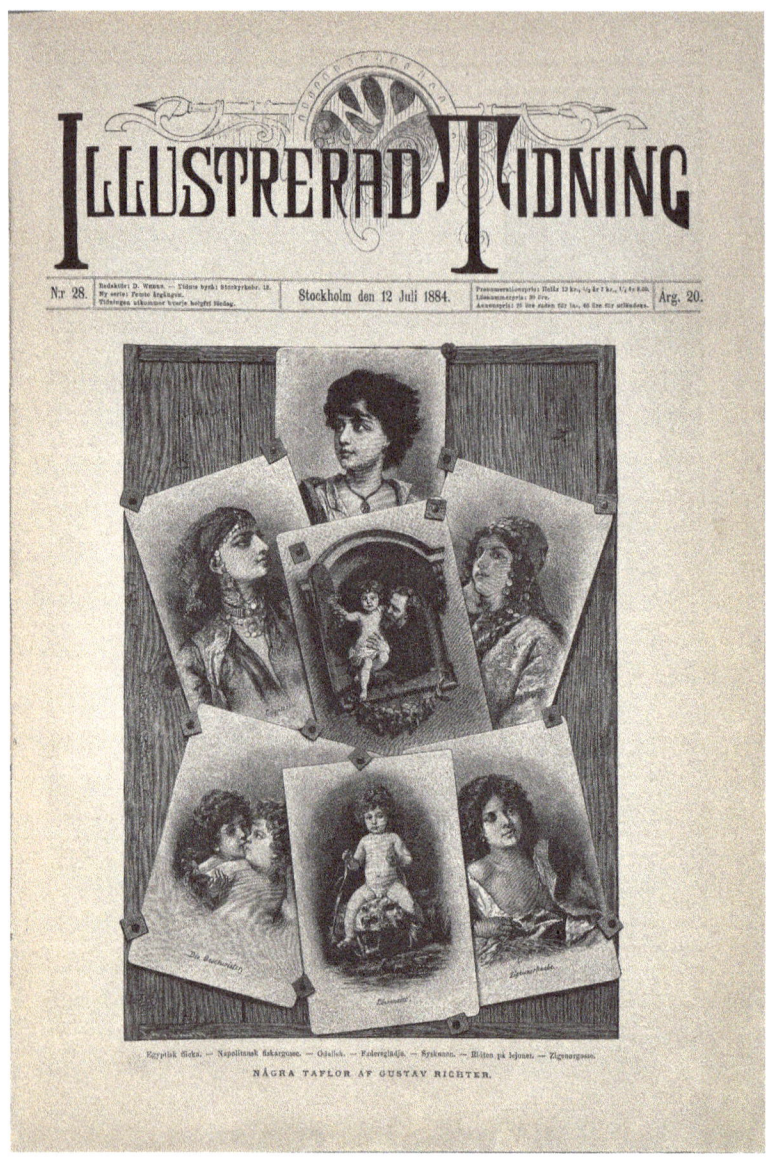

Figure 1. Front page of *Ny Illustrerad Tidning*, 1884. Reproduction: National Library of Sweden/Kungliga biblioteket, Stockholm. License: CC-BY-NC-ND.

surface as distinct from *in* the motif (as the German titles beneath the motifs on the prints represented). It signifies reproduction not so much because of what it says (although "XA" means xylographic atelier) but because of the fact that it is reversed, a not unusual accident in production when the marks from one surface were transferred to another.[31] But here, it is noteworthy not as a reference to the practice of production but as a sign of reversibility itself, which could alternately be called not static, changeable, transposable, unfixed. And there is still another contemporary media of pictorial reproduction referred to by the montage manner of the front page, namely photography. This reference hence builds on the formal organization of the motif, and parallels the practice of mounting photographs into albums in similar arrangements.[32]

And more, to this assemblage of media, the illustration also adds itself. By the xylographic surface, the genre of illustration is alluded to as the culturally defined product of xylography in journalistic print media, which is the same connotative relationship as that between the depicted lithographic prints and the medium of painting. Together with the article inside the magazine, to which the picture as an illustration is conventionally expected to refer, the picture on the front page presents the combined mediality of the genre. The material presence of picture and text as a pertinent feature of illustration could be thought of as so obvious that it does not at all provide a source of attention. But then the point of the overall exposure of media would be missed. In being framed by the media genres of lithography, xylography, painting, and photography, the combined mediality of the illustration is enhanced precisely as a presence of media.

The traditionally honourable medium of painting is then, with Mitchell's expression, "nested" within the illustration's continuous assemblage of new media of pictorial reproduction, including

---

[31] About reversals in the printing process, see Antony Griffiths, *The Print Before Photography: An Introduction to European Printmaking 1550–1820* (London: The British Museum Press, 2016), 35–38.

[32] For illustrations, see Anna Dahlgren, *Ett medium för visuell bildning: Kulturhistoriska perspektiv på fotoalbum 1850–1950* (Stockholm: Makadam, 2013), 96, 105.

itself as a new and combined medium.³³ In this, the illustration on the front page and the article inside the magazine both conjoins and diverts. The latter introduces the twice "reproduced" motifs *on* the lithographic prints (named "Gipsy boy," "Neapolitan fisher boy" and so on) as the art of the painter and his most popular idealizing subjects, which are contextualized by an account of their reception and the painter's biography. The theme of reproduction is not the overall theme of the article, even though it typically begins by commenting on the wide circulation of Richter's prints, "one sees them in reproduction everywhere."³⁴ Both article and front page can thus be said to conjoin in the reference to the medium of painting, although with different angles. The article points to the art of the *painter* and the illustration to the medium of *painting*. They also make use of different means: the article narrates the story of the artist's life and reception whereas the illustration represents painting as reproduced in lithography. The emphasis on painting is further doubled by another pictorial reference to the same medium. The first-order motif of the wooden board is reminiscent of a particular *trompe l'œil*-genre of illusory depictions of wooden wall boards with an assemblage of pinned-up letters, drawings, prints, booklets, and other pieces of paper, a genre practiced from the seventeenth through the nineteenth centuries.³⁵ Painting, with its art-historical status as an "auratic" non-reproductive medium, is in various ways nested within the combined media of the illustration, which hence actualizes itself as a media genre in relation to painting, and further shows painting as contained within lithography, moulded by a xylographic surface, and placed aside photography.³⁶

This exposure of media (materially present in combination and by the surface, represented by the motif, imitated in style, alluded

---

[33] Mitchell, *Picture Theory*, 48, 56; Mitchell, *Image Science*, 131–132.
[34] "Till Gustav Richters taflor," *Ny Illustrerad Tidning*, no. 28 (1884): 237.
[35] For illustrations, see *Lura ögat: Fem seklers bländverk*, ed. Karin Sidén, exh. cat., (Stockholm: Nationalmuseum, 2008), 20–30.
[36] For the concept of "aura," see Walter Benjamin's classical essay "The Work of Art in the Age of Mechanical Reproduction," in *Illuminations*, ed. Hannah Arendt, trans. Harry Zohn (New York: Schocken Books, 1968), 217–251.

to by organization), makes the illustration move beyond the content of the article. It does not so much illustrate the work of the painter as the assemblage of new media of pictorial reproduction placed in a continuous relation to the art of painting and to the new and combined media of the genre of illustration itself. In sum, the media involved in and on the front page are exposed by an internal series of pointing and emphasizing: the inscription on the surface enhances its status as xylographic reproduction, which in its turn points to the genre of illustration, the montage manner doubles photographic practices with a genre of painting, painting further recurs in the idea of the originals to the motifs on the lithographs depicted, and the lithographic media is emphasized by the mimicked style, except by being part of the first-order motif.[37]

The continuous model exposed by the illustration importantly opposes the historiographic divide between illustration as art and as pictorial reproduction (of textual and/or artistic sources). More precisely, I understand continuity as the semantic outcome produced by the illustration's pictorial and textual parts. When this outcome is turned to face the idea of a divide, it not only opposes it, but in that very opposition makes the latter more uncertain. The illustration on the front page then follows the pattern of ambivalence of intersecting conceptual propositions studied in the previous section. In that sense it further underlines the modern concept of illustration as an only provisional entity or an unstable set of related but incoherent notions.

---

[37] The differences between the orders of re/presentation indicated in the paragraphs above correspond to Bolter and Grusin's broad distinction between "immediacy" and "hypermediacy" or the cooperative forces of remediation, that captures, on the one hand, the perception of and immersion in representational content and erasure of media (seeing lithography and painting represented), and, on the other, enhancement of media by making multiple acts of mediation perceptible (the xylographic mimicking of the lithographic tonal style, the reversed signature, the organization or the montage manner). This means that Bolter and Grusin's terms are employed here to theoretically inform the concept of new media drawn from Gitelman (note 11), but they are, because of lack of precision, not made operative in the details of the analysis. Cf. Bolter and Grusin, *Remediation*, 21–44, 54–55, 70–71.

But besides accommodating the instability of the modern concept of illustration as a historiographic entity, the illustration also exposes *another* kind of ambivalence, analytically building on properties that are not so much derived from preconceived words as from the illustration itself and relating to metalanguage sideways. The front page gives rise to questions about media and genre borders and their transgression partly provoked by my, at first, naïve reference to it as a front page—which is not completely wrong. It is the first page of the number, complete with letterhead and cover illustration. But the untheorized referring to it as a given unit actually entails the problem of the illustration's own borders. To simplify a bit, the intuitive delimitation of the illustration as a *picture* is the thin outline surrounding the wooden board (which is nonetheless broken by the outbreaking drawing pins), whereas the intuitive delimitation of the *illustration* in the combined media sense, is the picture placed in relation to the title beneath it and the article further on. What the illustration in its combined media sense does *not* include is the elements belonging to the front *page*, like the letterhead, the ornamental motif of shield and spear or the white margins. These elements thus have in common that they are conventionally excluded from the illustration's physical extension on the page and from the textual units it is conventionally expected to illustrate, which is an exclusion shared by a particular quality of the pictorial *surface* that can be called its "graphicness" or its many parallel and crossed strokes. It is this particular quality that gives rise to the questions of border transgression, once it is recognized that it is a quality the pictorial surface have in common with some elements on the *page*, or elements *within* the illustration's immediate proximity but *without* its conventional borders: the horizontal bar that runs beneath the letterhead and the vertical strokes intersecting the ornament behind the accentuated name of the magazine.

The communality between the pictorial surface, the horizontal bar, and the vertical strokes, however, hinges upon a restricted sense of graphicness as material forms that are neither textual nor pictorial. The graphic qualities that now have been pointed out are not pictorial in the same figurative way as depictions of things (like lithographs and drawing pins) or figures (like the second-order motif of the "Egyptian girl") or scenery (like the architectural frame in the middle print or the river shore in the lower). Neither are they textual in the material sense of being shaped like letters or narrative in the same straightforward way as the subject entitled "Father's joy" is pictorialized by the man holding/showing a child and helping it to raise a cup in a gesture of celebration. Consequently, the strokes of the pictorial surface should be distinguished from, for instance, the similar strokes of the wooden board, or strokes that are ceasing to be graphic the moment they are recognized and accounted for as "grainings in wood"—which is almost automatically done. The graphic elements of the pictorial surface are not as easily accountable for, but still not beyond conceptualization. The latter is actually achieved already by calling them "traces after graphic tools" or "graphic qualities."[38] Of course, it could be objected that the bar and the traces after graphic tools are not in all aspects similar cases. The former organizes the textual units within it by grouping, dividing, and outlining, and are thereby connected to the qualities Johanna Drucker more broadly calls "information graphics,"[39] while the latter makes out the overall pictorial surface and gives texture to depicted figures, things, etc. The vertical strokes behind the letterhead is still another case of filling in space. One reason to separate this graphic quality from more textual and pictorial counterparts and make it into a category of its own is, however, to make a point of its in-betweenness. While the combined-media approach targets text and picture, the graphic elements are neither the one nor the other. And from the conventional point of view, they are not recognized as the essential, meaning-producing elements of the

---

[38] I am here distancing my terminology from James Elkins's "graphic marks." Like me, Elkins recognizes the traces after tools as analytical units but refuses them sign function by calling them "marks," in an argument completely opposed to the project I am committed to. Elkins's critical agenda is to estrange pictures as non-textual, whereas mine is to verbalize and communicate the semantic dimension *also* of graphic qualities. James Elkins, *On Pictures and the Words That Fail Them* (Cambridge: Cambridge University Press, 1998), 3–46, 73, 213, 215.

[39] Johanna Drucker, *Graphesis: Visual Forms of Knowledge Production* (Cambridge: Harvard University Press, 2014), 64–137.

genre, as long as the idea of a textual counterpart corresponding to narrative parts of motifs serves as the parameter for what is essential to illustration's meaning production.

Now, the graphicness of both surface and page invites a metalanguage that accounts for their transgressive status. This is to be found in Derrida's concept of "parergon," which terms the frame (parergon) of a work (ergon) and conceptualizes it as the double work of de/composing borders. The frame is recognized as the dual device that aligns the inside with the outside, while it also cuts off. Derrida characterizes it as an intervening third, which is both exterior and interior to the object framed. The frame is exterior in being, from the point of view of the essential qualities of the work, imposed from without. But when it is brought onto the work, it is not only annexed to it but is also made operative on its inside.[40] When graphic qualities are now recognized as parergonal qualities, their border transgression can be qualified in two ways. Firstly, in being conceptualized as the parergonal framework from which to consider combined mediality. In their very difference, graphic qualities make the distinctions between textual and pictorial media both visible and transgressed. This idea builds on the simple fact that to speak about graphic qualities as different already presupposes the definition of illustration as a combination of textual and pictorial media. The point, however, is that when graphic qualities by differing point to the notion of textual and pictorial distinctness, they in the same move transgress the concept of combined mediality, as being omitted from the combination, but still "there," in the illustration. This is the parergonal duality of a framework that is both interior and exterior. Graphic qualities have been brought to, imposed upon, the illustration as a combined medium, and made operative on its

---

[40] Jacques Derrida, *The Truth in Painting*, trans. Geoff Bennington and Ian McLeod (Chicago: University of Chicago Press, 1987 [1978]), 37–82, esp. 54–56, 69–74. In the discussion here, "parergon" is used as a concept evoked by and therefore also guided by the illustration, which has made me leave out considerations of the supplementary function Derrida assigns to it. My pictorial example warrants questions of borders and transgressions, but not necessarily questions of supplementarity. Cf. Derrida, *Truth in Painting*, 56, 57, 59–60, 64, 71, 78–79.

inside when understood as a question of border transgression. Remember "not beyond verbalization" above; graphic qualities are here made to "speak" about how they exceed the constraints of the combined medium. If this first aspect has to do with how the illustration is allowed to give rise to words, to content, the second aspect has to do with the illustration's concrete transgression of its conventional extension on the page. The graphicness of the pictorial surface mimics the graphicness of the horizontal bar and the vertical strokes of the page. Their graphic qualities have different material realizations but are nonetheless aligned in their in-between status and in that respect traverses the cut of the combined-media approach. In other words, what has now been attended to via the parergonality of the graphic surface is a parallel case of the ambivalence of intersecting models discussed above.

To summarize what has happened in the analysis in this section, there is both seriality and a change of positions involved. Initially, the ambivalence of the modern concept of illustration suggested by the historiographic readings pointed out the direction of analysis, paired with the attention to the surface suggested by the concept of new media. These two guides were in their turn conditioned by my approach to the illustration as self-referential. Also initially, and derived from the concept of new media, came the stress on the surface's visibility. I made a point of the transgression of the historiographic divide between art (represented by painting) and illustration as a new medium of pictorial reproduction (represented by the exposure of the whole assemblage of media genres) that, taken as a "text" or something I textualized by verbalizing it as a conceptual entity (a model of continuity), stresses the conceptual unfixedness in the first section and throws equivocal light on the (presumed) divide. Then, the (xylo)graphic quality of the surface, initially pointed out by the concept of new media, needed further attention as graphic. The surface did not, so to speak, completely fit the frame. With recourse to the concept of parergon I pointed to graphicness as a hybrid between textual and pictorial media and a bridge between pictorial surface and page that intersects the conventional borders of the genre of illustration. From this it can be said that the concept of ambivalence has indeed been illustrated by the front page, *but* that the analytical process of making it illustrate has included an oscillation between a concept that is the outcome of historiographic readings, reliance on convention, and concepts drawn from media studies and philosophy, or an oscillation where the illustration is both used as an object made to accommodate preconceived words and allowed to give rise to further adjustments of analysis.

Conclusion

One of the study's preconditions was to recognize that the two basic positions of illustrated and illustrating need not be tied to any particular type of object, whether pictorial or textual. With this in mind, "basic positions" are more properly called *functions* than "positions," since the latter have unhappy associations to something stable and fixed once and for all. The entity that is allowed to function as either illustrated or illustrating is exchangeable, the functions can be activated both simultaneously and serially, and the "same" object could in the course of analysis occupy both at different stages.

Thinking illustration as two exchangeable and reversible functions does not propose a passive and in the stronger sense mimetic task for the object that for the moment is illustrating. This has been exemplified by attending to the transmedial processes by which a semantic outcome has been allowed to deviate from its initial shape. Ambivalence was first modelled out in historiographic readings and then adjusted by the confrontation with the front page, used as an illustration of it. The illustration, however, offered *both* a "new" content to the initial term while still keeping in accordance with it, *and* an ambivalence of its own as a point from which to further understand the initial concept. It turned ambivalence from an issue of intersecting conceptual models to a graphic issue about its own (imposed) borders or "frame-up" as illustration, in the *serial* course of the study.

Although my study in a less-specified sense has dealt with one illustration, it must be stressed that it is nonetheless a *composite* object also in other ways than is suggested by its semantic equivocality and media combination. Additionally, it has been compartmentalized into the parts of surface, (parts of) motif(s), graphic qualities, organization, and further into different levels of re/presentation. These parts were dealt with in the same, more or less *simultaneous*, step and were used to counter the serially elaborated combination of concepts (new media and ambivalence from the start and subsequently parergon, when the front page was already understood in terms of the former concepts). In other words, neither the "object" employed for the (reversible) purpose of illustrating, nor the "object" employed to be illustrated is one-dimensional.

All in all, the operational definition of illustration that preconditions the study has been slightly elaborated. I started by pointing to the relationship between combined mediality and metalanguage and the reversibility of the basic positions. I have ended up with understanding the latter as two analytical functions occupied by exchangeable and reversible composite objects.

References

Bal, Mieke. *Reading "Rembrandt": Beyond the Word-Image Opposition*. Cambridge: Cambridge University Press, 1991.

Bal, Mieke. *Travelling Concepts in the Humanities: A Rough Guide*. Toronto: University of Toronto Press, 2002.

Barthes, Roland. *Image Music Text*. Translated by Stephen Heat. London: Fontana, 1977.

Benjamin, Walter. "The Work of Art in the Age of Mechanical Reproduction." In *Illuminations*. Edited by Hannah Arendt, translated by Harry Zohn, 271–251. New York: Schocken Books, 1968.

Blackburn, Henry. *The Art of Illustration*. London, 1896 [1894].

Bland, David. *A History of Book Illustration: The Illuminated Manuscript and the Printed Book*. London: Faber and Faber Limited, 1958.

Bolter, Jay David, and Richard Grusin. *Remediation: Understanding New Media*. Cambridge: MIT Press, 1999.

Burén, Jan af. *Det mångfaldigade originalet: Studier i originalgrafikbegreppets uppkomst, teori och användning*. PhD diss. Stockholm: Carlssons, 1992.

Crane, Walter. *Of the Decorative Illustration of Books Old and New*. London, 1896.

Curtis, Gerard. *Visual Words: Art and the Material Book in Victorian England*. Aldershot: Ashgate, 2002.

Dahlgren, Anna. *Ett medium för visuell bildning: Kulturhistoriska perspektiv på fotoalbum 1850–1950*. Stockholm: Makadam, 2013.

Derrida, Jacques. *Of Grammatology*. Translated by Gayatri Chakravorty Spivak. Baltimore: Johns Hopkins University Press, 1997 [1967].

Derrida, Jacques. *The Truth in Painting*. Translated by Geoff Bennington and Ian McLeod. Chicago: University of Chicago Press, 1987 [1978].

Drucker, Johanna. *Graphesis: Visual Forms of Knowledge Production*. Cambridge: Harvard University Press, 2014.

"Editorial." *Journal of Illustration Studies* (December 2007). Accessed August 18, 2015. http://jois.uia.no/articles.php?article=42.

Elkins, James. *On Pictures and the Words That Fail Them*. Cambridge: Cambridge University Press, 1998.

Elleström, Lars. *Media Transformation: The Transfer of Media Characteristics Among Media*. Basingstoke: Palgrave Macmillan, 2014.

Frankel, Nicholas. *Masking the Text: Essays on Literature & Mediation in the 1890s*. High Wycombe: The Rivendale Press, 2009.

Gitelman, Lisa. *Always Already New: Media, History, and the Data of Culture*. Cambridge: MIT Press, 2006.

Gitelman, Lisa, and Geoffrey B. Pingree, eds. *New Media, 1740–1915*. Cambridge: MIT Press, 2003.

Griffiths, Antony. *The Print Before Photography: An Introduction to European Printmaking 1550–1820*. London: The British Museum Press, 2016.

Hamerton, Philip Gilbert. *The Graphic Arts: A Treatise on the Varieties of Drawing, Painting, and Engraving in Comparison with Each Other and with Nature*. Boston, 1882.

Helsinger, Elizabeth, Martha Tedeschi, Anna Arnar, Allison Morehead, Peyton Skipwith and Erin Nerstad. *The "Writing" of Modern Life: The Etching Revival in France, Britain, and the U.S., 1850–1940*. Exhibition catalogue, Smart Museum of Art. Chicago: University of Chicago, 2008.

Hodnett, Edward. *Image & Text: Studies in the Illustration of English Literature*. London: Scolar Press, 1982.

Janzen Kooistra, Lorraine. *Poetry, Pictures, and Popular Publishing: The Illustrated Gift Book and Victorian Visual Culture 1855–1875*. Athens: Ohio University Press, 2011.

Korda, Andrea. *Printing and Painting the News in Victorian London: The Graphic and Social Realism*. Burlington: Ashgate, 2015.

Lund, Hans. *Mötesplatser: Ord och bild i samverkan*. Lund: Intermedia Studies Press, 2013.

Lura ögat: Fem seklers bländverk. Edited by Karin Sidén. Exhibition catalogue, Nationalmuseum. Stockholm: Nationalmuseum, 2008.

Miller, Hillis J. *Illustration*. London: Reaktion Books, 1992.

Mitchell, W. J. T. *Image Science: Iconology, Visual Culture, and Media Aesthetics*. Chicago: University of Chicago Press, 2015.

Mitchell, W. J. T. *Picture Theory: Essays on Verbal and Visual Representation*. Chicago: University of Chicago Press, 1994.

Pennell, Joseph. *Modern Illustration: Its Methods and Present Conditions*. London, 1898.

Rajewsky, Irina O. "Intermediality, Intertextuality, and Remediation: A Literary Perspective on Intermediality." *Intermediality: History and Theory of the Arts, Literature and Technologies*, no. 6 (2005): 43–64.

Schapiro, Meyer. *Words and Pictures: On the Literal and the Symbolic in the Illustration of a Text*. The Hague: De Gruyer Mouton, 1973.

"Till Gustav Richters taflor." *Ny Illustrerad Tidning*, no. 28 (1884): 237–238.

Yousif, Keri. *Balzac, Grandville, and the Rise of Book Illustration*. Burlington: Ashgate, 2012.

Song as Event: On Intermediality and the Auditory
Erik Wallrup

Abstract

The background of intermedial studies related to language and tone or sound, reaching all the way back to the comparative literature of the 1950s, can be discerned still today in the tendency to focus upon matters of signification and treating music as a medium of communication (indeed as a semiotic system). Through a critique of the typologies or models of intermedial relations afforded by Werner Wolf and Lars Elleström, followed by a discussion on an auditory model presented by Calvin Scott, this article suggests that song should be understood as an event, a both linguistic and musical event that takes place in time and in sound, where the semiotic character of music cannot be taken at face value. With the fourteenth song from Arnold Schoenberg's *15 Gedichte aus Das Buch der hängenden Gärten von Stefan George* op. 15 and its George poem as touchstones, the different typologies and models are scrutinized, ending with the suggestion that a promising intermedial investigation would be the elucidation of the differences and similarities between the world of the song and the world of the poem. In the earlier case, this world is primary to the ensuing sign relations as well as the relation between the basic media that are parts the qualified medium song.

How to cite this book chapter:
Wallrup, Erik. "Song as Event: On Intermediality and the Auditory." In *The Power of the In-Between: Intermediality as a Tool for Aesthetic Analysis and Critical Reflection*, edited by Sonya Petersson, Christer Johansson, Magdalena Holdar, and Sara Callahan, 349–374. Stockholm: Stockholm University Press, 2018. DOI: https://doi.org/10.16993/baq.n. License: CC-BY.

Introduction: Schoenberg and George as Touchstones

One of the most intriguing questions concerning musical modernism is why Arnold Schoenberg in 1907 turned to Stefan George (or, perhaps, George's poetry chose Schoenberg) in his urge to free himself from the restrictions of tonality. He prided himself of being a song composer who did not with care read the poems to be set: "I had composed many of my songs straight to the end without troubling myself in the slightest about the continuation of the poetic events."[1] The act of composition, so he maintains, took place only with the impact from the first sounds of the poems. At the time deeply involved with asymmetric composition (or, "musical prose," as he would term it later[2]), he was seemingly at odds with the strict verses of so much of George's poetry. Schoenberg loosened the grip of meter, rhyme, and assonance, decomposing all those linguistic traits that are often hailed as "musical" characteristics of Stefan George's poems. His treatment of the texts was the composer's version of how, with George Steiner's famous phrase, the "contract between word and world" can be broken,[3] here, however, understood as the contract between word and music in the German *Lied*. One should also bear in mind that it was precisely George who brought Hugo von Hofmannsthal into the distress that lead to the writing of the Lord Chandos letter,[4] that painful report on the separation between language and world with silence as its ultimate consequence.

This breach of contract is certainly not an affair for music historians only. It has an impact on intermedial studies as well,

---

[1] Arnold Schoenberg, "The Relationship to the Text," in *Style and Idea* (Berkeley: University of California Press, 1984), 144.

[2] Arnold Schoenberg, "Brahms the Progressive," in *Style and Idea*, 415. An authoritative account of the term can be found in Carl Dahlhaus, "Musikalische Prosa," in *Gesammelte Schriften*, vol. 8, *20. Jahrhundert* (Laaber: Laaber, 2005).

[3] George Steiner, *Real Presences: Is There Anything in What We Say* (London: Faber and Faber, 1989), 8. Later (93) he writes: "*It is this break of the covenant between word and world which constitutes one of the very few genuine revolutions of spirit in Western history and which defines modernity itself.*" (Italics in the original.)

[4] Hugo von Hofmannsthal, "Ein Brief," in *Gesammelte Werke: Erzählungen, Erfundene Gespräche und Briefe, Reisen* (Frankfurt: Fischer, 1979), 461–472.

not at least since it calls for reflection upon the history and prehistory of the discipline. If we turn back to the emergence of the interdisciplinary study of literature and music from comparative literature, with Calvin S. Brown's *Music and Literature: A Comparison of the Arts* (1948) as a kind of starting point for what was to become interart studies and later intermedial studies related to language and tone or sound, then we can see that the possible connections between music and text highlighted by Brown—primarily concerning form but also the imitating "literal setting" and the suggestive "dramatic setting"—fall outside the field opened up by Schoenberg.[5] However, precisely as Jørgen Bruhn suggests in an introduction to the discipline of intermedial studies, this kind of interart-related question is not a very promising one for the understanding of intermedial relations,[6] even if there is many an example of studies of that vein still existing in the field.

An important branch of intermedial studies, including investigations of the relation between music and language, has had semiotics as its theoretical underpinning. In a most general formulation, medium is here understood as something that diffuses information or signs, and that might explain why musicology has responded reluctantly to intermediality and why there are not that many musicologists who have turned to intermedial studies.[7] It is true that music can be a sign when incorporated in film (only the slightest touch of non-Western scales signifies something exotic and foreign in Hollywood productions), intended musical intertextuality can be found in Medieval music already (perhaps in the music of the Antiquity, too, but we do not know much about the actual compositions), and of course there is musical semiotics (of different kinds). However, the ordinary musicologist

---

[5] Calvin S. Brown, *Music and Literature: A Comparison of the Arts* (Athens: The University of Georgia Press, 1949). The formal aspects dominate his discussion, on "literal" and "dramatic" setting, see 53–86.
[6] Jørgen Bruhn, "Intermedialitet: Framtidens humanistiska disciplin?," *Tidskrift för litteraturvetenskap* 38:1 (2008): 21–38.
[7] Mats Arvidson points out this reluctance, with Sweden as his example, in the article "Music and Musicology in the Light of Intermediality and Intermedial Studies," *STM-Online* 15 (2012), unpaginated.

looks with some suspicion at these different fields, taking them for being perhaps interesting, but in one way or another missing the point of music.

Exactly this suspicion leads back to Arnold Schoenberg, who did not only reflect upon his own music when he said that to him reading the text of a song is of no importance for the understanding of the actual song. He had then the texts to Schubert's *Lieder* in mind: "when I had read the poems it became clear to me that I had gained absolutely nothing for the understanding of the songs thereby, since the poems do not make it necessary for me to change my conception of the musical interpretation in the slightest degree."[8] Then, it seems that there is hardly any reason at all for a composer to include a text in a composition, but that is not what Schoenberg means. Later he writes: "I had completely understood the Schubert songs, together with their poems, from the music alone, and the poems of Stefan George from their sound alone, with a perfection that by analysis and synthesis could hardly have been attained, but certainly not surpassed."[9]

It is exactly here a critical intermedial scholar should intrude, saying that the most interesting thing to know is precisely the relationship—parallels and analogies, but more interestingly the differences—between the poem as poem and the poem in the song. The words in the poem and the words in the song are often more or less identical but as we shall see they are not one and the same.[10] Schoenberg's own George settings show that most emphatically. Accordingly, the intermedial relation to be focused upon here is the one between a poem and a song that is the setting of that same poem. Two media, poem and song, are put forth and are being interrelated to each other.

What I would like to show theoretically in this article is that in some of the most influential thoughts about intermediality and songs, music is mistaken for a semiotic system, which leads to a

---

[8] Schoenberg, "The Relationship to the Text," 142.
[9] Schoenberg, "The Relationship to the Text," 144.
[10] Yet, sometimes the composer has changed the text, deliberately or by mistake. Other deviances, quite common, are reiteration of words or whole verses due to structural or expressive reasons and the neglect of following the periods of the verses (which otherwise give the poem a sense of order both visually and acoustically—when read aloud or with the inner voice).

biased view on songs in general. Both Werner Wolf's highly diversified typology and Lars Elleström's elaborated reflections, the latter relying on Peircean semiotics, are to be discussed from this perspective. That does not lead to a dismissal of their thinking. Wolf's many distinctions are often useful, and Elleström's broad understanding of media gives insights into subtle intermedial relations, but the main problem concerning music and semiotics still remains. As I will explain, music should not be understood as a semiotic system, even if semiotics with no doubt has a lot to say about certain perspectives on music. I shall argue that a song ought to be understood as an *event*, a both linguistic and musical event that takes place in time and in sound, where the semiotic character of music cannot be taken at face value. Doing so, references are made to an auditory-oriented model of intermediality in song, presented by Calvin Scott, but his suggestion is also criticized for its shortcomings.

The intent is, therefore, to elaborate conceptually both positive and negative interrelations between poem and song. This is carried out through the introduction of concepts that may seem to be alien to an intermedial context—such as "event," the "world" of an artwork, and the "tone" of a text—but such that can overcome the semiotic bias, which hinders the understanding of auditory-based intermediality. I will more than once come back to Schoenberg and his George settings, this in order to counteract the tendency in much theoretical writing to lose contact with the concrete, but also due to the fact that Schoenberg's songs from the period 1907–09 put a pressure on the stable and unproblematic relation between the poem as it can be read on paper and the same words as a constituent part of a song. In short, these songs are exemplary because of the liberties Schoenberg allows himself.

The Semiotic Overstatement

Even if Werner Wolf is totally aware of the fact that the background of intermedial studies in comparative literature has had repercussions upon the field,[11] his view on the relation between

---

[11] Cf. Werner Wolf, "Intermedialität als neues Paradigma der Literaturwissenschaft? Plädoyer für eine literaturzentrierte Erforschung von

music and language is determined by his way of seeing media as belonging to the sphere of communication and the work to be investigated defined by its signification or the semiotic structure/complex of the work.[12] Having started within the frames of interart studies, where the object of research is first of all the multi- or plurimedial artwork itself, he has broadened the scope through allowing relations outside the work of art. What he calls "intracompositional intermediality" (or intermediality in the narrow sense) can be supplemented by "extracompositional intermediality" (such as transmediality and intermedial transposition).[13]

An obvious problem is, however, that Wolf recognizes that "music cannot unambiguously refer to a reality outside itself, let alone to such abstract concepts as a different medium"[14] at the same time as he stresses the semiotic character of the work. Here, the point to be made is not that there is nothing such as an "unambiguous reference" between a sign and reality; instead, the problem lies in the circumstance that music is held to be both semiotic and without reference (neither to reality, nor to any other semiotic system outside itself, whereas the self-reference is unclear). Music would then be semiotic but without signs referring to other signs or to reality. As already suggested, music may have

---

Grenzüberschreitungen zwischen Wortkunst und anderen Medien am Beispiel von Virginia Woolfs 'The String Quartet,'" *Arbeiten aus Anglistik und Amerikanistik* 21:1 (1996): 85–116 and "Intermediality Revisited," in *Essays in Honor of Steven Paul Scher on Cultural Identity and the Musical Stage*, ed. Suzanne M. Lodato, Suzanne Aspden, and Walter Bernhart, *Word and Music Studies* (Amsterdam: Rodopi, 2002), 21.

[12] Wolf defines "intermediality" in the narrow sense as "a direct or indirect participation of more than one medium of communication in the signification and/or semiotic structure of a work or semiotic complex, an involvement that must be verifiable *within* this semiotic entity." Wolf, "Intermediality Revisited," 17.

[13] Wolf's most developed description of "intracompositional intermediality" can be found in the chapter "'Intermediality': definition, typology, related terms" in his *The Musicalization of Fiction: A Study in the Theory and History of Intermediality* (Amsterdam: Rodopi, 1999), 35–50. "Extracompositional intermediality" is introduced in the article "Intermediality Revisited."

[14] Wolf, "Intermediality Revisited," 24.

a semiotic character, most obvious in film and opera, often clear in programme music, but the major characteristics of music is not dependent on semiotic relations.

When we turn to Lars Elleström's intricate model for intermedial relations, the main problem concerning song and music is still there. Elleström asserts that song (or, more specifically, the pop song) is a qualified medium combining and integrating two basic media, where a sounding text is combined with organized non-verbal sound. Both basic media have a common material interface, but the semiotic modalities of theirs differ: meaning in the sounding text is said to be determined first of all in a decoding of conventional signs whereas the organized non-verbal sound is mainly interpreted in terms of iconicity.[15]

As far as I know, Elleström has not developed a more detailed account for the iconicity of music, even if he touches upon the theme in an article on iconicity and miming.[16] However, in an anthology, which happens to be co-edited by Elleström, we find an article by the Swiss semiotic scholar Costatino Maeder, who describes three different iconic strategies that tie music to the linguistic arts when combined in opera and oratorio. Of course, these strategies do not have to be totally in accord with Elleström's views, but they lead in a direction that affords us with a better understanding of the semiotic character—and possibilities—music may have from time to time. Maeder says that music is a "semiotic system that differs drastically from the functioning of human language,"[17] but when he describes the three main strategies, he is quite close to the sounding elements of language. Firstly, "music mimes the prosody of human speech (rhythm, stress, and intonation)," secondly, it "mimes linguistic and psychological behaviour of human beings

---

[15] Cf. Lars Elleström, "The Modalities of Media: A Model for Understanding Intermedial Relations," in *Media Borders, Multimodality and Intermediality*, ed. Lars Elleström (London: Palgrave Macmillan, 2010), 29.

[16] Lars Elleström, "Iconicity as Meaning Miming Meaning and Meaning Miming Form," in *Signergy*, ed. Jac Conradie et al. (Philadelphia: John Benjamins, 2010), 73–100.

[17] Costantino Maeder, "Opera, Oratorio, and Iconic Strategies," in *Iconic Investigations*, eds. Lars Elleström, Olga Fischer, and Christina Ljungberg (Philadelphia: John Benjamins, 2013), 275.

under pressure," and thirdly, it "mimes and models communicative processes; for example, dialogue, argumentation."[18] Of these, the first two strategies are foremost bound to imagic iconicity, and the third one to diagrammatic iconicity.

Maeder's approach allows him to not get stuck on the question of whether music alone, that is, instrumental music without a programme, has any iconic characteristics or not (he does, however, describe different views on the matter, from Eduard Hanslick's and Carl Dahlhaus's notions of "absolute music" to Jean-Jacques Nattiez's declaration that music has at least a weak capacity of transferring propositional content[19]). Yet, what he has to say about iconicity in opera and oratorio has a lot to do with the problem put forward by me. In the context of a scene in an opera or an oratorio, music may mime prosody, behavior, and verbal structure. It is also true that these elements have a close relation to the characters on a scene (in an oratorio, we also most often find characters). However, much of the musical activity in the orchestra usually does not have something to do with how the characters speak, behave and communicate directly. The same counts for the short "scene" of a song. We can of course find a poetic I or a persona of the poem, but the relevance of Maeder's iconic strategies are limited when it comes to that poem set to music and then especially concerning the accompaniment.

The Formalistic Overstatement

What kind of alternatives do we have to an iconic foundation of music's relation to its text in songs? In *"Ich löse mich in tönen…": Zur Intermedialität bei Stefan George und der Zweiten Wiener Schule*, Calvin Scott tries to free the conception of intermediality from both its background in literary studies and the visual dominance in much writing in the field. The reason for him to carry out his investigations is precisely Stefan George's poetry, which has been set to music by composers such as Arnold Schoenberg, Anton Webern, and Alban Berg, but which in itself stands in

---

[18] Maeder, "Opera, Oratorio, and Iconic Strategies," 275–276.
[19] Cf. Maeder, "Opera, Oratorio, and Iconic Strategies," 277.

intermedial relations beyond referentiality. One of the aspects is visual, due to George's awareness of the designing of his literary production, realizing a new sans-serif font for his books and collaborating with the painter and designer Melchior Lechtor, who did the decoration for a series of George's books. However, even if Lechtor's work made George's collections of poems into artworks in their own right, being opulent expressions of the *art noveau* style, Scott is able to show that George's typography and even orthography give support to the auditory aspects of the poems. The typographic design estranges the reader from the words,[20] whereas the spelling has a tendency to come as close as possible to spoken words (for instance is "*-tzt*" in "*zuletzt*" reduced to "*-zt,*" non-pronounced letters such as "*h*" in "*wohl*" are omitted, and long vowels such as "*-o-*" in "*los*" are written with double letters, "*loos*").[21] Both the physical books, being highly elaborated art objects, and the visual characteristics of their typography point at Stefan George's urge to make his poetic words into a cult. The readings within the George circle were of vital importance for his poetic activities, and they should be understood in terms of events, taking place in time, within a space and in a community. George's texts can therefore be seen as scores for performances. When set to music, this circumstance does not change.

Calvin Scott underscores that the aural phenomenon is always temporal and spatial, and if such a thing as a song is to be investigated, then it must be seen as an event and a process. Distancing himself expressly from the conception of intermediality to be found in Wolf's writings, Scott suggests the following:

> A concept of intermediality, which should answer to something as fugitive-unstable as acoustic-sounding phenomena, demands first of all the discharge of the idea that matters of "intermedial" interrelationships should be about the presence of available and

---

[20] Scott refers to the Germanist Armin Schäfer, who has shown that the typography obstructs word identification: "'Gelesen' werden lediglich Buchstabengruppen statt Wörter." Calvin Scott, *"Ich löse mich in tönen…": Zur Intermedialität bei Stefan George und der Zweiten Wiener Schule* (Berlin: Frank & Timme, 2007), 49, n. 119.
[21] Scott, *"Ich löse mich in tönen…,"* 48.

concrete artefacts, in which the "establishment of contact" between "media of communication" or a "conceptual togetherness" of "medial quotes and elements" are at hand statically. "Intermediality" denotes from now on a phenomenon that "takes place" in an utterly temporary, dynamical way.[22]

Scott's criticism is probably directed at earlier stages of the development of intermedial studies, when the transformation of a drama or a novel into a film or an opera was a typical theme for research, but he actually wants to re-establish some of the earliest formulations of intermediality, namely by the scholar of Slavic studies Aage Hansen-Löve, who in his investigations of the relation between literature and pictorial art suggested a formalistic understanding of the intermedial correlation between these forms of art. The correlations were said to take place in between, in an oscillation between the preconceived art forms.[23]

It is, however, through turning to the sociologist Niklas Luhmann that Scott finds his solution. In Luhmann's definition of "medium," the relation to "form" is of vital importance: "A medium consists of loosely coupled elements, whereas a form brings these same elements into a tight coupling."[24] From this follows

---

[22] Scott, *"Ich löse mich in tönen…,"* 27 (my trans.): "Ein Intermedialitätskonzept, das etwas so Flüchtig-Instabilen wie dem Akustisch-Lautlichen gerecht werden will, erzwingt zunächst die Verabschiedung der Vorstellung, es würde sich bei der Frage nach 'intermedialen' Wechselbeziehungen um jederzeit verfügbare und handfeste 'Artefakte' handeln, in denen eine 'Kontaktaufnahme' von 'Kommunikationsmedien' oder ein 'konzeptuelles Miteinander' von 'medialen Zitaten und Elementen' statisch vorliegt. 'Intermedialität' bezeichnet nunmehr ein äußerst temporäres, dynamisch 'stattfindendes' Phänomen."

[23] Scott refers to an article that Aage Hansen-Löve published for the first time as "Intermedialität und Intertextualität: Probleme der Korrelation von Wort- und Bildkonst – Am Beispiel der russischen Moderne," in *Dialog der Texte: Hamburger Kolloquium zur Intertextualität*, Wiener slawistischer Almanach, Sonderband 11, eds. Wolf Schmid and Wolf-Dieter Stempel (Wien: Gesellschaft zur Förderung slawistischer Studien, 1983), 291–360.

[24] Niklas Luhmann, *Die Gesellschaft der Gesellschaft* (Frankfurt: Suhrkamp, 1997), 198 (my trans.): "Ein Medium besteht in lose gekoppelten Elementen, eine Form fügt dieselben Elemente dagegen zu strikter Kopplung zusammen." Quoted by Scott, *"Ich löse mich in tönen…,"* 30.

that the loosely coupled elements are tightly coupled by the medium in an event: the form is not everlasting but takes place in time. Further, there is an hierarchic relation where that which is a medium in one instance (for example sound) is tightly coupled by the form of words, whereas these words in the medium of language is arranged in the form of sentences, and these sentences in their turn can be elements within the medium of literature.[25] Scott's conclusion, when it comes to the relation between different media such as language and music, is that it would be possible to see how the media at some point are coupled to each other through having elements in common, whereas they in other instances may lack such joints. Since, according to Scott, language is characterized by having a reference to the outer world whereas music is self-referential, the intermedial relation between language and music is restricted to those formal arrangements that are supposed to exclude meaning. Forms such as metrical schemes and specific poetic forms (sonnet, ottava rima, etc.), as well as rhythmical figurations and melodic phrasing can be mirrored in the different media.

Let us see, then, what this means when Scott reaches the concrete works. I shall turn to a George setting by Schoenberg that has the advantage of having been richly commented upon by scholars of different strands, the fourteenth song of *15 Gedichte aus Das Buch der hängenden Gärten von Stefan George* op. 15 (Figure 1).[26] The short lines, the rich but often not symmetric rhymes, but especially the stern meter and a choice of words giving prominence to the vowels "*-au-*" and "*-i-*" are characteristics that come to mind.

---

[25] Cf. Niklas Luhmann, *Die Kunst der Gesellschaft* (Frankfurt: Suhrkamp, 1995) quoted and commented by Scott, *"Ich löse mich in tönen...,"* 32.

[26] The poem reads *in toto*: "Sprich nicht immer / Von dem laub · / Windes raub · / Vom zerschellen / Reife quitten · / Von den tritten / Der vernichter / Spät im jahr · / Von dem zittern / Der libellen / In gewittern / Und der lichter / Deren flimmer / Wandelbar." Stefan George, *Werke: Ausgabe in zwei Bänden* (Stuttgart: Klett-Cotta, 1984), 109. Schoenberg has normalized the text and made it into prose. Cf. Arnold Schoenberg, *15 Gedichte aus Das Buch der hängenden Gärten von Stefan George* (Wien: Universal, 1908–09), 32: "Sprich nicht immer von dem Laub, Windesraub; vom Zerschellen reifer Quitten, von den Tritten der Vernichter spät im Jahr. Von dem Zittern der Libellen in Gewittern, und der Lichter, deren Flimmer wandelbar."

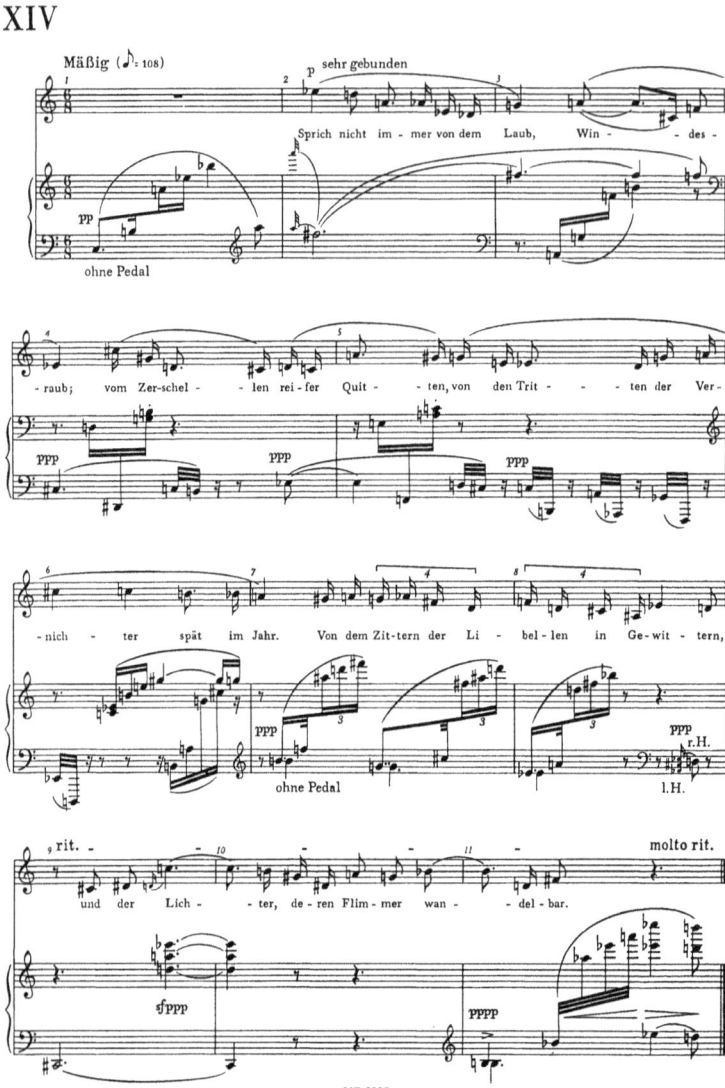

Figure 1. "Sprich nicht immer … ." Arnold Schoenberg, 1908–09. From Schoenberg's *15 Gedichte aus Das Buch der hängenden Gärten von Stefan George für Stimme und Klavier* op. 15. Copyright: Copyright 1914, 1941 by Universal Edition A.G. Vienna UE 5338. License: CC-BY-NC-ND.

However, these textual traits are not emphasized in Schoenberg's song; instead, it is one of the instances when he composes a kind of "musical prose," preventing symmetries and affording asymmetries. As Scott readily points out, the setting is totally at odds with all that which is associated with George's priestly readings within his circle. Indeed, the image of Schoenberg's textual distortion in scholarly comments on the George cycle are singled out by Scott (Harald Krebs speaks about "distortive inflections" whereas Karl Heinrich Ehrenfort points out a "breaking" through "barriers"[27]). From Scott's point of view Schoenberg misses all those joints that can appear (and then disappear) in the relation between music and text. Instead, Scott lapses into "non-musical" alternatives such as symbolism or even ciphers: the opening half-tone steps downward are seen as a returning motive that in its movements illustrate autumn leaves twisting and dancing in the wind.[28]

Yes, we have by then reached the process of musical semiosis. Scott is, however, not satisfied. The reason why is that all those "musical" and formal aspects that are of importance to George are almost wiped out by Schoenberg. The shaping forces of the song are only musical, whereas the intermedial relation is unmusical, according to Scott. And, of course, his own model for intermedial relations is not being activated by Schoenberg's setting.

The Evasive Musical Meaning

We should, however, not forget that Elleström's model covers all the relations that Scott highlights. The major difference is that

---

[27] Harald Krebs, "Three Versions of Schoenberg's Op. 15 No. 14: Obvious Differences and Hidden Similarities," *Journal of the Arnold Schoenberg Institute* 8:2 (1984): 131 and Karl Heinrich Ehrenforth, *Ausdruck und Form: Arnold Schönbergs Durchbruch zur Atonalität* (Bonn: Bouvier, 1963), 47 (my trans.): "'Durchbrechen' von 'Schranken.'" Scott quotes them in *"Ich löse mich in tönen…,"* 107 and 110 respectively.

[28] Scott writes: "Hierin liegt das musikalische Hauptmerkmal von Schönbergs Ausdrucks- und Formideal der 'musikalischen' Prosa: Die Gestaltung der Gesangsstimme und die 'pointillistischen' Gesten der Klavierbegleitung sollen tonmalerische und tonsymbolische *Chiffren* für das sich im Gedicht entfaltende, herbstliche Bild konstituiren." Scott, *"Ich löse mich in tönen…,"* 109.

Scott is only interested in the auditory aspects, since they have been downplayed by earlier theorists and since he has an investigation on the relation between George and the Second Vienna School in mind. One of the consequences is Scott's own lack of interest in musical semiosis. Elleström, on his part, tries to find a general model for intermediality, founded on a clarification of what a medium is. He avoids theoretical one-liners such as Marshall McLuhan's phrase that every medium is an "extension of man."[29] No, Elleström suggests a multi-facetted understanding, where any medium is said to be material, sensorial, spatiotemporal, and semiotic; a four-fold that he calls "modalities."[30] Further, he adds two qualifying aspects, firstly the contextual qualifying aspect that puts the medium into a historical, cultural, and social context, and secondly the operational qualifying aspect that is given by its communicative and aesthetic characteristics. Such media that are dominated by their modal appearances are called "basic media" and those dominated by their qualifying aspects are called "qualified media."[31]

For me in this article, not discussing intermediality in general, but the intermedial relation between poem and the setting of that poem to music, it is of great importance that Elleström does not see a song as being constituted by the relation between text and music (a combination that Wolf would call "intracompositional intermediality"). As already mentioned, Elleström says that song is a qualified medium, constituted by two basic media, "auditory text" and "organized non-verbal sound." The combination and integration of these two basic media in a song happens through their common material interface, sound waves, and they are both fundamentally temporal and share spatial characteristics, too. However, the striking difference between these two basic media is according to Elleström that "the process of signification in auditory texts is mainly a question of decoding conventional signs, whereas the meaning of the organized non-verbal sound first and

---

[29] Marshall McLuhan, *Understanding Media: The Extensions of Man* (Cambridge: MIT Press, 1994), 24.
[30] Elleström, "The Modalities of Media," 15.
[31] Elleström, "The Modalities of Media," 27.

foremost is a result of interpreting the sounds in terms of resemblance and contiguity."[32] Again, we see that the distinction between words and music is based on semiotic differences. But the song intended by Elleström is not any song, but a pop song. If his analysis up to this point can be said to be general for any song—art songs, folksongs, Gregorian chant, singing incantations—the next qualifying step is said to be specific for pop songs:

> The qualities of qualified media become even more qualified, so to speak, when aspects of genre are involved; a genre might therefore be called a sub-medium. Indeed, we usually deem that the lyrics produced by the singer are in themselves music, as is the sound produced by the mechanical and electronic instruments. The integration of the two basic media in a pop song is consequently in effect very deep, since the two media are more or less identical when it comes to three of the four modalities, and concerning the fourth modality, the semiotic, it is perfectly normal to integrate the symbolic and the iconic sign-processes in the interpretation of both literature and music. Texts are generally more symbolic and music is generally more iconic but the combination and integration of words and music stimulates the interpreter to find iconic aspects of the text and to realize the conventional facets of the music.[33]

There is much to comment on in this quotation. Firstly, the slightly surprising supposition that "we" take the lyrics sung by someone as music in itself, but one can presume that Ellerström intends the "musical" aspects of auditory texts. The fact is that the hovering status of language in a pop song lies behind the heated discussion on Bob Dylan as receiver of the Nobel Prize 2016: the texts by Dylan can of course be read in a book, but there is always something missing in silent reading of lyrics. A genuine kind of intermediality can be found here, since it is almost impossible to bring Dylan's voice into silence during the act of reading his texts once you have heard him singing a specific song. The assertion that auditory texts and organized non-verbal sound are more or less identical concerning the material, sensorial, and spatiotemporal modalities can be seen as an overstatement, but, in fact, we have

---

[32] Elleström, "The Modalities of Media," 29.
[33] Elleström, "The Modalities of Media," 29.

in both cases to do with sound waves being perceived by the ear (if the music is loud, by the body, too) in temporal flow that takes place in a shared space. However, the difference between tone in non-musical auditory texts (such as spoken-word poetry) and tone in musical auditory texts, where that which Roger Scruton calls the musical "field of force" is active, must be taken into account.[34] This field of force is dependent on musical phenomena such as the logic of melody and more or less obvious harmonic progression, both of them related to cultural factors, but yet vital to most if not all music cultures. There is a difference between a singing person and a person who speaks with a singing voice, with a number of shadings in between, such as *Sprechgesang* and rap, but in both cases the floating in between is seldom or never achieved.

Or do we find this opposition in the semiotic modality? Well, even if Elleström is totally right when saying that a song may impel the listener to find iconicity in the lyrics and conventional symbols in music, his reasoning it totally blank concerning musical phenomena such as mobility and spatiality, when these are not relating to a situation that might take place in reality. Music moves even if it does not move *like something*, and this movement may take place in a space that has nothing or very little to do with physical space. This is in fact the essential problem with any semiotic understanding of music. Music can obviously be an icon, reflecting the movement downward in a sigh, and that sign can also have a symbolic function when it is used as a standardized musical figure in an aria full of sorrow. Music can even be treated as an Peircean "index,"[35] at least if we trust the major part of non-formalistic musical aesthetics that accepts that music is the language of feeling and that the composer expresses him- or herself in music. (I believe that this standard view must be accepted, even if most contemporary composers do other things

---

[34] Scruton writes: "A tone is a sound which exists within a musical 'field of force.' This field of force is something that *we* hear, when hearing tones." Roger Scruton, *The Aesthetics of Music* (Oxford: Oxford University Press, 1999), 17.

[35] On the musical index, see, e.g., Vladimir Karbusicky, "The Index Sign in Music," in *Semiotics of Music*, ed. Eri Tarasti, special issue of *Semiotica* 66 (1986): 25–35.

than expressing themselves and their affective state when they sit in front of their computer screen.) But most of the time, music does not stand for anything else, it does not function as a sign, it is nothing semiotic. There are even some problems with an interesting notion that Elleström has picked up in another context, namely music as an "empty sign,"[36] which can attract different meanings in different contexts, but which does not have a meaning of its own. Most often, music is no sign at all, be it empty or not.

However, a great advantage with Elleström's model is that it tends both to blur the borders between the media and to rely on a simple distinction between them. Let me explain this paradoxical statement. Saying that song, indeed, pop song, is a medium of its own, that is, a qualified medium, Elleström allows a song to be a song, that is, something that hovers in between linguistic and musical traits—where "linguistic" elements are of "musical" relevance and where music seems very close to language. He keeps at the same time the distinction between language and music as basic media. The problem is that he either overemphasizes music's iconicity, or disregards that important field of musical meaning, which has not to do with semiotics at all. Musical meaning? Well, that is the meaningful interplay between tones and rhythms, which cannot be articulated outside music.[37] Meaning related to signification has to do with a relation where something stands for something else, whereas a tone or note often does not stand for anything, even if it has meaningful relations to other tones or notes. The understanding of the pronounced musical meaning has been the hallmark of the connoisseur (*Kenner*) in comparison with

---

[36] Concerning "empty signs," Elleström refers in his 2002 book on irony in the arts, *Divine Madness*, to Kevin Barry, who in his turn has observed it in eighteenth-century texts on musical aesthetics. In *Divine Madness*, Elleström discusses the problem with musical meaning with care, showing that he is well read in musical aesthetics. That makes it much harder to understand his later stance on music and semiosis. Cf. Lars Elleström, *Divine Madness: On Interpreting Literature, Music, and the Visual Arts Ironically* (Lewisburg: Bucknell University Press, 2002).
[37] Cf. Matthias Vogel, "Nachvollzug und die Erfahrung musikalischen Sinns," in *Musikalischer Sinn: Beiträge zu einer Philosophie der Musik*, eds. Alexander Becker and Matthias Vogel (Frankfurt: Suhrkamp, 2007), 316.

the amateur (*Liebhaber*) ever since the eighteenth century,[38] and it is still working in silence in Theodor W. Adorno's typology of listeners and further on.[39] The difference lies between someone who understands the logic of musical unfolding from the perspective of compositional technique and someone who only reacts upon this logic, be it in a very sensitive way, or even tries to understand the music as an expression of feeling with the consequence that the music becomes signs for inner states.

Song as Event

What takes place in a song, then? We cannot generalize this kind of event into a law, but at least we should be able to see that Goethe's famous praise of Carl Friedrich Zelter's settings, saying that they were identical with his poems, is a problematic way of describing a (successful) song.[40] At the other extreme, we find Luigi Nono's string quartet *Fragmente—Stille, An Diotima*, which can be seen as a variant of Schoenberg's George settings in the last two movements of his Second String Quartet, with the obvious difference that Nono excludes vocal singing, but includes fragments of Hölderlin poems in the score to be "sung" in silence by the musicians ("*The players should 'sing' them* [the fragments] *inwardly, in their autonomy*").[41]

The relation between poem and music in art song has been open for debate ever since Socrates's demand in Plato's *Republic*

---

[38] Cf. the entry "Kenner" in Johann Georg Sulzer, *Allgemeine Theorie der Schönen Künste*, vol. 3 (Leipzig: Weidmannsche Buchhandlung, 1793), 5–14.

[39] Theodor W. Adorno, *Einleitung in der Musiksoziologie*, in *Gesammelte Schriften*, vol. 14 (Darmstadt: Wissenschaftliche Buchgesellschaft, 1998).

[40] In a letter to Zelter he writes: "Deine Kompositionen fühle ich sogleich mit meinen Liedern identisch, die Musik nimmt nur, wie ein einströmendes Gas, den Luftballon mit in die Höhe. Bei andern Komponisten muß ich erst aufmerken wie sie das Lied genommen, was sie daraus gemacht haben." Johann Wolfgang von Goethe, *Sämtliche Werke nach Epochen seines Schaffens: Münchner Ausgabe*, vol. 10:1 (Munich: Hanser, 1999), 601.

[41] Luigi Nono, *Fragmente—Stille, An Diotima* (Milan: Ricordi, 1980), unpaginated (at the beginning of the score, italics in the original).

that mode and rhythm must follow the words in a song[42]—if not further back in history. A contrast to the naïve attitude formulated by Goethe has been Suzanne Langer's and Edward T. Cone's suggestion that music appropriates the poem,[43] instead of trying to translate or just accompany it.[44] Pierre Boulez, reflecting upon his own practice when using texts in his compositions, draws this position to its extreme when he says that the formal traits of the poem might be of great importance for the construction of the work, whereas the poem is absent in the work.[45] Langer's and Cone's amalgamation, steered by musical principles, is further put in doubt by Lawrence Kramer, who rather speaks about an agonic relation between words and music: "the song is a 'new creation' only because it is also a de-creation."[46] If especially Cone would say that the composer uses a reading of the text, Kramer underscores that this reading then is both critical and performative. In his view, a struggle between word and music takes place in the art song, giving space to a very interesting question about intermediality concerning the original poem and the musical setting of it.

If we keep using the Schoenberg song as a litmus test for the different stances accounted for above, we can see that he in his composition has appropriated George's poem in an almost violent way. Nearly all rhythmical patterns are wiped out, the assonances and rhymes do not have a structuring function, and the text seems to be reduced to prose. It is through a thorough reconstruction of the circumstances around George's text that we can see how far

---

[42] Cf. Plato, *Republic, Books 1–5* (Cambridge: Harvard University Press, 2013), 270.

[43] Cf. Susanne K. Langer, *Feeling and Form: A Theory of Art developed from Philosophy in a New Key* (London: Routledge and Kegan, 1953), 153; Edward T. Cone, *The Composer's Voice* (Berkeley and Los Angeles: University of California Press, 1974), 19.

[44] Here and in the following comments on Pierre Boulez and Lawrence Kramer, I am indebted to Håvard Enge's introduction to the dissertation *Music Reading Poetry: Hans Zender's Musical Reception of Hölderlin* (PhD diss., University of Oslo, 2010), 9–27.

[45] Pierre Boulez, "Poésie – centre et absence – musique," in *Points de repère, Tome I: Imaginer* (Paris: Christian Bourgois Éditeur, 1995).

[46] Lawrence Kramer, *Music and Poetry: The Nineteenth Century and After* (Berkeley and Los Angeles: California University Press, 1984), 127.

the musically performed words have been taken from the imagined readings of the poem in the solemn meetings of the George circle.

However, we do find an element that seems to have almost such qualities that it can be ranked as an instance of transmediality, namely the tone. In another context, I have developed the characteristics of this both fugitive and pervasive phenomenon in George's lyrical output.[47] It has been witnessed and discussed by sensitive readers such as Friedrich Gundolf and Hans-Georg Gadamer,[48] but it was also decisive to Schoenberg in his choice of George during the period when he released himself from tonality and tried to find something that could organize a composition without the tonal reference.[49] Being freed from concrete materialization in rhythm and sound, being an "intonation" of the words rather than a melodic contour, its shortest formulation can be seen in a quotation from one of George's own poems: it is the "droning of the sacred voice" (*Dröhnen der heiligen Stimme*).[50] Gundolf quotes these words by George in a context where he discusses the difference between the young poet and the mature one, where the young poet is said to not proclaim a world with his word, whereas the mature poet installs such a world.[51]

When trying to elucidate his concept of "tone," Gundolf rather says what it is not, and not what it is. When absent, even the most sublime words seem to be empty; when present, an inauguration takes place. According to Gundolf, George has a tone, as well as Shakespeare, and, surprisingly, Napoleon, all of them persons who, in different media, have installed worlds.[52] If we try

---

[47] Erik Wallrup, "From Mood to Tone: On Schoenberg and Musical Worlds," *Danish Musicology Online*, special edition, 17th Nordic Musicological Congress (2016): 123–144.
[48] Cf. Friedrich Gundolf, *George*, 3rd ed. (Berlin: Bondi, 1930) and the following essays by Hans Georg Gadamer: "Der Dichter Stefan George" and "Hölderlin and George," in *Gesammelte Werke*, vol. 9, Tübingen: Mohr Siebeck, 1993.
[49] Cf. the following texts by Arnold Schoenberg: "Composition with Twelve Tones (1)," in *Style and Idea*, and "The Relationship to the Text."
[50] Stefan George, "Entrückung," in *Werke*, 293.
[51] Gundolf, *George*, 61.
[52] Gundolf, *George*, 61.

to find out what he actually means, then the answer must be that "tone" is not something, it is not a thing, yet it can be traced in the order of the poem. This world is not set up by the tone, but it is "in tone," according to an intonation. Neither tone, nor world, can be made into objects for an investigation, since they are not objects: the world is that which gathers things together, not being a thing itself, and the gathering is made in accordance with the tone. Gadamer, in his turn, refers to George's tone as "the melodic substance of Gregorian chant,"[53] and that gives another clue: the intonation that takes place can be likened with the intonation in plainchant, namely an initial melodic phrase sung by the priest before the other voices joins the singing—a defining and stabilizing motion.

Here we find a new turn of the metaphor of a contract. A successful artwork installs a world, and this world is primordial in relation to the elements that can be found within it. If the contract was broken, then a new one is written, establishing new kinds of relations between the words and the tones. This is also what happens in Schoenberg's song: the establishment of a world, now not made of words only, but a new order for all relations between words and tones as well as for words and words and tones and tones.

What clearly is a very meagre material for generalizations—a song with a duration of 40 seconds—cannot be seen as anything else than a hint. But what this hint says is that we must start with concrete works of art if we want to understand the way in which basic media such as "auditory text" and "organized non-verbal sound" are combined in a "qualified medium" as an art song. The song is to be taken as an event. So I said from the start, but then without elaborating the meaning of the word. Being a primordial event, the song cannot be taken as an object, which can be decomposed into its simpler, constituent elements. Instead, it is something that happens through opening up a world, which allows the listener to be a part of it, exposing him or her for a changed order. It invites the listener to stand out in another sphere than the customary one. Now, the point has been reached where

---

[53] Gadamer, "Der Dichter Stefan George," 222.

it is possible to insert the intermedial notions already put in play: the event lets a world take place, a world that lets the signs be signs (be they symbolic, iconic, or indexical) and determines the relations between the basic media that are parts of the qualified medium. Here, the intermedial investigation should be directed at elucidating the differences and similarities between the worlds of the poem and the song, both of them emerging as events which take place under specific historical and aesthetic circumstances.

Every time the song is sung (or, for the *Kenner*, read vividly), the world emerges, at least as long as it achieves an impetus that displaces the expectations of the listener. Schoenberg's music has still that capacity, strangely enough. How can it then be that the song sounds so different, sung by different singers (both male and female), and played by different pianists? The solemn melancholia is obvious when Christian Gerhaher sings with Gerold Huber at the piano. Brigitte Fassbaender sounds more like a singer who has escaped from *Pierrot Lunaire*, when she, together with the pianist Aribert Reimann, makes a theatrical interpretation. Glenn Gould's dropping, capricious piano playing and Helen Vanni's operatic mezzo-soprano emerges in one stroke, a contrast that only can be fathomed with a reflective act after its appearance.[54] Yet, all these different concretizations give a hint of the tone of the poem, and this tone should not be confounded with the actual voice in the performance. The tone of the poem is an in-between, a potentiality. The successful interpretation (all those mentioned here are successful, but in very different ways) keeps something of the tone, though not making it manifest: it is an affecting absence.

In three steps, I have turned from a quite common notion of the language-music interrelations in intermedial studies grounded upon semiotics (afforded by Werner Wolf and Lars Elleström), over an auditory model (developed by Calvin Scott), arriving at an understanding of the relation between a poem and a song set

---

[54] The following recordings of the song are referred to: Christian Gerhaher and Gerold Huber, Sony Classical 88691935432, 2012; Brigitte Fassbaender and Aribert Reimann, His Master's Voice 1C 067 1466851, 1983; Helen Vanni and Glenn Gould, Columbia Masterworks, M2S 736, 1966.

to that same poem as one between two different emerging worlds. That which has been suggested does not gainsay the fact that songs and indeed music alone may communicate something semiotically, or that music may have formal aspects that cannot be reconciled with linguistic meaning. Instead, a more primordial point is reached where a song (here exemplified with one song only, by Arnold Schoenberg, leaving much to be done before the position taken can be said to be well grounded) is grasped as an event where a world is opened up. This world installs the possible relations between words and words, tones and tones, as well as words and tones; it allows signs to be signs, and it determines the basic media as parts of the qualified medium that a song is. In this way, we can begin to investigate how this world of a song is related to the world of the poem to which music has been set. The words in the song and those in the poem may be identical, but they are not the same. Yet, the song might preserve something of the tone of the poet, that extremely elusive phenomenon that in an intermedial investigation can be said to be transmedial.

References

Adorno, Theodor W. *Einleitung in der Musiksoziologie*, in *Gesammelte Schriften*, vol. 14. Darmstadt: Wissenschaftliche Buchgesellschaft, 1998.

Arvidson, Mats. "Music and Musicology in the Light of Intermediality and Intermedial Studies." *STM-Online* 15 (2012).

Boulez, Pierre. "Poésie – centre et absence – musique." In *Points de repère, Tome I: Imaginer*. Paris: Christian Bourgois Éditeur, 1995.

Brown, Calvin S. *Music and Literature: A Comparison of the Arts.* Athens: The University of Georgia Press, 1949.

Bruhn, Jørgen. "Intermedialitet: Framtidens humanistiska disciplin?" *Tidskrift för litteraturvetenskap* 38:1 (2008): 21–38.

Cone, Edward T. *The Composer's Voice*. Berkeley and Los Angeles: University of California Press, 1974.

Dahlhaus, Carl. "Musikalische Prosa." In *Gesammelte Schriften*, vol. 8, *20. Jahrhundert*, 361–374. Laaber: Laaber, 2005.

Ehrenforth, Karl Heinrich. *Ausdruck und Form: Arnold Schönbergs Durchbruch zur Atonalität*. Bonn: Bouvier, 1963.

Elleström, Lars. *Divine Madness: On Interpreting Literature, Music, and the Visual Arts Ironically*. Lewisburg: Bucknell University Press, 2002.

Elleström, Lars. "Iconicity as Meaning Miming Meaning and Meaning Miming Form." In *Signergy*, edited by Jac Conradie et al., 73–100. Philadelphia: John Benjamins, 2010.

Elleström, Lars. "The Modalities of Media: A Model for Understanding Intermedial Relations." In *Media Borders, Multimodality and Intermediality*, edited by Lars Elleström, 11–48. London: Palgrave Macmillan, 2010.

Enge, Håvard. *Music Reading Poetry: Hans Zender's Musical Reception of Hölderlin*. PhD diss., Department of Musicology, University of Oslo, 2010.

Gadamer, Hans Georg. "Der Dichter Stefan George." In *Gesammelte Werke*, vol. 9, 211–228. Tübingen: Mohr Siebeck, 1993.

Gadamer, Hans Georg. "Hölderlin and George." In *Gesammelte Werke*, vol. 9, 229–244. Tübingen: Mohr Siebeck, 1993.

George, Stefan. *Werke: Ausgabe in zwei Bänden*. Stuttgart: Klett-Cotta, 1984.

Goethe, Johann Wolfgang von. *Sämtliche Werke nach Epochen seines Schaffens: Münchner Ausgabe*, vol. 10:1, 601. Munich: Hanser, 1999.

Gundolf, Friedrich. *George*. 3rd ed. Berlin: Bondi, 1930.

Hansen-Löve, Aage. "Intermedialität und Intertextualität: Probleme der Korrelation von Wort- und Bildkonst – Am Beispiel der russischen Moderne." In *Dialog der Texte: Hamburger Kolloquium zur Intertextualität, Wiener slawistischer Almanach*, Sonderband 11, edited by Wolf Schmid and Wolf-Dieter Stempel, 291–360. Wien: Gesellschaft zur Förderung slawistischer Studien, 1983.

Hofmannsthal, Hugo von. "Ein Brief." In *Gesammelte Werke: Erzählungen, Erfundene Gespräche und Briefe, Reisen*, 461–472. Frankfurt: Fischer, 1979.

Karbusicky, Vladimir. "The Index Sign in Music." In *Semiotics of Music*, special issue of *Semiotica* 66 (1986): 23–35.

Kramer, Lawrence. *Music and Poetry: The Nineteenth Century and After*. Berkeley and Los Angeles: California University Press, 1984.

Krebs, Harald. "Three Versions of Schoenberg's Op. 15 No. 14: Obvious Differences and Hidden Similarities." *Journal of the Arnold Schoenberg Institute* 8:2 (1984): 131–140.

Langer, Susanne K. *Feeling and Form: A Theory of Art developed from Philosophy in a New Key*. London: Routledge and Kegan, 1953.

Luhmann, Niklas. *Die Kunst der Gesellschaft*. Frankfurt: Suhrkamp, 1995.

Luhmann, Niklas. *Die Gesellschaft der Gesellschaft*. Frankfurt: Suhrkamp, 1997.

Maeder, Costantino. "Opera, Oratorio, and Iconic Strategies." In *Iconic Investigations*, edited by Lars Elleström, Olga Fischer, and Christina Ljungberg, 275–289. Philadelphia: John Benjamins, 2013.

McLuhan, Marshall. *Understanding Media: The Extensions of Man*. Cambridge: MIT Press, 1994.

Plato, *Republic, Books 1–5*. Cambridge: Harvard University Press, 2013.

Schoenberg, Arnold. "The Relationship to the Text." In *Style and Idea*, 141–145. Berkeley: University of California Press, 1984.

Schoenberg, Arnold. "Composition with Twelve Tones (1)." In *Style and Idea*, 214–245. Berkeley: University of California Press, 1984.

Schoenberg, Arnold. "Brahms the Progressive." In *Style and Idea*, 398–441. Berkeley: University of California Press, 1984.

Scott, Calvin. *"Ich löse mich in tönen…": Zur Intermedialität bei Stefan George un der Zweiten Wiener Schule*. Berlin: Frank & Timme, 2007.

Scruton, Roger. *The Aesthetics of Music*. Oxford: Oxford University Press, 1999.

Steiner, George. *Real Presences: Is There Anything in What We Say*. London: Faber and Faber, 1989.

Sulzer, Johann Georg. "Kenner." In *Allgemeine Theorie der Schönen Künste*, vol. 3, 5–14. Leipzig: Weidmannsche Buchhandlung, 1793.

Wallrup, Erik. "From Mood to Tone: On Schoenberg and Musical Worlds." *Danish Musicology Online*, special edition, 17th Nordic Musicological Congress (2016): 123–144.

Vogel, Matthias. "Nachvollzug und die Erfahrung musikalischen Sinns." In *Musikalischer Sinn: Beiträge zu einer Philosophie der Musik*, edited by Alexander Becker and Matthias Vogel, 314–368. Frankfurt: Suhrkamp, 2007.

Wolf, Werner. "Intermedialität als neues Paradigma der Literaturwissenschaft? Plädoyer für eine literaturzentrierte Erforschung von Grenzüberschreitungen zwischen Wortkunst und anderen Medien am Beispiel von Virginia Woolfs 'The String Quartet'." *Arbeiten aus Anglistik und Amerikanistik* 21:1 (1996): 85–116.

Wolf, Werner. *The Musicalization of Fiction: A Study in the Theory and History of Intermediality*. Amsterdam: Rodopi, 1999.

Wolf, Werner. "Intermediality Revisited." In *Essays in Honor of Steven Paul Scher on Cultural Identity and the Musical Stage*, Word and Music Studies, edited by Suzanne M. Lodato, Suzanne Aspden, and Walter Bernhart, 13–34. Amsterdam: Rodopi, 2002.

Musical Works

Nono, Luigi. *Fragmente— Stille, An Diotima*. Milan: Ricordi, 1980.

Schoenberg, Arnold. *15 Gedichte aus Das Buch der hängenden Gärten von Stefan George*. Wien: Universal Edition, 1908–09.

Recordings

Schoenberg, Arnold. *Das Buch der hängenden Gärten*. Helen Vanni (song) and Glenn Gould (piano). Columbia Masterworks, M2S 736, 1966.

Schoenberg, Arnold. *Das Buch der hängenden Gärten*. Brigitte Fassbaender (song) and Aribert Reimann piano. His Master's Voice 1C 067 1466851, 1983.

Schoenberg, Arnold. *Das Buch der hängenden Gärten*. Christian Gerhaher (song) and Gerold Huber (piano). Sony Classical 88691935432, 2012.

Old and New Media: On the Construction of Media History

Christer Johansson

Abstract

This chapter investigates how one of the central intermedial relations of media studies, the relation between old and new media, has been conceptualized in media-historical contexts. More specifically, the study discusses how digital media was received, when it was new by the turn of the millennium, by leading media theorists at the time, Jay David Bolter and Richard Grusin and Lev Manovich. A metatheoretical and conceptual analysis is used to uncover the rhetorics and mechanics of media theory and show how old (analogue) and new (digital) media are historically constructed. The analysis of Bolter and Grusin's *Remediation* and Manovich's *The Language of New Media* shows how these seminal books, situated in intellectual history, are a mix of traditional theorizing relying on essential definitions of concepts, binary oppositions, and conceptual metaphors such as the container metaphor, and more postmodern strategies such as paradoxical reasoning, a spatial description of history, and conceptual blends of the old and the new. The conclusion discusses how the relation between old and new media should be explored within the field of media theory. The author suggests that we approach media as (metaphorically speaking) hybrids, and focus our intermedial investigations on media-specific phenomena and actual (instead of symbolic) relations between media.

How to cite this book chapter:
Johansson, Christer. "Old and New Media: On the Construction of Media History." In *The Power of the In-Between: Intermediality as a Tool for Aesthetic Analysis and Critical Reflection*, edited by Sonya Petersson, Christer Johansson, Magdalena Holdar, and Sara Callahan, 375–406. Stockholm: Stockholm University Press, 2018. DOI: https://doi.org/10.16993/baq.o. License: CC-BY.

One of the central concerns of media theory, emanating from the writings of scholars such as Harold Innis and Marshall McLuhan has, since the early days of the discipline in the 1950s and '60s, been the relationship between so-called old media and new media, recently equated with analogue and digital media, respectively.[1] Media are thus theorized as a conceptual field consisting of two, more or less, conflicting phenomena—on the one hand, old media, on the other hand, new media.[2] The conceptual construction of media history, in terms of old and new, is the topic of this text.

More precisely, this chapter has a threefold purpose: 1) to discuss how media history has been theorized in intermedial terms, as the interrelations between old and new media; 2) to investigate how digital media were received, when it was new by the turn of the millennium, by leading media theorists at the time; 3) to suggest how the relation between old and new media should be explored within the field of media theory.

More specifically, I will try to uncover the conceptual structures and rhetorical strategies of two well-known studies of new media, two prominent academic books published by the turn of the millennium: Jay David Bolter and Richard Grusin's *Remediation: Understanding New Media* (1999) and Lev Manovich's *The Language of New Media* (2001). They share a common subject matter as they try to describe and define the characteristics of "new," digital media, and how these relate to "old" media. The books are also different from each other in that Bolter and Grusin explicitly continue and develop (in a more scientific direction) the media-theoretical tradition of Marshall McLuhan, while Manovich is more influenced by and addresses the tradition of (structuralist) semiotics. These two books are probably among the most-cited works on mediality, still being read and used as

---

[1] See Harold A. Innis, *Empire and Communications* (Toronto and New York: Dundurn Press Limited, 2007 [1950]); Marshall McLuhan, *Understanding Media: The Extensions of Man*, critical ed. (Corte Madera: Ginko Press, 2003 [1964]). In this chapter, the term "new" digital media refers to media such as the Internet, digital television, interactive multimedia, virtual reality, mobile communication, and video games.

[2] See, e.g., Innis, *Empire and Communications*, 75–105; McLuhan, *Understanding Media*, 9–35.

textbooks at universities all over the world. They are thus an important part of the (early) academic reception and construction of "new" digital media and its place in media history.[3] In addition, the books under scrutiny are, I will argue, in certain important aspects characteristic of how the relations between old and new media are conceptualized in media theory. The theories presented in these studies rely on a number of core concepts designed to enable the writing of media history: remediation, immediacy and hypermediacy (Bolter and Grusin), the language of media (digital media and cinema), interface and database (Manovich). I will demonstrate the intermedial functions of these and other related concepts, that is, how they describe, define, and construct old and new media and how these media are related to each other.

My approach is conceptual and cognitive. Following Mieke Bal, I believe that concepts (thought of as miniature theories, relating to both objects and larger theoretical complexes) should be our focal point of attention when analyzing how theories are constructed and developed, migrated and transformed.[4] To be able to investigate the concepts of (old and new) media, fundamental to the theories of Bolter and Grusin and Manovich, as well as other important theoretical notions of mediality, I have developed a method of analysis, relying on tools from four different disciplines investigating concepts and conceptual analysis: 1) theories of the concept of concept, that explore phenomena such as definitions, basic-level concepts and prototypes;[5] 2) cognitive theories of mapping and blending,

---

[3] In the introduction to *New Media, Old Media: A History and Theory Reader*, Wendy Hui Kyong Chun mentions Bolter and Grusin and Manovich as two of the most important contributors to the early critical debate within new media studies. Wendy Hui Kyong Chun and Anna Watkins Fisher with Tomas W. Keenan, eds., *New Media, Old Media: A History and Theory Reader*, 2nd ed. (New York: Routledge, 2016), 3. On the "newness" and historical context of new media, see Lisa Gitelman and Geoffrey B. Pingree, eds., *New Media, 1740–191* (Cambridge: MIT Press, 2003), xi–xxii.

[4] Mieke Bal, *Travelling Concepts in the Humanities: A Rough Guide* (Toronto: University of Toronto Press, 2002), 5–14.

[5] See George Lakoff, *Women, Fire, and Dangerous Things: What Categories Reveal About the Mind* (Chicago: University of Chicago Press, 1987); Gregory L. Murphy, *The Big Book of Concepts* (Cambridge and London:

focusing on conceptual metaphors, metonymies, and other varieties of mental projection and integration, implying certain entailments and inferential structures;[6] 3) semantic (or conceptual) field theory, that describes different kinds of relations between concepts, such as clusters, doublets, proportional series, and hierarchies;[7] 4) theories of the transfer of concepts (or "travelling concepts"), that demonstrate how concepts from one (media) discipline are used in, adapted to, and transformed within the confines of another (media) discipline.[8]

It is my contention that these are the important aspects to analyse when investigating and outlining a certain theory and its fundamental concepts. They describe and explain what a concept is (in its literal as well as metaphoric facets) and how the concept of concept has been approached in different traditions, how concepts relate to other concepts and to different scientific contexts. I will explain and demonstrate these and other metatheoretical notions and how they contribute to our understanding of different concepts of mediality, as the conceptual analysis of the two studies targeted in this chapter progresses.

First, I will analyse the concept of medium (including new media), the theory of remediation as a conceptual field of media history and three conceptual metaphors underpinning Bolter and Grusin's theory of intermedial relations; second, after a short

---

MIT Press, 2002); Eleanor Rosch and Barbara B. Lloyd, *Cognition and Categorization* (Hillsdale: Erlbaum, 1978), 27–48.

[6] See George Lakoff and Mark Johnson, *Metaphors We Live By* (Chicago and London: The University of Chicago Press, 2003 [1980]); George Lakoff and Mark Johnson, *Philosophy in the Flesh: The Embodied Mind and its Challenge to Western Thought* (New York: Basic Books, 1999); Gilles Fauconnier and Mark Turner, *The Way We Think: Conceptual Blending and the Mind's Hidden Complexities* (New York: Basic Books, 2002).

[7] See David Bordwell, *Making Meaning: Inference and Rhetoric in the Interpretation of Cinema* (Cambridge: Harvard University Press, 1989); Alan D. Cruse, *Lexical Semantics* (Cambridge: Cambridge University Press, 1986); Eve Feder Kittay, *Metaphor: Its Cognitive Force and Linguistic Structure* (Oxford: Clarendon, 1990).

[8] See Bal, *Travelling Concepts*; Birgit Neumann, Ansgar Nünning, and Mirjam Horn, eds., *Travelling Concepts for the Study of Culture* (Berlin: Walter de Gruyter & Co, 2012).

comparison between the two books, I will show how Manovich investigates relations, analogies and similarities, between old and new media, by way of different kinds of conceptual transfers, described in terms of conceptual mapping and blending. Whenever the analysis touches upon what I consider to be a question or pattern of a more general scope, of importance for media theory and related disciplines, I will address it. Lastly, in a conclusion, I will try to situate the two studies in intellectual history, summarize and evaluate how the constellation of concepts in the analysed theories function to delineate the interrelation between old and new media and construct media history, and finally suggest some alternative approaches.

Bolter and Grusin's Theory of Remedation

The Concept of (New Digital) Medium

The core concept of *Remediation* is the concept of remediation, closely related to the concepts of medium, mediation, and new media.[9] These four terms, at times, seem to constitute a small cluster, a conceptual field of synonyms, that is, four different but equivalent descriptions of the same concept.[10] Bolter and Grusin offer the following definition of "medium":

> a medium is that which remediates. It is that which appropriates the techniques, forms, and social significance of other media and attempts to rival or refashion them in the name of the real. A medium in our culture can never operate in isolation, because it must enter into relationships of respect and rivalry with other media.[11]

---

[9] On the relationship between intermediality and remediation, see Irina O. Rajewsky, "Intermediality, Intertextuality, and Remediation: A Literary Perspective on Intermediality," *Intermediality: History and Theory of the Arts, Literature and Technologies*, no. 6 (2005): 43–64.
[10] A cluster is a conceptual field in which items have a semantic overlap and a low degree of contrastiveness. Bordwell, *Making Meaning*, 115–116; Cruse, *Lexical Semantics*, 265–270; compare Kittay, *Metaphor*, 237–242.
[11] Jay David Bolter and Richard Grusin, *Remediation: Understanding New Media* (Cambridge: MIT Press, 1999), 65.

Consequently, a medium is, by definition, that which remediates. In a similar fashion, the authors argue that all "mediation is remediation."[12] And the same is true of new digital media, which has as a defining characteristic the "representation of one medium in another" (for example a website representing moving images), that is, "*remediation*."[13] The synchronic interrelations between media, old and new ones, in specific media objects and cultural networks at large, and the diachronic developments of media history are built into the concept of medium. This way of thinking is deeply rooted in the North American media-theoretical tradition and more specifically, Bolter and Grusin admit, incited by McLuhan, who contends that the "content" of any medium is always another medium, "one medium is itself incorporated or represented in another medium"; the content of writing is speech, the written word is the content of print, print is the content of the telegraph, and so on.[14] Furthermore, this figure of thought is obviously akin to the academic discourses of intertextuality (all signs and texts are related to other signs and texts) and intermediality (all media are mixed media).[15] The defining characteristic of medium and mediation is thus, according to Bolter and Grusin, a relational (in distinction to an intrinsic), even intermedial, property of sorts.[16] At the same time, this definition of *medium* appears to be an essential definition, remediation being a necessary and perhaps even sufficient condition for medium, mediation, and, above all,

---

[12] Bolter and Grusin, *Remediation*, 55.
[13] Bolter and Grusin, *Remediation*, 45.
[14] Bolter and Grusin, *Remediation* 45; cf. 66; see McLuhan, *Understanding Media*, 17–35.
[15] See Ferdinand de Saussure, *Cours de linguistique générale* (Lausanne: Payot, 1916), 155–169; Charles S. Peirce, "Logics as Semiotic: The Theory of Signs," in *Semiotics: An Introductory Anthology*, ed. Robert E. Innis (Bloomington: Indiana University Press, 1985), 1–23; Gérard Genette, *Palimpsests: Literature in the Second Degree* (Lincoln: University of Nebraska Press, 1997), 1–7; W. J. T. Mitchell, "There Are No Visual Media," in *MediaArtHistories*, ed. Oliver Grau (Cambridge: MIT Press, 2007), 395–408, and Julia Kristeva's famous coinage of the term intertextuality, referred to in Peter Gillgren's chapter.
[16] Cf. Noël Carroll, "Fiction, Non-fiction, and the Film of Presumptive Assertion: A Conceptual Analysis," in *Film Theory and Philosophy*, eds. Richard Allen and Murray Smith (Oxford: Clarendon Press, 1997), 179.

new digital media.[17] However, Bolter and Grusin take great pains to avoid the fallacy of media essentialism.[18] The authors stress that in arguing that all mediation is remediation they do not mean that remediation is "the irreducible essence of either digital media or mediation generally," but rather that at our historical moment, remediation is the predominant convention at work in establishing the identity of new digital media. With a different but related move, Bolter and Grusin argue that the remediation of new digital media is both what is "unique to digital worlds" and what denies the possibility of that uniqueness.[19] The definition of new media as remediation is thus formulated as a paradox. Finally, remediation is described as "a spectrum of different ways in which digital media remediate their predecessors."[20] The tension between new and old media varies from zero (a website faithfully rendering an old movie) to an aggressive will to transform and absorb (old television clips distorted in digital video art), and remediation operates in both directions.[21] Remediation, the defining characteristic of media, mediation, and new media, is not only a relational property, but a graded series of possibilities, depending on the shifting interrelations between old and new media.[22]

To avoid media essentialism, Bolter and Grusin employ three different strategies to make their central concept of (new) digital media fuzzier and bring it closer to the notions of family resemblance and culture dependent (proto)typicality: historical contextualisation, the use of paradox and the graded series.[23] Their

---

[17] On definitions and essences, necessity and sufficiency, see Murphy, *Big Book on Concepts*, 12; cf. Lakoff and Johnson, *Philosophy in the Flesh*, 379–382.
[18] On media essentialism, see, e.g., Lisa Gitelman, *Always Already New: Media, History, and the Data of Culture* (Cambridge: MIT Press, 2006), 8–10.
[19] Bolter and Grusin, *Remediation*, 50.
[20] Bolter and Grusin, *Remediation*, 45.
[21] Bolter and Grusin, *Remediation*, 27, 45–48.
[22] Conceptual fields can be structured hierarchically, either in branching or nonbranching forms. See Bordwell, *Making Meaning*, 120–124; Cruse, *Lexical Semantics*, 112–118, 136–196.
[23] On the fuzziness of concepts, family resemblance and prototypes, see Murphy, *The Big Book on Concepts*, 16, 17, 20–22; Ludwig Wittgenstein, *Philosophical Investigations* (Oxford: Blackwell, 1953), paragraphs 65,

definition of *medium* and description of the relations between new digital media and older forms of media hover between essence and deliberate fuzziness. Perhaps we could conclude that the concept of medium, in the theory of Bolter and Grusin, grows out of an, at times, unresolved tension (or double logic) between media essentialism (the old way to define concepts and describe phenomena) and non-essentialist strategies (the new approach to concepts and definitions), a tension corresponding to their understanding of the charged interrelations between old and new media.

Remediation, and the Relations between Old and New Media, as a Conceptual Field

It is not surprising then that the paradoxical notion of remediation, thought of as a conceptual field, is structured by a doublet or binary opposition.[24] Already in the introduction to *Remediation*, Bolter and Grusin discuss our culture's "contradictory imperatives for immediacy and hypermediacy" and what they call "a double logic of *remediation*."[25] Bolter and Grusin's theory is thus structured by this fundamental binary opposition, the contradictory relation between two different media phenomena characterising the interrelations between old and new media: immediacy (the putative erasure of the sign vehicles of media, for example realistic cinema) and hypermediacy (the multiplying of and self-referential highlighting of media, for example montage film). All media, old and new, grow out of these opposing modes, they are the driving forces behind remediation and the development of media history.

To construct a theory about cultural objects, of some sort, and their history by way of binary oppositions is probably one of the most common and traditional methods of theorising in Western thought.[26] More specifically, Bolter and Grusin's double logic of

---

67; Rosch, *Cognition and Categorization*, 36; cf. Lakoff, *Women, Fire, and Dangerous Things*, 5–57.

[24] See Bordwell, *Making Meaning*, 117–118; Cruse, *Lexical Semantics*, 197–264; Kittay, *Metaphor*, 20–22; cf. Daniel Chandler, *Semiotics: The Basics* (London: Routledge, 2002), 101–118.

[25] Bolter and Grusin, *Remediation*, 5. Italics in the original.

[26] See, e.g., Bordwell, *Making Meaning*, 117–118, 122; Chandler, *Semiotics*, 101–118; John Bell, *Oppositions and Paradoxes: Philosophical Perplexities in*

remediation is akin to, or perhaps even inspired by, age-old aesthetic doublets such as mimesis versus diegesis, showing versus telling, and realism versus self-reflexivity or defamiliarisation.[27] The opposition between immediacy and hypermediacy is developed, by the authors, into a series of doublets, a propositional series, organized as parallel clusters of associated terms:[28]

> immediacy, transparence, looking through, gaze, product, unified, window, erasure, effacement, reality, experience, presence, content, reproduction, autonomy
>
> hypermediacy, opacity, looking at, glance, process, heterogeneous, windowed, sign, mediated, medium, surface, agency, material, representation, multiplicity

To organize a theory as a series of doublets forming parallel clusters is, again, a very common strategy in many areas of the human sciences, especially in media theory.[29] We find it not only in McLuhan, who to a large extent structures his discourse as series of connected doublets (old and new media, industrial age and electronic age, hot and cold media, high and low definition,

---

Science and Mathematics (Peterborough: Broadview Press, 2016); Jonathan Culler, *On Deconstruction: Theory and Criticism after Structuralism* (Ithaca: Cornell University Press, 1982), 85–226; Jacques Derrida, *Positions* (Chicago: University of Chicago Press, 1982), 41; Roman Jakobson and Moris Halle, *Fundamentals of Language*, 2nd rev. ed. (The Hague: Mouton, 1971); Irena Rima Makaryk, ed., *Encyclopedia of Contemporary Literary Theory: Approaches, Scholars, Terms* (Toronto: University of Toronto Press, 1993), 511.

[27] See, e.g., *The Living Handbook of Narratology*, accessed June 9, 2017, http://wikis.sub.uni-hamburg.de/lhn/index.php/Diegesis_-_Mimesis; Winfried Nöth and Nina Bishara, eds., *Self-reference in the Media* (Berlin: Mouton de Gruyter, 2007), 3–30; Marie-Laure Ryan, *Narrative as Virtual Reality: Immersion and Interactivity in Literature and Electronic Media* (Baltimore: Johns Hopkins University Press, 2001), 1–21.

[28] See Bordwell, *Making Meaning*, 118–120; Cruse, *Lexical Semantics*, 118–135.

[29] In their book *Social Semiotics*, under the heading "Saussure's rubbish bin," Robert Hodge and Gunther Kress uncover the binarism of Saussure's semiology and build their social semiotics of the conceptual opposites that Saussure excludes from his theory. Robert Hodge and Gunther Kress, *Social Semiotics* (Cambridge: Polity, 1988), 15–18; cf. Bordwell, *Making Meaning*, 117–120, 124–126.

and so on),[30] but also for example, and perhaps more surprisingly, in the texts of a postmodern and posthumanist scholar such as Katherine Hayles, who in her study *How We Think: Digital Media and Contemporary Technogenesis* (2012), discusses the discourses, methods and institutions of so-called digital humanities (and its relation to print-based equivalents) in terms of doublets and tensions: digital humanities versus print-based humanities, quantitative/qualitative, text-based/time-based, machine/brain, algorithmic analysis/hermeneutic close reading, linear temporal causality/ spatialized grids, narrative/database, argumentation/embodiment, and so on.[31]

Bolter and Grusin are of course aware of the tradition and problems of binarism. Consequently, they have the ambition to deconstruct, or at least qualify or soften, the binarism of their media historiography. In order to accomplish this, Bolter and Grusin employ the strategy of paradoxical reasoning. The authors describe the conceptual field of remediation, and the relationship between immediacy and hypermediacy, in paradoxical terms; the so-called double logic of remediation seems to be a paradoxical one: "Our culture wants both to multiply its media and to erase all traces of mediation: ideally, it wants to erase its media in the very act of multiplying them."[32] This major paradox is the result of a series of synthesising strategies and minor paradoxes. The history of media and remediation is defined as an interplay between immediacy and hypermediacy, new digital media is said to oscillate between transparency and opacity, and the seemingly contradictory logics are "mutually dependent."[33] The opposites seem to include each other; hypermedia strive for immediacy, the quest for immediacy leads to hypermediacy:

---

[30] McLuhan, *Understanding Media*, 39–50, 73–81, 215–221.
[31] Katherine N. Hayles, *How We Think: Digital Media and Contemporary Technogenesis* (Chicago and London: The University of Chicago Press, 2012), 23–54. To be fair, Hayles is conscious and critical of the binarism of the digital humanities discourse and approaches the field with a deconstructive ambition. Still, her discussion is permeated by binary thinking.
[32] Bolter and Grusin, *Remediation*, 5.
[33] Bolter and Grusin, *Remediation*, 17, 6; cf. 84.

> Although each medium promises to reform its predecessors by offering a more immediate or authentic experience, the promise of reform inevitably leads us to become aware of the new medium as a medium. Thus, immediacy leads to hypermediacy.[34]

Bolter and Grusin's argument is that immediacy and hypermediacy are somehow causally connected, the one leads to the other through the process of remediation, and drives media history.

Moreover, transparent media and hypermedia are opposite expressions of the same ambition to achieve the real and the authentic.[35] Bolter and Grusin try to pinpoint common features that immediacy and hypermediacy share, and thus to find some overarching category that might include both of them:

> Hypermedia and transparent media are opposite manifestations of the same desire: the desire to get past the limits of representation and to achieve the real. [...] Transparent digital applications seek to get to the real by bravely denying the fact of mediation; digital hypermedia seek the real by multiplying mediation so as to create a feeling of fullness, a satiety of experience, which can be taken as reality.[36]

The excess of digital hypermedia becomes, according to the authors, an "authentic experience," not in the sense that it corresponds to an external reality, but because it "does not feel compelled to refer to anything beyond itself."[37] Consequently, both immediacy and hypermediacy lead to the authentic, all new media remediate the real.[38] This move is realized by widening the extension of the concepts of the real and the authentic to cover more than they initially seem to cover, not only contents but forms and sign vehicles as well.[39]

---

[34] Bolter and Grusin, *Remediation*, 17; cf. 37, 54.
[35] Bolter and Grusin, *Remediation*, 53, 59, 70.
[36] Bolter and Grusin, *Remediation*, 53.
[37] Bolter and Grusin, *Remediation*, 53–54; cf. 58, 59.
[38] Bolter and Grusin, *Remediation*, 59.
[39] The widening of the extension of the real and the authentic is a restructuring of the conceptual field of remediation by way of categorisation by branching hierarchy; see Bordwell, *Making Meaning*, 120–124; Cruse, *Lexical Semantics*, 112–118.

To summarize, Bolter and Grusin construct their theory of media history, and the relations between old and new media, as a binary system consisting of parallel clusters of oppositions, and then try to undermine this system by way of paradoxical reasoning. The theory of remediation and new media is thus characterized by the tension between conceptual essentialism and fuzziness, on the one hand, and the parallel tension between binarism and the paradoxical, on the other.

The Conceptual Metaphors of Remediation and Media History

According to cognitive theorists George Lakoff and Mark Johnson most of our thinking and all our abstract categories are structured by conceptual metaphors (or metaphoric concepts), which means "understanding and experiencing one kind of thing in terms of another."[40] This observation is valid for scientific theories as well as everyday concepts.[41] Bolter and Grusin make extensive, intermedial use of conceptual metaphors. To describe the relations between old and new media, and the processes of remediation and media history, they employ three central conceptual metaphors, two ontological ones describing media as such and a spatial metaphor structuring the temporality of media history: the conduit or container metaphor, personification and the metaphor of resonance.

One of the most powerful metaphors in *Remediation* is also one of the most discussed conceptual metaphors, the so-called conduit or container metaphor, common in descriptions of communication and representation.[42] I have already touched upon McLuhans importance for the concept of remediation. His influence is also discernable when it comes to the metaphoric concept of containment. Bolter and Grusin write:

---

[40] Lakoff and Johnson, *Metaphors We Live By*, 5, 10–12, 246; Lakoff and Johnson, *Philosophy in the Flesh*, 128.

[41] See Lakoff and Johnson, *Philosophy in the Flesh*, 335–548.

[42] The container metaphor is a kind of entity/substance metaphor which allows us to understand our experiences "in terms of objects or substances of a uniform kind." Lakoff and Johnson, *Metaphors We Live By*, 25.

On the opening page of *Understanding Media* (1964), Marshall McLuhan remarked that "the 'content' of any medium is always another medium. The content of writing is speech, just as the written word is the content of print, and print is the content of the telegraph." As his problematic examples suggest, McLuhan was not thinking of simple repurposing, but perhaps of a more complex kind of borrowing in which one medium is itself incorporated or represented in another medium. Dutch painters incorporated maps, globes, inscriptions, letters, and mirrors in their works.[43]

Following and revising McLuhan, Bolter and Grusin contend that the "content" of any medium is another medium; computer games remediate, that is, contain the medium of film, and so on.[44] In a similar fashion, one of the poles on the axis of remediation, the extreme where an older medium is represented in digital form without any real tension, is described by way of the container metaphor. In cases such as websites that offer texts and pictures for download, the digital medium is not set in opposition to other media like painting, photography, or printing; instead, the computer is functioning as a new means of gaining access to these older media, "as if the content of the older media could simply be poured into the new one."[45] Media, old and new, are thus metaphorically treated as objects and substances and are related to each other, both synchronically and diachronically, as container and contained.

As I have already touched on, the conduit/container metaphor is one of the most fundamental traditional conceptual metaphors in scientific as well as non-scientific descriptions of communication and representation. As Michael Reddy demonstrates in a seminal article, the default conceptual metaphor in English describing linguistic communication is the conduit metaphor. The speaker puts ideas (objects) into words (containers) and sends them (along a conduit) to a hearer who takes the idea/objects out of the word/containers.[46] Bolter and Grusin thus reuse (or remediate) one of

---

[43] Bolter and Grusin, *Remediation*, 45.
[44] Bolter and Grusin, *Remediation*, 45.
[45] Bolter and Grusin, *Remediation*, 45–46; cf. 48, 68.
[46] Michael Reddy, "The Conduit Metaphor," in *Metaphor and Thought*, ed. A. Ortony (Cambridge: Cambridge University Press, 1979), 284–324; Lakoff and Johnson, *Metaphors We Live By*, 29–32. An influential scientific

the most important traditional cultural and scientific metaphors for communication and representation to describe the relations between old and new media. This conception of remediation entails that media have "meanings" in themselves (an old medium such as cinema is, for example, present in a new medium like computer games), independent of any context, a figure of thought that downplays the contextual aspects of mediality.

As is evident in the quotation above, where Bolter and Grusin discuss McLuhan, the concept of remediation and the relationship between media are also formulated in terms of personification (media acting as agents);[47] remediation is, for example, described as a kind of "borrowing."[48] However, the most important personifications revolve around a never-ending power struggle between media. The spectrum of remediation is said to be dependent on "the degree of perceived competition or rivalry between the new media and the old media."[49] The interrelations between old and new media (such as cinema and computer games) are frequently described in terms of action, honour, response, acknowledgement, reaffirmation, challenge, aggression, attack, invocation, and remake. Old and new media are brought to life and made into the participants in a media-historical drama about the power over culture.

---

manifestation of this conceptual metaphor is linguist Loius Hjelmslev's sign model, a development of Saussure's signifier/signified dichotomy, which in Hjelmslev's terminology becomes a distinction between expression plane and content plane on the one hand, and between form and substance, on the other; there is thus a form of the content and a form of the expression, a substance of the content and a substance of the expression. Louis Hjelmslev, *Prolegomena to a Theory of Language*, rev. English ed. (Madison: University of Wisconsin Press, 1961 [1943]), 47–60. Hjelmslev's sign model has been transmediated, i.e., applied to other and different media than natural languages, by, e.g., narratologist Seymour Chatman, investigating literary, cinematic and potentially all kinds of narratives. Seymour Chatman, *Story and Discourse: Narrative Structure in Fiction and Film* (Ithaca and London: Cornell University Press, 1978), 22–27.

[47] On personification, see Lakoff and Johnson, *Metaphors We Live By*, 33.
[48] Bolter and Grusin, *Remediation*, 45.
[49] Bolter and Grusin, *Remediation*, 45; cf. 5, 14–15, 46, 55, 86.

This theoretical strategy is not only common in media theory and history,[50] but also of central importance in the more ideologically tainted branch of intermediality studies, most notably represented by W. J. T. Mitchell. In the chapter "What is an image" in his *Iconology* (1986), a classic in the field of intermediality studies, Mitchell describes the relations between media, in this case pictorial and linguistic signs, and the development of cultural history by way of personification and the metaphor of power struggle:

> The dialectic of word and image seems to be a constant in the fabric of signs that a culture weaves around itself. [...] The history of culture is in part the story of a protracted struggle for dominance between pictorial and linguistic signs, each claiming for itself certain proprietary rights on a "nature" to which only it has access.[51]

Mitchell does not want to "heal the split" between words and images, but to see what "interests and powers it serves."[52] The figurative struggle between personified media is thus one of the fundamental metaphors of research on media history.

To describe the relations between media from different historical periods Bolter and Grusin refer to Michel Foucalt's notion of genealogy, but choose another metaphor when stating that "we too are looking for historical affiliations or resonances and not for origins."[53] To avoid the supposed misleading notions of origins and chronology, Bolter and Grusin introduce the concept of

---

[50] Cf. Gitelman *Always Already New*, 8–10.
[51] W. J. T. Mitchell, *Iconology: Image, Text, Ideology* (Chicago: Chicago University Press, 1986), 43.
[52] Mitchell, *Iconology*, 44. In a later work by Mitchell, *What Do Pictures Want?*, the personification of media and pictorial representations is presented as a conscious method of media analysis. Mitchell's poetics of pictures is a study of "'the lives of images,' from the ancient idols and fetishes to contemporary technical images and artificial life-forms, including cyborgs and clones." The question to ask of pictures from the standpoint of poetics is not just what "they mean or do but what they *want*—what claim they make upon us, and how we are to respond." W. J. T. Mitchell, *What Do Pictures Want?: The Lives and Loves of Images* (Chicago: University of Chicago Press, 2005), xv.
[53] Bolter and Grusin, *Remediation*, 21, note 1.

"historical resonances (to Renaissance painting, nineteenth-century photography, twentieth-century film, and so on)" that will be offered to "help explain the contemporary situation."[54] To describe the relations between new digital media and older forms of media, "resonances," a physics and acoustics concept, is used, entailing that different media in different historical circumstances can be thought of as connected physical objects or systems, in continuous space, affected by the same forces. This non-chronological, antinarrative and antiteleological approach to media history has become a staple in recent media studies disciplines such as media archaeology (see 392–397).[55]

In conclusion, the relations between old and new media are thus described, by Bolter and Grusin, as containers containing objects, as interactions between living beings, and as physical strata connected by acoustic phenomena in a continuous space. One might wonder how these metaphors go together in the theory of remediation. One answer is that they don't. Most theories are probably built on conflicting, or inconsistent, conceptual metaphors. Various metaphorical configurations of a concept serve different purposes by highlighting different aspects of a concept (in this case remediation).[56] But there may still be metaphorical coherence. The three metaphors of remediation, two ontological metaphors and a time metaphor, all imply and highlight an essentialist understanding of media.[57] Media are conceived of as agents, forces and objects with essences that can affect and be incorporated in other media with other essences. To complicate things, the "resonances" metaphor also has a non-essentialist and postmodern quality, since it challenges the traditional notion of media history as a chronological narrative.

---

[54] Bolter and Grusin, *Remediation*, 21; cf. 34–35.
[55] See, e.g., Erkki Huhtamo and Jussi Parikka, "Introduction: An Archaeology of Media Archaeology," in *Media Archaeology: Approaches, Applications, and Implications*, eds. Erkki Huhtamo and Jussi Parikka (Berkeley: University of Carlifornia Press, 2011), 1–21. Huhtamo and Parikka contend that Bolter and Grusin's endeavor has "affinities with the ways media archaeologists draw parallels between seemingly incompatible phenomena." Huhtamo and Parikka, *Media Archaeology*, 5.
[56] Lakoff and Johnson, *Metaphors We Live By*, 96, 100–105.
[57] Cf. Gitelman *Always Already New*, 8–10.

Manovich and the Language of New Media

Manovich's study has some fundamental features in common with the media theory of Bolter and Grusin. His investigation of new media and their relation to old media, is structured by similar binary systems, forming clusters of associated concepts:

> viewer – user, perceiving – acting, transparent – opaque, representation – control, illusion – interactivity, immersion – direct address

Manovich describes new media as remediations of old media, refers explicitly to Bolter and Grusin,[58] and uses various metaphors of containment (cinema is "poured" into the computer),[59] personification and media rivalry. The computer screen is described as a "battle field" for a number of opposites, such as window and control, depth and surface, transparency and opaqueness.[60] Human culture is, in a similar vein, represented as a struggle between database and narrative:

> As a cultural form, the database represents the world as a list of items, and it refuses to order this list. In contrast, a narrative creates a cause-and-effect trajectory of seemingly unordered items (events). Therefore, database and narrative are natural enemies. Competing for the same territory of human culture, each claims an exclusive right to make meaning out of the world.[61]

There seems to be a common scientific "language" for the study of the "language" of new media, current at the time (by the turn of the millennium), shared by Bolter and Grusin and Manovich. Interestingly enough the two studies rely on contrasting metaphors for the temporality of media history. Manovich's view of media history is more traditional than the "spatial" one, represented by the metaphor of resonance, presented by Bolter and Grusin. The historical relations of and between old and new media are, in Manovich's description, much more of a plot-driven,

---

[58] Lev Manovich, *The Language of New Media* (Cambridge: MIT Press, 2001), 71, 79, 83, 84.
[59] Manovich, *Language of New Media*, 86.
[60] Manovich, *Language of New Media*, 90–91, 216.
[61] Manovich, *Language of New Media*, 225; cf. 89, 228, 231, 234.

even teleological, narrative. There is chronology, movement, progression, causality, and shifts. Manovich discusses, for example, the "general evolution of all media types toward increased modularity, and the particular evolution of the moving image in the same direction [...]."[62] Two different temporal metaphors, with different inferential logics, structure the two studies. Bolter and Grusin delineate media history as simultaneity in a unified space (a version of the Time as Space metaphor), Manovich represents media history as a vehicle moving through space, towards a destination (an instance of the Time's Landscape metaphor).[63]

So, Manovich presents a more traditional view of media history, at least as regards his choice of temporal metaphor. However, one of Manovich's most important theoretical strategies is more in line with the resonance metaphor used by Bolter and Grusin, that is, his (media-archaeological) tendency to observe and/or create relations, analogies and similarities, between old and new media, by way of different kinds of conceptual transfers. Following cognitive theory, I will discuss this fundamental theoretical approach in terms of conceptual mapping and blending.

Travelling Concepts and the Construction of Media History

Manovich's study sets in motion different varieties of conceptual transfer (or travelling concepts), that is, the transfer of concepts across the borders of media and media disciplines:[64] transmediation, conceptual remediation, anachronistic mapping, and conceptual blending.

The introduction to Manovich's book clearly demonstrates some of the author's most important transmedial strategies. Manovich uses Dziga Vertov's avant-garde classic *Man with a*

---

[62] Manovich, *Language of New Media*, 140; cf. xvii, 133, 148.
[63] See Lakoff and Johnson, *Philosophy in the Flesh*, 145–146, 160.
[64] Conceptual transfer (or travelling concepts, a term coined by Mieke Bal) demonstrates how concepts from one (media) discipline are beeing used in, adapted to and transformed within the confines of another (media) discipline. See Bal, *Travelling Concepts*, 3–55; Neumann, Nünning, and Horn, eds. *Travelling Concepts for the Study of Culture*, 1–22.

Movie Camera as "our guide to the language of new media."⁶⁵ The prologue consists of a series of stills from the film. Each still is accompanied by a quote from the text, summarizing a particular principle of new media:

> A hundred years after cinema's birth, cinematic ways of seeing the world, of structuring time, of narrating a story, of linking one experience to the next, have become the basic means by which computer users access and interact with all cultural data. In this respect, the computer fulfills the promise of cinema as a visual Esperanto—a goal that preoccupied many film artists and critics in the 1920s, from Griffith to Vertov.
>
> And in contrast to cinema, where most "users" are able to "understand" cinematic language but not "speak" it (i.e., make films), all computer users can "speak" the language of the interface.⁶⁶

These passages communicate a complex combination of conceptual transfers. Most importantly, Manovich transmediates the concept of language, mapping it onto both (old) cinema and new media, comparing the logics behind the developments of "film language" and "the language of new media." By transmediation I mean the use of a concept, rooted in a certain media-studies discipline, as the vehicle for an overarching and generalized notion, supposedly valid for all or most kinds of media.⁶⁷ The transmediation of "language" is one of the most well-known, most productive, and most devastating scientific mappings in the history of the humanities. I am of course thinking of the structuralist paradigm, initiated by Ferdinand de Saussure, treating all kinds of meaningful signs (literature, film, theatre, fashion, advertising, and so on) as languages of sorts.⁶⁸ Manovich is highly aware of this, and his use of the language metaphor is a conscious move:

---

[65] Manovich, *Language of New Media*, xiv.
[66] Manovich, *Language of New Media*, xv, 78–79; cf. xxvi–xxvii.
[67] On the concept of transmediality, see, e.g., Lars Elleström, *Media Transformation: The Transfer of Media Characteristics Among Media* (Basingstoke: Palgrave Macmillan, 2014); Jan-Noël Thon, *Transmedial Narratology and Contemporary Media Culture* (Lincoln: University of Nebraska Press, 2016).
[68] de Saussure, *Cours de linguistique générale*, 23–35, 97–113. See also,

> In putting the word *language* into the title of the book, I do not want to suggest that we need to return to the structuralist phase of semiotics in understanding new media. However, given that most studies of new media and cyberculture focus on their sociological, economic, and political dimensions, it was important for me to use the word *language* to signal the different focus of the work: the emergent conventions, recurrent design patterns, and key forms of new media.[69]

Manovich thus takes pains to distance himself from the "structuralist phase" of semiotics. Still, the metaphoric projection of "language" onto cinema and new media is a transmedial semiotic project akin to the structuralist one, and a prerequisite for Manovich's comparisons between old and new media. Manovich uses "language" as "an umbrella term" to refer to "various conventions" used by designers of new media objects and representations to "organize data" and "structure the user's experience."[70] The metaphoric use of "language" thus highlights the conventional, formal, and logical qualities of the media in question, while downplaying iconic and indexical media aspects, as well as context-dependent features of meaning and mediality.[71] The mapping of "language" onto cinema and new media also paves the way for the mapping of traditional (structuralist) semiotic concepts, such as codes (or conventions) for communication, syntagm (sequential relations between elements) and paradigm (mutually exclusive choices), originally designed, by scholars such as Roman Jakobson and Louis Hjelmslev, to describe and explain the workings of natural languages and literature, onto other and different media.[72] Consequently, the computer interface is discussed in terms of codes:

---

e.g., John Sturrock, *Structuralism,* 2nd ed. (Oxford: Blackwell Publishing, 2003), 25–47, 74–97.

[69] Manovich, *Language of New Media*, 12.

[70] Manovich, *Language of New Media*, 7.

[71] Iconicity (meaning production by way of similarity) and indexicality (meaning production by way of contiguity) are of course central concepts in the semiotic tradition emanating from Charles Sanders Peirce, see, e.g., Peirce "Logics as Semiotics," 8–19.

[72] See, e.g., Roman Jakobson, "Language in Relation to Other Communication Systems," in *Selected Writings,* vol. 2 (The Hague: Mouton, 1971),

> In semiotic terms, the computer interface acts as a code that carries cultural messages in a variety of media. When you use the Internet, everything you access—texts, music, video, navigable spaces—passes through the interface of the browser and then, in turn, the interface of the OS. In cultural communication, a code is rarely simply a neutral transport mechanism; usually it affects the message transmitted with its help. [...] Most modern cultural theories rely on these notions [...]. For instance, according to the Whorf-Sapir hypothesis [...] human thinking is determined by the code of natural language; the speakers of different natural languages perceive and think about the world differently. [...] when we think about the case of the human-computer interface, applying a "strong" version of this idea makes sense.[73]

The interface is a semiotic code, the vehicle of cultural messages, and it provides (the Whorf-Sapir hypothesis being refashioned and mapped) its own model of the world, its own bias. To reiterate, Manovich's theoretical strategy for the construction of media history is an abundantly clear instance of conceptual transmediation: concepts from one area of mediality and media studies (language, linguistics/structuralist semiotics) being mapped onto other and all kinds of media objects and communicative devices. This transmediation, recycling the old structuralism project, is the basis for a series of more radical conceptual transfers structuring Manovich's study.

As indicated in the quoted passages above, Manovich observes and investigates affinities between the historical developments of cinema and new media. This analogy between media evolutions is detected, demonstrated, or perhaps created by way of a combination of two kinds of conceptual transfer I would like to call conceptual remediation and anachronistic mapping. Early in his book Manovich states that "the theory and history of cinema serve as the key conceptual lens though [sic!] which I look at new media."[74] Manovich thus employs film theory (and film

---

697–710; Hjelmslev, *Prolegomena*, 73–76; Chandler, *Semiotics*, 83–84, 147, 148.
[73] Manovich, *Language of New Media*, 64; cf. 65, 229–233.
[74] Manovich, *Language of New Media*, 9; cf. 11, 287.

history) as a means of analysing new media.[75] Consequently, new media are described and defined by concepts transferred from cinema studies, such as screen, montage, mobile camera and point of view, and the subject of realism in 3-D computer animation is treated with reference to the arguments advanced in film theory about cinematic realism.[76] This is an instance of conceptual remediation (thus myself transferring and transforming Bolter and Grusin's concept in a metatheoretical context): concepts specifically developed, within a certain discipline, to describe, define and analyse a certain medium and its characteristics, are mapped onto a different (usually younger) medium, within the confines of a new discipline.

The second strategy, anachronistic mapping, travels in the opposite direction, from new media and media disciplines to old ones. Manovich discusses Vertov's *Man with a Movie Camera* in terms of computer technology and science. Vertov is described as a major "database filmmaker" and his famous movie is proclaimed the most important example of a "database imagination in modern media art."[77] The concepts of interface and database are mapped onto Vertovs's work:

> In his research on what can be called "kino-eye interface," Vertov systematically tried different ways to overcome what he thought were the limits of human vision. [...] *Man with a Movie Camera* is not only a database of city life in the 1920s, a database of film techniques, and a database of new operations of visual epistemology, but also a database of new interface operations that together aim to go beyond simple human navigation through physical space.[78]

The compound expression "kino-eye interface" is a brilliant manifestation of the strategy of anachronistic mapping, that is, a transfer of concepts from the discipline of computer studies, developed for the analysis of new digital media, to the analysis of (the older medium of) film.

---

[75] Manovich, *Language of New Media*, 11.
[76] Manovich, *Language of New Media*, 9, 78, 84, 184–187, 320–326.
[77] Manovich, *Language of New Media*, xxiv, 239.
[78] Manovich, *Language of New Media*, xxx; cf. 62.

The combination of anachronistic mapping, projecting concepts from computer science onto cinema, and conceptual remediation, mapping concepts from cinema studies onto new media, generates something akin to a so-called conceptual blend: relations and properties from different domains of mediality (cinema and cinema studies, new digital media and computer studies), and scenarios (cinema as new media, new media as cinema) are imaginatively integrated, resulting in apparent analogies between media.[79] This method is an important part of the media-archaeological enterprise (with Manovich as one of its forerunners), focusing on historical ruptures and a discontinuous media history analysed by way of unexpected analogies.[80]

To summarize, Manovich uses different methods for conceptual transfer and mapping to communicate his view of media history and the interrelations of old and new media. Travels and mappings move in all directions and the overriding objective seems to be the detection, demonstration, or perhaps creation of analogies between media and historical contexts. This strategy is akin to the resonance metaphor set in motion by Bolter and Grusin and closely related to the media-archaeological project mentioned above.

Conclusions

Old and New Media in the Digital Age

The scientific reception, or construction, of digital media and media history, as it is manifested in the works of Bolter and Grusin and Manovich by the turn of the millennium, is formulated as an intermedial relation, the relation between old analogue media and new digital media. The concept of medium is defined in relational and intermedial terms as well: all media must be understood through their relations to other media,

---

[79] The theory of conceptual blends is an extension of cognitive metaphor theory. See Fauconnier and Turner, *The Way We Think*, 261, 263.
[80] See Huhtamo and Parikka, *Media Archaeology*, 13; cf. 3, 4, 6, 7, 9–10, 15.

mediation is always remediation. The overarching conceptual field, the doublet of old and new, is systematically analysed and broken down into multiple doublets. Remediation, the driving force of media history, defined by Bolter and Grusin and adopted by Manovich, is structured by the fundamental binary opposition between immediacy and hypermediacy. This opposition is developed into series of doublets, organized as parallel clusters of associated terms. The relations between old and new media, and the processes of remediation, are also, in both Bolter and Grusin and Manovich, structured by way of two fundamental ontological conceptual metaphors, the conduit (or container) metaphor and personification. Media are, on the one hand, related to each other as container and contained (the computer contains cinema), on the other hand personified and described as agents or forces involved in an endless struggle for power and control (the narrative and the database).

These three related strategies, mediation (essentially) defined as remediation, (re)mediation structured as a conceptual field consisting of series of binaries, and media connections described by way of the ontological metaphors of containment and personification should, I think, be viewed as traditional conceptual devices deployed to control the chaotic and all-encompassing domain of new, digital mediality. Media are thought of as oppositions, objects or forces characterized by discernible essences. The same is true of Manovich's transmediation of language, turning both old analogue media and new digital media into codes and conventions. The unfamiliar is made familiar by the use of traditional analytic and theoretical methods and models.

There is, however, an opposite tendency in both works under scrutiny, a postmodern (for lack of a better term) ambition to undermine and deconstruct traditional notions of concept definition, representation, and history. Bolter and Grusin try to reach beyond the traditional logics of the concept of medium, binarism, and chronological media history by a consistent use of paradoxical reasoning and spatialized analysis. Manovich achieves a similar effect by way of an analytical method consisting of a multidirectional conceptual transfer (a combination of conceptual remediation and anachronistic mapping), ultimately resulting in the creation of conceptual blends of old and new media. These postmodern strategies intentionally make things fuzzier and more complex, to meet the requirements of the new and unfamiliar, with a blurring of traditional analytic clarity as one of their side effects.

So, situated in intellectual history, these two closely related constructions of media history and conceptualizations of digital media are characterized by a tension between the use of traditional scientific approaches and postmodern strategies defying traditional scientific logic, a tension corresponding to the tension between old analogue and new digital media. Let us leave this tension unresolved since it is, I believe, as close as we can get to the non-essentialist essences of these important books.

Remediation and *The Language of New Media* are still relevant as they manifest some of the most important tendencies and productive ideas in both past and contemporary media theory: media and mediation defined as the interrelations between media, the metaphoric understanding of the interrelations between old and new media in terms of objects and containers, animate beings and power struggle, the use of clusters of binaries to describe the conceptual fields of media, and the deployment of strategies like anachronistic mapping or a spatialization of temporality to write a non-chronological and antiteleological media history. To end this chapter I will try to challenge some of these ideas, both traditional and postmodern, by once more returning to Bolter and Grusin's and Manovich's books. Let us downplay some of the central notions and highlight some less central ones, pose some questions and hint at some alternative solutions.[81]

---

[81] Two recent attempts to discuss and reformulate central notions in media theory (the concept of content, media and meaning, binarism, media, and agency) are W. J. T. Mitchell and Mark B. N. Hansen, eds., *Critical Terms for Media Studies* (Chicago: The University of Chicago Press, 2010), vii–xxii and John Durham Peters, *The Marvelous Clouds: Toward a Philosophy of Elemental Media* (Chicago: The University of Chicago Press, 2015), 13–52.

Media as Hybrids, Media Specificity, and Historical Literalness

One of the less central conceptual metaphors in *Remediaton* seems to me much more important and productive than metaphors such as media as containers and the struggle between media conceived of as agents or the metaphor of resonance. Bolter and Grusin write:

> Futhermore, media technologies constitute networks or hybrids that can be expressed in physical, social, aesthetic, and economic terms. Introducing a new media technology does not mean simply inventing new hardware and software, but rather fashioning (or refashioning) such a network.[82]

Interestingly enough, the same metaphor can be found in Manovich's book: "The language of cultural interfaces is a hybrid. It is a strange, often awkward mix between the conventions of traditional cultural forms and the conventions of HCI [...]."[83] I suggest that we focus on the hybrid metaphor, MEDIA and MEDIA HISTORY ARE HYBRIDS, and highlight it (while at the same time downplaying the metaphors mentioned above).[84] Media "are" hybrids, that is, physical, social, aesthetic, and economic phenomena and relations, and to describe them, and the interrelations between old and new media, accurately, we must take all these aspects into consideration. This is not, by any means, an original suggestion; MEDIA ARE HYBRIDS is part of Mitchell's argumentation against media purity in "There Are No Visual Media," and already set in motion by McLuhan.[85] It is also closely related to current theories on media as multimodal and heteromedial conglomerates.[86] Even if not an original suggestion, I find the metaphor and its entailments and inferential structures (indicating

---

[82] Bolter and Grusin, *Remediation*, 17.
[83] Manovich, *Language of New Media*, 91.
[84] I also suggest that we avoid the network metaphor since it is so closely related to the all-present and dominant internet.
[85] Mitchell, "There Are No Visual Media," 396, 398; McLuhan, *Understanding Media*, 71–81.
[86] See, e.g., Elleström, *Media Transformation*, 36–45; Jørgen Bruhn, *The Intermediality of Narrative Literature: Medialities Matter* (London: Palgrave Macmillan, 2016), 15, 42.

the multifacetedness and context of the phenomena) useful: it says that media and its interrelations are something complex and complicated that we must investigate very carefully and in detail. The MEDIA ARE HYBRIDS metaphor thus fits our experiences of media and the relations between old and new media better than alternative metaphors.[87] Instead of, metaphorically, turning media and media history into objects, containers, and persons playing different roles in a binary power struggle, I think we should view them as the multifaceted, strange, and awkward phenomena that they are.

Another thing I would like to promote is the notion of medium specificity and the necessary transformation of travelling concepts and avoidance of anachronistic mappings and analogies. Manovich discusses the concept of "operation," a new concept for new media: "it would be a mistake to reduce the concept of an operation to a 'tool' or 'medium.' In fact, one of the assumptions underlying this book is that these traditional concepts do not work very well in relation to new media, and thus we need new concepts like 'interface' and 'operation.'"[88] New media, new environments, and new historical circumstances call for new and different concepts. Moreover, following the same logic, concepts transferred from the discourse of one medium to another medium, from one discipline to another discipline, must not only be transferred and applied, they must also be transformed to do their job in the new scientific environment.

Finally, I want to argue for historical literalness (the methodological and literal counterpart of the "media are hybrid" metaphor), for lack of a better term. Bolter and Grusin are aware of the problem of personification and the figurative wars of media. They admit that when writing something like "'digital media are challenging the status of television and film' we are asking readers to treat this as shorthand." The longer version would include individuals, groups, and institutions that create and use digital media as improved forms of television and film.[89] In the introduction

---

[87] See Lakoff and Johnson, *Metaphors We Live By*, 139–146.
[88] Manovich, *Language of New Media*, 121.
[89] Bolter and Grusin, *Remediation*, 78; cf. criticism in Gitelman, *Always Already New*, 9.

to her seminal study, *Always Already New: Media, History, and the Data of Culture* (2006), media historian Lisa Gitelman criticizes this theoretical tendency to essentialize and naturalize media by way of treating them as if they were "unchanging, 'immutable objects with given, self-defining properties,'" as well as the parallel tendency to describe media as "self-acting agents of their own history."[90] According to Gitelman media are very particular sites for very particular, importantly social as well as historically and culturally specific experiences of meaning.[91] And what we should investigate, Gitelman seems to recommend, is the real and literal agency of mediality: authors, designers, engineers, entrepreneurs, programmers, investors, owners, or audiences.[92] Conceptual metaphors, analogies, and mappings of different kinds are, not only unavoidable but also highly useful when employed in a systematic way, but let us avoid misleading shorthand and distorting conceptual fields and mappings, whenever we can, and describe and explore actual interrelations between old and new media (mediated by real agents and actions) instead of symbolic ones.

References

Bal, Mieke. *Travelling Concepts in the Humanities: A Rough Guide*. Toronto: University of Toronto Press, 2002.

Bell, John L. *Oppositions and Paradoxes: Philosophical Perplexities in Science and Mathematics*. Peterborough: Broadview Press, 2016.

Bolter, Jay David, and Richard Grusin. *Remediation: Understanding New Media*. Cambridge: MIT Press, 1999.

Bordwell, David. *Making Meaning: Inference and Rhetoric in the Interpretation of Cinema*. Cambridge: Harvard University Press, 1989.

Bruhn, Jørgen. *The Intermediality of Narrative Literature: Medialities Matter*. London: Palgrave Macmillan, 2016.

---

[90] Gitelman, *Always Already New*, 8, 9.
[91] Gitelman, *Always Already New*, 8.
[92] Gitelman, *Always Already New*, 9–10.

Carroll, Noël. "Fiction, Non-fiction, and the Film of Presumptive Assertion: A Conceptual Analysis." In *Film Theory and Philosophy*, edited by Richard Allen and Murray Smith, 173–202. Oxford: Clarendon Press, 1997.

Chandler, Daniel. *Semiotics: The Basics*. London: Routledge, 2002.

Chatman, Seymour. *Story and Discourse: Narrative Structure in Fiction and Film*. Ithaca and London: Cornell University Press, 1978.

Chun, Wendy Hui Kyong, and Anna Watkins Fisher, with Tomas W. Keenan, eds. *New Media, Old Media: A History and Theory Reader*. 2nd ed. New York: Routledge, 2016.

Curse, Alan D. *Lexical Semantics*. Cambridge: Cambridge University Press, 1986.

Culler, Jonathan. *On Deconstruction: Theory and Criticism after Structuralism*. Ithaca: Cornell University Press, 1982.

Derrida, Jacques. *Positions*. Translation and annotation by Alan Bass. Chicago: University of Chicago Press, 1982 [1972].

Elleström, Lars. *Media Transformation: The Transfer of Media Characteristics Among Media*. Basingstoke: Palgrave Macmillian, 2014.

Fauconnier, Gilles, and Mark Turner. *The Way We Think: Conceptual Blending and the Mind's Hidden Complexities*. New York: Basic Books, 2002.

Genette, Gérard. *Palimpsests: Literature in the Second Degree*. Lincoln: University of Nebraska Press, 1997.

Gitelman, Lisa. *Always Already New: Media, History, and the Data of Culture*. Cambridge: MIT Press, 2006.

Gitelman, Lisa, and Geoffrey B. Pingree, eds. *New Media, 1740–1915*. Cambridge: MIT Press, 2003.

Hayles, Katherine N. *How We Think: Digital Media and Contemporary Technogenesis*. Chicago and London: The University of Chicago Press, 2012.

Hjelmslev, Louis. *Prolegomena to a Theory of Language*. Rev. English ed. Madison: University of Wisconsin Press, 1961 [1943].

Hodge, Robert, and Gunther Kress. *Social Semiotics*. Cambridge: Polity, 1988.

Huhtamo, Erkki, and Jussi Parikka. "Introduction: An Archaeology of Media Archaeology." In *Media Archaeology: Approaches, Applications, and Implications*, edited by Erkki Huhtamo and Jussi Parikka, 1–22. Berkeley: University of California Press, 2011.

Innis, Harold A. *Empire and Communications*. Toronto and New York: Dundurn Press Limited, 2007 [1950].

Jakobson, Roman. "Language in Relation to Other Communication Systems." In *Selected Writings*, vol. 2, 697–708. The Hague: Mouton, 1971.

Jakobson, Roman, and Moris Halle. *Fundamentals of Language*, 2nd revised edition. The Hague: Mouton, 1971 [1956].

Kittay, Eve Feder. *Metaphor: Its Cognitive Force and Linguistic Structure*. Oxford: Clarendon, 1990.

Lakoff, George. *Women, Fire, and Dangerous Things: What Categories Reveal About the Mind*. Chicago: University of Chicago Press, 1987.

Lakoff, George, and Mark Johnson. *Philosophy in the Flesh: The Embodied Mind and its Challenge to Western Thought*. New York: Basic Books, 1999.

Lakoff, George, and Mark Johnson. *Metaphors We Live By*. Chicago and London: The University of Chicago Press, 2003 [1980].

The Living Handbook of Narratology. Accessed June 9, 2017. http://wikis.sub.uni-hamburg.de/lhn/index.php/Diegesis_-_Mimesis.

Makaryk, Irena Rima, ed. *Encyclopedia of Contemporary Literary Theory: Approaches, Scholars, Terms*. Toronto: University of Toronto Press, 1993.

Manovich, Lev. *The Language of New Media*. Cambridge: MIT Press, 2001.

McLuhan, Marshall. *Understanding Media: The Extensions of Man*. Critical ed. Corte Madera: Ginko Press, 2003 [1964].

Mitchell, W. J. T. *Iconology: Image, Text, Ideology.* Chicago: University of Chicago Press, 1986.

Mitchell, W. J. T. *What Do Pictures Want?: The Lives and Loves of Images.* Chicago: University of Chicago Press, 2005.

Mitchell, W. J. T. "There Are No Visual Media." In *MediaArtHistories*, edited by Oliver Grau, 395–408. Cambridge: MIT Press, 2007.

Mitchell, W. J. T., and Mark B. N. Hansen, eds. *Critical Terms for Media Studies.* Chicago: The University of Chicago Press, 2010.

Murphy, Gregory L. *The Big Book of Concepts.* Cambridge and London: MIT Press, 2002.

Neumann, Birgit, Ansgar Nünning, and Mirjam Horn, eds. *Travelling Concepts for the Study of Culture.* Berlin: Walter de Gruyter & Co., 2012.

Nöth, Winfried, and Nina Bishara, eds. *Self-reference in the Media.* Berlin: Mouton de Gruyter, 2007.

Peirce, Charles S. "Logics as Semiotic: The Theory of Signs." In *Semiotics: An Introductory Anthology*, edited by Robert E. Innis, 1–23. Bloomington: Indiana University Press, 1985.

Peters, John Durham. *The Marvelous Clouds: Toward a Philosophy of Elemental Media.* Chicago: The University of Chicago Press, 2015.

Rajewsky, Irina O. "Intermediality, Intertextuality, and Remediation: A Literary Perspective on Intermediality." *Intermediality: History and Theory of the Arts, Literature and Technologies*, no. 6 (2005): 43–64.

Reddy, Michael. "The Conduit Metaphor." In *Metaphor and Thought*, edited by A. Ortony, 284–324. Cambridge: Cambridge University Press, 1979.

Rosch, Eleanor, and Barbara B. Lloyd. *Cognition and Categorization.* Hillsdale: Erlbaum, 1978.

Ryan, Marie-Laure. *Narrative as Virtual Reality: Immersion and Interactivity in Literature and Electronic Media.* Baltimore: Johns Hopkins University Press, 2001.

Saussure, Ferdinand de. *Cours de linguistique générale*. Lausanne: Payot, 1916.

Sturrock, John. *Structuralism*. 2nd ed. Oxford: Blackwell Publishing, 2003.

Thon, Jan-Noël. *Transmedial Narratology and Contemporary Media Culture*. Lincoln: University of Nebraska Press, 2016.

Wittgenstein, Ludwig. *Philosophical Investigations*. Oxford: Blackwell, 1953.

About the Authors

Staffan Bergwik is associate professor and senior lecturer of history of science and ideas at Stockholm University. His research focuses on the cultural history of nineteenth- and twentieth-century natural science. He has previously studied science and gendered family life. His current research project is entitled *Elevated Views: Sven Hedin's Expeditions and the World from Above 1900–1935* and is funded by Riksbankens jubileumsfond (The Swedish Foundation for Humanities and Social Science).
ORCID: https://orcid.org/0000-0002-3475-6899

Jørgen Bruhn is professor of comparative literature at Linnaeus University, Sweden. Bruhn's latest books are *The Intermediality of Narrative Literature: Medialities Matter* (2016) and, with Anne Gjelsvik, *Cinema Between Media: An Intermedial Approach* (2018).
ORCID: https://orcid.org/0000-0003-2685-9510

Sara Callahan is enrolled in the PhD program in art history at the Department of Culture and Aesthetics at Stockholm University. She received her master's degree in art history at Södertörn University (Stockholm) in 2013. Prior to that she has worked at numerous private and public art galleries in Stockholm and Seattle.
ORCID: https://orcid.org/0000-0001-9521-5167

Anna Dahlgren is professor of art history at Stockholm University. She has published on different aspects of photography and visual culture including the digital turn, fashion and advertising photography, nineteenth-century print culture and albums, archives, and museum practices. Recent publications include *Travelling Images: Looking Across the Borderlands for Art, Media and Visual Culture* (2018) and *Representational Machines: Photography and the Production of Space* (2013, co-edited).
ORCID: https://orcid.org/0000-0001-7772-2739

Elina Druker is professor at the Department of Culture and Aesthetics, Stockholm University. Her primary research interests are modernist aesthetics and children's literature, especially picture-book studies. She is co-editor for *Children's Literature and the Avant-garde* (2015) and is currently working with representations of consumerism in Swedish children's literature during the first half of the twentieth century.
ORCID: https://orcid.org/0000-0002-0592-9228

Johanna Ethnersson Pontara is associate professor in musicology at the Department of Culture and Aesthetics, Stockholm University. She received her PhD in musicology (2003) and her research has thereafter focused on opera with particular emphasis on performance theory and the representation of gender. She is currently working on the research project *Classical Music for a Mediatized World: Visual and Audio-visual Representations of Western Art Music in Contemporary Media and Society*.
ORCID: https://orcid.org/0000-0003-1731-0366

Peter Gillgren is professor of art history at Stockholm University. His publications include several articles and books on renaissance and baroque art, as well as on methods and theories of art history. His book *Siting Michelangelo: Spectatorship, Site Specificity and Soundscape* was released by Nordic Academic Press in 2017.
ORCID: https://orcid.org/0000-0002-9922-819X

Magdalena Holdar is senior lecturer in art history at the Department of Culture and Aesthetics, Stockholm University. Former director of its Curating Art international master's programme, her research involves the performative aspects of art, exhibition making, and the curatorial. Currently, she is investigating Fluxus from the perspective of its organization as a transnational network.
ORCID: https://orcid.org/0000-0003-3452-1050

Rikard Hoogland is a senior lecturer in theatre studies at Stockholm University. His two recent publications are one article about popular theatre and one about historiography, both in

Nordic Theatre Studies. They both resulted from a project funded by the Swedish Research Council. In 2017 he also published a chapter "'How close is Angola to us?' Peter Weiss's Play Song of the Lusitanian Bogeyman in the Shadow of the Cold War" in an anthology published by Palgrave Macmillan. During spring 2017 he was a visiting researcher at the Freie Universität in Berlin.
ORCID: https://orcid.org/0000-0002-5350-6916

Christer Johansson is a research officer and senior lecturer at the Department of Culture and Aesthetics, Stockholm University. He received his PhD in literary studies (2008) and is currently working on the research projects *Concepts of Mediality: A Metatheoretical Investigation of Intermedial Studies and Media Theory* and *The Materialised Word: Medium and Meaning in Eyvind Johnson's Prose Fiction*.
ORCID: https://orcid.org/0000-0002-5350-6916

Fredrik Krohn Andersson is a senior lecturer in art history at the Department of Culture and Aesthetics, Stockholm University. He received his PhD in art history (2012) and his research is currently focusing on questions on the construction of cultural heritages and uses of them as political, cultural, and economical resources.
ORCID: https://orcid.org/0000-0001-5825-7042

Sonya Petersson is a postdoctoral researcher and senior lecturer at the Department of Culture and Aesthetics, Stockholm University. She received her PhD in art history (2014) and is currently working on the research project *Graphic Illustration: Concepts and Combined Mediality from the Point of View of Mechanical Reproduction* (2016–2018).
ORCID: https://orcid.org/0000-0003-1335-1080

Daria Skjoldager-Nielsen is a PhD candidate in theatre studies, Stockholm University, working on a project about audience development in public theatres. She is vice-chairwoman of the Rococo Foundation researching cultural institutions' management and performance. Her research interests lie in audience development, the theatrical event, new approaches to marketing and theatre, and cultural policy.

ORCID: https://orcid.org/0000-0003-2616-2289

Kim Skjoldager-Nielsen is currently a PhD candidate in theatre studies, Stockholm University, finishing his dissertation *Over the Threshold, Into the World: Experiences of Transcendence in the Context of Staged Events*. With International Federation for Theatre Research (IFTR), he is an elected ExComm member and founding co-convener of the working group Performance, Spirituality and Religion, as well as founding co-editor of the e-journal *PRS – Performance, Religion and Spirituality*. He is a member of the Performance Studies international (PSi) working group Performance and Science and a participant in the Performance Studies Space Programme (PSSP). His research interests are performative aesthetics, spirituality, science and theatre, and contemporary staged events.

ORCID: https://orcid.org/0000-0002-2577-9538

Henriette Thune is Vice Dean of Research at the Faculty of Health Sciences, University of Stavanger, Norway. She obtained her PhD in literature and aesthetics in 2012 with a thesis on Mikhail Bakhtin's aesthetic object and Sara Stridsberg's novel *The Dream Faculty* (2005). Thune is affiliated with *Network of Gender Studies* and the research project *Death: Emotions, Relations and Constructions* (DERC), amongst others.

ORCID: https://orcid.org/0000-0001-8349-8227

Erik Wallrup is a co-ordinator of the Critical Studies master's programme at the Department of Culture and Aesthetics, Stockholm University, where he also teaches in musicology. He received his PhD in musicology 2012. Wallrup has published the book *Being Musically Attuned: The Act of Listening to Music* (2015) and he is currently working on the research project *The Affective Shift of Music in the Gustavian Era*.

ORCID: https://orcid.org/0000-0002-9218-2029

Index

15 *Gedichte* (Schoenberg) 359, 360

A

Adorno, Theodor W. 366
advertising 257
  designing consumers 256
  overview 241, 257
  picture books 17, 244
  sentient machines 251
  short films 17
aesthetic object 27, 29, 30, 41, 43, 47
aesthetic strategy 2, 160, 178
Albers, Kate Palmer 309
Allen, R. E. 291
anachronistic mapping 397, 398, 399
analogue
  analogue/digital binary 295
  copy, original, and reproduction 311
  death of a medium 314
  intermediality as analytic tool 294
  materiality of analogue and human body 305
  notion of the analogue 301
  original and copies 300
  overview 291
  photographing the invisible 307
  postconceptual art and photography 292
  temporality and history 309
  the unphotographable; unphotographable 299
  truth claims 297
Analogue (Leonard project) 312, 314
analogue media 376, 397
analogue photography 17, 300, 307, 310
Andersen, Hans Christian 135
Anderson, Joel 138, 144
Anderson, O. 134, 141
animation 253, 396
anthropomorphism 241, 243
Antonsson, Lotta 311
Arab Image Foundation (AIF) 314
architectural history 265
Ars Poetica (Horace) 3
art
  and reproduction; reproduction 16
  and science; science 201
  art, image, and media studies 219
  instruction art 107, 111, 118, 119, 121, 125
  postconceptual art and photography 292
art exhibitions 36, 152
art history 12, 216, 217, 334

Art of Illustration, The
 (Blackburn) 324, 328
Arvidson, Mats 351
Assmann, Aleida 134
Assmann, Jan 8
Audebert, Nicholas 88
August, Prince 219, 221
authorship 122
avant-garde 250, 251

B

Baetens, Jan 295, 296
Baigent, Elisabeth 208
Baker, Thomas 144
Bakhtin, Mikhail
 aesthetic object 27, 29, 41, 43
 Calle's *Rachel, Monique* 27, 29,
  41, 43, 44
 intersubjectivity 16
 intertextuality 77
Bal, Mieke 75, 119, 167, 326, 377
Balme, Christopher B. 132
Barkan, Leonard 84
Barral, Xavier 33
Barry, Kevin 365
Barthes, Roland 77, 230, 296,
 299, 303, 324
basic media 291, 362, 365,
 370, 371
Batchen, Geoffrey 297, 299, 300
Baudrillard, Jean 241, 251, 256
Bay-Cheng, Sarah 152
Beardsley, Aubrey 328
Becker, Colleen 92
Bellman, Carl Michael 227,
 228, 229, 231, 233
Belting, Hans 217

Belvedere Cleopatra 82, 83, 94
Belvedere court 82, 94
Benjamin, Walter 12, 299, 304
Bennett, Jane 115
Berg, Alban 50, 356
Berggren Torell, Viveca 252
Bergman, Gösta M. 139
Bergman, Ingmar
 Hour of the Wolf, The 56, 59,
  61, 63, 64, 66, 70
 Images (Bilder) 55
 Lanterna Magica 60
 overview 13, 15
 Persona 52, 54, 55, 69
 Sawdust and Tinsel 69
Bergström, Lasse 56, 60
Bernhardt, Sarah 143
Bigg, Charlotte 187, 201
Billing, Johanna 113
Binkley, Timothy 299
biopolitics 266
Bird, Michael 56
Bishara, Nina 383
Bishop, Claire 300, 301
Bjurström, Per 214
Blackburn, Henry 324, 328,
 329, 330, 334
Bland, David 328, 333
Bleeker, Maaike 157, 161,
 167, 168
Blomdahl, Karl-Birger 69
Boccaccio, Giovanni 85
Bocchi, Francesco 88
Bolter, Jay David
 illustration and new media
  326, 339
 intermediality 9, 17, 18

language of new media 391, 392
media as hybrids 400, 401
old and new media 377, 382, 386, 398
remediation 142, 150, 169, 262, 382, 386, 387, 388, 390
Bordwell, David 378, 379, 381, 382, 383, 385
Boulez, Pierre 367
Bournonville, August 135, 136
Boyd, Harriet 51
Brandt, Frish 298
Braun, Joseph 90
Brembeck, Helene 252
Bremmer, Magnus 195, 205, 233
Broman, Per F. 51, 65
Brown, Calvin S. 351
Bruhn, Jørgen 5, 27, 32, 52, 263, 351, 400
Burén, Jan af 334

C

Cage, John 106, 111
Calle, Sophie
 background and oeuvre 32
 Prenez soin de vous (Take care) 32, 44
 Rachel, Monique as aesthetic object 43
 Rachel, Monique exhibition experience 36
 Rachel, Monique formal content 41
 Rachel, Monique inventory of medialities 40
 Rachel, Monique overview 11, 15, 16, 31, 47
Campano, Gianantonio 83
Carroll, Noël 380

Cartier-Bresson, Henri 227
Castiglione, Baldassare 83, 93
Cattrall, Kim 33, 36, 43
Cavalier of the Rose, The (Strauss) 51
Celsing, Peter 265, 273
Chandler, Daniel 306
Chapple, Freda 152, 153, 154
Chatman, Seymour 388
children's literature 241, 244, 246, 255
Chinese Compass (Hotel Pro Forma) 162
Christoffersen, Erik Exe 150, 151, 158, 159
Chun, Wendy Hui Kyong 377
cinema 54, 249, 393, 394, 397
cinematic mode 55, 62
Citron, Marcia 61, 63
Cleopatra, Belvedere 82, 83, 94
Close, Rebecca 109
cognitive theory
 and conceptual analysis; conceptual analysis 378
 and metaphor; metaphor 386
conceptual blending 392
Coleridge, Samuel Taylor 103
combined medium 325, 338, 343
Comment, Bernard 187, 190
computer interface 395, 397
Concannon, Kevin 101, 118
conceptual analysis 15, 18, 379, 402
conceptual art 315
conceptual fields 378, 384
conceptual metaphor 378, 390

conceptual remediation 396, 397, 398
Condivi, Ascanio 81
conduit/container metaphor 388, 390, 391, 398
Cone, Edward T. 367
consumerism 16, 256, 257
Cook, Daniel Thomas 252
Cook, Nicholas 66
Cooperative Union 242, 246, 255
Corliss, Richard 50, 60
counterculture 103, 108, 125
coupling, loose/tight 359
Crane, Walter 324, 332
Crawford, Lawrence 158
Crisp Bread Parade (Knäckebrödsparaden) xiii, 244, 245
Cruse, Alan D. 378, 379, 381, 382, 383, 385
cultural policy 280
    collapsing representations 279
    documents 271
    Kulturhuset (*Culture house*) 275
    overview 17, 264, 279
    points of departure 269
    previous studies 266
culture 262, 264, 391
culture houses 262, 275, 276, 279
Cupers, Kenny 272
Curran, Brian 81, 83
Curtain Up (exhibition) 151
Curtis, Gerard 323

D

Dahlgren, Anna 132, 142, 245
Dahlhaus, Carl 356
Damaged Negatives Scratched Portrait of Mrs. Baqari (Zaatari); 288, 289, 305, 314
database 391, 396
de Wahl, Andres 135, 143
Dean, Tacita 313
death 26, 37, 41, 43, 46, 84
Dehlholm, Kirsten 151, 159, 163, 167, 171, 177, 178
Derrida, Jacques 306, 329, 342, 383
descriptive layering 16, 188, 197, 207
Deswarte-Rosa, Sylvie 82
Dewey, John 110
digital media
    and analogue; analogue 301, 310, 313, 314
    digital hypermedia 385
    media as hybrids 401
    old and new media 376, 377, 382, 387, 399
    remediation and media history 9, 387
digital photography 13, 17, 288, 303, 306, 310
Discipline and Punish (Foucault) 266
discipline, and security 269
Doppelbegabungen 4
Dovey, Kim 267
Drucker, Johanna 341
Druker, Elina 242, 243
Duchamp, Marcel 164
dying 26, 28, 37, 43, 46
Dylan, Bob 363

E

Edenman, Ragnar 268
Edström, Mauritz 56, 60, 64
Ehrenforth, Karl Heinrich 361
Eisenstein, Sergei 164
ekphrasis 4, 106
El Madani, Hasham 288, 304, 305
Elkins, James 297, 341
Elleström, Lars
  analogue 292, 315
  dimensions 52
  modalities 7, 27, 362, 364
  qualified media 39
  remediation 263
  song as event 353, 355, 363, 364, 365
embodiment 156, 157, 305
Emerson, Caryl 30
En levnads teckning (Sven Hedin as Artist) 201
end of life care. *See* death; dying
Enge, Håvard 367
Ernst, Wolfgang 216
Et Folkesagn (play) 136
Ethnersson Pontara, Johanna 51, 69
Ettlinger, L. D. 87
event
  and intermediality; intermediality 294, 353, 357, 370
  and the work of art; work of art 119, 153, 156, 157, 307
  and world; world 369, 370, 371
  song as event 353, 357, 359, 370
Experiments in Art and Technology (E.A.T.) 102
external work 29, 42

F

Fagerlin, Ferdinand 226
Fauconnier, Gilles 378, 397
Feldman, Martha 55
Fernández-Carracedo, Daniel 265
Filliou, Robert 124
film
  advertising 249, 253
  Hour of the Wolf 56, 60, 63, 67, 70
  language of new media 393, 397
  media as hybrids 401
Fischinger, Oskar 250
Fisher, Anna Watkins 377
Florman, Gösta 133, 219, 221
Fluxus
  and Dick Higgins; Dick Higgins 102, 103, 105, 108
  and instruction art; instruction art 114, 121
  and network; network 114, 124
  and performance; performance 114, 121
  and Yoko Ono; Yoko Ono 112, 113, 114, 124
  intermedia in artistic practice 121, 122
  overview 14, 15
folk tales 136, 142
formal content 27, 40, 41
formal imitation 52, 60, 63, 70
Foster, Hal 164
Foucault, Michel 267, 269, 389
Fraenkel, Jeffrey 298
Frankel, Nicholas 328
Frenander, Anders 264, 270
Fried, Michael 296
Frye, Northrop 278

G

Gadamer, Hans-Georg 368, 369
Gade, N. W. 136
Gaehtgens, Thomas. W. 219
Ganter, Brian 302
Genette, Gérard 380
geography 16, 192, 194, 197
George, Stefan 350, 352, 357, 361, 362, 369
Giannotti, Donato 86
Gitelman, Lisa 8, 13, 14, 300, 326, 402
Gjelsvik, Anne 4, 32
Godard, Jean-Luc 51
Godfrey, Mark 301, 309, 313
Goethe, Johann Wolfgang von 366
Gorbman, Claudia 51
governmentality 266, 268, 273, 279
Grabow, Carl 134, 139
Grapefruit (Ono) 118, 124
Green, David 309
Greenberg, Clement 234
grief 41, 45
Group Zero 102
Grundell, Vendela 299
Grusin, Richard
    conceptual metaphors 387, 388, 390
    illustration and new media 326, 339
    language of new media 391, 392
    media as hybrids 400, 401
    old and new media 377, 382, 386, 398
    overview 9, 17, 18
    remediation 142, 150, 169, 262, 382, 386, 387, 388, 390

Gundolf, Friedrich 368
Gunning, Tom 54, 55
Guthrie, William Keith Chambers 85

H

Häger, Olle 185
Hagman, Justus 133 138, 140
Hallberg, Kristin 243
Hamerton, Philip Gilbert 334
Hamilton, Peter 226
Hansen, Mark B. N. 10
Hansen-Löve, Aage 358
Hanslick, Eduard 356
Hanssen, Eirik Frisvold 4, 32
Harding, Tobias 264
Hargreaves, Roger 226
Harren, Natilee 120, 121, 122
Harris, Verne 305
Hartmann, P. E. 136
Harvard, Jonas 144, 217
Havelock, Eric A. 8
Hawkins, Joyce 291
Hayles, Katherine N. 384
Hedberg, Frans 135
Hedin, Sven
    anchoring meaning 207
    descriptive layers and media formats 209
    figures 196, 199, 202, 206
    overview 16
    panoramic genre, geography, and imperialism 192
    photographic panoramas 197
    Southern Tibet 189, 198, 200, 203, 204, 206
    Transhimalaya 189, 200, 203, 205, 207

understanding whole
landscape 194
visual layers 203
Heineman, Hans-Erland 271, 272
Heise, Ursula 209
Helsinger, Elizabeth 335
Heraclitus 83
Here and Now Story Book (Mitchell) 254
Hi Red Center 102
Higgins, Dick
and intermedia chart; intermedia chart 104, 110, 121
and intermedia; intermedia 14, 103, 106, 111, 120, 121, 122, 124, 125
Higgins, Hannah 106
Hillis Miller, J. 332
history 309
Hitler, Adolf 186
Hjalmar the Brave (lithograph) 223 224
Hjalmar's Farewell (painting) 223
Hjarvard, Stig 218
Hjelmslev, Louis 388, 394
Hodell, Frans 130
Hodge, Robert 383
Hodnett, Edward 329
Hoffmannsthal, Hugo von 350
Holquist, Michael 27, 30
Hoops, Jonathan 50, 60
Horace 3
Horn, Mirjam 378
Hotel Pro Forma
overview 15, 178
theatre performance 151, 152, 166
Today's Cake is a Log 167, 168, 171, 173, 174, 175, 177

Hour of the Wolf, The (film) 71
formal imitation through music, sound and images 67
formal imitation through opera 63
formal imitation through speech/sound 60
medial mixedness and purity 70
opera 51
overview 13, 15, 56, 71
synopsis and key scenes 57
Huhtamo, Erkki 187, 190, 208, 217, 390, 397
Hultén, Pontus 272, 275
Humphray, Caroline 163
Huron, David 249
Hutcheon, Linda 32
hybrid metaphor 401
hypermediacy 177, 382, 383, 385, 398
hypermediality 154

I

I Only Appear to be Dead (Hotel Pro Forma) 172
icon 296, 364, 394
Ideal Baking Powder, The (advert) 247, 248, 251
illustration 345
as combined media; combined media 325, 341
conventional concept of 17, 325, 334
definitions 322, 329, 334
functions of 345
Hedin's visual layers 203
historiographic ambivalence 327
illustrated/illustrating 326, 344
modern concept 333

new media 327, 344
overview 327, 345
photomontage 141
supplementarity 329
illustration studies 324, 328, 333
imagetext 316, 326
immediacy 382, 383, 385, 398
imperialism 192, 208
in-between 11, 13, 76
index 220, 292, 296, 297, 301, 309, 364, 394
Ingemann, Bruno 150
Innis, Harold A. 376
instruction art 107, 111, 118, 119, 121, 125
interart studies 5
interface 396, 401
intermedia chart 104, 110, 121
intermedia theory 108, 110, 111, 125
intermedial reference 5, 53, 65
intermedial studies, history of 351, 353, 358, 370, 389
intermediality
    aesthetic analysis and critical reflection 14
    analogue 294, 316
    and film; film 53, 70
    and intertextuality; intertextuality 4, 15, 78, 94, 380
    and transmediality; transmediality 263
    artefacts, networks and concepts 18
    cultural contexts 76
    definitions 2, 3, 293
    descriptive layers and media formats 209
    hyper- and intermediality in theatre performance 154
    intermedial experience in post-dramatic theatre 157
    new digital medium 380
    performance of perception 168
    song as event 351, 353, 354, 358, 362
    theatre performance 152, 158, 166
intermediality studies 3, 5, 10
intersubjectivity 16, 77
intertextuality 4, 15, 78, 94, 380
Irvin, Sherri 164
Isaksson, Curt 144
Iversen, Margaret 296, 304

J

Jakobson, Roman 394
Jämlikhet – för handikappade? (Equality – for the Handicapped?) film 262, 279
Janzen Kooistra, Lorraine 323
Jenkins, Henry 8, 188, 218
Jensen, Carston 162
Jeongwon, Joe 50
Jerichau-Baumann, Anna Maria Lisinska 224 225
Joannides, Paul 86
Johnson, Mark 386
Jørgensen, Dorthe 176
Joselit, David 113
Jürgensen, Knut Arne 135

K

Kaprow, Allan 106
Karlholm, Dan 219, 290
Kattenbelt, Chiel 153, 157, 158, 160, 177

Keenan, Tomas W. 377
Keller, Kevin 248
kino-eye interface 396
Kiss, Stroke, Grip (Ganter series) 303
Kittay, Eve Feder 378, 379, 382
Kittler, Friedrich 8
Klockar Linder, My 265
Koester, Joachim 303, 306
Korda, Andrea 323
Koskinen, Maaret 55, 70, 71
Kragh-Jacobsen, Svend 136
Kramer, Lawrence 367
Krauss, Rosalind 295
Krebs, Harold 361
Kress, Gunther 383
Kristeva, Julia 11, 15, 78, 94
Krøgholdt, Ida 164
Kubiak, Daria 169
kulturhus (culture houses) 262, 266, 275, 276, 279
Kulturhuset (*Culture house*) building, Stockholm 262, 263, 265, 266, 269, 276, 279

L

LaBelle, Brandon 119
Lager Vestberg, Nina 295, 296
Laidlaw, James 163
Lakoff, George 377, 386, 388
Langer, Suzanne K. 367
language
　of new media; new media 395, 397
　old and new media in digital age 398
　remediation and media history 388
　song as event 356, 359, 365
　transmediation of 398
Language of New Media, The (Manovich) 376, 399
Laocoön (Lessing) 3, 234
Larsson, Lars Olof 265
Lavender, Andy 152
Lechtor, Melchior 357
Lehmann, Hans-Thies 155, 160
Lennon, John 114, 124
Leonard, Zoe 313, 314
Leonardo da Vinci 82
Lessing, Gotthold Ephraim 3, 234
Levine, Gabriel 101
Liapunov, Vadim 27
Lind, Maria 113
Lister, Martin 294, 313
Lithographic Album (*Litografisk album*)
　art, image, and media studies 217, 218
　figures 215, 221, 229, 230
　lithography overview 216
　paintings 227
　photographs 222
　statues 231
　transparency, media specificity, and print culture 235
lithography 235
　art, image, and media studies 219
　illustration and new media 334, 337, 338, 339
　overview 16, 216
　paintings 227
　photographs 222
　statues 231
　transparency, media specificity, and print culture 235

Ljungby horn (play)
  figures 130, 133
  photomontage 136, 139, 141, 142
Lloyd, Barbara B. 378
Lowry, Joanna 309
Luhmann, Niklas 358
Luko, Alexis 52, 56, 59, 68
Lulu (Berg) 50
Lund, Hans 218, 324
Lundby, Knut 218
Lundell, Patrik 144, 217
Lutter, Vera 308

M

Maciunas, George 114, 122
Madonna sculpture (Michelangelo) 89, 91
Maeder, Costatino 356
Magic Flute, The (Mozart opera) 50, 55, 58, 62
Man with a Movie Camera (film) 393, 396
Manghani, Sunil 217
Manoff, Marlene 295, 297
Manovich, Lev
  analogue 295
  language of new media 397
  media as hybrids 401
  old and new media 377, 399
  overview 17, 18
  travelling concepts 397
Marchesano, Louis 219
Mariotti, J. Rogers 91
Markus, Thomas A. 267
material modality 7, 363
Mattsson, Helena 250
McCauley, Elizabeth Anne 143

McGee, Vern W. 30
McLuhan, Marshall
  media as hybrids 400
  media history 376
  musical meaning 362
  old and new media 380, 383
  oral and written media 8
  remediation and media history 387
  Something Else Press 106
Medelius, Hans 227
media archaeology 8, 216, 390, 397
media history 2, 8, 14, 379, 390, 392, 398
media specificity 13, 401, 402
media theory
  analogue photography 292
  and intermediality; intermediality 3, 8
  old and new media 383
  song as event 362
medial combinations 5, 53, 61, 322
mediality 7, 26, 40, 44, 46, 70, 402
mediation 263, 264, 379, 381, 398
mediatization 218
Medici chapel
  figures 79, 86, 89, 90
  Michelangelo and intertextuality 81, 84, 86, 91, 94
Medici family 79, 81, 86
medium
  analogue photography 13, 17, 294
  definition 382
  digital photography 13, 17, 301

media specificity 13, 401, 402
old and new media 381, 382, 387, 397
Merx, Sigrid 156, 161, 178
Message from Andrée (Koester animation) 302, 304, 308
metareferentiality 11
metatheory 17, 378, 396
Meyer, Annette 169
Michelangelo Buonarroti, and Night 15, 81, 82, 85, 87, 91, 94
migration 94
   cultures of migration 76
   figures 92
   Kristeva's intertextuality 78
   Night and the *Belvedere Cleopatra* 82
   Night overview 81, 94
   Night soundscapes 91
   pathos formula 92
   sculpture and poetry 86
Miller, Peter 267
miming 355
Mini, Antonio 79, 80
Mitchell, Lucy Sprague 254
Mitchell, W. J. T. 7, 10, 14, 105, 293, 298, 316, 325, 337, 389, 400
mixed media 6, 104, 380
mobility of music 364
modalities 7, 362, 364
modernity 218, 255
Molin, Johan Peter 228, 229, 231
Molin's fountain (*Molins fontän*) 230, 231, 232, 233
montage 134, 135, 144, 145, 164
Moorman, Charlotte 102

Moreni, Domenico 87, 88
Morris, Christopher 54, 68
Moxey, Keith 216
Mozart, W. A. 50, 55, 63
Müller, Jürgen E. 4
multilayer montage 135
multimedia 51, 76, 93, 158
music
   advertising 246
   and film; film 56, 63, 67, 70, 71
   evasive musical meaning 366
   formalistic overstatement 361
   Ono's *Space Transformer* 111
   Schoenberg and George as touchstones 353
   semiotic overstatement 356
   song as event 17, 371
musical semiotics 351, 353, 356
musical sign 351, 355, 365
Mussell, James 219

N

Nadar (photographer) 143
Nagel, Alexander 90
Nattiez, Jean-Jacques 356
Navigare (Hotel Pro Forma) 162
Nedbal, Martin 58, 60
Nelson, Robin 152
networks 15, 17, 264
Neumann, Birgit 378, 392
new media
   and illustration; illustration 327, 344
   and old media; old media 9, 17
   and pictorial surface; pictorial surface 327, 335, 341, 343
   conceptual metaphors of remediation and media history 387, 390

Manovich and language of new media 397
media as hybrids, media specificity and historical literalness 402
media history 379
new digital medium 382
old and new media in digital age 399
Nibbelink, Lisbeth Groot 156, 161, 178
Night (Michelangelo sculpture) 15, 79, 81, 82, 86, 91, 94
Nilsson, Lars 113
Nilsson, Louise 248
Nilsson, Sven 266, 271
nineteenth century
analogue photography 300
illustration 324
lithography 213, 214, 220, 222, 224, 226, 232
panoramic genre and geography 187, 191, 195, 201, 205, 208
theatre photography 130, 134, 137
Noë, Alva 156
Nono, Luigi 366
Nöth, Winfried 383
Nünning, Ansgar 378, 392
Ny Illustrerad Tidning (magazine) 327, 335, 336, 337
Ny kulturpolitik (*New cultural policy*) report 262, 263, 271, 274
Nyblom, Andreas 144
Nyström, Bengt 227
Nyström, G. Alfred 227, 229

O

O'Flynn, Siobhan 32
Obrist, Hans Ulrich 117, 118
Oetterman, Stephan 187
Of the Decorative Illustration of Books Old and New (Crane) 324, 332
old media
and new media; new media 9, 17
Manovich and language of new media 392, 397
media history 379
new digital medium 381
old and new media in digital age 399
remediation and media history 387, 390
Olszewski, Marek Titien 85
On This Site Landscape in Memoriam (Sternfeld series) 309
One Who Whispers, The (Hotel Pro Forma) 176
Ong, Walter 8
Ono, Yoko
and Higgins' intermedia theory; Higgins' intermedia theory 103, 107, 108
and John Lennon; John Lennon 114, 124
Bed Peace 124
Cut Piece 124
Grapefruit 118, 124
instruction art 107, 111, 118, 121
intermedia in artistic practice 122
Painting to Hammer a Nail 110
performativity 15
Space Transformer 14, 15, 101, 118, 125
War Is Over campaign 115, 116
White Chess Set 118, 123
op de Beeck, Natalie 241, 253, 255, 256

opera
- and film; film 13, 51, 52, 54, 56, 70, 71
- formal imitation through music, sound and images 67
- formal imitation through speech/sound 60
- formal imitation through use of opera 63
- semiotic overstatement 355, 356
- visual opera 164

operation concept 401
Optical Poem (film) 250
oral media 8, 142
Örn, Johan 265
Orphism 86, 91, 94
Oscar II, King of Sweden 219
Osborne, Peter 290, 292
overview media 187, 192

P

Paik, Nam June 112
painting 12, 227, 232, 300, 335, 337, 339
Painting to Hammer a Nail (Ono) 110
Panopticon 266
panoramic visions
- anchoring meaning 207
- descriptive layers and media formats 209
- figures 196
- overview 16, 209
- panoramic genre, geography, and imperialism 192
- photographic panoramas 197
- understanding the whole landscape 194
- visual layers 203

parasocial interaction 144
parergon 342, 343, 345
Parikka, Jussi 8, 217, 390, 397
Pastille Dance, The (Pastilldansen) 240, 241, 245, 246, 249, 250
pathos formula 92
Peirce, Charles S. 7, 296, 297, 309, 394
Pelizzari, Maria Antonella 188
Pennell, Joseph 334
Per and Lisa's Christmas Kitchen (Per och Lisas julkök) 243
perception 157, 168, 178
performance. *See also* theatre performance
- hyper- and intermediality 154
- intermedia in artistic practice 119
- of perception; perception 157, 161, 168, 178
- performing the exhibition 177
- photomontage 138, 143
- unlimited performance and performativity 125

performative exhibition 160, 167, 169
performativity
- intermedia in artistic practice 119, 122
- of perception; perception 168, 178
- Ono's *Space* Transformer 113, 114, 116, 117, 125

Persona (film) 52, 54, 55, 69
personification 389, 391, 398, 401
Peters, John Durham 10
photo albums 132, 214

photography. *See also* analogue; digital photography
   analogue/digital binary 295
   analogue photography 17, 300, 307, 310
   anchoring meaning 207
   and postconceptual art; postconceptual art 292
   descriptive layers and media formats 209
   illustration and new media 337
   indexicality 297
   lithography 232
   overview 13, 16, 17
   photographic panoramas 197
   photographing the invisible 307
   visual layers 203
photomontage
   examples 134
   flash lighting 141
   illustrative drawings 141
   multilayer 135
   overview 15, 16, 145
   play script 136
   remediation 144
   theatre photographs 139
picture books 241, 244, 254
Picture of Snow White, The (Hotel Pro Forma) 162
Pingree, Geoffrey B. 14
play scripts 136
Plutarch 83
poetry
   Michelangelo's *Night* 86, 87, 93
   Schoenberg and George 350, 352, 353, 357, 359, 369
Pontara, Tobias 51
pop songs 363, 365

postconceptual art 290, 292, 315, 316
Prenez soin de vous (Take care [of yourself]) (Calle) 32, 44
print culture 218, 235
Przyblyski, Jeannene M. 219
punctum 298, 304

Q

qualified media
   analogue 292, 315
   Elleström dimensions 39, 52
   song as event 362, 363, 365, 370, 371
Qvarnström, Carl Gustaf 228
Qvortrup, Lars 159, 160

R

Rachel, Monique (Calle)
   as Bakhtinian aesthetic object; Bakhtinian aesthetic object 43
   Calle's oeuvre 32
   exhibition experience 36
   figures 26, 34, 35
   formal content 41
   inventory of medialities 40
   overview 11, 15, 31, 47
Rajewsky, Irina O. 1, 5, 12, 13, 27, 53, 61, 65, 166, 292, 293, 322
Rake's Progress, The (Stravinsky opera) 55
Ranft, Albert 130, 131, 134, 135, 139, 141
Reddy, Michael 387
remediation
   and binarism; binarism 9, 386
   and conceptual metaphor; conceptual metaphor 390

cultural policy 263
illustration 339
new digital medium 382
old and new media as conceptual field 386
old and new media in digital age 398
photomontage 130, 144
theatrical performance 15, 151, 164, 169, 178
Remediation (Bolter and Grusin) 376, 399, 400
remembrance 27, 42
resonance 390, 391, 392, 397
Richter, Gustav 335, 338
Richter, Hans 250
Ridout, Nicholas 54, 62, 63
Rittsel, Pär 132, 140, 143, 229
ritualization 163
Robic, Marie-Claire 188, 194
Robillard, Valerie 4, 78
Rosch, Eleanor 378, 382
Rose, Nikolas 267
Rose, Theresa 50
Rosenberg, Raphael 87, 88
Rosenqvist, Claes 139
Ruchatz, Jens 137
Runsten, Lars 69
Ryan, Marie-Laure 383
Rydin, Axel 140

S

Saint Cosmas sculpture (Michelangelo) 89, 91
Saint Damian sculpture (Michelangelo) 89, 91
Sandberg, Mark B. 56

Sans Titre (hommage á B. Lategan) (Antonsson diptych) 311
Santini, Andrea 51
Saussure, Ferdinand de 383, 388, 393
Sawdust and Tinsel (film) 69
Schäfer, Armin 357
Schapiro, Meyer 324
Schechner, Richard 150
Schechter, Joel 136
Schildt, Jurgen 56, 60
Schoenberg, Arnold 17, 353, 356, 361, 371
Schubert, Franz 352
Schwartz, Vanessa R. 219
science, and art 201
Scott Brown, Timothy 108
Scott, Calvin 353, 356, 358, 361, 362
Scruton, Roger 364
sculpture 86, 233
Seattle Art Museum (SAM) 110
security, and discipline 268, 269
self-reflexivity 157, 160, 167, 290, 316, 383
semantic field theory 378, 384
semiotic modality 6, 363
semiotics
    and intertextuality; intertextuality 3, 77
    mixed media 6
    old and new media 376, 395
    social semiotics 383
    song as event 351, 353, 356, 362, 365
Senelick, Laurence 144
sensorial modality 7, 363

sentient machines 241, 251, 254
sentient products 252, 256, 257
Shklovsky, Victor 158
sign-value 251
Siljeström, Per Adam 234
Silverman, Kaja 289, 296, 304
simple orchestration 165, 166, 171, 172, 173
Sindler, Monique 27, 28, 31, 35, 37, 43, 45
Skjoldager-Nielsen, Kim 163, 169
sleep 76, 84, 92
social semiotics 383
Söderberg, Rolf 132, 140, 229
Söderlind, Solfrid 220
Söndags Nisse (magazine) 130, 131
song as event 371
   evasive musical meaning 366
   formalistic overstatement 361
   overview 17, 371
   Schoenberg and George as touchstones 353
   semiotic overstatement 356
Sontag, Susan 296
sound
   film and opera 55, 57, 60, 63, 67, 70, 71
   Michelangelo's *Night* soundscapes 91, 93
Southern Tibet (Hedin) 189, 198, 200, 203, 204, 206
Space Transformer (Ono)
   figure 100
   Higgins' intermedia theory 108
   intermedia in artistic practice 122
   itinerary of things and actions 118
   overview 14, 15, 101
   unlimited performance and performativity 125
spatiality 357, 364, 391
spatiotemporal modality 7, 363
speech 60
Spencer, Herbert 331
staging
   advertising 248
   hyper-and intermediality in theatre 153
   theatre photography 139
   theatrical performance 159, 160, 161, 163
statues 231, 233
Sturrock, John 394
Stavenow-Hidemark, Elisabet 227
Steiner, Evgeny 254
Stott, Tim 118
Steiner, George 350
Sternfeld, Joel 309
Stilwell, Robynn 62, 64, 65
Stina's Peculiar Birthday Journey (book) 254
Strauss, Richard 51
Stravinsky, Igor 55
Strindberg, August 68, 192, 277, 278
Strozzi, Giovanni 86
structuralism 394
Sulzer, Johann Georg 366
supplementarity of illustration 329, 342
Svennberg, Tore 143
Svenstedt, Carl Henrik 57
symbol 6, 256, 296, 363, 364

T

Take care [of yourself] (*Prenez soin de vous*) (Calle) 32, 44
Talbot, William Henry Fox 194
Tarkovsky, Andrei 51
technical media 53, 54, 59, 60, 61, 63, 291, 293
temporality 309
Tenor & Figaro (advertising film) 249
theatre 136, 154, 157
theatre performance 178
    approaching *Today's Cake is a Log* 168
    hyper- and intermediality 154
    intermedial experience in post-dramatic theatre 157
    introducing Hotel Pro Forma 166
    overview 152
    photomontage 130, 138, 143
theatre photography 130, 139, 141, 143
theatrical mode 55, 62
Theil, Per 151
Thieles, Just M. 135
Thon, Jan-Noël 393
Thune, Henriette 27, 29, 40, 41
Tobeck, Christina 68
Today's Cake is a Log (exhibition)
    hyper- and intermediality 152
    overview 15, 151, 178
    performing the exhibition 177
tone 369, 370, 371
transformation 5, 114, 121, 123, 153, 246, 263, 401
Transhimalaya (Hedin) 189, 200, 203, 205, 207
transmediality 263, 354, 368, 393
transmediation 257, 393, 395, 398
transparency 233, 385
travelling concepts 10, 378, 397
Turner, Jane 214
Turner, Mark 378, 397
Turvey, Malcolm 249
typography 357

V

Vargtimmen. See Hour of the Wolf, The
Vasari, Giorgio 80, 82, 84, 85, 91
Vertov, Dziga 392, 396
Vieillefon, Laurence 85
Villius, Hans 185
visiting card photos 132, 143
visitor as performer 178
visual opera 154, 164
visual perception 234
vital materialism 115
Voegelin, Salomé 87
Vogel, Matthias 365
von Rosen, Georg 219

W

Wagner, Meike 153
Wallenstein, Sven-Olov 266
Wallrup, Erik 368
Wang, Wilfried 265, 273
War Is Over (if you want it) campaign 115, 116
War Sum Up (*manga*-opera) 165, 166, 171

Warburg, Aby 91
Ward, Gerald W. R. 214
Warhol, Andy 44
Weber, Max 163
Webern, Anton 356
welfare state 14, 252, 255, 262
Wennerholm, Eric 193
Werle, Lars Johan 52, 56, 63, 64, 66, 69, 71
White Chess Set (Ono) 118, 123
Whorf-Sapir hypothesis 395
Why Does Night Come, Mother (Hotel Pro Forma) 161, 163, 174
Wieselgren, Oscar 130
Wilke, Jürgen 218
Wind, Edgar 84
Winge, Mårten Eskil 224, 232
Winkelhorn, Kathrine 151, 159
Without Borders exhibition 250
Wittgenstein, Ludwig 381
Wolf, Werner 4, 5, 11, 13, 52, 353, 354, 362
Wollen, Peter 308
wood engraving (xylography) 214, 334, 337, 339
world
and event; event 369, 370, 371
and intermediality; intermediality 159
and the work of art; work of art 63, 108, 115, 175
as outer world; outer world 359
panoramic visions 191
sonic world 64, 67
waking and sleeping 84
Wounded Danish Soldier, A (Jerichau-Baumann) 226

X

xylography (wood engraving) 214, 334, 337, 339

Y

Young, La Monte 102, 112
Yousif, Keri 323

Z

Zaatari, Akram 288, 289, 304, 305, 310, 314
Zelizer, Viviane A. Rotman 252
Zelter, Carl Friedrich 366
Zen For Head (Paik) 112
Zeppelin (Lutter image) 308
Zodiak (Werle ballet) 69
Zurbrugg, Nicolas 103
Zylinska, Joanna 293

www.ingramcontent.com/pod-product-compliance
Lightning Source LLC
Chambersburg PA
CBHW040519220526
45473CB00013B/2916